Deleuze's *Cinema* Books

In memory, Antony
for Anna and Robert

Deleuze's *Cinema* Books

Three Introductions to the Taxonomy of Images

David Deamer

EDINBURGH
University Press

Edinburgh University Press is one of the leading university presses in the UK. We publish academic books and journals in our selected subject areas across the humanities and social sciences, combining cutting-edge scholarship with high editorial and production values to produce academic works of lasting importance. For more information visit our website: edinburghuniversitypress.com

Edinburgh University Press Ltd
The Tun – Holyrood Road
12 (2f) Jackson's Entry
Edinburgh EH8 8PJ

Typeset in Arno and Myriad by
R. Footring Ltd, Derby, UK, and
printed and bound in Great Britain by
CPI Group (UK) Ltd, Croydon CR0 4YY

A CIP record for this book is available from the British Library

ISBN 978 1 4744 0767 0 (hardback)
ISBN 978 1 4744 0768 7 (paperback)
ISBN 978 1 4744 0769 4 (webready PDF)
ISBN 978 1 4744 0770 0 (epub)

Contents

Figures and frames

Figures (Sections I and II) are tables and diagrams which serve to support the text, and, correspondingly, the text to explicate. Frames (Section III) are images from the films explored functioning as a visual orientation.

Acknowledgements

I owe deep gratitude to the people who have read and offered comments on sections of this book over the last six or so years: Ian Buchanan, Felicity Colman, Rob Lapsley, Patricia Pisters, Anna Powell and Henry Somers-Hall. Also, to the readers of and commenters on my online *cineosis* project (2010–16) – thank you for everything: you know who you are, even if I don't. Thanks are likewise due to the MMU students (especially year III, 2013–14) and Cornerhouse scholars (2013) who allowed me to explore aspects of these *Three Introductions* in lectures and classes. Many conversations at seminars, in reading groups, coffee shops and bars contributed to my ongoing thinking about Deleuze and cinema (in wider philosophical debates), and thanks go in particular to Matt Barnard, Ullrich Hasse, Joanna Hodge, Robert Jackson, Wahida Khandker, Maxime Lallement, Rob Lapsley, Anna Powell and Mark Sinclair. Thanks to all at – and those associated with – EUP: to Gillian Leslie who commissioned the book and championed the format; to Richard Strachan for early editorial support and Eddie Clark who saw the project through to the end; to Emma Rees in marketing and Rebecca Mackenzie for cover production; to copy-editor Michael Ayton; and to designer and typesetter Ralph Footring who rose to the challenge of organising all the diverse elements which make up the text. Thanks also to Krishna Stott (again!) at Bellyfeel for sorting out the film frames. To Aleks and crew at Caffè Nero, Oxford Road – thanks for the Americanos. And to Nyah – as always – thank you for the inspiration and encouragement.

Section I, Chapter 3 is based on my essay 'A Deleuzian cineosis: cinematic semiosis and syntheses of time', in *Deleuze Studies*, vol. 5, no. 3 (Edinburgh University Press, 2011); it has, however, been much revised and expanded, going beyond the synthesis of time to the syntheses of space and consciousness – all from Deleuze's *Difference and Repetition* (1968). The chapters on the films *Five*, *Russian Ark* and *Self Made* also appear in print elsewhere (the first two in much-extended form): 'Look? Impure optical and sound situations: Ozu – (Deleuze) – Kiarostami' in *Ozuesque: Ozu and His Influence* (ed. Jinhee Choi, Oxford University Press, 2017); 'Time travel and temporal paradox: Deleuze, the time-image and *Russian Ark*' in *Time Travel in Popular Media: Essays on Film, Television, Literature and Video Games* (ed. Jones and Ormrod, McFarland, 2015); and 'Now you see me … Gillian Wearing's *Self Made*' in *Gillian Wearing* (Ridinghouse, Whitechapel, Pinakothek der Moderne and K20, 2012). My thanks to the editors and publishers for kind permission to appropriate material from the above-mentioned journal and collections. Sections II and III take their impetus from my online *cineosis* project; Section II from *cineosis.com* (2010), which provided short definitions of each image and sign through a hyperlinked map (a version of which is reproduced at the centre of this book; the online map now linking to the film explorations in the accompanying *cineosis blog* – see below). These sections have been entirely rewritten and expanded for the *Three Introductions*. They have also been augmented with a series of diagrams developed over a number of years, earlier versions (action-image large form, recollection-image, sheets of the past) appearing in 'An imprint of *Godzilla*: Deleuze, the action-image and universal history' in *Deleuze and Film* (Edinburgh University Press, 2012) and '"Watch out! Recollection": the spectre of impossibility in Kaneto Shindo's *Children of the Atom Bomb*' in *A/V* (Manchester Metropolitan University, 2007). Section III began as occasional posts at *cineosis.blogspot.co.uk* (2010–16), the idea being to popularise Deleuze's film-philosophy by affirmative explorations of cinematic releases as they hit the screens (of Manchester). In due course, films encountered at special screenings, on DVD and TV snuck in. Why not? These films have been revisited and rewatched during the composition of the *Three Introductions*, and the engagements revised and rewritten. Accordingly, the original texts have been redacted from the *cineosis blog*; the films discussed online that did not make it into the book remain.

Abbreviations

Gilles Deleuze

B   *Bergsonism*
C1   *Cinema 1: The Movement-Image*
C2   *Cinema 2: The Time-Image*
DI   *Desert Islands and Other Texts: 1953–1974*
DR   *Difference and Repetition*
LS   *The Logic of Sense*
NP   *Nietzsche and Philosophy*
TRM   *Two Regimes of Madness: Texts and Interviews 1975–1995*

Gilles Deleuze and Félix Guattari

AO   *Anti-Oedipus: Capitalism and Schizophrenia*
K   *Kafka: Toward a Minor Literature*
TP   *A Thousand Plateaus: Capitalism and Schizophrenia*
WP   *What Is Philosophy?*

Gilles Deleuze and Claire Parnet

D2   *Dialogues II*

Henri Bergson

CE   *Creative Evolution*
MM   *Matter and Memory*

Charles Sanders Peirce

As per tradition in Peirce scholarship, reference to Peirce's writings in collected volumes will be designated by an abbreviation for the text, followed by volume and paragraph number.

CP 1   *Collected Papers of Charles Sanders Peirce: Volume I, Principles of Philosophy*

CP 2   *Collected Papers of Charles Sanders Peirce: Volume II, Elements of Logic*

CP 5   *Collected Papers of Charles Sanders Peirce: Volume V, Pragmatism and Pragmaticism*

CP 8   *Collected Papers of Charles Sanders Peirce: Volume VIII, Reviews, Correspondence, and Bibliography*

SS   *Semiotic and Significs: The Correspondence between Charles S. Peirce and Victoria Lady Welby*

SW   *Charles S. Peirce: Selected Writings (Values in a Universe of Chance)*

Preface: a Deleuzian cineosis

The usefulness of theoretical books on cinema has been called into question. (C2: 280)

The *Cinema* books of Gilles Deleuze are a maze of mirrors. An encounter between film and philosophy where philosophy and film produce ideas: film through images, philosophy through concepts. The *Cinema* books enmesh images and concepts developing a complex taxonomy of signs: a cinematic semiosis – a cineosis. Always an alliance between the two intensive surfaces, sometimes the cineosis is a shining path, sometimes a trajectory through convex and concave recursions. Deleuze is Daedalus, the cunning architect and builder of labyrinths. And the reader sometimes the Minotaur, sometimes Ariadne, sometimes Theseus. Film philosophy (film theory, cinematic thought) – for Deleuze – is neither the site of a privileged discourse by philosophy on film, nor film finding its true home as philosophy. Neither discipline needs the other. Yet together philosophy and film can create adventures: correspondences, resonances, relations – coalesce, discover secret escapes, silences and ellipses. This is the cineosis: a complex matrix of ideas, concepts and images, signs. And this complexity is a consequence of the complexities of both film and philosophy. Accordingly, while the *Cinema* books outline a rigorous development and proliferation of elements (appropriated, displaced, half-forgotten and neologistic), they are also composed through elusive and allusive writing processes. Deleuze wants the reader to explore, become lost, find their way once more, be tested and test themselves: for this is the purpose of his film philosophy – to create an atmosphere for thought.

The *Three Introductions to the Taxonomy of Images* explicates and exposes some of the complexities of Deleuze's cineosis. To do so, each of the introductions takes a different approach, exploring the cineosis from one of three different standpoints: a philosophical genealogy of the taxonomy; a serial procession of component elements; and a dynamic encounter between the cineotic signs and the movies. These films are all taken from the first two decades of the second century of cinema, a period as vibrant and creative as any in the history of film: they include *Inception* (Christopher Nolan, USA | UK, 2010); *Uncle Boonmee Who Can Recall His Past Lives* (Apichatpong Weerasethakul, Thailand *et al.*, 2010); *Doctor Who – The Day of the Doctor* (Nick Hurran, UK, 2013); *Minions* (Kyle Balda and Pierre Coffin, USA, 2015); *The Human Centipede (First Sequence)* (Tom Six, the Netherlands, 2009); *Self Made* (Gillian Wearing, UK, 2010); *marxism today (prologue)* (Phil Collins, UK | Germany, 2010); *Harry Potter and the Deathly Hallows: Part 1* and *Part 2* (David Yates, USA | UK, 2010; 2011); *Se7en* (David Fincher, USA, 1995); and *Five* (Abbas Kiarostami, Iran *et al.*, 2003) – wondrous blockbusters, cutting edge arthouse, comedies, thrillers, horror, fantasy and documentary from the world of cinema. There will be forty-four such encounters, each corresponding to a designated, described and diagrammed sign. These signs emerge as a serial procession of concepts from Deleuze's *Cinema* books. And this series has a genesis in a taxonomical framework. Accordingly, this structure necessitates an in-depth genealogical exploration of the primary philosophical texts that inspire such cineotic coordinates: Henri Bergson's *Matter and Memory* (1896), Charles Sanders Peirce's *Pragmatism and Pragmaticism* (1903) and Deleuze's own foundational text *Difference and Repetition* (1968). Such is the approach of the *Three Introductions*.

Why Deleuze's *Cinema* books? Why as a taxonomy? And why three introductions? These questions will be explored in this Preface to the *Introductions*. To anticipate the argument, however, these questions are – for me, in a way – one and the same enquiry. Or rather, different aspects of the same investigation. Over the last thirty or so years the study of Deleuze's film-philosophy has slowly, relentlessly, exploded. Readers, writers, filmmakers, theorists and philosophers have engaged with the *Cinema* books in ways it is difficult to believe Deleuze could have envisioned. There have been introductions, applications, extensions and critiques – conferences convened, journals launched, book series created. And this may only be the beginning. As such, it seems likely that readers, writers, filmmakers, theorists and philosophers will continue to return – again and again – to the *Cinema* books: to explore their ideas, to think about their consequences, to be inspired by their originality and creativity. In other words, even with all this work on Deleuze's film-philosophy, the *Cinema* books remain relevant and resist becoming exhausted. It is such a consideration that begins to answer my first question, for despite the fifteen or so years over which I have been thinking about the *Cinema* books, I see no end in sight for my encounters with them. On the contrary – the more I read, the more I discover: the books are fractal. To fully respond to my first question, however, I must refer to my second. The *Cinema* books are fundamentally taxonomical – Deleuze's originary move is to create a cinematic semiosis, a cineosis. Yet very little study exists in this area. Ask a 'Deleuzian film philosopher' how many images or signs there are, what all these elements designate, or indeed, how the underlying framework is structured, and you are as likely as not to get a shrug of the shoulders, to be told that it doesn't really matter, that such questions risk vacuous pedantry at best, that at worst you might be missing the point, that the taxonomy is a toolbox from which you can select the most appropriate implement for the job at hand (see e.g. O'Toole, 2005). Without doubt, there is much truth in such comebacks. Deleuze himself – and saying this, of course, could equally put the noses of some very serious philosophers out of joint – encouraged and was fine with such an approach to his work. Nevertheless, I don't believe we should in this way leave the question of the taxonomy. When I began reading the *Cinema* books it was immediately apparent they were founded upon an encounter with a semiotic, and – just as significant – that this taxonomy was riven with ellipses and lacunas. I wanted to lay my hands on some kind of explication – something that admitted the taxonomy as fundamental, something that explored the semiotic elements in such a context, and something that would engage with those lacunas and ellipses. The *Three Introductions* is a bit like the text I wanted all those years ago, and still wish was out there in the world. Which brings me to my final question. Why *three* introductions? Over the last decade or so of my thinking and rethinking the cineosis, there seems to me three different aspects to such an investigation, each aspect requiring a different approach: a genealogy of the philosophies that Deleuze appropriated in order to construct the underlying framework and structure; a naming of signs with definitions and mutual dependencies between the elements of the series; and (last, but by no means least), an exploration of a particular movie through each of the signs of the taxonomy. The differentiation, individuation and dramatisation of the cineosis (to exploit three related Deleuzian concepts encountered a little later in this book). All the aspects are – of course – inextricably interrelated. Yet each benefits from its own approach owing to the procedural problems inherent in each respectively. The genealogy may provide the theory with a structure; however, the derivation of each of the actual names and definitions of the elements does not follow from this framework. The arrangement of the series of images and signs – reciprocally – provides clues to the structure, yet is as much a pragmatic extraction of elements from the text. And given the nexus of the structure and the series, cinema risks becoming merely an illustration or example of the concept deployed if we do not begin with the film. To have brought the three approaches together would have been to effectively efface these problems (as differenciation). This book is composed of three different introductions (as de-differenciation) to allow the investigations to remain disparate and at the same moment resonate.

The framework through a genealogy, the elements as a serial procession, and films as an encounter of signs: each receives its own treatment. Accordingly, the sections of this book can be read in any order. If you are new to Deleuze and his *Cinema* books, a good way to begin would be with the films. Read the *Three Introductions* backwards: the third section, before exploring the serial logic of images and signs, then the structural framework for the wider concerns of Deleuze's project. Perhaps you prefer to engage with the complexities of the genealogy in order to contextualise the logic of the elements and their capturing in their deployment: if so, begin with the first section and read through to the end. You can even orient yourself from the middle and go on to either the third or first sections as you please and as the moment dictates. Or even pass back and forth between the various chapters of the book (the movement-images then the time-images across each of the sections, for instance) – this seems, to me, as good an approach as any.

Thinking cinema

It is often claimed that filmmakers believe theoretical books on cinema to be unnecessary, a mutilation even. Robert Lapsley and Michael Westlake's seminal exploration *Film Theory: An Introduction* kicks off with a commentary on a famous statement from movie director Alan Parker: '"Film needs theory … like it needs a scratch on the negative." The supposition is not an uncommon one: directors, calling on inspiration and imagination, don't need it, and neither do audiences, who have only to watch and respond' (Lapsley and Westlake, 2006: vi). '[F]ilm theorists', echoes Tony Miller in *A Companion to Film Theory*, appear to 'unravel the magic and escape of cinema' (Miller, 2004: 3). Such resistance is perhaps overstated. Filmmakers themselves, after all, have been writing on cinema from the earliest of days – for every Parker there is a Sergei Eisenstein, Paul Schrader, Robert Bresson, Andrei Tarkovsky, Pier Paolo Pasolini and so on. Furthermore, academic disciplines engaging with cinema are well entrenched in universities across the world, there is an ongoing proliferation of journals, books and online content; and cineastes seem willing to expose themselves – more than ever – to film theory, film philosophy, cinema studies, whatever we may call such thinking cinema. Even so, it would be naive to believe such resistance is illusory or can be pushed aside. Many writers, accordingly, will offer robust, articulate and convincing defences of the discipline, Lapsley and Westlake (2006) and Miller and Stam (2004) among them. *We need film theory because …* We have needed and need film theory because it confronts cinema, allows us to think about cinema, even accentuates our enjoyment and the pleasure of cinema. And film philosophy is ever-evolving, research does not sleep – there are fundamental disagreements, revolutions, counter-revolutions, expansions, linkages. Cinema studies is exciting, and vital. How to approach a retrospective, and where to begin?

A–B–C–D–E–F–G: these seven letters – the first seven primary letters of the French alphabet – spell out a moment in a revolution in thinking cinema. In 1969, Jean-Louis Comolli and Jean Narboni published an editorial in the French film journal *Cahiers du cinéma* entitled 'Cinema/Ideology/Criticism' (*Cahiers du cinéma* no. 216, October 1969). '*Every film is political*', write Comolli and Narboni, 'inasmuch as it is determined by the ideology which produces it' (Comolli and Narboni, 1996: 45). As every film is part of the economic system from which it arises, so every film is ideological. Cinema does not capture reality, but rather 'the vague, unformulated, untheorized, unthought-out world of the dominant ideology' (Comolli and Narboni, 1996: 46). Thus the task of the cinema theorist is to 'elaborate and apply a critical theory of cinema' by way of 'a rigidly factual analysis of what governs the production of a film' (Comolli and Narboni, 1996: 46, 50). This is scientific criticism, a socio-political analysis. Theory is opposed to ideology; theory is the tool to crack open ideology. In this way, the critical theorist is in the vanguard of the producing and consuming populace, who are all caught up in the ideology of the cinema. On the one hand, write Comolli and Narboni, the cinema-consuming public 'can only express itself via the thought-patterns of the ideology' (Comolli and Narboni, 1996: 47). So, the job of theory is to decode and reveal for the viewer. And – furthermore – it should be troublesome to and an inspiration for the production of cinema itself: 'the film-maker's first task is to show up the cinema's so-called "depiction of reality"', thus 'a chance that we will be able to disrupt or possibly even sever the connection between the cinema and its ideological function' (Comolli and Narboni, 1996: 46). Accordingly, Comolli and Narboni believe in films which are directly political in content ('they do not just discuss an issue, reiterate it, paraphrase it, but use it to attack') and radical in form ('breaking down the traditional way of depicting reality') (Comolli and Narboni, 1996: 47). Such films would become the cinematic subject matter of *Cahiers*, and thus the ascension of what has become known as film theory, employing the trinity of Saussurian semiology, dialectic materialism and psychoanalysis. As Stephen Heath once put it, 'the encounter of Marxism and psychoanalysis [Freud and Lacan] on the terrain of semiotics' (Heath in Easthope, 1996: 8). Film theory would go on to revolutionise the way in which cinema was conceived, produced and consumed – its tenets entering into the university system as film courses and through academic texts, eventually becoming an accepted discipline over the years that followed.

Yet film theory was not the beginning of serious and engaged thinking about movies: far from it. Writers, critics, filmmakers, theorists and philosophers had been exploring the image since very early on in the history of cinema. '[P]erhaps arguably', comments Noël Carroll in *The Philosophy of Motion Pictures* (2008), 'with the publication in 1916 of *The Photoplay: A Psychological Study* by Hugo Munsterberg' (Carroll, 2008: 1). In this way, film theory was perhaps not so much a revolution in thinking cinema as a reorientation or paradigm shift: a turning away from certain lines of dominant thought, and a turning towards other aspects through rediscovery and extension. On the one hand, the *Cahiers* factor was a reaction to what has since become known as 'classic film theory', broadly aligned with philosophical realism. While it is rarely in doubt that cinema will always work upon the image, the various exegeses of cinematic realism were concerned with the representation of the real through film. The previous regime at *Cahiers*, for instance, had been led by André Bazin, who developed a theoretical position dependent upon an 'evolution' of filmmaking arising from two intertwined propositions: the long take and deep focus (Bazin, 1997: 23). Long takes with an active depth-of-field create sequence-shots giving 'a sense of the ambiguity of reality', mirroring the real (Bazin, 1997: 36). However, '[c]lassic film theory', comments Antony Easthope, 'is superseded' when such an 'assumption gets overthrown' (Easthope, 1996: 5). On the other hand, the new theory was just as often inspired by other aspects of classical theory, such as the writing of the early Soviet filmmakers and academics, Lev Kuleshov, Vsevolod Pudovkin, and – of course – Sergei Eisenstein. Bazin's formulation was in itself a reaction to such montage theorists, who believed the editing of images to be primary, cutting techniques utilised to force an exposure of the real. And as *Cahiers* geared up for its change of direction, the magazine published and celebrated Eisenstein's writing on cinema in a retrospective. In other words, the rise of the new film theory was not simply a break with the past; and the first wave of so-called classic film theory was never a homogeneous field, but incredibly rich and heterogeneous.

As, indeed, became – very soon, inevitably – film theory itself. Lapsley and Westlake comment: there is 'nowhere outside of theory, in that any thinking, however anti-theoretical', will draw 'on a background of suppositions, beliefs and judgements'; yet, there are 'two possibilities' (Lapsley and Westlake, 2006: 214): the Marxist-Althusserian line of *Cahiers*, that 'it was possible to escape from this into a realm of knowledge (science) … a discourse free of determination by other social practices'; and – alternatively – that there was no escape from ideology, 'thought as inextricably bound up with social practice' (Lapsley and Westlake, 2006: 214). As the authors summarise: 'having begun with a Marxist structuralist confidence in the possibility of knowledge it found itself increasingly inclined towards … views of post-structuralism and postmodernism' (Lapsley and Westlake, 2006: 214). Film theory began to fragment into an expansive and fertile domain of disparate practices – feminist film theory, post-colonial film theory, queer film theory, third cinema theory, postmodernist film theory and so on. These disciplines could often share some basic assumptions (for example, taking a broadly Marxist foundation) yet were just as likely to reject or see some aspects of film theory as reactionary and symptomatic (for example, Freudian and Lacanian psychoanalysis as not exposing but reifying patriarchy). A myriad of disciplines emerged and developed, departing from each other, sometimes returning to the fold, sometimes inspiring new practices which in turn rejoined with now established specialities.

Yet film theory – in both these guises, its core and extension – would soon be put under a very different type of critique, this time from the outside. As Slavoj Žižek commented back at the turn of the century: 'the principal contradiction of today's cinema studies' is between what has become known as Theory, the 'deconstructionist/feminist/post-Marxist/psychoanalytical/sociocritical/cultural studies etc. approach ... and the so-called "Post-Theory", the cognitivist and/or historicist reaction to it' (Žižek, 2001: 1). In *Mystifying Movies: Fads and Fallacies in Contemporary Film Theory* (1988), Carroll aligned film theory with continental philosophy against his own cognitivist approach and the analytical tradition, in so doing, turning away from Lacanian, Marxist and structuralist inspirations towards cognition-based models of spectatorship exploring the ontology of film. Carroll, and colleagues such as David Bordwell, aimed at a grounded film philosophy, a study of the cinema anchored in properly scientific disciplines such as logic and neuroscience, and used established empirical philosophical procedures to progress the field through reasoned dialectics. Here is a film: 'you said that it is good; I said that it is bad' (Carroll, 2008: 209). Who is right? 'An overall evaluation – a.k.a. an "all-things-considered judgement" – of a motion picture should take into account not only the movie's success or failure by its own (category-relative) lights, but the value or disvalue of the purpose or purposes to which the category is committed' (Carroll, 2008: 209). Designating a hierarchy of film types and forms, accordingly, can be seen to echo the procedures (if not the political aims) of *Cahiers*; and there was an eventual semi-rapprochement with film theory by film philosophy. In *The Philosophy of Motion Pictures* (2008) Carroll writes, 'by the 1980s cinema studies, like other branches of the humanities, took what has come to be called "the cultural or social turn" ... academics in cinema studies decided to reorient their field in the direction of what came to be known as "cultural studies"' (Carroll, 2008: 2). Film philosophy becomes the 'legitimate heir ... not a usurper' of film theory proper, although 'the end product' of the analytic-cognitivist approach 'is in nowise as unified as the philosophies of our very distinguished predecessors in film theory. Instead our results are pluralistic' (Carroll, 2008: 5). Of course, while Grand Theory is given a reprieve, cinema studies is now seen in terms of anti-intellectual and non-philosophical degeneration accompanying the inexorable marketisation of our university systems. Yet, the cultural studies/cinema studies nexus – with its focus on the socio-historical and political-economic foundations of disparate everyday phenomenon – was an active force in demanding a critical response to the corporatisation of culture, and – furthermore – had pluralistic aims just like film-philosophy. Film theory from core to extension is inspired by, inspires and merges with cinema studies – and it takes some serious entrenchment to designate where one may end and the other begin. As Žižek maintains, and as we have seen, 'Theory' is 'ironically nicknamed' in the singular but 'of course, is far from a unified field' (Žižek, 2001: 1). Accordingly, as Robert Sinnerbrink has recently proposed, 'we should move beyond the adversarial battle between "Grand Theory" and "Analytic-Cognitivist" paradigms, and attempt instead … to synthesize' (Sinnerbrink, 2011: 1). It is clear – even by Carroll's account – such things are possible and are already happening, have always happened.

Classical film theory, film theory, cinema studies, film philosophy: such is one version of the last one hundred years of thinking cinema. It is thus tempting to consider the domain as a univocal field composed of a multiplicity of disciplines. And the disciplines push ever onwards through endless confrontation, re-invention, evolution, revolution and eventual rapprochement; and then, once again …

Deleuze, Deleuzian philosophy and the *Cinema* books

I began, however, by asking why there should be resistance to such thinking cinema. Parker's scratch on the negative. Sinnerbrink, in *New Philosophies of Film: Thinking Images*, concludes with a wonderful image from Orson Welles' *Don Quixote*, an unfinished film. Quixote is in a cinema watching a movie, when he slashes the cloth of the screen, annihilating the image completely. 'Quixote', writes Sinnerbrink, 'destroys the very thing he loves'; and concomitantly, the 'film, in an ironic gesture of self-sacrifice, invites philosophy, which would rather dominate the image, to relinquish its mastery and learn to see' (Sinnerbrink, 2011: 196). In other words, classical film theory, film theory, cinema studies, and film philosophy can appear and be practised as cinephobia, cineicism (a fear of film, a cynicism – or nihilism – regarding cinema). From *Cahiers* rejection of popular movies to Carroll's *a priori* hierarchisation of forms, thinking cinema appears as a discourse about film, a lifting of the veil, rendering movies as an (often bad) object. It is almost as if the actual film becomes an inconvenience to theory, philosophy, study, these disciplines turning in upon themselves and turning against cinema.

Cinema 1 – The Movement-Image (1983) and *Cinema 2 – The Time-Image* (1985) are – above all – a celebration of cinema, a celebration by way of beautiful films by great filmmakers. There are bad films – of course – yet explicating the judgement of such an evaluation is not the task of Deleuze's cinema philosophy. Rather, the project is one of affirmation. 'One cannot object' to such a project, writes Deleuze, 'by pointing to the vast proportion of rubbish in cinematographic production – it is no worse than anywhere else' (C1: ix). But neither does a cinematic triumph depend upon an unobtainable ideal, the positing of which is only possible in the wake of a film's creation. We have the films we have. 'The history of cinema', for Deleuze, 'is a long martyrology' where filmmakers have been 'able to invent and get screened, in spite of everything' (C1: ix). Accordingly, Deleuze's perspective on bad films begins with a Nietzschean prerogative: 'let looking away be my only negation!' (Nietzsche, 2003: 157). The *Cinema* books do not discuss any films which Deleuze considers shit. The 800 or so movies in the books – from Hollywood to Japan, from Senegal to France, from the USSR to Mexico; from the beginning of cinema to the early 1980s – are all 'masterpieces to which no hierarchy of value applies' (C1: x). In this way, Deleuze's film-philosophy is one where cinema awakens thought and thought conjoins with cinema. Reflecting upon the project between *Cinema 1* and *Cinema 2*, Deleuze wrote: 'film was no pretext or field of application'; rather, philosophy and cinema appear as an 'active and interior alliance' (TRM: 219). 'It does happen', comments Deleuze, 'that I feel like I "absolutely need" to see some film or other, and that if I don't, I won't be able to continue the work. And then I give up – I'm forced to do without it'; reciprocally, '[i]t also happens that when I go see a film, if it seems really beautiful, I know I will want to write about it. This changes the writing conditions' (TRM: 220–1). Philosophy inspires the cinematic engagement, and cinema transforms the philosophical trajectory. Deleuze begins with a love of cinema, as much as with the love of philosophy. Lapsley and Westlake conclude: 'Deleuze has no desire to arrive at the final truth about cinema. The cinema books, in their celebration of difference, are not an attempt at the creation of a new paradigm within which more detailed analyses can proceed; rather, they are examples of experiment and invention … Their message is, "This is what I made of cinema. What can you make of it?"' (Lapsley and Westlake, 2006: 253). Deleuze's *Cinema* books thus occupy a strange place in thinking cinema, appear difficult to position in the history of film theory, cinema studies, film philosophy and so on. Indeed, Deleuze's approach to such applied disciplines is one of appropriation, overturning, reversal, sidestepping, incorporation. Žižek has written: 'Deleuze was well known for his aversion toward debate' (Žižek, 2004: ix). And according to Alain Badiou (using a very loaded term!), Deleuze prefers "'collaboration" … in a context of convergence … [and/or] divergence' (Badiou, 2000: 5). Furthermore, Deleuze will never cease to exploit the history of philosophy for more ideas to incorporate, to twist, to rebirth. In the *Cinema* books, Deleuze creates an adventure in cinema, film theory and philosophy as a disruptive image of thought.

It would, in this way, be a mistake – perhaps – to see Deleuze as a film theorist; or better put, to approach his study of cinema without considering it in the context of his wider philosophical trajectory. Deleuze began – long before the *Cinema* books – by writing on key figures from the history of philosophy, although he followed an alternative line of flight to academic proclivities at the time: David Hume (*Empiricism and Subjectivity* [1953]); Friedrich Nietzsche (*Nietzsche and Philosophy* [1962]); Henri Bergson (*Bergsonism* [1966]); and Baruch Spinoza (*Expressionism in Philosophy: Spinoza* [1968]; *Spinoza: Practical Philosophy* [1970; 2nd exp. edn, 1981]). Not so much developing a method, his concerns can be seen as an exploration of the problems of modern philosophies caught between empiricism (the experiential knowledge advocated through the sciences) and metaphysics (the nature of the world and being as a non-empirical enquiry). Yet, as Deleuze writes in *Nietzsche and Philosophy*, in the wake of Nietzsche, 'empiricism … is almost indistinguishable from philosophy itself … the only guarantor of freedom in the concrete spirit, the only principle of a violent atheism' (NP: 4). Freedom is possible because 'a thing is sometimes this, sometimes that, sometimes something more complex' – empiricism is thus an affirmation of pluralism, and pluralism is 'philosophy's greatest achievement' depending upon 'philosophy's highest art – that of interpretation' (NP: 4). This is Deleuze's philosophy, developed in his work on Bergson through the multiplicity in the univocity of being-becoming (as we will explore in much more detail in Section I, Chapters 1, 3 and 4). Accordingly, Deleuze will abandon much of the traditional language of philosophy for his own creation of concepts.

Such engagements resulted in two early – and intimately allied – masterpieces: *Difference and Repetition* (1968) and *The Logic of Sense* (1969). Of the former, Deleuze famously said this was the first book where he did philosophy, and all his work in the wake of this text is related to it. The basic argument is that there are two images of thought: the classical and the disruptive – and while they interweave throughout the history of philosophy, the tendency is for the classical to dominate. This image of thought is one of common sense and good sense – an image of thought that pronounces natural judgement. Deleuze – in the wake of his work on Nietzsche, Bergson and Spinoza – will claim each age has to rediscover and reinvent the disruptive image of thought anew, rereading the past in the present for the future. Accordingly, *Difference and Repetition* itself is such an image – elusive and allusive, exploring philosophy and science. Deleuze would go on, with co-author Félix Guattari, to develop these two images of thought in *Anti-Oedipus* (1972) and *A Thousand Plateaus* (1980) through concepts such as territorialisation and deterritorialisation (*Anti-Oedipus*) and (*A Thousand Plateaus*) the arborescent and the rhizomatic. The crucial aspect here is that these images are polarities, and create interim states. 'There is no ... ontological dualism here', write Deleuze and Guattari, and 'no axiological dualism between good and bad ... There are knots of arborescence on rhizomes, and rhizomatic offshoots in roots' (TP: 22). Conversely, 'there are despotic formations of immanence and channelization specific to rhizomes, just as there are anarchic deformations in the transcendent system ... *The important point* is that the root-tree and canal-rhizome are not two opposed models' (TP: 22; my emphasis). To explore the interweavings of these images of thought Deleuze and Guattari refine a serial procedure of composition in their co-writing – exploring a series of disparate events that are made to resonate with one another. Such a complex, however, can be seen as being founded in Deleuze's *Logic of Sense*, which followed, or created, a series of paradoxes framed through sense and non-sense/nonsense. Such paradoxes can be seen in the Stoics' notion of time and in – among other literary texts – Lewis Carroll's *Alice* books. In this way, with *Logic of Sense*, art comes to the foreground alongside philosophy for the investigation of the two images of thought – the classical and the disruptive – through multiple interweavings. *Logic of Sense*, furthermore, develops the forays into art and philosophy Deleuze had begun with *Proust and Signs* (1964; 2nd exp. edn, 1976) and through Sacher-Masoch in *Masochism: Coldness and Cruelty* (1967); and would continue with his treatise on painting in *Francis Bacon: The Logic of Sensation* (1981). The acentred discourses of philosophy, science, art; the univocity, multiplicity and two polarities of the images of thought therein, as well as their infinite matrixes – this is what constitutes the Deleuzian project, unequivocally confronted in Deleuze and Guattari's final work, *What Is Philosophy?* (1991).

The *Cinema* books can thus be seen – on the one hand – as a pragmatic employment of *Difference and Repetition*; and – on the other hand – as a productive repetition of *Logic of Sense*. With respect to *Difference and Repetition*, Deleuze writes two books of film philosophy, each of which correlates to a kind of cinema that aligns with the two images of thought (classical and disruptive, arborescent and rhizomatic, and so on). *Cinema 1 – The Movement-Image* explores classical cinema; while *Cinema 2 – The Time-Image* explores new waves, modernism, and so on. Yet the *Cinema* books echo the form and continue the project on art set out in *Logic of Sense* and developed through *A Thousand Plateaus* – both *Cinema 1* and *Cinema 2* are composed in a serial format of short chapters and sections that create an ongoing taxonomical unfolding of complex interweavings of the two images of thought, explored through an alliance of philosophy and film.

The core argument of the *Cinema* books, accordingly, is that there are two images of cinematographic thought – two regimes of cinema: movement-images and time-images. Deleuze will create this division through a return to Bergson's investigations of image and duration from *Matter and Memory* (1896). And Deleuze will extend each moment of the polarity – in the first place, with the movement-image – through the semiotics of Charles Sanders Peirce; and – in the second place, with the time-image – through *Difference and Repetition* (or so I will claim in Section I, Chapter 3). In this way, the two regimes – in the wake of Peirce and *Difference and Repetition* – form a vast taxonomy of signs describing different types of movement-image and time-image. Such a description might immediately seem to indicate that Deleuze is setting up an argument in which the movement-image will be condemned and the time-image affirmed. Indeed, claims such as this abound in Deleuzian cinema studies. And it is easy to see why: the tradition of film theory, cinema studies and film philosophy – as explored above – tend to operate in just such a way, to create an *a priori* hierarchy of value of cinematic forms. Similarly – again, as explored above – philosophy loves its dualisms. It is thus perhaps no surprise that the *Cinema* books have been explored within such traditions, and that this perspective has come to dominate the reception and application of Deleuze's film philosophy. I take another view – and this view forms the argument of the *Three Introductions*. As we have seen, Deleuze has already affirmed the films appearing in the *Cinema* books as masterpieces. He will write in *Cinema 2*: 'it cannot be said' of movement-images and time-images 'that one is more important than the other, whether more beautiful or profound' (and there will – of course – be garbage produced in both regimes: making a time-image film is no guarantee of beauty, of profundity, of a masterpiece) (C2: 270). With the movies of the *Cinema* books, evaluation has already been made – but through an affirmation, not by way of an incorporation of *ressentiment* into the text, and without a nihilistic belief in the death of cinema. Films both of the movement-image and of the time-image are encountered in all their wonders. This is because great films of the movement-image and the time-image – in themselves – already explore the two images of thought, their interweavings and interrelations. Cinema does not need philosophy to explicate this – it already knows. Cinema is not the object of Deleuze's film philosophy, but rather, great films – be they movement-images or time-images – can resonate with philosophy, with Deleuze's philosophical project.

'What led me to start writing on film', says Deleuze, 'was that I had been wrestling with a problem of signs for some time', and in cinema Deleuze saw 'the proliferation of all kinds of strange signs' (TRM: 219). Accordingly, the approach of the *Three Introductions* is to foreground the twofold cineosis as a series of images and signs. The concern is how – in different times, at different places, under different circumstances – cinema creates a film that can invite us to think. No doubt, approaching the *Cinema* books as a cineosis – as a taxonomic system, as a series and as a serial filmic encounter (a semiotic unfolding and cinematic enfolding) – is a reading of Deleuze's film philosophy. Yet this is a perspective that has not as yet received the focus it is due. In the thirty or so years since the publication of *Cinema 1* and *Cinema 2*, there have been several great commentaries. There have been some really beautiful books, including D. N. Rodowick's *Gilles Deleuze's Time Machine* (1997), Barbara M. Kennedy's *Deleuze and Cinema: The Aesthetics of Sensation* (2002), Ronald Bogue's *Deleuze on Cinema* (2003), Paola Marrati's *Gilles Deleuze: Cinema and Philosophy* (2008), Felicity Colman's *Deleuze and Cinema: The Film Concepts* (2011), and Daniala Angelucci's *Deleuze and the Concepts of Cinema* (2012/2014). Each of these books has brought something new to the study of Deleuze's film philosophy. And I am indebted to every one of these authors; they have guided me and accompanied me over the years, made me think about Deleuze's film philosophy in a multitude of different ways. The *Three Introductions* would not exist without them. Yet if these books have something in common, it is this – while each touches upon the taxonomy in its own way, none takes the cineosis as its starting point, and then attempts a full exploration of the elements therein. This is the project of the *Three Introductions* – to begin again, to begin with the taxonomy and explore it in three different ways: through a philosophical genealogy, as a serial procession, and with dynamic encounter with the movies. In so doing, I present here another way through the *Cinema* books. I have always been taken by the opening salvo of one of Deleuze's favourite texts, Pierre Klossowski's *Nietzsche and the Vicious Circle* (1969): 'This is a book …' – check it out …

Deleuze's *Cinema* books: Three Introductions to the Taxonomy of Images

Cinema – for Deleuze – is movement-images and time-images. Two regimes of the cinema: each regime divergent, yet between the two many connections, interrelations, exchanges and transformations. The two regimes, in this way, unfold into a series of interconnected filmic signs. '[W]hat has seemed fundamental to us', writes Deleuze towards the end of *Cinema 2*, 'is the distinction between two kinds of images with their corresponding signs, movement-images and time-images'; correspondingly, 'there are many possible transformations, almost imperceptible passages, and also combinations between the movement-image and the time-image' (C2: 270). This is the cineosis: a univocal cinema diverging into two regimes of images explicated through serial multiplicity – a twofold cinematic semiosis of signs. And it is the objective of the *Cinema* books to create this cineosis through the conjunction of philosophy and film. Here is the opening of *Cinéma 1*'s 'avant-propos' (in the English translation, 'Preface to the French edition'): 'This study is … a taxonomy, an attempt at the classification of images and signs' (C1: xiv). A taxonomy is a system which organises a field into elements according to a logic, the aim being to provide a coherent conceptual framework to be used in an exploration of that field. Yet while the *Cinema* books create and describe such a taxonomy, this description is deeply complex; it is also, by turns, haunted by ambiguities, disjunctions and silences. These features – without doubt – are some of the most courageous and wondrous aspects of the *Cinema* books: not only admitting to Deleuze theorising cinema at the very limit of his extraordinary capacity as a thinker and writer; but simultaneously allowing openings for readers, writers, filmmakers, theorists and philosophers to interpret and extend Deleuze's arguments in any number of ways. For all that, however, such complexities can obscure the rigour of Deleuze's approach. In this way, it is necessary to return to this logic and its many ambiguities. To discover the concealed and absent structures and elements of the taxonomy; to better understand the framework of the two regimes and the series of images and signs which compose it. To map, as Deleuze writes, the 'differentiation' and 'specification' of the cineosis (C2: 29). For it is only then that we can fully appreciate the multitude of ways in which to 'interweave concrete analyses of images and signs with the "monographs" of great directors who have created or renewed them' (C1: x). Such an interweaving is the aim of Part Two of this book; Part One must first respond to the logic – to the complexities, disjunctions, ambiguities and silences of both the structure and the series.

Accordingly, two reciprocal approaches inspire the objectives of Part One. Section I explicates the logic of the cineosis through a genealogy. In other words, exploring the essential philosophies which inspire the structure of the taxonomy: the thinking which grounds the differentiation of cinema into the two regimes, the schemas which organise the internal coordinates of the movement-image and the time-image, and – at the heart of things, finally – the fundamental relation between the two regimes. Section II, in comparison, begins with the consequences of the final investigation of the previous section, and focuses upon the cineosis as a filmic series. Here the perspective is that of the taxonomy as a cinematic continuum (image to image, sign to sign, sign to image and image to sign). The concern will be the specification of the elements by way of the cinematic procedures which allow Deleuze to provide each with a definition. Accordingly, Sections I and II approach the cineosis from very different perspectives: perhaps best conceived as a vertical structure and as a horizontal serialisation. And neither approach fully determines the other: the structure of the cineosis cannot be fully reconstructed from the series of images and signs that compose the two regimes; nor can the full description of each of the elements of the series be derived from the overall philosophical structure. However – and at one and the same moment – each approach is dependent upon the other. It is only by way of simultaneously working through the structure and the series that the coordinates of the genealogy can be identified and theorised, and that each element of the series can be named and defined. The cineosis is a cat's cradle of philosophy and film – the philosophical coordinates inspired by an engagement with cinema, the cinematic coordinates inspired by an engagement with philosophy. This is a reason for Part One being divided into two sections – to ensure that precedence is given neither to philosophy nor to cinema; or better put, that both cinema and philosophy are given preference in their own way. A second – and perhaps more important – reason for the division is to ensure that the procedures of the two enterprises – genealogy and serialisation – can focus upon the complexities, disjunctions, ambiguities and silences appropriate to each.

Movement-images and time-images – the two great regimes of the cineosis – are created by Deleuze in the wake of the philosophy of Henri Bergson. Bergson explicates a world encountered by its bodies in terms of a sensory-motor system (the retentions of perceptions, affects and actions) founded upon pure-spontaneous thought. The first chapter of Section I investigates how Deleuze adopts the sensory-motor system to define the cinema of the movement-image, and pure-spontaneous thought to define the cinema of the time-image. While such a philosophical derivation of the taxonomy appears uncontroversial, the complexity here, rather, concerns how Bergson's ontology is appropriated as Deleuzian methodology. It is, however, with the extension of this fundamental Bergsonian background that the obscurities really begin to accumulate. On the one hand, as will be explored in Chapter 2, the elements of the movement-image will be expanded through an iteration of Charles Sanders Peirce's pragmatic semiosis (a science, or logic, of signs). Peirce describes three primary categories and nine sign divisions resolving into a decalogue of sign classes each composed of three combinatory sign functions. The problem in describing Deleuze's full taxonomy of movement-images is not only the alignment of Bergson's sensory-motor system with Peirce's three categories, but also the generative account of the new elements allowed via Peirce. Deleuze gives several overviews of the expanded movement-image cineosis, each iteration different (in terms of the number and arrangement of elements), and none of the individual accounts (apparently) tarrying with Peirce. Yet, as Chapter 2 will claim, many of these issues can be elucidated if

Peirce's procedural unfolding of categories is followed. Accordingly, reading Deleuze's movement-image in the wake of such an engagement allows not only for a full differentiation of the structure of the images and signs of the movement-image, but also for a deeper appreciation of the relations between the coordinates thereof.

The obscurities of the time-image, on the other hand, are even more accentuated. While Deleuze creates a number of elements, there is no explanation for their derivation, an uncertainty as to their number and relation, and little sense of a taxonomical framework. Chapter 3 sets out to posit an order to the coordinates of the time-image, and – in consequence – propose an underlying structure. The claim is that the time-image can be considered as a reification of Deleuze's ontology in *Difference and Repetition* (1968) – the three constitutive syntheses of time, space and consciousness. In the wake of such an investigation, not only do the *Cinema* books offer the opportunity to explore the arguments of Deleuze's foundational philosophical text through their embodiment in the practice of cinema, but they also provide an account of how time-images relate to movement-images. Such an account will be fleshed out in Chapter 4 by way of a return to Bergson's sensory-motor system and pure-spontaneous thought – the initial foundation of Deleuze's division of cinema into the two fundamental regimes. Deleuze's ontology exposes a secret hidden in Bergsonian theory, something that remained silent in the first chapter of this section, and something that immediately impacts the cineosis. This concerns the apparent dualism of Bergson's method: the sensory-motor system as the processes of matter, and the esoteric realm of pure-spontaneous thought. After Deleuze, Bergson's dualism is revealed as a ruse, a provocation and method rather aimed at explicating a monism as multiplicity. All cinema is composed of matter-images, both movement-images (as described in the wake of Peirce's pragmatic semiosis) and time-images (as explicated through Deleuze's constitutive syntheses). And all cinema creates images of thought. The two regimes of the movement-image and the time-image can thus also be considered as a singular continuum of signs as multiplicity, every element describing an image of thought appropriate to each.

This idea of the cineosis as a multiplicity of images and signs can also be derived immediately via the taxonomy itself. Section II of this book explicates just such a Deleuzian perspective by exploring each image and sign in turn along the trajectory of its logical unfolding. The sixteen chapters here focus upon each image and sign complex in turn – pursuing a line from the first of the movement-images to the last of the time-images through a multitude of mutual interdependences. Signs constitute images, and images constitute avatars and domains of images, which in turn interpenetrate and transform one another in any number of ways. The sign series is all resonance and ricochet, a mosaic of elements. The obscurities in this description are thus very different from those exposed in Section I. If the genealogy of the structure gave an account of the number of elements of the series, each element of the cineosis should be able to be identified, named and described. Yet – in the movement-image – ellipses are revealed. However, close reading of the *Cinema* books as a logical series can point to these missing elements and their descriptions. And if these unnamed signs can be described, each can be given a name appropriate to its function (to signal such a designation, these names will remain italicised throughout Section II). In the time-image, the problem appears in a slightly different way: an overabundance of elements and an indeterminacy of their relations. Yet once again, a close reading of the *Cinema* books as a logical series (similarly in reference to the structural framework) resolves the trajectory, with elements revealed as aspects of other concepts viewed from different perspectives. Accordingly, the cineosis can be specified in all its anarchic magnificence as a multiplicity of cinematic forms.

I have chosen not to illustrate the mappings of Part One with any films. This may seem a strange approach to take in an engagement with film-philosophy, one immediate consequence being to render the discussions abstract. Such is the risk, no doubt – but it is more than mitigated, I believe, in freeing these explorations of structure and series from any anchor to a particular film or set of films (either the movies chosen by Deleuze in his *Cinema* books, or ones of my own choice). In Sections I and II such a procedure, in the context of these investigations, would amount to using cinema as an example – the crime *par excellence* of a so-called film-philosophy that sees a movie as a passive object convenient for the mere illustration of philosophy; or conversely, a film somehow embodying, rendering or exhausting a philosophical concept – the flailing of theoretical applications which sees theory as a conceptual pick 'n' mix. It is hoped this approach to the structure and the series of the cineosis similarly frees the reader to think and rethink their own filmic moments as structure and series are explored. Part One, instead, illustrates and captures its arguments through tables and diagrams: predominantly tables in Section I and diagrams in Section II. The tables of Section I are used to illustrate sometimes quite complex structural relations between the concepts in a particular theory and between different philosophical models. In comparison, the diagrams of Section II can be seen as an attempt to capture the essence of a sign and the resonances between the different images of the series, the text that accompanies each diagram – perhaps – here taking on the function of illustration.

Concrete filmic interactions are provided in the third section, Part Two of the book – the third introduction. Here cinematographic image and cineotic sign are made to interact as a contingent and momentary collaboration (and not – it is hoped – to exemplify or illustrate the film through philosophy or philosophy through the film). Each of the 44 chapters begins with the movie, and through the film approaches the cineosis, reaches out for a sign. The film choices are from 1995 to the present, and from the whole world of cinema, as much as my viewing practices and serendipity allowed. The project began by using films as they were released during the writing of this book, but the timespan was opened up to the first two decades of the second century of cinema to celebrate the ongoing life of the movies and provide a wider canvas. I also wanted to avoid retreading any of the ground of the *Cinema* books, and discussing any films Deleuze had engaged with, so a date after the mid-1980s seemed necessary. In a way, all these chapters have a fundamental serendipity. If I enjoyed a film, be it at the cinema or by some other means, I took this as impetus to write. Of course – as Deleuze tells us – some categories 'are crowded, and others are empty' (TRM: 285). Accordingly, there are many films I would have loved to have written on here, but was unable to. And while many films aligned with some sign categories, it was also the case that some other sign categories were less easy to stumble across – although none proved entirely empty. Surely a wonderful litmus test of the state of world cinema. It goes without saying, in an *Introduction* of this scope, that the space available for each engagement is limited. However, I have attempted to give each as much time as necessary for the film in the context of the sign – some of the chapters are thus fleet of foot, others take a little longer to wander through an argument. In each case, the aim has been to bring a sign to a film in order to explore the cinematographics – be that an image, the narration or the narrative; be it a sequence of a film, the whole film or even a series of films. It is beyond the remit of the project, and would make this book far too long, to engage with writers, theorists and philosophers who have already explored the films herein – I thus invite the reader to make their own connections. Finally, I also wanted to ensure that the choices in Section III resonated with, expanded upon or even challenged Sections II and I. In all these ways, the movies explored are not exemplary of the sign – none is a perfect fit (as if such a thing were possible). Rather, the film allowed itself – to my mind – to be exploited by a sign in order to think the film, for a moment, that is all. You may well have other ideas.

*
*   *

There is – finally – a third reason for dividing this book into three introductions. In *A Thousand Plateaus*, Deleuze (and co-author Félix Guattari) compare mapping with tracing, cartography with decalomania. Mapping prepares us for an exploration; while tracing is merely a copying out – 'organised, stabilized, neutralised … multiplicities' (TP: 15). Mapping is a 'reverse, but non-symmetrical, operation'; mapping undoes tracing, not only sustaining but propagating multiplicity through interpretation – and the method is to 'combine several maps' (TP: 15). The structural and serial investigations of Part One and the filmic explorations of Part Two are three different attempts at a mapping: all disparate and all resonating. Part One – a survey and a peregrination; the vertical and the horizontal; a deep dive into the ocean while the other skips stones across its surface. And both sections propagate further mappings. Section I maps Bergson, Peirce, the Deleuze of the *Cinema* books and the Deleuze of *Difference and Repetition*; and Section II maps a world of varied cinematic forms through a diverse series of images and signs; and through, in turn, a series of diagrams. Part Two – a reverse procedure, maps cinema to the many images and signs of the cineosis to explore a question, a problem, a void, ellipsis in the sequences and movies encountered, encounters that were left open to chance. Mapping is interpretation. Perhaps another – perhaps a more appropriate – title for this book would have been *Three Interpretations*.

Part One

Unfolding the Cineosis

A classification scheme is like the skeleton of a book: it's like a vocabulary ... a necessary first step. (TRM: 285)

What we call cinematographic concepts are ... the types of images and the signs which correspond to each type. (C1: ix)

Section I

First Introduction

Two Regimes of Images

There are – for Deleuze – two regimes of images in the cinema: movement-images and time-images. Two kinds of cinema each with its own distinct filmic semiotic, a system of signs as a twofold logic. The First Introduction explores, develops but also challenges this aspect of Deleuze's film theory through a genealogy of the philosophies that inspire and organise the cineosis. Chapter 1 is concerned with the creation of the two regimes as a response to Henri Bergson's investigations of image and duration from Matter and Memory. *Chapter 2 focuses upon the taxonomy of the movement-image, which unfolds in the wake of the semiosis of Charles Sanders Peirce from* Pragmatism and Pragmaticism. *Chapter 3 turns its attention to the time-image, where the sign system can be seen as a playing out of Deleuze's syntheses of time, space and consciousness from his own foundational text* Difference and Repetition. *Chapter 4 returns to Bergson in the aftermath of the explorations of the previous chapters to orient the investigation away from the primacy of the two regimes, and – in anticipation of Section II and Section III – towards an alternative understanding of the cineosis as a univocal series describing a multiplicity of signs.*

1

Movement-images and time-images: Bergson, image and duration

Cinema – for Deleuze – is the movement-image and the time-image. Two regimes of the cinematic image, where the fundamental division is theorised in the wake of the philosophy of Henri Bergson. In *Matter and Memory* (1896) Bergson explores – and, as the title suggests, asserts – the radical difference in kind between pure matter and pure memory; between image and duration; between the sensory-motor system and spontaneous thought; between the body (its flesh, bone, nervous system and brain) and the mind (as degrees of consciousness). Deleuze's appropriation of Bergson's philosophy and its application to cinema will consist of using the coordinates of the sensory-motor system to designate the movement-image, and an examination of pure memory and spontaneous thought to designate the time-image. In other words, Bergson's philosophy gives the cineosis its fundamental taxonomy. Yet such a taxonomical appropriation must immediately be considered as only a filmic tendency. For all cinema is necessarily a matter-image and an image of matter; and all cinema inescapably – in some way – captures, expresses and engenders memory and thought. Accordingly, while Bergson's *division* of the sensory-motor system and memory-thought provides the taxonomical coordinates of the movement-image and the time-image, it is the *relation* between the sensory-motor system and memory-thought that inspires the integrated philosophy of the cineosis. Movement-images and time-images are thus two polarities: the movement-image as a tendency of the cinema to describe ways in which the world and its bodies capture up, organise, and structure pure memory and spontaneous thought through the sensory-motor system; the time-image as a tendency of the cinema to discover means to escape, unground, disrupt and disturb the sensory-motor system through pure memory and spontaneous thought. This double articulation of the two cinematic regimes comes as no critique of Bergsonism, but rather, for Deleuze, is the very essence of Bergson's philosophy. There can be no sensory-motor system without pure-spontaneous thought, and no pure-spontaneous memory without the sensory-motor system; no image without duration, no duration without image. Bergson explicates such a division and relation in any number of ways, including the dimensions of space and time, and the properly philosophical concepts of the actual and the virtual. And it is this division and relation that Deleuze extends into the art of the cinema through the concepts of the movement-image and the time-image.

The sensory-motor system and pure memory

Bergson's account of the sensory-motor system describes the processes of a living body located at the centre of its universe. Both body and world are made of and are in matter; and matter – for Bergson – is an image and forms assemblages as images. The body is an image at the centre of the image of the universe; a universe composed of a multitude of images at every scale, images which are in constant interaction with one another. Accordingly, this body is subject to the never-ending collisions and contacts – movements – from images on its outside. These movements are received as perception. Such perceptions obey the laws of physics, chemistry and biology and will thus determine appropriate reactions, the world in turn becoming subject to the actions produced by bodies. Here we encounter the formula: perception → action. In visual perception light particles collide with a light-receiving device: a retina, perhaps. Such visual perception is not different in kind from that, say, of an auditory, tactile or olfactory perception: all are the reception of movement, all are interactions of and in matter. These perceptions – light hitting a retina describing a visual image; sound waves banging the drum of the ear, the hammer striking the anvil and describing an auditory image – pass through the body, its nervous system and brain producing an act in response to the sensory field. Electrical potentials and chemical balances change and the organic body moves (turns towards, turns away), becoming a motor in the world effecting a transformation in and upon the images of that world.

This fundamental sensory-motor formula, however, is purely nominal. Between perceptions and actions is another domain: affect. 'Affects', for Bergson 'always interpose themselves between the excitations that I receive from without and the movements which I am about to execute' (MM: 17–18). Between extensive perceptions and extensive actions are intensive affects. '[T]he afferent nerves are images', writes Bergson, 'the brain is an image, the disturbance travelling through the sensory nerves and propagated in the brain is an image too' (MM: 24). The body is matter, an image like any other; but one that distributes external perceptions as intensive forces through a nervous system and brain to component parts of that body for an externalised reaction. In this way, a more complex sensory-motor trajectory becomes apparent: perception → affect → action. Life – from unicellular to multi-cellular organisms – describes an ever-complexifying nexus of pathways from perception to action. And this complexity affirms the possibility of diverse reactions. Bergson thus calls the body as affect a centre of indetermination (MM: 41). This body and its affects bring indetermination to determination – actions are open to variation, deviation, aberration and chance.

Such indetermination would immediately appear to be subject to a twofold limit. So far as the complex trajectory is concerned, the possibility of in-determination is derived from a prior perception which operates as a field of necessity; and the range of responses to such a field would thus tend towards the functional.

On the one hand, perception operates at the level of aggregate images in order to better define and recognise an outline of an object (a solid visual image, a solid tactile image, a solid auditory image, and so on). Bergson writes, 'we have no reason … for representing the atom to ourselves as a solid, rather than liquid or gaseous' (MM: 199). Yet perception does indeed tend towards binding and effacing molecular distributions as and for solid molar entities, the better to order, classify and organise. Natural organic perception operates at a certain scale, functioning to limit any tendency towards molecular indetermination for instantaneous recognition and identity. Concomitantly – and on the other hand – recognition and identity indicate that indetermination will become caged to ever more encompassing determinations as actions become habitualised, responses to received perceptions proving more or less effective – if less, rejected; if more, retained. In this way the sensory-motor trajectory is developed beyond a linear trajectory, a development Bergson names as the memory-image. The body, then, is a memory-image, an image composed of habituated memories, not only oriented as perception → affect → action, but also as perception ← affect ← action. From the vast swathes of a universe composed of matter and innumerable images, certain coalescences are selected for us by our perceptions. Just as from all possible reactions a certain action will tend towards preference, perception becomes oriented towards recognition, what affects us as a centre. World and body, body and world form relay loops of extensive and intensive forces; perceptions, affects, and actions as memory-images; determination and indetermination, indetermination and determination. Accordingly, the sensory-motor schema is no longer a trajectory, but a full and complex reciprocal system of movement with the formula: {perception ↔ affect ↔ action} ↔ memory-image.

This conception of memory as image, for Bergson, is 'effected in two different ways' (MM: 237). Sometimes, as has been outlined, recognition is 'acted rather than thought, the body responds to a perception that recurs by a movement or attitude that has become automatic' (MM: 237). Sometimes, however, Bergson sees that 'recognition is actively produced by memory-images which go out to meet the present perception' (MM: 237–8). Such an active production of memory-images seemingly creates a paradox: memory-images produced not from the movements of matter, but from memory itself. How can memory derive from memory? For Bergson, the explication of this paradox begins with 'complexity' (MM: 222). In complex organisms and as the organism becomes more complex – as affects bring increasing indetermi-nation to determination and actions open up to variation, deviation, aberration and chance – life appears to free itself, become independent from matter. While such indeterminations are subject to refinement through habituation, memory-images are always exposed, in turn, to further indeterminations under the ongoing processes of affect. And affect, as a centre of indetermina-tion, as a centre of complexity, introduces the interval. On the one hand – this interval appears between perception and action as delay (which extends the moment of response away from instantaneity). On the other hand – this interval appears between memory-images for possible actions (the selection of different responses). Accordingly, complexity, for Bergson, is 'the material symbol of ... independence itself ... a symbol of the inner energy which allows the being to free itself from the rhythm of the flow of things' (MM: 222). Complexity is a symbol for the interval – and the interval is derived from inner energies, the differential physical, chemical and biological processes of the body and its brain: spontaneous thought, arising consciousness, pure memory. It thinks nothing and remembers nothing, but is the vitality shaping memories and thinking. 'The intellect', writes Bergson, is 'forever moving in the interval' between memory-images, and 'unceasingly finds them again or creates them anew' (MM: 242). Consciousness is at the centre of life. Con-sciousness is life. It is that which flows from the centre of indetermination to be ordered and structured through the sensory-motor system. And it is that which selects and creates – or rather re-creates – memory-images, embodying images of pure memory and spontaneous thought in the body through affects; as and for recognition in perceptions; as and for the selection of actions. Spontaneous thought, pure memory, is that which both founds and frees itself from the sensory-motor system. This is the 'opposition between ... consciousness and

perception	affect	action
memory-image		
sensory-motor system		
pure memory		

Figure I.01 Bergson: the sensory-motor schema and pure memory

movement', between 'freedom and necessity' (MM: 245, 247). Hence the full Bergsonian formula: {{perception ↔ affect ↔ action} ↔ memory-image} ↔ pure memory. This relation can be described as in Figure I.01.

Image and duration, space and time, actual and virtual

These concepts of the sensory-motor system and pure memory are clarified by Bergson, their division and their relation, through explications of various corresponding and resonating couplings. Correlates include 'the reality of matter' and 'the reality of spirit'; 'body' and 'soul'; 'movement' and 'duration'; 'space' and 'time'; 'brain' and 'thought'; and 'the actual' and 'the virtual' (MM: 9, 10, 11, 15, 23, 131, 217–19). These coordinates are fundamental in developing and further exploring the radical nature of Bergson's argument, and – as will be seen – for the appropriations of Deleuze's movement-image and time-image. Beginning with space and time, we can explore movement and duration, then conclude with the actual and the virtual. To anticipate this trajectory, the distribution of these correlates and their conceptual developments can be expressed as in Figure I.02.

Sensory-motor system	Pure memory
space	time
… or rather, spatialised time	… or rather, temporalised space
movement	duration
matter (bodies, brains)	consciousness (spirit, soul)
image	thought
actual	virtual

Figure I.02 Bergson: correlates of the sensory-motor system and pure memory

The sensory-motor system describes an organic organisation of life in and of the world: an emergent centre in comprehensive space and chronological time. That is to say, a body experiences space and time as space-time. Space is inseparable from time, and time inseparable from space for a body in the universe. As the body moves through space it moves in time, and as the body experiences time it does so through subsisting in space. Yet while space has three apparent dimensions (forwards–backwards, upwards–downwards, right–left), time here is rendered in one dimension. Time is unidirectional and linear, the ever-present instantaneous now. Accordingly, the past, the present and the future appear as homogeneous moments of now: the now-itself, a now to come, and a now that has passed. The now to come and the now that has passed, however, are different from the now-itself as they do not exist in the space which the body occupies. Time, in this way, is defined by space. The now is derived purely spatially: the famous example of the hands on a clock which move through space, and from which an image of time is derived. Space-time appears as space and space appears as movement (perceptions, affects, actions and memory-images as movements of matter). Kimberley and Dittmer put it beautifully, writing that time is measured in 'the movement of a star across the sky, in the development of wrinkles in a face, in the passage of sand through an hourglass' and concluding: 'even the idea of measuring time at all implies its spatialization' (Kimberley and Dittmer, 2015: 64). Here the formula is: space = spatialised temporality as movement.

Yet there is another experience of time. Here the reciprocal formula would be: time = temporalised spatiality as duration. In the space-time of the present (which is the only time of space) everything is experienced in the now; duration then is properly of the past and the future. This is the past and the future as that which bring a new kind of temporality to the present as time. When we look out at the stars, we see the present overwhelmed by the past – thousands upon millions of years are in the present as simultaneous shining points of many pasts. The future, in distinction, is fundamentally and radically unknowable: a darkness without any points of light. Such a consideration describes a very different kind of present. Here time overwhelms space – spatiality becomes temporalised. This is the present as duration. Kimberley and Dittmer once again: this 'present cannot be understood as the "dot" on a timeline that signifies "now". Rather, the present must be understood as elastic, capable of expanding itself to include what from the past and immediate future it requires to remain in continuity with itself' (Kimberley and Dittmer, 2015: 68). Accordingly, this present 'has no measurable length ... it takes as long as it takes ... it may stretch itself to include minutes, hours, days, and even longer. When, for example, we talk of geological or evolutionary duration, we may define the present in terms of centuries or millennia' (Kimberley and Dittmer, 2015: 68). This is duration, the coalescence of shining points and radical darkness.

Accordingly, there are two kinds of present – one present which moves and composes time as the immediate flow of now (effacing the past and an effaced future); one present which encompasses the past and the future (an effective effacement of the present as now). These two presents are thus both badly named. The former is really movement (as space, spatialised temporality); the latter is really duration (as time, temporalised spatiality). Movement describes the sensory-motor system of a body – perception, affects, actions and memory-images. Duration describes pure memory and spontaneous thought – the retention of memory-images of actions, affects and perceptions; and the possibility of searching, jumping, falling between the dark intervals of memory-images for perceptions, affects and actions.

Such a consideration of space and time as movement and duration in reference to the sensory-motor system and pure-spontaneous thought foregrounds the radical nature of Bergson's philosophy. This radical nature concerns the memory-image and memory. Every scar is accompanied by its durations. Every dancer imprisons movements within the body as physical, chemical and biological modification; and each rehearsal and each performance has its own duration. Duration is the whole of the past and the future within the present, which are returned to the body as memory-images. Such a return is not a reconstitution but a constitution, the memory-image will have intermixed with other memory-images, memory-images colour one another and are created anew. As Patrick McNamara writes, classical accounts of memory would seem to see 'the sequence of events ... [as] an external cue and then a search process'; yet 'Bergson argued against this empiricist approach to memory' (McNamara, 1996: 222). In other words, there is 'no notion of encoding' in Bergsonian accounts of memory (McNamara, 1996: 222). Consciousness is the body in duration. The body is in time: the body is not only in the spatial present of the now, but in the time of its past – all its past – oriented towards its future. Pure memory as a function of the brain is a spontaneous flow of energy which encounters the external world, the perception of which causes a break in that flow for the production of memory-images, affect and action in the now. McNamara puts it this way: 'most memories/rememberings are not triggered by external cues ... spontaneous rememberings, in fact, are the norm for human beings' (McNamara, 1996: 222). This pure memory, spontaneous thought, is not a consequence of the movements of matter, but a perspective towards the movements of matter. Bergson writes: 'pure memory is a spiritual manifestation. With [pure] memory we are, in truth, in the domain of spirit' (Bergson, 1991: 240).

In other words, duration describes consciousness, and movement the realm of the unconscious. Yet these concepts of duration and movement are not in reality pure: memory as pure memory is an impossibility, just as would be the concept of a pure sensory-motor system. Consciousness cannot exist without the body, and the body is always in consciousness to some degree. The sensory-motor system and pure-spontaneous thought interact in space and time, movements are always accompanied by duration, and duration by movements. As Bergson writes in *Creative Evolution*: 'matter, the reality which descends, endures only by its connection with that which ascends ... life and consciousness are this very ascension' (CE: 369). Matter endures in memory through duration, the virtual. The virtual is the realm of consciousness which is actualised in the body and its brain as memory-images, with affects, with perceptions, with actions. Memory is actualised through the sensory-motor system; and the duration of the actual movements of matter endure only through becoming virtual.

Movement-images and time-images

Cinema – for Deleuze – resonates with Bergsonism. Bergson's sensory-motor system and pure memory – image and thought, movement and duration, space and time, the actual and the virtual – give Deleuze both the philosophy and the coordinates of his cinema theory. Cinema is composed of images, matter-images of and in matter. Yet cinema also captures thought (the thought of filmmakers – directors, actors, musicians, cinematographers, writers and so on) and engenders thought (the thought of the audience – spectators, critics, theorists, philosophers and so on) across space and in time (geographical and historical; durational). Cinema does so through the transmission of visual and sound images. This is to say, the actualised images of cinema happen in the space-time of the immediate present. However, these actual images also have virtual correlates. A film has duration – it somehow captures up the durations of filmmakers and engenders the durations of audiences. It somehow captures up the time in which it was made, the time or times it describes, the time in which it is watched and rewatched, and the times in which it appears in thought. The matter-images of cinema have a reality which endures only as its ascension through consciousness.

From such a general proposition Deleuze decomposes the cinematographic image into two regimes: movement-images and time-images. Such a naming, after Bergson, refers to the two formulas of movement and duration: space = spatialised temporality as movement; and, time = temporalised spatiality as duration. Accordingly, movement-images describe Bergson's sensory-motor system; while time-images describe Bergson's spontaneous thought and pure memory. Deleuze here has shifted his focus from Bergson's philosophy to the descriptive coordinates of that philosophy. It is with such a shift that Deleuze inaugurates the cineosis. For movement-images and time-images will necessarily both be composed of actual visual and sound images of matter in space as movement. However, each regime will tend towards a different image of time. Movement-images tend towards an image of time as a dimension of space: what Deleuze calls an indirect image of time. Time-images will tend towards a direct image of time: the actual images of the film will be overwhelmed by their virtual correlates. From such principles the taxonomy of the cinema as movement-images and time-images will arise.

Movement-images describe on-screen the sensory-motor system: a cinema which extracts from the world a coherent centre, a centre such as a human character; a centre which can express emotions and then react to or act upon the world from which it was extracted – a centre where recollection, thought and imagination are reconstituted as memory-images of consciousness. In this way, movement-images are constituted through the linkage of four different domains of images: perception-images, affection-images, action-images and mental-images. The regime of the movement-image is thus a logic, flow and connection of domains: {perception-image ↔ affection-image ↔ action-image} ↔ mental-image.

Perception-images distil a character from all possible images of the universe, create a character that is perceived by and perceives the world. Such a distillation occurs – as we saw above in Bergson's formulation of perception – through a trajectory of the gaseous, liquid and solid. Gaseous perception is molecular and genetic in that it is the condition of all images vibrating upon each other – a montage of shots of landscapes, objects, people, animals, and so on. With liquid perception, centres begin to form – groups accumulate, privileged for a moment before the film flows on to other scenes, locations and times. Becoming solid is a leaving behind of a purely objective world (where all images interact with each other) for the creation of a central and privileged image: the character. The perception-image thus creates a solid subject through capturing images of that character, following that character, seeing and hearing with that character. A solid centre and privileged image around which exist, flow and vibrate the degrees of perception which they will organise and structure. This perception-image passes immediately into the affection-image. The affection-image is where the environment engenders affects in the character, these unfilmable internal intensities appearing as external expressions upon faces and bodies with respect to the mise-en-scène. The central and privileged image will be captured in close-up: and the close-up of the face is the expression of affects as determined feelings and emotions. From such affects the affection-image passes into the action-image. In other words, perceptions and affects are determined for a reacting to and an acting upon. The central and privileged image is now revealing the determinates of that world, resolving the situation of that world. Finally, mental-images capture images of thought on-screen (recollections as flashbacks; imaginings through dreams and nightmares; comprehension by way of the relations between the world, its characters and objects). In this way, perceptions, affects and actions appear as mental-images for the privileged centre: habitualised behaviours, haunted pasts, wishes for the future – such images actualised on the screen as the impetus and providence of the character.

Movement-images thus structure and organise the film through perception-images, affection-images, action-images and mental-images. The film is composed of moments of perception, affect, action and thought edited seamlessly together in long shot, medium shot and close-up centring upon a privileged character. A character whose perceptions, affects, actions and thoughts flow through all the images on-screen: comprehensive space and chronological time creating a coherent centre. These are the linkages, the process and the philosophy of the movement-image. And it is these linkages, processes and philosophy that (tend to) capture the audience.

The time-image is very different – and this difference can be articulated both as negation and affirmation. In the first instance, the time-image is an outcome of the collapse of the coordinates of the movement-image into an undifferentiated image. No longer can a film be said to be composed of perception-images, affection-images, action-images and mental-images; no longer is there a fixed and solid centre that can process affects as lucid expressions, a centre that can adequately react to and perform acts upon the world; a centre whose thoughts can be reliably traced, depicted and defined. Human centres are dispersed, comprehensive space displaced and chronological time becomes disjunctive. In the second instance – as a consequence of, and in consort with such a dissolution of the movement-image – the time-image sets free a new kind of cinematic image. Dispersed centres, disjunctive temporality and displaced spatiality are revealed as full and positive powers of affirmation: the affirmation of a new image of thought unshackled from the coordinates of determined and determinable perceptions, affects and actions. In other words, the actual images of the film encounter the virtual. Sequences may appear to have no relation; cuts between images stymie the flow; characters become ciphers, shadows, even disappear. The film decomposes itself – sound and colour become disruptive elements. Backgrounds remain amorphous or overwhelm the screen. The actual images of the film are punctuated by intervals of every kind: breaks, caesuras, repetitions with difference. And it is these intervals which open up the actual on-screen images to virtual correlates. Accordingly, the delinked nature of the film becomes an encounter in which the viewer cannot simply see the image of thought produced by the film, but must (if we do not turn away) think what the film does not actualise. The time-image is the possibility of the ascension of cinematic duration.

In one sense time-images are fundamental, coming before movement-images. If time-images are dispersive and perplexing, it is the movement-image function of cinema that will cut and link, select and organise (edit) these moments, give them a determined situation and a central character who can see, feel, think, and act. Correspondingly, time-images come after movement-images (are invented in the wake of movement-images). Time-images are a radical response to films which believe in a governed milieu, films through which people can understand and know the world, others, themselves; and a radical response also to films which believe that the chaos of the universe can be fully tamed and resolved. Making and discovering time-images takes an act of will that ungrounds the movement-image function which wants to assert itself at every moment: the time-image is both fundamental and difficult to reconstitute. Finally – such befores and afters are nominal (on the side of actualisation): movement-image and time-image films occur in cinema history in parallel and interpenetrate to greater and lesser degrees (are in duration). In this way, there would be no such thing as a pure movement-image film, and no such thing as a pure time-image film. All cinema is composed of matter-images that have duration. However, the tendency will be for the cohesion of the movement-image or the dispersals of the time-image to overwhelm the film. Either a movement-image or a time-image function will dominate the film – to a greater or lesser degree. Crucially, and accordingly – 'there is no value-judgment here', writes Deleuze, both movement-images and time-images can shape 'masterpieces to which no hierarchy of value applies' (C1: x). All that can be said is that movement-images and time-images conceive image, narration and narrative very differently. This relationship, echoing that of the Bergsonian model (Figure I.01), can be given as in Figure I.03.

perception-image	affection-image	action-image
mental-image		
movement-image		
time-image		

Figure I.03 Deleuze: the movement-image and time-image after Bergson

* * *

Movement-images and time-images derive their philosophy from Bergson's ideas on image and duration, and their taxonomic coordinates are derived from the explications of the sensory-motor system and pure memory/spontaneous thought. From such a philosophical and taxonomic origin Deleuze will go on to produce, in turn, two semiotics which explore cinema through an extended set of movement-image and time-image elements. Over the twenty-two chapters of the *Cinema* books Deleuze introduces an extraordinary amount of terminology. Much of this terminology is borrowed, reworked and redefined to form cinematic concepts which remap and re-encounter the cinema. With respect to the movement-image, the taxonomy will be grounded and expanded through the semiotic methodology of Charles Sanders Peirce. With respect to the time-image, the taxonomy will be a capturing of Deleuze's syntheses of time, space and consciousness from *Difference and Repetition*. Yet each taxonomy remains dependent upon its Bergsonian foundation, time-images foregrounding pure-spontaneous thought, and movement-images foregrounding the sensory-motor system.

2

Movement-images: Peirce, semiosis

Cinema – the cinema of the movement-image – begins for Deleuze with perception-images, affection-images, action-images and mental-images. The sensory-motor system as explicated by Bergson describes the world and its bodies as a nexus of perceptions, affects and actions; a nexus traversed, underlain and sustained with memory-images. These Bergsonian coordinates give Deleuze the fundamental taxonomic elements composing the cinema of the movement-image: perception-images extract from all the images of the world a body around which the film will revolve; affections-images express unfilmable internal intensive states through this centre as character emotions and feelings; action-images allow and obligate the privileged image to act in and upon the world; and mental-images permeate the film actualising the character's thoughts, dreams and memories. Deleuze – however – goes on to expand this fundamental taxonomy: 'there is every reason to believe that many other kinds of images can exist' (C1: 68). To create these new images, Deleuze unfolds the movement-image beyond the primary Bergsonian coordinates through a conjunction of identifying and determining interim states and devolving such images into a series of compositional signs. The movement-image cineosis becomes complex: a web of signs, images, avatars and domains. Such complexity, however, is haunted by ambiguity. Deleuze will give three iterations of the extended movement-image taxonomy – the text of *Cinema 1*, the glossary of *Cinema 1* and a recapitulation of images and signs early on in *Cinema 2* – and each iteration is different. Not only that, but after the supposed final summary in *Cinema 2*'s recapitulation there appears to be the designation of even more types of movement-image. Across the *Cinema* books, lucid expositions of the movement-image cineosis see repetitions interweaving with differences. This chapter attempts to explicate, justify and even resolve some of these ambiguities, as well as acknowledging the limit of such an enterprise. Either way, the aim is to present a full and complete framework for the coordinates of signs, images, avatars and domains of the movement-image regime, where all the different enunciations of that taxonomy appear as moments of a process of unfolding.

Such an exposition rests upon an engagement with the semiotics of Charles Sanders Peirce. Deleuze believes there to be a general agreement between the coordinates of Bergson's sensory-motor system and the logic of Peirce's semiotic, and that Peirce's method can be used to expand the movement-image taxonomy that began with Bergson's fundamental coordinates. Deleuze writes: '[w]e will frequently be referring to the American logician Peirce (1839–1914), because he established a general classification of images and signs, which is undoubtedly the most complete and the most varied' (C1: xiv). Peirce himself once commented (with respect to a proposed but never realised text on his semiotic): 'I feel confident the book would make a serious impression much deeper and surer than Bergson's, which I find quite too vague' (SW: 428). Yet while the expansion of the movement-image taxonomy is inspired by the semiotics of Peirce, it is with this appropriation that we encounter the heart of the problem with respect to the ambiguities of the cineosis. In the first place, the specifics of Peirce's semiotic can appear superfluous to the movement-image. Deleuze comments in *Cinema 2*: 'we borrowed from Peirce a certain number of terms whilst changing their meaning' (C2: 32). And he adds, '[w]e therefore take the term "sign" in a completely different way from Peirce', blithely advising the reader they can 'skip' the work on the semiosis in *Cinema 1* (C2: 32). This appears to indicate Deleuze has ridden roughshod through Peirce's methodology, and simply used terminology as a nomenclature reservoir, creating concepts willy-nilly. This has led Ronald Bogue to write: 'obviously, the tally [of signs] is insignificant … Deleuze is no ordinary system builder … his taxonomy is a generative device meant to create new terms for talking about new ways of seeing' (Bogue, 2003: 104). In the second place, the Peircian semiotic is itself complex and riven with obscurities. There are at least three different accounts (created over a forty-year period) in published and (originally) unpublished papers, lectures, notes and letters. Peirce scholars have been working through these accounts for decades, and certain aspects are still – and are likely to remain – under debate. However, despite the semiosis being passed off as peripheral and being complex in and of itself, exploring Peirce's method reveals it as essential for investigating the ambiguities in Deleuze's articulations of the extended movement-image cineosis as well as the ground for establishing the full set of images and signs as a relational framework. For while Deleuze may change the names and meanings of signs, and even the notion of the sign itself, the logic of Peirce's semiotic structural unfolding remains. Deleuze takes Peirce's universal semiosis and – in the wake of the already appropriated Bergsonian sensory-motor system – uses it to create a pragmatic cineotic matrix of movement-images.

Pragmatism and semiosis

In the introduction to *Pragmatism and Pragmaticism,* a series of lectures presented at Harvard in 1903, Peirce begins by saying he struck the term 'pragmatism' back in the 1860s, and while it has been brought into academic and popular consciousness through the work of William James, James's approach was not exactly what concerned Peirce. Hence the new term 'pragmaticism' to refer to his own version of pragmatism. Changing nomenclature is a continual theme in the work of Peirce, and something we see in particular with the semiosis. And indeed, it is the semiosis – the precision and procession of signs – that comes to underpin pragmaticism. Correspondingly, one way to approach the semiosis is through Peirce's pragmaticist doctrine. Peirce writes in 1903: 'pragmaticism is not a *Weltanschauung* but is a method of reflexion having for its purpose to render ideas clear' (CP 5.13). Accordingly, pragmaticism can be seen as a practical science, as having a practical experiential application in the world. This statement from *Pragmatism and Pragmaticism* is also a not-so-oblique reference to an early published paper, 'How to Make our Ideas Clear' (1878). Here Peirce describes thought as a 'thread of melody running through the succession of our sensations', and belief 'the demi-cadence which closes a musical phrase in the symphony of our intellectual life' (CP 1.292). This music of thought and belief has – for Peirce – three properties: '[f]irst, it is something that we are aware of; second, it appeases the irritation of doubt; and third, it involves the establishment in our nature of a rule ... or ... habit' (CP 1.292). In this way, 'the whole function of thought is to produce habits' (CP 1.292). The pragmaticist maxim, then, would be: 'Consider what effects, that might conceivably have practical bearings, we conceive the object of our conception to have. Then, our conception of these effects is the whole of our conception of the object' (CP 1.292). Lest we think such a maxim vague, this is for Peirce the basis of a logic. In lecture one of the Harvard series, in reference to this maxim, Peirce says: 'the question of the nature of belief [is] ... the question of what the true logical analysis of the act of judgement is' (CP 5.28). And it is the semiotic that becomes the logical analysis for Peircian pragmaticism. 'Logic, in its general sense, is ... only another name for semiotic ... the quasi-necessary, or formal, doctrine of signs' (CP 2.227). As Bonnie Meyer comments, 'pragmaticism is essentially a method for interpreting a certain type of sign – the concept – by looking for a certain type of interpretant – the practical effects' (Meyer, 2008: 152). Peirce later reflected: 'it has never been in my power to study anything – mathematics, ethics, metaphysics, gravitation, thermo-dynamics, optics, chemistry, comparative anatomy, astronomy, psychology, phonetics, economics, the history of science, whist, men and women, wine, metrology, except as a study of semeiotic' (SS: 85–6). Peirce did indeed write on many of these subjects, and underlying these writings his ever-developing semiotic can be felt, glimpsed and encountered.

The first seeds of this semiotic were sown around the same time as pragmatism was first conceived in a published paper called 'On a New List of Categories' (1868), and Peirce would explore the semiotic up until his death. As Albert Atkin neatly summarises: 'Peirce continually returned to and developed his ideas about signs and semiotic and there are three broadly delineable accounts' (Atkin, 2008: 1). There is 'a concise Early Account from the 1860s; a complete and relatively neat Interim Account developed through the 1880s and 1890s and presented in 1903 [the aforementioned Harvard lectures]; and his speculative, rambling, and incomplete Final Account developed between 1906 and 1910' (Atkin 2008: 1). We can compare Atkin's schematic overview with Peirce's own take (from around 1903): '[a]ll that you can find in print of my work on logic are simply scattered outcroppings here and there ... a rich vein of which remains unpublished. Most of it I suppose has been written down; but no human being could ever put together the fragments. I could not do so myself' (CP 2: introductory statement). Of course, the desire to trace the semiotic, to put together the versions and the fragments, has captured many a Peirce scholar. The first paper to attempt a configuration of the trajectory across the three accounts is Paul Weiss and Arthur Burks' 'Peirce's Sixty-Six Signs' (1945). Weiss and Burks are attuned to the complexity of such an enterprise, one of the problems being that the 'terminology is not constant, raising doubts as the whether or not he has changed his thesis with his terms' (Weiss and Burks, 1945: 383). More importantly: 'perhaps the greatest difficulties stem from the necessity of understanding and keeping clearly distinguished *(a)* Peirce's single trichotomy of "categories", *(b)* his triply trichotomous, and *(c)* decimally trichotomous "division" of signs as well as *(d)* his ten-fold and *(e)* sixty-six-fold "classification" of signs' (Weiss and Burks 1945: 383–4). Weiss and Burks use these five principles and follow the trajectory of the three accounts to construct a viable synopsis. Most, if not all, explications of the semiosis follow in their wake, no matter how different the outcome.

Three universal categories

The starting point of Peirce's semiosis is the categories. For Peirce, understanding the way in which we experience the world has been the reason for the creation of categories since Aristotle, and from Kant to Hegel (CP 5.43). Peirce, however, is 'dissatisfied' (as Meyer puts it) with these previous attempts, hence his own method (Meyer, 2008: 153). In the second lecture of the Harvard series Peirce writes that to adopt the pragmaticist doctrine is to 'open our mental eyes and look well at the phenomenon and say what are the characteristics that are never wanting in it' (CP 5.41). This phenomenon can be of diverse origin, 'something that outward experience forces upon our attention ... [our] wildest of dreams ... [or] the most abstract and general of the conclusions of science' (CP 5.41, 5.42). And our mental eyes that encounter the phenomenon, for Peirce, engage three faculties. So, while Peirce is dissatisfied with previous attempts at describing universal categories, he will refer to Hegel's 'three stages of thought' and 'the three categories of each of the four triads of Kant' as independent precursors to his work, and their existence, whatever the differences, as 'only go[ing] to show that there really are three such elements' (CP 8.329).

These three elements (faculties, categories or concepts – Peirce uses such terminology interchangeably) are described for the first time in 'On a New List of Categories'. 'The function of conceptions', writes Peirce, 'is to reduce the manifold of sensuous impressions to unity' (CP 1.545). This occurs through the three faculties (developing the three moments already seen in 'How to Make our Ideas Clear'). First as a quality, or feeling. This is the thing in its thisness: hard, red, round. Second, as a reaction, as difference, the thing is this because it is not that. Third, abstracted thought, habituation, or representation. Peirce will, in later writings, simplify the nomenclature and call these categories firstness, secondness and thirdness (CP 5.66). Firstness (quality) and secondness (reaction) come before thirdness (representation), yet can only be thought through representation. In thinking quality and reaction, they are no longer pure quality and pure reaction, but the thought of quality and the thought of reaction. Thus while there is quality in-itself and reaction in-itself, there is also quality in action, quality as part of thought, and reaction as part of thought. Correspondingly, there is nothing beyond the final category, no other categories are needed, thirdness (representation) 'suffices of itself to give the conception of True Continuity ... no conception yet discovered is higher' (CP 5.67). There is nothing beyond the laws of thought. Quality → Reaction → Representation, or Firstness → Secondness → Thirdness, are thus a synthesis: 'Category the First is the Idea of that which is such as it is regardless of anything else. That is to say, it is a Quality of Feeling' (CP 5.66). 'Category the Second is the Idea of that which is such as it is as being Second to some First, regardless of anything else and in particular regardless of any Law, although it may conform to a law. That is to say, it is Reaction as an element of the Phenomenon' (CP 5.66). 'Category the Third is the Idea of that which is such as being a Third, or Medium, between Second and its First. That is to say, it is Representation as an element of the Phenomenon' (CP 5.66). If thirdness is the final aspect of an encounter with a thing, but also inclusive of (and not separate from) firstness and secondness, it follows that there are (at least) three different types of encounter with an object: the quality of firstness; the reaction of secondness; and the representation of thirdness. It is with this realisation that Peirce inaugurates the semiosis.

And this realisation, once again, occurs in 'New List'. The quality of the object of firstness Peirce calls the likeness (later to be renamed the icon). This is where the quality of objects is shared, for example, the redness, roundness, hardness of things in-themselves. The reaction of secondness is the index, where two things relate, for example, by cause and effect. Examples include a weathercock to the wind; a killer to the killed, smoke to fire. The representation of thirdness is a symbol, where things relate by convention, for example the reference of language, as in 'man' referring to a certain type of human (CP 1.545). We can notate the three aspects of the object as a sign against the categories, as in Figure I.04. This matrix of categories and their signs is commonly known as Peirce's first trichotomy.

Sign ╲ Categories	Firstness (feeling)	Secondness (reaction)	Thirdness (representation)
object	icon (or likeness)	index	symbol

Figure I.04 Pierce: first trichotomy (1868)

Three trichotomies and ten classes of signs

After the publication of 'New List', however, Peirce began to encounter experiential evidence that there are signs which cannot be accounted for through the icon–index–symbol trichotomy. A sign is more complex than the bare encounter of an object. Over the years following this first account Peirce would think about and explore this idea and such complexities in a number of ways, eventually developing a second *a priori* description of signs: (1) there is the object, the thing; (2) there is the sign of the thing which arises from the thing and is related to the thing; (3) there is the mind (for example) that processes the sign. Peirce calls these: representamen (or sign in-itself); the object of a sign; and the interpretant of the relationship between a sign and its object (CP 1.541). A sign S = R → O → I. Peirce describes triadic semiosis a number of times over the years. Here is one such statement: '[a] sign, or representamen, is something which stands to somebody for something in some respect or capacity. It addresses somebody, that is, creates in the mind of that person an equivalent sign, or perhaps a more developed sign' CP 2.228). Thus, '[t]hat sign which it creates I call the interpretant of the first sign. The sign stands for something, its object. It stands for that object, not in all respects, but in reference to a sort of idea, which I have sometimes called the ground of the representamen' (CP 2.228). It is as if the sign were an encounter that can be considered as a matrix, nexus or procession of movement between the object, idea and interpretation.

The essential aspect is this: as we saw previously, an object is experienced as firstness, secondness and thirdness. Now, if we have two more aspects to the sign other than the object – the representamen and the interpretant – these too will also have firstness, secondness and thirdness. In other words, there will now be three trichotomies with nine sign elements (traditionally named in Peirce studies as divisions). In an annexe to the 'Syllabus' document called 'Nomenclature and Divisions of Triadic Relations' (that accompanied his 1903 lectures) Peirce describes these nine divisions thus: '[s]igns are divisible by three trichotomies'; first 'according as the sign in itself is a mere quality, is an actual existent, or is a general law'; second 'according as the relation of the sign to its object consists in the sign's having some character in itself, or in some existential relation to that object, or in its relation to an interpretant'; third 'according as its interpretant represents it as a sign of possibility or as a sign of fact or a sign of reason' (CP 2.243). Such descriptions allow Peirce to name each of the nine sign divisions (CP 224–50). These can be notated as in Figure I.05.

Sign \ Categories	Firstness (feeling)	Secondness (reaction)	Thirdness (thought)
Sign in itself (representamen)	Qualisign (1)	Sinsign (2)	Legisign (3)
Sign in relation to object	Icon (1)	Index (2)	Symbol (3)
Sign in relation to interpretant	Rheme (1)	Dicisign (2)	Argument (3)

Figure I.05 Pierce: the three trichotomies (1903)

As any 'full' sign is composed of three divisions (R + O + I), we should, however, describe their composition in another way, as a triadic combination (or class). In other words, as fulfilling firstness, secondness and thirdness. The three most obvious classes are seen if we read down each column. These triadic combinations indicate what Peirce calls genuine signs of firstness, secondness and thirdness. There will be other possible combinations, but – crucially – only those combinations that compose a full sign (R + O + I) are allowed. Logically, then, entities of firstness can only join up with other entities of firstness; entities of secondness can only join up with entities of firstness and other entities of secondness; while entities of thirdness can include any other entity: (1); (2(1)); (3(2(1))). Thus there are not 27 possible combinations (3³) but ten, each being a different level of interpretation to which any phenomenon can be submitted (CP 1.530). These combinations can be listed as in Figure I.06 (which also gives their reduced class name – based on removing redundant demarcations – as designated by Peirce).

#	Category	Rep.	Obj.	Int.	Num.	Reduced class name
I	Firstness	Qualisign	Icon	Rheme	111	Qualisign
II	Secondness	Sinsign	Icon	Rheme	211	Iconic sinsign
III	Secondness		Index	Rheme	221	Rhematic Indexical sinsign
IV	Secondness			Dicisign	222	Dicent sinsign
V	Thirdness	Legisign	Icon	Rheme	311	Iconic legisign
VI	Thirdness		Index	Rheme	321	Rhematic indexical legisign
VII	Thirdness			Dicisign	322	Dicent indexical legisign
VIII	Thirdness		Symbol	Rheme	331	Rhematic Symbol
IX	Thirdness			Dicisign	332	Dicent symbol
X	Thirdness			Argument	333	Argument

Figure I.06 Peirce: ten classes of full signs from nine sign divisions (1903)

Another way of putting this is to say that genuine signs (333 and 222, though not 111, which is indivisible) can have degenerate forms. As Floyd Merrell explains, Peirce's adoption of the term 'is from mathematics and divorced from pejorative meaning in ordinary language use. De-generate signs are actually more fundamental' (Merrell, 1995: 100). Genuine secondness (222) can have a strong and a weak form. The weak form is the firstness of secondness (211), while the strong form is secondness of secondness, which includes a relatively degenerate secondness (221) as well as genuine secondness (222). Genuine thirdness (333) can split into a strong form as well as degenerate and weaker degenerate forms. The weakest degenerate is the firstness of thirdness, thus one on its own (311). The degenerate form is the secondness of thirdness. Thus we have a double, what we might call the firstness of the secondness of thirdness (321) and the secondness of the secondness of thirdness (322). Genuine thirdness has three values of thirdness, a relatively degenerate firstness of thirdness (331), a relatively degenerate secondness of thirdness (332) and, finally, true genuine thirdness (333) (CP 5.68–72). Therefore, and once again, we have ten classes of sign. We can represent the genuine and degenerate relationships as in Figure I.07 (which corresponds exactly to Figure I.06).

No doubt, such logical explications of the ten sign classes – carried out either through generation or degeneration – are complex. Yet the point Peirce

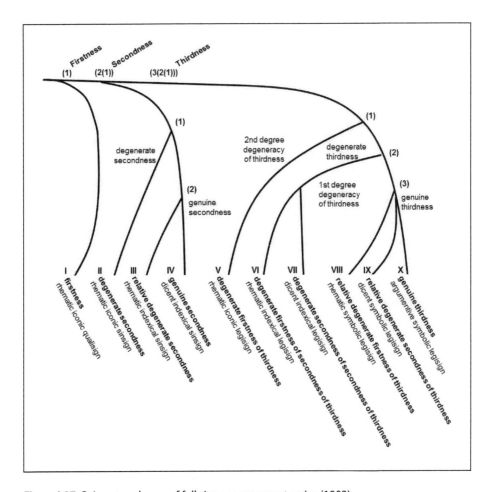

Figure I.07 Peirce: ten classes of full signs as emergent series (1903)

is making is relatively simple. First, the 'decalogue' – as Hing Tsang names the resultant list of classes – describes the level of engagement by the mind with the phenomenon through the sign of the encountered object (Tsang, 2013: 22). Peirce gives some examples, but the translation into levels given by Tsang (after work by Merrell) is particularly illuminating: see Figure I.08. Second, these levels are not static – the engagement by the mind with the phenomenon through the sign of the encountered object can rise and fall: see Figure I.09. Levels of attention can rise from feeling to realising; or descend from, say, awareness to the vaguest of feelings. The mind can become more or less attentive, more or less engaged, more or less exploratory. The semiosis is always in process, always in movement.

And so ends the semiosis of 1903. It is worth noting that, just as Peirce will replace combinatory divisional sign references, or classes, with new

#	Sign class	Examples from Peirce (CP2.254–263)	Examples from Tsang via Merrell (Tsang, 2013: 23)
X	Argument	a syllogism	realising
IX	Dicent symbol	a proposition	perceiving-saying
VIII	Rhematic Symbol	a common noun	seeing-saying
VII	Dicent indexical legisign	a street cry identifying individuals by tone	looking-saying
VI	Rhematic indexical legisign	a demonstrative pronoun	impressing-saying
V	Iconic legisign	a diagram, apart from its factual individuality	scheming
IV	Dicent sinsign	a weathercock or photograph	awaring
III	Rhematic Indexical sinsign	a spontaneous cry	sensing
II	Iconic sinsign	individual diagram	imaging
I	Qualisign	a feeling of red	feeling

Figure I.08   Peirce: ten classes with examples from Peirce and Tsang after Merrell

I	II	III	IV	V	VI	VII	VIII	IX	X	#
→	→	→	→	→	→	→	→	→	→	Semiotic generacy
←	←	←	←	←	←	←	←	←	←	Semiotic degeneracy

Figure I.09   Peirce: ten classes showing semiotic generacy and degeneracy

namings through redundancy (Figure I.06), he will also go on to rename some combinations, for instance rhematic indexical sinsigns become 'vestiges' and dicent symbols become 'propositions' (SS: 35–6). All of which adds further complexity – as Weiss and Burks pointed out – with respect to designation and meaning. However, the essential aspect is that the semiosis of 1903 consists of ten full classes of sign, each of which is composed of three sign elements. It is this version of the semiosis – the way in which full sign classes are composed of combinations of sign divisions, and sign divisions refer to three categories of signs – that will inspire the expansions of Deleuze's movement-image cineosis. However, before we return to Deleuze, Bergson and the movement-image, it is worth briefly exploring how Peirce will go on to enlarge his semiosis further still, for it is such mobility of the logic – along with Peirce's proclivity for renaming – which gives Deleuze licence to appropriate it for his own purposes.

For future explorers …

During 1903, Peirce began a correspondence with Victoria Lady Welby, the author of, among other texts, *Significs and Language* (1895). In two long letters, one sent 23 December 1908 (the other a different draft of the letter that appears to have been put aside and never posted), Peirce once again explicates his semiosis. These letters go on to expand the taxonomy of the semiosis further still. Rather than three trichotomies of the sign being delineated (representamen, object and interpretant), there are now ten, as in Figure I.10.

# Signs	Categories	Firstness	Secondness	Thirdness
01	Sign in itself	qualisign	sinsign	legisign
02	Immediate object	descriptives	designatives	copulants
03	Dynamic object	abstractive	concretive	collective
04	Relation of the sign to the dynamic object	icon	index	symbol
05	Immediate interpretant	hypothetical	categorical	relative
06	Dynamic interpretant	sympathetic	percussive	usual
07	Relation of the sign to the dynamic interpretant	suggestive	imperative	indicative
08	Normal interpretant	gratific	producing action	producing self-control
09	Relation of the sign to the normal interpretant	rheme	dicisign	argument
10	Triadic relation of the sign to its dynamic object and its normal interpretant	assurance of instinct	assurance of experience	assurance of form

Figure I.10 Peirce: the ten trichotomies (1908)

If we had, in 1903, nine sign elements over the three trichotomies giving 3^3 (27) possible combinations resolving to ten classes of sign; in 1908 we have ten trichotomies meaning 3^{10} (59,049) possible combinations. Of course, if we follow the logic of 1903, these must resolve into classes in exactly the same way, and 'these will only come to 66' (SS: 407). This development of the semiosis has been explored in a number of ways since the volumes of the *Collected Works* were published. Following Weiss and Burks, Gary Sanders' 'Peirce's Sixty-Six Signs?' is keen to show how there might not be 66 classes. Deciding upon an actual number of classes should really, according to Sanders and in the spirit of Peirce, be decided by experience (Sanders, 1970: 12). Peirce himself writes: 'in order to decide what classes of signs result from them I have 3^{10}, or 59,049, difficult questions to carefully consider; and therefore I do not undertake to carry out my systematic division of signs any further, but will leave that for future explorers' (CP 8.343). Among these explorers is Len Olsen, who, in 'On Peirce's Systematic Division of Signs' (2000), shows a number of ways to consider how the three trichotomies resolve to the ten classes, giving different results and thus impacting the third account, his work revisiting that begun by Sanders and taken up by Ralf Müller in 'On the principles of construction and the order of Peirce's trichotomies of signs' (Müller, 1993). As well as these taxonomic approaches, there are attempts to navigate the trajectory from a more historical, more philosophical angle. T. L. Short, in 'The Development of Peirce's Theory of Signs' (2004), is keen to understand why Peirce is spurred on to develop and continually transform the semiotic, and explore what is at stake in each of the accounts. At the other end of the spectrum are the mathematical attempts, the most extreme and fascinating utilising computer software to generate the trichotomy patterns of the 1903 and 1908 versions (Farias and Queiroz, 2003; 2004a,b; 2006). However, it is the general commentaries and explications that are of most interest and have travelled furthest outside the world of Peirce scholarship, for example Gérard Deledalle's many essays (some in English, some in French). So, despite Peirce saying no one could ever put together the fragments, that is exactly what this chapter, and all the essays and books mentioned above, have attempted to do. Furthermore, and perhaps most productively of all, some writers have gone on to use Peirce's semiosis as a basis for their own theoretical practices. This includes Merrell, in, for example, *Semiosis in the Postmodern Age* (1995), who reads the 1903 semiosis in spellbinding depth, before using it for his own ends. And more recently, Tsang's innovatory *Semiotics and Documentary Film* (2013), again based on the 1903 version.

Which brings us back to Deleuze. It is clear Deleuze is familiar with Peirce, and with Peirce scholarship of the time. For instance, he gives a sound, short overview of the 1903 semiotic schema – from categories to trichotomies to sign divisions and classes – as part of the recapitulation early in *Cinema 2*, even including in an endnote a version of the nine sign divisions table (see Figure I.05) (C2: 30, 287). *Cinema 1* and *2* also contain a number of references indicating a familiarity with Deledalle's commentaries (C1: 227, 231, 232; C2: 287). However, like Merrell and Tsang after him, Deleuze also wants to use Peirce for his own purposes.

On the alignment of Bergson and Deleuze with Peirce

'[T]here is every reason' – let Deleuze remind us – 'to believe that many other kinds of images can exist' beyond those specified in the wake of Bergson's sensory-motor system (C1: 68). Creating these new images can happen in one or both of two ways: 'they can result from a comparison of movement-images between themselves, or from a combination' (C1: 68). And for Deleuze, the productive machinery of comparison and combination has as inspiration the semiosis of Peirce. Yet, a word of caution from early in *Cinema 1*: '[w]e will have to compare the classification of images and signs that we propose with Peirce's great classification: why do they not coincide, even at the level of distinct images?' However, Deleuze continues: 'before this analysis – which can only be carried out later – we will constantly use the terms that Peirce created to designate particular signs, sometimes retaining their sense, sometimes modifying it or even changing it completely' (C1: 69). Deleuze will go on to give three iterations of this extended movement-image taxonomy – the text of *Cinema 1*, the glossary of *Cinema 1* and a recapitulation of images and signs early on in *Cinema 2* (Chapter 2). Each iteration (as will be seen) is different; furthermore, after the supposed final summary there is the designation of even more types of movement-image. The rationale for aligning Bergson and Peirce, as well as the explanation for all these differences (both between Peirce and Deleuze and between the versions of the movement-image), thus seems to centre on the comparison promised at the beginning of *Cinema 1*. This comparison, however, is deferred all the way until *Cinema 2*'s recapitulation. Accordingly, the recapitulation is perhaps the best place to start exploring the generative framework of the movement-image taxonomy, even if this will need to be re-evaluated later with respect to *Cinema 1*'s glossary and – most importantly – text. Finally, the full significance of the recapitulation is that – as was mentioned above – it convinces us that Deleuze's understanding of Peirce is sound through its explications of the 1903 account of the decalogue.

Deleuze's first move is to align Peirce's semiotic categories with Bergson's sensory-motor system and the resonant coordinates of his own movement-image taxonomy. As was explored in detail in Chapter 1 above, Bergson describes the world of matter through the movement of images. A body at the centre perceives the images of the world, is affected by these images through internal intensities, and then acts upon these affects in the process changing the images of the world. This trajectory becomes a system as the body is a memory-image of habituations: perceptions, affects and actions are a flux of indeterminations and determinations mediated as experience. Peirce's schema, according to Deleuze, can be considered in this way: first the image affects us; second, we act upon the image; third, the image becomes thought-habituations. Now, this account of Peirce's categories, while bearing a resemblance to that of Bergson's sensory-motor system, differs in one essential respect. Peirce's categories begin with how an image affects, whereas this is not the first category in Bergson, which is perception. In order to reconcile this difference Deleuze invents a corresponding term. He labels Bergsonian perception as having zeroness in reference to Peirce (C2: 31–2). For Deleuze, zeroness can be introduced into the Peircian schema as there is a silence in Peirce's approach: 'in his phenomenology, he claims the three types of image [firstness, secondness, thirdness] as a fact, instead of deducing them' (C2: 31). Bergson begins with 'mental eyes' (CP 5.41). For Deleuze, Peirce's claim is possible only because feeling (affection), reaction (action) and thought (memory-images) depend upon an initial perception. Peirce takes perception for granted.

Indeed, it is the productive consequence of this silence in Peirce that affirms Deleuze's approach to the perception-image. After Bergson, Deleuze's movement-image taxonomy appears to describe four domains: perception-images, affection-images, action-images and mental-images. Again, as was seen in Chapter 1, perception-images create a character that is perceived by and perceives the world; affection-images describe unfilmable internal intensities as external expressions upon the face and bodies of characters; action-images allow the character to transform the world; and mental-images capture images of thought on-screen. In the recapitulation – however – it becomes clear that perception does not exist as a domain for itself; rather, 'perception is strictly identical to every image' (C2: 31). In this way the perception-image disappears into all other movement-images instantaneously. Deleuze writes 'the perception-image will therefore be like a degree zero in the deduction which is carried out as a function of the movement-image: there will be a "zeroness" before Peirce's firstness' (C2: 31–2). We can thus tabulate the alignment of the Bergsonian, Peircian and Deleuzian schemas, at the level of image, as in Figure I.11.

Bergson	Perception	Affection	Action	Memory-image
Peirce	Zeroness (Perception)	Firstness (Feeling)	Secondness (Reaction)	Thirdness (Thought)
Deleuze	Perception-image	Affection-image	Action-image	Mental-image

Figure I.11 Deleuze: the correspondence between Bergson and Peirce

To conclude thus far – in the wake of the alignment of Peirce with Bergson at the beginning of the recapitulation, Deleuze has mapped the sensory-motor system with the semiotic categories, simultaneously supporting the domains of the movement-image cineosis while designating the perception-image as zeroness and as taking on a new and essential function. This function will have two important consequences: the first concerns the sign series that will be given to each of the images; the second concerns the generative method of Peirce's decalogue of sign classes as model for the full extended movement-image cineosis.

The first significance of zeroness: three signs for each movement-image

The recapitulation's designation of Bergsonian perception and the Deleuzian perception-image as zeroness is essential – in the first instance – for the series of signs that will be given to each of the different movement-images. Deleuze writes, after Peirce, that the 'degree zero, the perception-image, gives the others a bipolar composition appropriate to each case', this bipolar distribution becoming 'two signs of composition' and 'one sign of genesis for each type' (C2: 32). In other words, the perception-image will create a triad of divisions for each of the subsequent movement-images; the perception-image echoes the Peircian representamen–object–interpretant (R + O + I) unfolding that gave to the universal semiosis the three trichotomies. In order to follow just how this will be enacted, we must return to a moment in the explication of the Bergsonian sensory-motor system and Deleuze's movement-image (Chapter 1): the trajectory of gaseous, liquid and sold perception.

Deleuze, since early in *Cinema 1* and without reference to Peirce, gives each of the images of the movement-image three component signs. His argument for such a system of signs is laid out in his first engagement with the perception-image. Deleuze writes: 'an objective perception is one where, as in things, all the images vary in relation to one another, on all their facets and in all their parts', while '[a] subjective perception is one in which the images vary in relation to a central and privileged image' – accordingly, '[t]hese definitions affirm not only the difference between the two poles of perception, but also the possibility of passing from the subjective pole' to the objective, and from the objective to the subjective (C1: 76). This formula – which 'Bergsonianism suggested' – allows Deleuze not simply to specify the perception-image as a given molar body, but rather to describe it as the emergence of a molar body from the molecular universe (C1: 76). The body as a privileged image – that which is perceived as a body and that which as a body perceives – undergoing composition (C1: 84). Deleuze names the subjective pole solid perception, and the objective pole gaseous perception; between the two (the solid becoming gaseous, the gaseous becoming solid) is liquid perception. Once again, Deleuze (as we saw in the previous chapter) appropriates this gaseous ↔ liquid ↔ solid terminology (although this goes unsignalled in the *Cinema* books) from Bergson (MM: 199). Thus, Deleuze's mapping of the perception-image with signs operates simultaneously in three ways: (1) an image in-itself as monad; (2) a dyadic polarity of composition and genesis; (3) a triadic series of signs. This can be diagrammatised as in Figure I.12.

It is at this point that we can return to *Cinema 2*'s recapitulation, and the designation of the perception-image as zeroness in the wake of the Peircian semiotic alignment. For this zeroness means the perception-image does not exist for itself, but disappears into each of the other images, simultaneously giving the movement-images 'proper' a sign series as structure appropriate to each. The perception-image is designated as having 'zeroness', as disappearing or being 'identical' to the other three images (C2: 31–2). In short, the sign

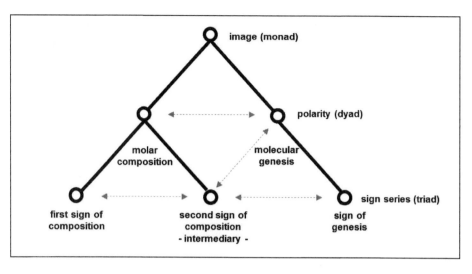

Figure I.12 Deleuze: image, polarity and triadic sign series

structure of the perception-image assures the sign structures of affection-images, action-images and mental-images. This cascade, that was merely assumed and taken for granted in *Cinema 1*, now receives an explication. The perception-image is purely functional with regards to the other images.

Accordingly, the dyadic polarity and triadic signs of the perception-image pass immediately into affection-images. The affection-image describes affects in the character in respect to the mise-en-scène, and such affects appear as internal intensities which are essentially unfilmable, appearing instead as external expressions upon faces and bodies. This image is captured in close-up, and in this way the expression of affects determined as feelings and emotions. These feeling and emotions flow to and from the character – through the people and places which surround the central and privileged image. Backgrounds become gaseous affective states (the pure beauty of the mountains; the dark horror of the forest; the banal monotony of the shopping mall) for the character who inhabits them. And from such affects the dyadic polarity and triadic signs of the perception-image pass into the action-image. Gaseous perception and its affective backgrounds become fully determined as social spaces. These social spaces are the coordinates in which the character will operate. In other words, perceptions and affects are determined in order for a reacting to and an acting upon. The central and privileged image is now transforming the world, revealing the determinates of that world, resolving the situation of that world. Finally, mental-images capture images of thought on-screen (memories as flashbacks; imaginings through dreams and nightmares; comprehension by way of the relations between the world, its characters and objects). Perceptions, affects and actions appear as memory-images for the privileged character: habitualised behaviours, a haunted past, wishes for the future – such images are actualised on the screen, pass through gaseous and liquid states to become the determining central impetus of the character. Taking this into consideration, we can tabulate the movement-image taxonomy as a framework as in Figure I.13.

Perception \ Images	Affection-image (firstness)	Action-image (secondness)	Mental-image (thirdness)
Solid perception: The first sign of composition	First sign of composition of the affection-image	First sign of composition of the action-image	First sign of composition of the mental-image
Liquid perception: The second sign of composition	Second sign of composition of the affection-image	Second sign of composition of the action-image	Second sign of composition of the mental-image
Gaseous perception: The sign of genesis	Sign of genesis of the affection-image	Sign of genesis of action-image	Sign of genesis of the mental-image

Figure I.13 Deleuze: movement-image logic of domains and sign divisions

Now, it will be noted that this table is structurally identical to Figure I.05 – Peirce's three categories and three trichotomies (1903). Yet it is here that we also understand what Deleuze meant when he wrote in the recapitulation: '[w]e ... take the term "sign" in a completely different way from Peirce' (C2: 32). For Peirce, each category (firstness – secondness – thirdness) is composed of representamen – object – interpretant (R + O + I): the aspect of a sign in-itself, the aspect of the sign referring to its object, and the aspect of a sign that will be encountered as interpretation. For Deleuze, however, each image (affection-image action-image–mental-image) is composed of gaseous–liquid–solid correlates, describing the dyadic poles of genesis and then composition (interim and full composition). Accordingly, this answers Deleuze's caveat in his appropriation of Peirce with respect to terminology: 'we borrowed from Peirce a certain number of terms whilst changing their meaning' (C2: 32). For Deleuze will give each of the movement-image signs a name, and these names will sometimes be derived from Peirce (although not necessarily be placed in the same coordinate) and sometimes will be neologisms, or taken from other philosophers. In this way, we should not – as will be seen, and further explored – expect Deleuze's 'special case' of a cinematic semiosis of movement-images to match Peirce's 'general' (universal) semiosis (C1: 76). For the divisions in Peirce and Deleuze are derived by different means. Deleuze uses the Bergsonian formula, and retains only the Peircian structure of the trichotomies through the zeroness of perception and the perception-image.

The second significance of zeroness:
a decalogue of movement-images

The three trichotomies of nine sign divisions was only the first move of Peirce's 1903 semiosis. The second move was to combine these nine sign divisions into classes. This occurred through an additive process of the divisions of representamen–object–interpretant; or, amounting to the same thing, the degenerative process of genuine signs. Either way, these processes allowed ten logical combinations. Thus, Peirce's decalogue resulted in ten sign classes each composed of a combination of three of the nine sign divisions. The recapitulation's designation as perception/perception-image as zeroness is thus similarly essential – in the second instance – for the creation of ten different types of movement-images.

However, such a correlation is not straightforward. In the recapitulation, Deleuze writes: '[b]etween the perception-image and the others there is no intermediary, because perception extends by itself into the other images. But, in the other cases, there is necessarily an intermediary which indicates the extension as passage' (C2: 32). Accordingly 'this is why, in the end, we find ourselves faced with six types of perceptible visible images': we thus now have two extra images: the 'impulse-image (intermediate between affection and action)' and the 'reflection-image (intermediate between action and relation [or mental-image])' (C2: 32). Impulse-images would describe nascent actions as immediate impulses; while reflection-images would be a more considered degree of action-image and a lesser degree of mental-image. Even if we bracket off perception-images as having zeroness and disappearing into the other images (as we must), the recapitulation leaves us with only five images, or, to put it in Peircian terms, five classes. Furthermore, in an endnote Deleuze comments 'in Peirce, there are no intermediaries, but only "degenerate" or "accretive" types' (C2: 287). It would appear that – in the recapitulation – Deleuze's method is very different from that of Peirce. Similarly, *Cinema 1*'s glossary (the second variation) also maintains only the six types (including, of course, the – as yet to be diagnosed as having zeroness – perception-image).

The actual textual descriptions of the *Cinema* books (the first variation), however, offer an alternative explication of the full extended movement-image taxonomy. *Cinema 1* begins in agreement with the glossary and recapitulation, with perception-images and affection-images (the latter specifically referred to in terms of Peircian 'firstness') (C1: 98). Yet with the action-image *Cinema 1* describes two distinct images. Deleuze conjures these two images in reference to the semiosis: 'according to Peirce's classification of images' the action-image is 'the reign of "secondness"' where 'everything … is two by itself' (C1: 142). And '[a]s the action-image on all its levels always brings together "two", it is not surprising that it should have two different aspects itself' (C1: 160). On the one hand, the large form action-image – SAS` – will describe how a situation engenders action which will then modify the situation. On the other hand, Deleuze also identifies the small form – ASA` – where the behaviours of characters rather reveal a situation, which will then necessarily modify their actions. It is as if Deleuze is restating Peircian genuine secondness, which, as we have seen, has a relatively degenerate form (221) connected to its genuine form (222). The large form action-image would correlate with the genuine form of secondness (222); while the small form action-image would correlate with the relatively degenerate form of secondness (221).

Deleuze also accounts for the impulse-image in Peircian terms: 'between the two [domains of affect and action], between firstness and secondness, there is something like the 'degenerate' affect, or the 'embryonic' action' (C1: 123). Accordingly, 'we must recognise that this new set is not a mere intermediary, a place of transition, but possesses a perfect consistency and autonomy' (C1: 123). In the recapitulation Deleuze signalled the impulse-image as an intermediary; in the text of *Cinema 1* the impulse-image takes on a Peircian derivation as a form of secondness, the firstness of secondness (211). Reflection-images ('figures' or 'the transformation of forms' as they are named in *Cinema 1*) are, by contrast, still specified as appearing as an intermediary between the action-image and the mental-image (C1: 178). Yet what is also clear is that reflection-images also create transformations between the two forms of the action-image (the large and the small). Deleuze identifies these transformations as 'attractions', 'inversions' and 'discursive figures' (C1: 178). Each of these figures goes on to describe its own way of working within the cinematic text; extending from action-images to mental-images proper by degree upon degree. Or rather, mental-images degenerating (in the Peircian sense) degree upon degree into action-images. Thus we have 'tropes … (metaphors, metonymies, synecdoches)' and 'imperfect tropes … (allegory, personifica-tion, etc.)' as attraction-images (C1: 183). Inversion-images describe '[l]iteral figures operating for example through reversal' (C1: 183). Finally, 'figures of thought' are filmic moments of 'deliberation, concession, support, prosopoeia, etc' (C1: 183, 190). In other words, these figures take on their own autonomy and consistency as what we can name attraction-images, inversion-images and discourse-images. With respect to the Peircian semiosis, these correlate to degenerate and weaker degenerate forms of thirdness: the firstness of thirdness (311) embodied by the attraction-image; the firstness of the secondness of thirdness (321) embodied by the inversion-image; and the secondness of the secondness of thirdness (322) embodied by the discourse-image.

Peirce's genuine thirdness – it will be remembered – also has three values: a relatively degenerate firstness of thirdness (331), a relatively degenerate secondness of thirdness (332) and, finally, true genuine thirdness (333). In *Cinema 1*, Deleuze writes, of the mental-image, that '[t]hirdness perhaps finds its most adequate representation in relation', indicating that Deleuze aligns what he specified as the relation-image with Peirce's genuine thirdness (C1: 197). Relation-images are designated by Deleuze as rendering symbolic thought on-screen – similar to the way Peirce's genuine thirdness indicated the law of the symbol as an argument. If relation-images are most adequate for thirdness, are there other possible images of thirdness that are not as 'adequate'? Or in Peircian terms, relatively degenerate? We could turn to recollection-images and dream-images in *Cinema 2*. It might initially appear that these two images are associated with the time-image taxonomy. This is understandable as they occur for the first time in *Cinema 2* and Deleuze does not mention them in the text of *Cinema 1*, in *Cinema 1*'s glossary, or in *Cinema 2*'s recapitulation of movement-images (which is presented prior to their appearance). Yet, for all that, it is clear that these two images are indeed movement-images (we will discuss the proof in more detail in Chapter 3). For instance, Deleuze writes: '[r]ecollection-images … still come within the framework of the sensory-motor situation' and 'dream-images … project the sensory-motor situation to infinity … but we do not, in this way, leave behind an indirect representation, even though we come close' (C2: 273). Recollection-images and dream-images (flashbacks of memory and dreamscapes of imagination) are actualised as thought on-screen. We could say, then, that we encounter here two more movement-images, two more images in the domain of mental-images. In Peircian terms, they would be relatively degenerate firstness of thirdness (331) and relatively degenerate secondness of thirdness (332).

There are now ten movement-images in total (taking perception-images as having zeroness). Accordingly, these ten movement-images can be mapped against Peirce's ten genuine and degenerate sign classes of the 1903 semiosis, as in Figure I.14 (which can be compared with the diagram of Peirce's genuine and degenerate forms in Figure I.07). Furthermore, in unfolding these ten images from the fundamental domains of Bergson's sensory-motor system (aligned with Peirce's categories) we encounter a state of avatars (between domains and images): affection-images; impulse-images; action-images; reflection-images; and, mental-images. In other words, the images of the glossary and recapitula-tion (excepting the zeroness of perception) which correspond to the five main branches of genuine and degenerate signs.

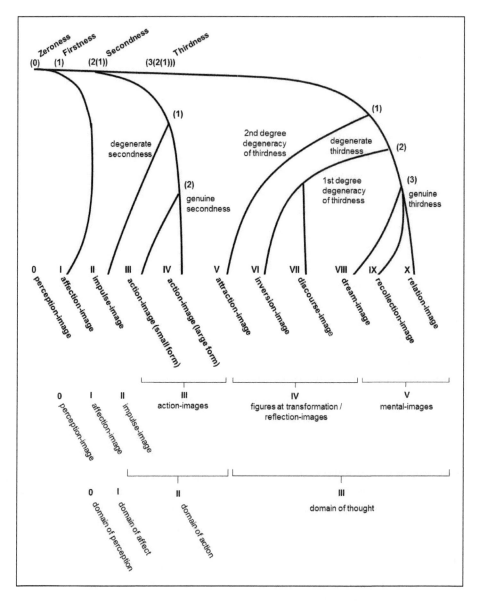

Figure I.14 Deleuze: ten images, five avatars, three domains of the movement-image (with perception as zeroness)

From images to sign series (and the limit of the appropriation of Peirce)

These two moments of the significance of the perception-image as zeroness – allowing the generation of ten images and giving a series of sign divisions to each image – now dovetail. With Peirce's semiosis of 1903, it will be remembered, the three categories (firstness, secondness, thirdness) corresponded with a trichotomy of signs (sign in-itself; sign to object; sign to interpretant) giving nine different sign divisions; through combination or degeneracy, these nine sign divisions generated ten classes of sign, with each of these sign classes composed of three of the nine sign divisions. Furthermore – for Peirce – each of these sign-classes could be named after the combinations from which it was composed (in entirety or through possible reduction), the position which it occupied in the trajectory (genuine or degenerate placement), and through new designations that capture its function (vestige, proposition, and so on). With the movement-image, the three fundamental images (affect, action and thought) that correspond with the three signs given through the zeroness of perception (solid, liquid and gaseous) giving nine sign divisions (as seen in Figure I.13) similarly follow such a logical unfolding. There will be ten movement-images composed of three signs, each of these one of the nine signs of the trichotomy. Such a logical composition (which echoes Peirce's combination of sign divisions in Figure I.06) could be constructed as in Figure I.15. Accordingly, the trajectory of these movement-images describes (depending upon which way we traverse the table) a graduated movement of types from the affection-image to relation-image, or relation-image towards affection-image. So, for instance, within the avatar of action we see the movement: impulse-image ↔ action-image (small form) ↔ action-image (large form). Such a movement designates how cinema becomes more and more dominated by action as we move away from the affective drives of the impulse-image (instincts) towards the determined situations and behaviours of the action-image (large form) as the genuine form of action. In this way, the table also indicates that the ten images are composed of three signs relative to each. So, while – for instance – the impulse-image is composed of solid affects, liquid affects and gaseous action, these signs which are derived and combined from the domains of affect and action would take on their own determinations as elements within the aegis of the impulse-image.

It is in consideration of this final point that Deleuze will give each sign of each image its own name and description. It is here that we reach the very limit of Deleuze's appropriation of Peirce, and – simultaneously – encounter one final problem with respect to the different iterations of the extended movement-image across the *Cinema* books. For none of the iterations

#	Domain (Category)	Perception-image (zeroness)			Num.	Reduced image name
		Genesis	Composition			
			2nd sign	1st sign		
I	Affect (Firstness)	Gaseous affect	Liquid affect	Solid affect	111	Affection-image (avatar of affect)
II	Action (Secondness)	Gaseous action	Liquid affect	Solid affect	211	Impulse-image (avatar of action)
III			Liquid action	Solid affect	221	Action-image (small form) (avatar of action)
IV				Solid action	222	Action-image (large form) (avatar of action)
V	Thought (Thirdness)	Gaseous thought	Liquid affect	Solid affect	311	Attraction-image (first reflection-image)
VI			Liquid action	Solid affect	321	Inversion-image (second reflection-image)
VII				Solid action	322	Attraction-image (third reflection-image)
VIII			Liquid thought	Solid affect	331	Dream-image (third mental-image)
IX				Solid action	332	Recollection-image (second mental-image)
X				Solid thought	333	Relation-image (first mental-image)

Figure I.15 Deleuze: movement-image logic of domains, avatars and images through sign combinations

corresponds to Peirce's namings, nor do they correspond with each other. And, furthermore, the number of signs given to each of the images varies in the iterations between two and five. These are listed in Figures I.16–19: the images and signs of the movement-image from the recapitulation of *Cinema 2* (I.16), the glossary of *Cinema 1* (I.17), the text of *Cinema 1* (I.18) and the text of *Cinema 2* after the recapitulation (I.19).

Images	Signs of Composition		Sign of Genesis
Perception-image	Solid	Liquid	Gaseous
Affection-image	Icon of quality	Icon of power	Qualisign/potisign
Impulse-image	Fetish of good	Fetish of evil	Symptom of an originary world
Action-image	Synsign	Index	Imprint
Reflection-image	Figures of attraction	Figures of inversion	Discursive figures
Relation-image	Mark	Demark	Symbol

Figure I.16 Deleuze: images and signs of the movement-image in the recapitulation of *Cinema 2*

Images	Sign(s) of Composition			Sign of Genesis	
Perception-image	Solid		Liquid	Gaseous	
Affection-image	Icon		Dividual	Qualisign/potisign	
Impulse-image	Fetish of an originary world			Symptom of an originary world	
Action-image	Synsign	Binomial	Index of lack or equivocity	Imprint	Vector
Reflection-image	Figures of reflection		Figures of inversion	Discursive figures	
Relation-image	Mark (demark)		Symbol	Opsigns and sonsigns	

Figure I.17 Deleuze: images and signs of the movement-image in the glossary of *Cinéma 1* (Deleuze, 2010)

Images	Signs of Composition		Sign of Genesis
Perception-image	Solid	Liquid	Gaseous
Affection-image	Icon of power; icon of quality; dividual		Any-space-whatever
Impulse-image	Relic; Vult; Symptom		Originary world
Action-image large form	Milieu	Binomial)	Imprint
Action-image small form	Index of lack	Index of equivocity	Vector
Figure of Attraction (first reflection-image)	Theatrical figure	Plastic figure	?
Figure of Inversion (second reflection-image)	Sublime figure	Enfeebled figure	Undifferentiated figure of the sublime and the enfeebled figures
Figure of Discourse (third reflection-image)	Limit of the large form action-image	Limit of the small form action-image	?
Relation-image	Mark	Demark	Symbol

Figure I.18 Deleuze: images and signs of the movement-image in the text of *Cinema 1*

Images	Sign(s) of Composition		Sign of Genesis
Recollection-image	Destiny		Forking paths
Dream-image	Rich dreams	Restrained dreams	Movement of world

Figure I.19 Deleuze: additional images and signs of the movement-image in the text of *Cinema 2*

It is at this point that the genealogy of the movement-image must conclude. For designating the signs appropriate to each image will only be able to be carried out by working through each of the signs, images, avatars and domains as a logical series (Section II). However, three observations already present themselves which will guide such work. First – where there are more than three signs for an image, such as for the action-image in the glossary, this can be seen as a moment of stasis in describing the avatar of the action-image before it is unfolded into large and small forms. Similarly, in the recapitulation, the three signs of the reflection-image can be seen as describing such an avatar-stasis before unfolding into attraction-images, inversion-images and discourse-images. The second observation concerns the situation where there are fewer than three signs. On the one hand, where only one sign of composition is listed, this can be seen as Deleuze operating at the level of dyadic polarity; and on the other hand, where there is no sign of genesis – as in the first and third of the reflection-images in the text of *Cinema 1* – we could be guided by the designation of the second reflection-image. Finally, while Deleuze may change the names, spellings (as in sinsign/synsign) and meanings of signs, and even the notion of the sign itself, the logic of Peirce's semiotic structural unfolding remains. As we have seen, Deleuze takes Peirce's universal semiosis and – in the wake of the already appropriated Bergsonian sensory-motor system – uses it to create a pragmatic cineotic matrix of movement-images.

*
*   *

Towards the end of the recapitulation of images in *Cinema 2*, Deleuze comments: 'a final problem arises: why does Peirce think that everything ends with thirdness and the relation-image and that there is nothing beyond?' (C2: 33). Peirce – as we have seen – believes his semiotic logic requires nothing beyond thirdness because there is nothing beyond thought, the laws of habituation: thirdness 'suffices of itself to give the conception of True Continuity ... no conception yet discovered is higher' (CP 5.67). It is in response to this problem that Deleuze returns to Bergson, and shifts his focus from the sensory motor-system to pure memory and spontaneous thought. For Peirce sees arising consciousness (the emergent trajectory of the semiotic) as a continuity, while Bergson believes such images are founded upon the interval derived from inner energies, the differential physical, chemical and biological processes of the body and its brain: spontaneous thought, arising consciousness, pure memory. 'The intellect', writes Bergson, is 'forever moving in the interval' between memory-images, and 'unceasingly finds them again or creates them anew' (MM: 242). Spontaneous thought, pure memory, is that which both founds and frees itself from the sensory-motor system. This allows Deleuze to propose a new cineotic, the time-image.

3

Time-images: Deleuze, syntheses

The cinema of the time-image – for Deleuze – describes disjunctive temporalities and displaced spatialities dissolving subjectivities. Such discords are the affirmation of a new image of filmic thought. The actual images on the screen undergo problematisations of every kind: preserving indeterminacies, creating caesuras, proliferating false continuities. In this way, the actual image opens up to virtual correlates forcing the propagation of perspectives and interpretations. This idea of the time-image begins with Bergson's exposition of spontaneous thought, pure memory, and duration – a nexus of correlates opposed to the matter-images and memory-images of the sensory-motor system. Deleuze appropriated Bergson's sensory-motor system to describe a cinema of the movement-image: perception-images as creating a body around which the film will revolve; affections-images expressing emotions and feelings through this centre; action-images obligating this privileged image to act in and upon the world; mental-images actualising the character's thoughts, dreams and memories. Such movement-images create a coherent consciousness in comprehensive space through chronological time. The time-image thus indicates the collapse of the domains and determinates of the movement-image. This collapse, however, is only the destructive moment of the ascension of a new regime of images, a regime that will propel Bergson's exposition of spontaneous thought, pure memory and duration into a new cinematic semiotic.

This new regime of the cinematographic image is described by Deleuze through a series of sign progressions. In the wake of the collapse of the movement-image there are opsigns and sonsigns (pure optical and sound situations), the undifferentiated image actualised on-screen. Opsigns and sonsigns are organised in a multitude of ways so as to open up the image to virtual correlates. Deleuze names these organisations 'hyalosigns', 'chronosigns' and 'noosigns'. The virtual appears through new conceptions of the image (the fragment in itself) as a hyalosign; narration (or coexistence of images) as a chronosign; and narrative (storytelling creating an indeterminate filmic event) as a noosign. Together these three aspects of the time-image are lectosigns: images which must be interpreted – the purest function of the virtual. Without doubt, this cineotic regime of time-images – opsigns/sonsigns; hyalosigns; chronosigns; noosigns; lectosigns – describes a logical development of the cinematic actual and virtual; yet, for Deleuze, '[c]inema's concepts are not given in the cinema' (C2: 280). Thus the question, from where do these coordinates of the time-image arise? The namings of the elements (neologisms all) betray no overall conceptual derivation, no established structure, no philosophical genealogy.

The problem here is both inverse to and more profound than that encountered with the taxonomy of movement-images. Deleuze, in the *Cinema* books, unequivocally announced the movement-image as a nexus of Bergson's sensory-motor system (developed as the domains of the perception-image, affection-image, action-image and mental-image) extended through the pragmatic semiotic processes of Peirce. The difficulties encountered with this extension concerned the alignment of Peirce's methodology with that of Deleuze, as well as a subsequent correlating of elements between the semiosis and cineosis. With the time-image, Deleuze announces no organising principles. There are general expositions of Bergson's investigations into duration through memory, thought, temporality and the virtual; and there are the coordinates of the time-image explicated in the text of *Cinema 2* – but no declaration of an explicit framework, no exposed method of organisation, no evident philosophical structure. The aim of this chapter is to detect and discover such a framework, organisation and structure; to explore how the cineosis of time-images – opsigns/sonsigns; hyalosigns; chronosigns; noosigns; lectosigns – resonates with and develops Deleuze's fundamental philosophical concerns. The argument is that this taxonomical organisation is founded upon the three syntheses of time, space and consciousness from Deleuze's *Difference and Repetition*. As Deleuze has stated: '*Difference and Repetition* was the first book in which I tried to "do philosophy". All that I have done since is connected to this book' (DR: xiii).

From the *Cinema* books to *Difference and Repetition*

For Deleuze, what marks the emergence of the time-image is the dissolution of the images and signs which cohere the movement-image. Perception-images are stymied in developing a central and privileged image, and – concomitantly – no longer organise the trajectory and domains of affection-images, action-images and mental-images. Time-images thus depict an undetermined and indeterminate world – a world resisting the common-sense mappings of space and time; a disruptive mise-en-scène destroying the coordinates of any given milieu and problematising the formation of characters. Broken, blank and banal landscapes are populated by people who are seers. They wander as witnesses, they disappear, they never existed, they fragment – appear as ciphers and shadows. Pasts, presents and futures intermix, remain undefined, undergo diverse repetitions. This is a cinema where bodies are not perceived as a subjective presence in reference to an objective world. This is a cinema where affects and memories are incongruous, absent or uncertain; where acts transforming or revealing the world become problematised. In this way, filmmakers discover and continually reinvent opsigns/sonsigns, hyalosigns, chronosigns, noosigns and lectosigns.

Opsigns and sonsigns – the terms a condensation of pure optical and pure sound situations – describe the indeterminacy of the images on-screen with respect to the domains of movement-images. According to Deleuze, opsigns and sonsigns are actualised images which have the potential to open up to virtual correlates, and this potential is generated in three ways. In the first place, the actual (on-screen) image is coerced to open up to the virtual through the creation of hyalosigns. Hyalosigns are named and inspired by the work of Gilbert Simondon, who uses the idea of the crystal (from which the prefix *hyal* – meaning 'glass' – is derived) as a new way of conceiving processes of individuation (TP: 19, 46, 66 n11, 573–4; DI: 86–9). For Deleuze, hyalosigns designate the way in which the image in-itself creates virtual correlates through delinking the flow of image to image, for a relinking of image to thought. In the second place, chronosigns operate by creating non-linear or serial narrations. Here the virtual appears as a function of the organisation of images across the whole of the film, the naming a synonym for the time-image (capturing up concepts of memory, the past and duration that emerge from Bergson's *Matter and Memory*). Chronosigns thus appear to be at the very heart of the time-image taxonomy disturbing the flows of chronological time. In the third place, noosigns 'constitute a new image of thought' as a perspectival narrative, the story or filmic event as virtual correlate. The naming is inspired by a short engagement with the work of Martin Heidegger in *What is Called Thinking?* (Heidegger, 1972: 3; C2: 156, 215, 308). Finally, lectosigns refer to the process of interpreting, or reading, time-images, again from the Latin, *lectio*. Lectosigns are the dovetailing of the three aspects of the virtual generated from opsigns and sonsigns through the images, narration and narratives of the time-image. Opsigns/sonsigns, hyalosigns, chronosigns, noosigns and lectosigns: each of these concepts displays a philosophical consonance and logically develops along a trajectory from the pure actual to the pure virtual through the necessary impurities of image and thought; yet Deleuze presents them without an exposed method of organisation and without betraying any evident philosophical structure.

The first clue in uncovering such a framework is that only hyalosigns, chronosigns and noosigns – not opsigns/sonsigns or lectosigns – can be decomposed into a triadic series of elements. Hyalosigns are decomposed into avatars which describe properties of crystalline formations in the cinematic image. Deleuze takes the example of the crystal and identifies how filmmakers have reflected the multiple facia of crystals, their fragments and growth. He identifies three broad trends which form the elements of the hyalosign: 'two mirrors face to face', 'the limpid and the opaque' and 'the seed and the environment' (C2: 71). Each performs exchanges between the actual on-screen image and its virtual connections. No longer does an actual image exist to flow seamlessly into the next actual image; but actual correlates to virtual, through different aspects of fragmentation, exchange and growth. The elements of chronosigns have a more direct relationship with the properties of pure memory discussed by Bergson in *Matter and Memory*, but are also extended by Nietzsche's concept of 'the will to power' (Nietzsche, 2008: 98–101; C2: 141). Deleuze specifies three types of chronosign that correspond to the three aspects of time in-and-for-itself. 'Sheets of the past' explore the way in which memories are 'no longer confused with the space which serves as its place' (C2: 100). Instead, memories explore duration – no longer functioning as a repository of the present, but as productive of the present. 'Points [or peaks] of the present' investigate the way in which any present moment is fundamentally divided between the present-in-itself, the past and the future (C2: 100). It is this aspect that can make time 'frightening and inexplicable' for the possibility of action is torn between living in the moment, reacting to the influences of the past and acting for future effects (C2: 101). Deleuze refers to these two aspects of chronosigns (sheets and peaks) as the 'order of time' in that they undermine the linear chronology (cause and effect) of past, present and future (C2: 155). The third avatar of the chronosign – which is oriented towards the future – is the 'power of the false' and Deleuze delineates this function as the 'series of time' (C2: 126, 133, 136, 155). A serial organisation once again disconnects the continuity of time that constructs the character in the film as locked into a narration where the present is a product of the past and the future a consequence. Rather than this closed circuit, a serial organisation is one in which time is organised into images which correlate as diverse virtual moments. Deleuze puts it thus: 'the power of the false exists only from the perspective of a series of powers, always referring to each other and passing into one another' (C2: 133). As in serialism in music, which attempts to overthrow traditional harmonics without descending into chaos, fundamental elements are continuously rearranged exploring the difference in repetition and the repetitions of difference. Finally, the avatars of the noosigns capture thought on-screen. Not the representation of thought – but the problems of thought. With noosigns, therefore, we encounter thought as a series of disjunctions: the disparate states of a body; the dissonance between bodies in their distinct states; and the discord between these bodies and the world, the world in-itself as absonant. This formula refers us to the three aspects of the noosign. First aspect: the attitude of the body, its differences. Second aspect: the connection between these disparate states, the body and bodies in coexistence. 'It is a cinema of bodies', comments Deleuze, which has broken all the more with the sensory-motor schema through action being replaced by attitude, and supposedly true linkage by the *gest* which produces … [time-image] storytelling' (C2: 276). Third aspect: the relation between attitude-*gest* and world which appears through the mise-en-scène as an image of the brain. As Deleuze puts it, 'the internal sheets of memory and the external layers of reality will be mixed up, extended, short circuited and form a whole moving life, which is at once that of the cosmos and the brain' (C2: 209). This is not a return to the mental-images of the movement-image: 'thought no longer appears on the screen as function of the body: flashbacks, symbols and dreams, but rather is strictly identical to every image – it is cerebral space' (C2: 211). The film itself is an image of thought for the brain.

That only hyalosigns, chronosigns and noosigns can be decomposed into constitutive elements is more than a detail. It intimates not only the way in which the components of the time-image are organised, but also the difference at a conceptual level between these time-images and the aspects of opsigns/sonsigns and lectosigns. Opsigns and sonsigns describe the actual visual and auditory images of a time-image film after the collapse of the coordinates of the movement-image. Deleuze writes: 'we gave the name opsign (and sonsign) to the actual image cut off from its motor extension' (C2: 69). They are 'slivers', the images resulting in the despecification of movement-images prior to rejoining each other as time-images (hyalosigns, chronosigns and noosigns) (C2: 69). Similarly, it is clear in Deleuze's discussion of lectosigns that this term is used for the way in which time-images need to be read – interpreted – rather than simply be seen. This is the 'final aspect of the direct time-image, the common limit' (C2: 279). This limit is that which 'force[s] us to read so many symptoms of the image, that is, to treat the optical and sound image like something that is also readable' (C2: 24). In this way, the domains of the time-image that appear between opsigns/sonsigns and lectosigns can be called the three time-images proper: the impurities of actual images with the virtual. Hyalosigns, chronosigns and noosigns are, on the one hand, complex compositions of opsigns and sonsigns. On the other hand, the images and signs of the time-image constitute an accumulation of lectosigns. Such a configuration of images and signs can be tabulated as in Figure I.20.

Images	Signs		
0 Opsigns and sonsigns			
1 Hyalosigns	Limpid and opaque	Mirrors face to face	Seed and environment
2 Chronosigns	Sheets of the past	Peaks of the present	Powers of the false
3 Noosigns	Body of gest	Body of attitude	Cinema of the brain
			Lectosigns ∞

Figure I.20 Deleuze: time-image images and signs

The three time-images proper: hyalosigns, chronosigns and noosigns – a taxonomy of three series of three images of indetermination. Where do we discover such a structure in Deleuze's philosophy? It is tempting to suggest – perhaps through intuition alone, to begin with – the three constitutive syntheses of time, space and consciousness in *Difference and Repetition*.

The central concern of *Difference and Repetition* is to attack concepts of identity and overturn philosophies of representation in order to set free an alternative 'image of thought' (DR: 164). Deleuze's approach is to conduct a number of sorties into the many and varied instances of identity and representation from Aristotle, via Kant and Hegel to Freud and beyond. The concept of identity, for Deleuze, is problematic because it relies upon reconstituting the same at the expense of the different. It is a concept that depends upon annulling difference in-itself. It is a concept that depends upon exclusion. It is a concept that relies upon the negative – this is this because it is not that. The concept of identity is fundamental to representation which proposes – firstly – an object and its representation as separate but – secondly – that there is a verisimilitude between the two. Representational relationships pretend to truth through identity. Deleuze's program is to replace the philosophy of representation with expression, another kind of image of thought that arises through an alternative series of philosophies, from the Stoics to Spinoza, Nietzsche and Bergson (DR: 346). Fundamental to achieving this is replacing identity with difference and repetition: the repetition of difference, the difference in repetition, taking the concepts of difference and repetition 'together rather than separately' (DR: xiii). For Deleuze both concepts have suffered the same fate, which is to say, neither had been fully developed as concepts in-and-of-themselves. Both concepts, in their own way, have been explicated in relation, opposition and subordination to the concept of identity. Setting these concepts free is thus the major activity of the book. Deleuze approaches this from a number of directions (though, crucially, they are not designed to 'add up', so much as create a nexus). One of the ways in which such a task is enacted is through the taxonomic unfoldings of the three constitutive syntheses of time, space, and consciousness. Each synthesis is composed of three elements; and each of the three elements resonates across each synthesis: the first passive synthesis of the present, distance and individuation; the second passive synthesis of the past, depth and differentiation; and the third impassive synthesis of the future, intensity and dramatisation. Together, these nine signs of the three syntheses describe the dispersal of a central and privileged consciousness through disjunctive temporality and displaced spatiality: atemporal, aspatial and ahuman forces. And it is these three constitutive syntheses that can be seen to inspire the structure of the time-image taxonomy. In other words, the domains of the three time-images of hyalosigns, chronosigns and noosigns are a repetition of each of the three different atemporal, aspatial and ahuman syntheses.

Deleuze's syntheses of time

Bodies and world are time: temporality, a weft and warp of presents, pasts and futures. Such is one expression, in Deleuze's *Difference and Repetition*, of bodies and world – the world and the body explored through the logic of the syntheses of time. We emerge as material elements gathered from the universe, born to organic life. And we perpetually discover ourselves in the present moment, an arising consciousness of the now, an axis that impales our mortal bodies to the Earth over which we wander, upon which we settle. Our conscious presence in the present appears eternal to our lives; however – at one and the same moment – we encounter falling-aways. We cascade into memory, recollecting images from our past (perceptions of childhood; affects of love and fear; actions celebrated and regretted) and the as-it-was (histories of our families and of the world; works of art, philosophic concepts, revelations of science). We trouble the future, projecting ourselves into the yet-to-come through understanding (the desires and dreads for ourselves, those around us and peoples of the world) and beyond the timespan of our bodies into the aeons ahead (nuclear or environmental devastation, the rise of the machines; a human golden age, journeys to the stars). In the living present we thus encounter a presence inscribed with recollection and understanding: an apparent consciousness of our body and world organised through chronological time.

We are – in this way, according to Deleuze – with the living present as organic matter with active consciousness: I am, I think? Yet, this 'I' self-aware of its materiality is merely a surface of constitutive processes. 'We are made', synthesised, 'of contracted water, earth, light and air not merely prior to the recognition or representation of these', writes Deleuze, 'but prior to their being sensed' (DR: 93). This sensing is thought as a passive synthesis, passive in that it happens to us and explicates consciousness as active synthesis. Thus the three syntheses of the living present: the organic, the passive and the active – where each and every body in the world 'is a sum of contractions' (syntheses), where 'the lived present constitutes a past and a future in time' (DR: 93). At the level of organic synthesis, the lived present constitutes the past 'in the form of cellular heredity', vital presence where 'need is the manner in which the future appears' (DR: 93). At the level of passive synthesis, the lived present is a 'succession of instants' and 'to it belong both the past and the future: the past in so far as the preceding instants are retained in the contraction; the future because its expectation is anticipated in this same contraction' (DR: 91). At the level of active synthesis, by 'combining' the organic and passive, the living present supports presence, subsidising the past and future as 'psycho-organic' recollection and understanding (DR: 93).

The levels of organic and passive synthesis are sub-representational and therefore 'can be represented only by the active synthesis' (DR: 106). Reciprocally, this active synthesis is the surface of the syntheses of forces arising from the organic body with the world; and these constitutive forces are in time. Thus the essential nature of the passive synthesis of the living present is twofold: constitutive and temporal. It is constitutive of presence in active synthesis: passive synthesis 'is not carried out by the mind', writes Deleuze, 'but occurs *in* the mind' (DR: 91). And it is the now, a now that retains the past and anticipates the future, placing these instants into a relation of before and after in the present (and for presence). It is thus a passive succession that is 'essentially asymmetrical: it goes from the past to the future in the present … thereby imparting direction to the arrow of time' (DR: 91).

Must time occur only from the perspective of the pure present? If the present is always passing, what allows such a passing? And what gives us active recollection? Deleuze puts it this way: 'this is the paradox of the present: to constitute time while passing in the time constituted. We cannot avoid the necessary conclusion – *that there must be another time in which the first synthesis of time can occur*' (DR: 100). This is the second constitutive synthesis of time, concerning the past. If the first passive synthesis of succession is the foundation upon which presence has grounding, the second passive synthesis is the very ground within which the foundation is set. We are pure memory – not the becoming-conscious recollections of active synthesis, but constitutive memory from which recollection can be generated. And if the first passive synthesis was a perspective of time, the same must be said of the second. From this perspective we are of the pure past, our present moment a dilation of the past as focal point – this way appearing as 'destiny' or fate (DR: 105. I have translated the French 'destin' with respect to the time-image as fate to distinguish it from the movement-image sign of destiny. See Deleuze, 2011: 68; Deleuze, 2009: 67). Not as *telos* (end and purpose), but in the sense that all of the past led to this. We can also say that the future is an aspect of the past, the past projected onto ourselves as 'reminiscence' (DR: 107). Reminiscence deploys the past into the future as soothsayer, prophecy, prediction and foretelling.

If there is a constitutive temporality of the past as pure memory and of the present as succession, we cannot but conclude there is a synthesis of the future. The case of the future is the 'empty form of time' (DR: 108). The future is radically unknowable, indeterminate, open. In this sense it is disruptive not only of the first and second temporal syntheses but also of the active synthesis: 'a fault or fracture of the I and a passivity of self' (DR: 109). It performs an ungrounding upon the grounded as much as the ground and foundation. It is thus neither passive nor active. This third temporal synthesis is 'impassive' (as Deleuze puts it in *Logic of Sense*), allowing 'the active and the passive to be interchanged more easily, since it is neither one nor the other' (LS: 10). Furthermore, just as with the two passive syntheses, the third constitutive synthesis is a perspective of time giving us the elements of the futureness of the present and the futureness of the past. The former sees the present as a break in the flow of time; the latter sees the past as an empty abyss, the forgotten, a 'dark precursor' (DR: 111–12, 145).

Series \ Dimensions	Past	Present	Future
Active synthesis Chronological time	Recollection	Presence	Understanding
First passive synthesis Succession of the present	Presentness of past (retention)	Presentness of present	Presentness of future (expectation)
Second passive synthesis Pure past	Pastness of past	Pastness of present (fate)	Pastness of future (reminiscence)
Third impassive synthesis Empty form of the future	Futureness of past (dark precursor)	Futureness of present (caesura)	Futureness of future
Organic synthesis Matter	Cellular heredity	Vitality	Need

Figure I.21 Deleuze: syntheses of time

The coordinates of Deleuze's syntheses of time can be deployed as in Figure I.21, as series of organic, impassive, passive and active syntheses. For Deleuze, these series explicate how we arise from the organic and are captured in chronological time. This is an ascension of active synthesis. Accordingly, the three constitutive series of temporality are atemporal paradoxes which are resolved in active synthesis. 'Active synthetic identity' is where the 'fracture [of the third synthesis] is quickly filled' and 'the successive presents [of the first synthesis] are organised into the circle of time [of the second synthesis], so that the pure past which defines them is itself still necessarily expressed in terms of a present' (DR: 109–10). Such resolution gives order to the world and its bodies.

From *Difference and Repetition* to the *Cinema* books

That the syntheses of time correlate – in some way – with the time-image has antecedents. For example, David Martin-Jones, Richard Rushton, Joe Hughes and Patricia Pisters have all explored such connections. In a short discussion in *Deleuze, Cinema and National Identity*, Martin-Jones argues that the first passive synthesis aligns with the movement-image components of perception-, affection- and action-images; while the second passive synthesis aligns with the mental-image category of recollection-images discussed early in *Cinema 2*. Thus, the third synthesis of time correlates with the time-image (Martin-Jones, 2006: 60–2). Correspondingly, in a more sustained format, Rushton, in 'Passions and Actions: Deleuze's Cinematographic Cogito', similarly sees the spectator of the modern cinema encountering film through the third synthesis (Rushton, 2008). Hughes' 'Schizoanalysis and the Phenomenology of Cinema' takes a rather different approach, the argument encompassing not only *Difference and Repetition*, but also *The Logic of Sense* and *Anti-Oedipus*. Hughes schematises thus: (1) material field = plane of immanence; (2) first passive synthesis = perception-image; (3) second passive synthesis = affection-image; (4) third passive synthesis = action-image; (5) failure of the third synthesis = crisis of the action-image; (6) pure thought, empty time = time-image (Hughes, 2008: 25). The most recent – and radical – contribution comes from Pisters in 'Synaptic Signals: Time Travelling through the Brain in the Neuro-Image' (2001) and, more fully, in *The Neuro-Image* (2012). Pisters aligns the movement-image with the first passive synthesis and the time-image with the second passive synthesis, and creates a new image – the 'neuro-image' – for the third synthesis (Pisters, 2011: 261). This exciting conceptual creation describes, for Pisters, the 'temporal dimensions of schizoanalysis' (Pisters, 2011: 261). The idea of an echoing of the three constitutive syntheses with the *Cinema* books thus has real pedigree, but little consensus. The crucial aspect – and that which will act as a guide here – is that none of these accounts appears to address the role of active synthesis. Accordingly, it is perhaps D. N. Rodowick with *Gilles Deleuze's Time Machine* who comes closest to the position adopted in what will follow. In his seminal exploration of the philosophical connectives of Deleuze's work on film, Rodowick writes: '[c]inematic movement-images emerge from the regime of universal variation where "matter=image" … Alternatively, time-images emerge from what Deleuze calls, in *Difference and Repetition*, the three passive syntheses of time' (Rodowick, 1998: 127). Rodowick leaves it, more or less, at this. His surfacing of the correlate is a general one. However – and as will be demonstrated – in the wake of delineating the elements of the time-image proper, each of the three constitutive syntheses of time can be seen to be explicated through these hyalosigns, chronosigns and noosigns. The essential aspect will be this: such an alignment rests upon first demonstrating that the movement-image correlates to active synthesis; and after that, all the three constitutive syntheses of time correspond to time-images.

To begin with, let us briefly remind ourselves of the organising principles of the movement-image. Deleuze sets up a correspondence between Bergson's concepts that describe the world of matter (perception—affection—action) and the films of a cinema of the sensory-motor response: a character sees, feels and reacts and the act changes the world of the film. From this correspondence Deleuze formulates the initial coordinates of the movement-image: perception-images, affection-images and action-images. Perception-images describe the central image of the character. Affection-images are close-ups of the face, unfilmable internal intensities expressed through emotions and feelings. Action-images return movement to the world through reactions and acts. These images are supported and sustained by mental-images. In Bergsonian terms this can be seen as a labelling of what Bergson calls 'habitual memory' or the memory-image (MM: 85). For Bergson, the memory-image underpins the sensory-motor schema (perceptions—affections—actions) causing recognition and invoking automatic responses. The automatic response is a habit stored up in the body but 'set in motion … by an initial impulse' (MM: 80). Simply put, our bodies obey habitual laws on the basis of a repetition of the perception—affections—action trajectory. Together, these four domains of images make possible the fundamental description of different types of movement-images. Mental-images are essential here, and have three coordinates: relation-images, which depict the thoughts of characters on-screen in symbolic form; recollection-images, which depict thought through flashbacks; and dream-images, which depict thought as hallucinations from fantasy to nightmares. Thus, for Deleuze, the movement-image actualises thought in a number of ways. In the first instance 'action, and also perception and affection, are framed in a fabric of relations … [a] chain of relations' (C1: 200). Or, thought on-screen is actualised through the flashback which indicates 'a causality which is psychological, but still analogous to a sensory-motor determinism, and, despite its circuits, only confirms the progression of linear narrative' (C2: 48). Finally, with dream-images there is a weakening of the bonds between perception, affection and action yet at the same time they are reconstituted in another space as an elsewhere. As Deleuze comments, 'dream-images … project the sensory-motor situation to infinity … but we do not, in this way, leave [it] behind' (C2: 273). Mental-images may find their 'most adequate representation in relation', yet the images of recollection and dream also operate in this domain; recollection-images 'seize a former present in the past and thus respect the empirical progression of time' while dream-images conjure up a 'metamorphosis of the situation' by linking dream situation to waking situation and so negotiating the latter through the former (C1: 197; C2: 273). While it is not difficult to assign these mental-images to three aspects of time – the present (relation), the past (recollection) and the future (dreams) – they reconstitute duration indirectly in the movement-image: they are spatialised, actualised, expressed as matter-images of time.

The question is this: do not mental-images – Bergsonian habitual memory-images – correspond exactly to the first passive synthesis of time? The first passive synthesis constitutes, for Deleuze, the 'lived, or living, present' and views the past as retention and the future as expectation (DR: 91). It is time's arrow, the passive synthesis that gives direction to time, structures the past, present and future in succession. Is this not recollection-image, relation-image and dream-image? Is the first passive synthesis not the classical image of thought that Deleuze sets up to overturn with the second and third passive synthesis?

Jay Lampert, in *Deleuze and Guattari's Philosophy of History*, seems to point the way here: 'Deleuze's first synthesis of time … is not as well known. When discussed at all, succession is generally treated as the false or superficial notion of time that co-existence is meant to replace'; yet 'Deleuze's description of succession is not merely a standard account of time setting the stage for his original contributions concerning coexistence; it is full of provocative and original arguments in its own right' (Lampert, 2006: 12). Let us return to *Difference and Repetition* and be reminded of what Deleuze has to say of the first passive synthesis, and the way in which it extends itself. On the one hand it extends into the second passive and third impassive syntheses. From the succession of the present to the pure memory of the past and finally to the empty, creative future. On the other hand, the first passive synthesis also extends into active synthesis. At the same time as the first passive synthesis of time is happening, something else occurs: 'the past is no longer the immediate past of retention but the reflective past of representation, of reflected and reproduced particularity' (DR: 92). And 'the future also ceases to be the immediate future of anticipation in order to become the reflexive future of prediction' (DR: 92). The past of the present (retention) and the future of the present (expectation) become – in active synthesis – recollection and understanding. Deleuze summarises thus: 'in other words, the active synthesis of memory and under-standing are superimposed upon and supported by the passive synthesis' (DR: 92). There are thus three types of the habitual present, the organic and active psychological present and the first passive synthesis of succession. As Deleuze writes, 'it concerns not only the sensory-motor habits that we have (psycho-logically), but also, before these, the primary habits that we are; the thousands of passive syntheses of which we are organically composed' (DR: 95).

There is a double aspect to the three syntheses of time: the temporal layers of the three constitutive syntheses and the spatialised temporality structuring the active synthesis that is built upon them. The first passive synthesis of time 'redeploys in the active synthesis of a psycho-organic memory and intelligence (instinct and learning)' (DR: 93). And this redeployment occurs for both the second and the third passive syntheses as well: '[w]e must therefore distinguish not only the forms of repetition in relation to passive synthesis but also the levels of passive synthesis and the combination of these levels with one another and with active syntheses'; accordingly '[a]ll of this forms a rich domain of *signs* which envelope heterogeneous elements and animate behaviour ... Each contraction, each passive synthesis, constitutes a sign which is interpreted or deployed in active synthesis' (DR: 93–4). Active synthesis binds passive and impassive syntheses through the sensory-motor system and its mental-images.

In short – and with respect to the twofold cineosis – the movement-image corresponds to active syntheses. In other words, the active and constitutive syntheses are another way of figuring Bergson's '*two forms of memory*', habitual memory and pure memory (MM: 79). On the one hand, habitual memory, which underpins the sensory-motor system and is of the movement-image and specified by relation-, recollection- and dream-images. On the other hand, pure memory, which underpins the time-image. The time-image is 'non-chronological time, Cronos and not Chronos', the latter corresponding to the movement-image (C2: 81). This difference is marked by the absence of a single consonant: so close and so difficult to separate. Perhaps this is why Deleuze chooses to use these similar (and often confused) terms in *Cinema 2*, rather than the more familiar Chronos and Aion. This interaction is one of the fundamental themes running throughout Deleuze's work. For instance, *The Logic of Sense*, written at the same time as *Difference and Repetition*, takes as its central paradox the Stoics' 'two kind of things' (LS: 7). The first kind of thing is the body, the second kind of thing impassive entities. The division is figured in this way: '[t]here are two times ... one is cyclical, measures the movements of bodies and depends upon the matter which limits and fills it out; the other is a pure straight line at the surface, incorporeal, unlimited, an empty form of time, independent of all matter' (LS: 71). And '[w]hereas Chronos expressed the action of bodies and the creation of corporeal qualities, Aion is the locus of incorporeal events, and the attributes which are distinct from qualities' (LS: 189). Deleuze concludes: 'this new dualism of bodies or states of affairs and effects or incorporeal events entails an upheaval in philosophy' (LS: 9). It is this upheaval that Deleuze, in all his work, is keeping alive. Chronos and Aion (Cronos) from the Stoics, matter and memory from Bergson; the active and constitutive syntheses of *Difference and Repetition*, the movement-image and time-image of the *Cinema* books. As Deleuze writes of *Cinema 2*: 'the whole aim of this book is to release ... [temporal structures] that the cinematographic image has been able to grasp and reveal, and which echo the teachings of science … or what philosophy makes understandable for us, each in their respective ways' (C2: xii).

Mapping the syntheses of time with time-images

It is not simply the case that the three time-images proper exemplify the three constitutive syntheses of time in general. The correspondence can be shown at the level of the philosophical concepts of the nine dimensions of the past, present and future as embodiments of the nine cinematographic elements of hyalosigns, chronosigns and noosigns. These three constitutive syntheses of time and elements of the time-image can be mapped as in Figure I.22.

Images	Cineotic elements and temporal elements			Syntheses
1 Hyalosigns	Past of the present (retention)	The living present	Future of the present (expectation)	First passive synthesis: succession
	Limpid and opaque	Mirrors face to face	Seed and environment	
2 Chronosigns	The pure past	Present of the past (fate)	Future of the past (reminiscence)	Second passive synthesis: pure memory
	Sheets of the past	Peaks of the present	Powers of the false	
3 Noosigns	Past of the future (dark precursor)	Present of the future (caesura)	The empty future	Third impassive synthesis: empty future
	Body of gest	Body of attitude	Cinema of the brain	

Figure I.22 Deleuze: syntheses of time and time-images

Hyalosigns can be seen to correspond with the first passive synthesis of time. This first passive synthesis is that of 'lived, or living, present', the 'thousands of habits of which we are composed' (DR: 91, 100). Hyalosigns are cinematographic images that appear in the now, where 'the actual [image] is cut off from its motor linkages', instead exploring 'the coalescence of an actual image and *its* virtual image' (DR: 127). This image in the now, this hyalosign, is a crystal-image and Deleuze identifies three aspects. First, the actual image describes a mirroring: 'oblique mirrors, concave and convex mirrors and Venetian mirrors', 'two facing mirrors', and a 'palace of mirrors' (C2: 70). Here the body and environment appear in the mirror, indiscernible (is this the actual? is this the virtual?) – the contraction of fragmentation that we are, our living present. Second, actual and virtual images enter into an exchange: one becoming limpid as another becomes opaque. Back and forth, an 'exchange' that is (once again) indiscernible (C2: 70). The actual image is in the present, but the virtual image is a past of the present, a retention. The virtual image appears with the actual image, constituting the 'smallest internal circuit' (C2: 70). Third, actual and virtual images appear as the seed and the environment. The present is the seed, the future of the present an environment in relation to that seed, an expectation, an anticipation – though not as a sensory-motor extension (actual chronological time) but rather as an indeterminate (virtual) illumination. The future is now: 'as pure virtuality, it does not have to be actualised' (C2: 79). The three images of the hyalosign thus describe the three dimensions of the first passive synthesis of time: the living present, the past as retention and the future as expectation. 'What we see … in the crystal is time, in its double movement of making presents pass, replacing one by the next while going towards the future, but also preserving all the past, dropping it into an obscure depth' (C2: 87).

Chronosigns can be seen to correspond with the second passive synthesis of time. This second synthesis is 'memory', the 'pure, general, *a priori* element of all time' (DR: 101, 103–4). Chronosigns, unlike hyalosigns, which appear as images in the now, are narrations: the film is a reconstitution involving the dimensions of the past. As Deleuze puts it, chronosigns 'no longer concern … description, but narration', a narration of 'false continuity' where 'crystalline narrations will extend crystalline description' (C2: 127). These false continuities take three forms. First, the 'coexistence of all the sheets of the past' which disrupt the order of time (C2: 99). The film resists linear organisation but jumps between circles of the past. The film is the pure past, an 'infinity of levels' (C2: 105). Second, some films are chronosigns in that they explore the present of the past, as Deleuze puts it, the peaks of the present. He writes: 'narration will consist of the distribution of different presents to different characters, so that each forms a combination that is plausible and possible in itself, but where all of them together are "incompossible"' (C1: 101). This kind of film also disrupts the order of time, 'gives narration a new value, because it abstracts it from all successive action' (C2: 101). Rather, the narration appears in the repetitions of the different presents. In this way the past(s) dominate(s) the present(s). This is the past as the fate of the present – not in the sense of prescription (a retroactive now which would require an unambiguous and actualised linear trajectory) but rather in the sense of 'setting time free' (C2: 102). Fate is freedom. And freedom is choice, the choice between 'inextricable differences' (C2: 105). Third, films can also explore the power of the false. Narration 'becomes fundamentally falsifying', it 'ceases to be truthful, that is, to claim to be true' (C2: 131). Crucially, as Deleuze puts it, 'this is not a simple principle of reflection or becoming aware: "Beware! This is cinema". It is a source of inspiration' (C2: 131). This chronosign is no longer content simply to disrupt the order of time; instead the strategy is one of a series of images, images that refer to each other and pass into one another in every way.

Difference and repetition, the repetition of themes, events, symbols, bodies, positions, objects, environments in difference: serialism. Reminiscences – the past in service of the future, interweaving, transformational memory. The three images of the chronosign thus describe the three dimensions of the second passive synthesis of time: the pure past, the present as radical fate and the future as vital reminiscence. Chronosigns are narrations that 'shatter the empirical continuation of time, the chronological succession, the separation of before and after' (C2: 155).

Noosigns can be seen to correspond with the third impassive synthesis of time. This third synthesis is a 'caesura' exploring the future as an 'empty form of time' (DR: 111, 108). Noosigns are thus events which 'force … us to think', events which 'force … us to think what is concealed from thought, life' (C2: 189). While hyalosigns are images and chronosigns are narration, noosigns are events that occur through the bodies and environments of the film: the mise-en-scène and actors. This is the narrative. Thought, then (our thought, the spectator's thought), is not engendered as a consequence of a sensory-motor linkage between the character and the situation, and the concomitant identification of character to subject and filmic situation to real milieu, but rather through the absence of such relations. In the absence of such a link, thought becomes us. These thought-images can occur in three ways. First, the actor does not perform an act of mimesis, but adopts 'the everyday body', a body of 'daily attitude' (C2: 191). This involves strategies such as exposing the fatigues, the ticks, the inabilities of the body. Here the body is circumscribed by the present. Second, the actor can foreground a performance, execute a 'ceremonial body' (C2: 191). This is the body of the 'gest' and 'carries out a direct theatricalisation of bodies' (C2: 192, 194). These bodies occur 'independently of the plot' and in this sense are an accumulation of the past (C2: 194). The final image of the noosign involves the mise-en-scène, the environment. It does not depend upon the physical presence of an actor, but the backgrounds, the lighting, the colours and sounds of the world of the film. Deleuze names this the 'cinema of the brain' (C2: 205). For Deleuze, certain films explore the 'identity of the brain and world' where 'landscapes are mental states, just as mental states are cartographies' and form a reciprocal 'noosphere' (C2: 205). The noosphere is a zone of nothingness that fractures the coordinates of the film. It is here, in this final aspect of the noosign, in this final aspect of the time-image, that cinema explores the future as terrifyingly opaque, as an unending night … and conversely, as infinitely open, vital. For the environment is immense, without horizon, without bounds. The three coordinates of the noosign thus describe the three dimensions of the third impassive synthesis of time: the past as experience, the present as caesura and the future as infinitely empty. Noosigns are the events of cinema that transpire between bodies and environments: 'the brain gives orders to the body which is just an outgrowth of it, but the body also gives orders to the brain which is just a part of it' (C2: 205).

The three time-images proper resonate with the three constitutive syntheses of time. Not in general, but at both the level of syntheses with images and the level of the nine dimensions of the past, present and future with the nine elements of hyalosigns, chronosigns and noosigns. Furthermore – such a correspondence between the time-image and *Difference and Repetition* exhausts neither text. The time-image is not simply a reification of the atemporal syntheses, for the synthesis of time is only the first of three taxonomic explications of the body and world, one moment of a wider series that also encompasses what Deleuze calls the syntheses of space and the syntheses of consciousness. And – as will be seen – both these syntheses can also be aligned with the three time-images proper, creating an ever richer series of cinematic resonances.

Deleuze's syntheses of space

'We should not be surprised', writes Deleuze in *Difference and Repetition*, that 'pure spatial syntheses … repeat the temporal syntheses previously specified' (DR: 289). That is to say – as Henry Somers-Hall comments – the atemporal series 'introduced … a synthesis that constituted a subject rather than presupposing one. Just as there were three syntheses of time, so there are three spatial syntheses' (Somers-Hall, 2013: 171). Space describes environments and places, organic life and non-organic objects. Such space is encountered in three dimensions – x, y, z: height (up ↔ down), width (back ↔ forth) and breadth (side ↔ side). Here I stand, these coordinates of extensity defining my place in the universe, on the Earth and in relation to others and the things that surround me. And such space – with an I at the centre – is an equivalent to the active synthesis of time: an active synthesis of space. The organic synthesis of matter is gathered up as three-dimensional spatiality. In thinking extensity, then, we already appear as a subjective spatial presence within an objective space. Yet these coordinates of extensity trace points, volumes, qualities, lines and curves constituted by space. It is here we encounter correlates of the three syntheses of time. These are the *extensio* of distance; the *implex* of depth and the *spatium* of intensity (DR: 288–9). Atemporal and aspatial series can be compared as in Figure I.23.

The first passive synthesis of space concerns extension (*extensio*), whereby extensity (*extensum*: x, y, z) is framed. It is 'the explication of extensity [that] rests upon the first synthesis, that of … the present' (DR: 289). *Extensio* (extension) is the foundation of *extensum* (extensity) – it is the plane of

Types Series	Syntheses of time	Syntheses of space
Active synthesis	Chronological time	Comprehensive space Extensity (extensum)
First passive synthesis	Living present of succession Presentness of present, past and future	Extensio of distance
Second passive synthesis	Pure past of memory Pastness of past, present and future	Implex of depth
Third impassive synthesis	Open future of emptiness Futureness of future, present and past	Spatium of intensity
Organic synthesis	Matter	

Figure I.23 Deleuze: syntheses of time and space

all-encompassing space across an ever extending (or infinite) distance. The second passive synthesis of space concerns depth – 'the implication of depth rests upon the second synthesis, that of Memory and the past' (DR: 289). If extension is the plane of distance in the now, depth is space as the whole past. This is 'depth itself, which is not an extension but a pure *implex*' (DR: 288). This *implex*, complex space, is the ground – all space since (for example, the big bang of) the beginning. Accordingly, space flows from this depth: 'depth envelops in itself distances which develop in extensity' (DR: 289–90). Finally, the third impassive synthesis of space concerns intensity, 'an intensive quality: the pure *spatium*' where 'the proximity and simmering of the third synthesis make themselves felt, announcing the universal "ungrounding"' (DR: 289). Here we encounter quantum fields, m-dimensions, molecular genesis: the very forces out of which space always will be forged. 'The strangest alliance', writes Deleuze, 'is formed between intensity and depth ... [and] out of this intensive depth emerge at once the *extensio* and the *extensum*' (DR: 290). Spatiality is constituted by the plane of the *extensio* of distance; the whole of the *implex* of depth and the genesis of the *spatium* of intensity: the three constitutive syntheses of space.

Of course – just as was seen with the three constitutive temporal syntheses – the three constitutive spatial syntheses are simultaneously disruptive of extensity within space: they are aspatialities. Distance as the indistinct at the moving edge of the beyond of the event horizon (creating the fragment); depth as the shifting imperceptible beneath the surface that obscures the whole (creating strata); intensity as a beyond of the molar threshold, at the always approximate mathematical realm, at the indeterminations that generate determinable states (the interstice). The indistinct, the imperceptible and the indeterminate nature of *extensio*, *implex* and *spatium* are aspatialities; the aspatiality concealed, cloaked and eclipsed by comprehensive space.

Mapping the syntheses of space with time-images

The question of such aspatialities is first announced in the *Cinema* books as early as *Cinema 1* through the concept of the any-space-whatever. The any-space-whatever is the genetic sign of the affection-image, the correlate of gaseous perception in the domain of affects, what Deleuze calls non-human affect. The environment creates affects in the character as external expressions upon faces and bodies. Affects are thus designated through unfilmable internal intensities appearing as affection-images. Here the close-up of the face of the central and privileged image expresses affects as determined feelings and emotions. These feelings and emotions flow to and from the character – through the people and places which surround the central and privileged image. Backgrounds – the any-space-whatever – appear for the character who inhabits and traverses them, who perceives, reflects upon and reacts to them. Accordingly, the affection-image is gathered from the perception-image and passes into the action-image and memory-image; and affective backgrounds – any-space-whatevers – become fully determined as social spaces within which the character will operate: revealing and transforming the milieu.

However, in the wake of the collapse of the movement-image, any-space-whatevers are set free from the sensory-motor system. The any-space-whatever is no longer an affective background for the character. Rather, '[t]he affect is now directly presented in … a space which is capable of corresponding to it' (C1: 109). In other words, the background subsumes all other images which may be within it, and is no longer there for a central image. These are deconnected and empty spaces. The central image disperses into the any-space-whatever which consumes the screen, and any extension from perception-images or into action-images or mental-image dissipates. 'Space', for Deleuze, 'is no longer a particular determined space, it has become any-space-whatever' (C1: 109). Deleuze appropriates the term 'any-space-whatever' from Pascal Augé; and Augé, writes Deleuze, 'would prefer to look for their source in the experimental cinema. But it could equally be said that they are as old as cinema itself' (C1: 109). 'How can [the] any-space-whatever be constructed (in the studio or on location)?' – asks Deleuze (C1: 111). The immediate answer is through shadowy darkness, white screens, and colourism (where a colour singularity permeates everything) (C1: 111–20). In such a way, comprehensive space is dislocated, space is displaced and the screen becomes the site of aspatiality, an aspatiality that – within the regime of movement-images – will nevertheless become bound up in extensity (matter-images and memory-images). Accordingly, the any-space-whatever is not an abstract universal; rather, '[i]t is a perfectly singular space, which merely has lost … the principle of its metric relations or the connection of its own parts, so that linkages can be made in an infinite number of ways.

It is a space of virtual conjunction' (C1: 109). Space becomes heterogeneous, unstable, and – crucially – sets the 'prior conditions of all actualisation, all determination' (C1: 109). The any-space-whatever correlates to the aspatial syntheses of the *extensio* of distance; the whole of the *implex* of depth and the genesis of the *spatium* of intensity: that which is gathered up in the affection-image through movement-images as comprehensive space.

Towards the end of the discussion of the any-space-whatever in *Cinema 1* Deleuze indicates that he will return to such aspatialities in *Cinema 2*, the concept to be developed in the regime of the time-image. Accordingly, in the first few pages of the second volume Deleuze writes: '[t]he space of a sensory-motor situation is a setting which is already specified and presupposes an action which discloses it, or prompts a reaction which adapts or modifies it. But a purely optical or sound situation becomes established in what we might call "any-space-whatever"' (C2: 5). In this way, the any-space-whatever accompanies opsigns-sonsigns as the undifferentiated image to be explicated as aspatial coordinates corresponding to hyalosigns, chronosigns and noosigns through cinematic fragmentation, stratification and intersticialisation: aspatial correlates of the atemporal image in-itself, the narration of the film and the narrative of the filmic event. This is the fragmented space of the image, the strata of coexisting images and the interstices within, without and between images. Fragmentation can be seen to correlate to the plane of the *extensio* of distance (first synthesis); strata to the whole of the *implex* of depth (second synthesis); and interstices to the genesis of the *spatium* of intensity (third synthesis). These correspondences and correlates can be mapped as in Figure I.24.

Series \ Types	Syntheses of space	Time-images
First passive synthesis	Extensio of distance	Hyalosigns Fragments and fragmentation
Second passive synthesis	Implex of depth	Chronosigns Strata and stratification
Third impassive synthesis	Spatium of intensity	Noosigns Interstices and intersticialisation

Figure I.24 Deleuze: syntheses of space and time-images

Hyalosigns are the image in-itself as crystalline description, decomposed through the elements of the mirror face to face, the exchange of the limpid and opaque, and the growth of the seed into the environment. These hyalosigns are actual images cut off from each other and relinked to their virtual correlates. This is fragmentation, the image retaining its status and affirming the fragment as fragment. The mirror image captures space, which is then duplicated, triplicated and so on. A hall of mirrors, a corridor of reflections create a fundamental aspatiality. It may be one image is distorted, that the reflection and what is reflected are indeterminate, that the reflection occupies the entire image, that the image is cracked, a cobweb of splinters. Whatever the case – the image fragments as if reflected through the facias of the crystal. This 'actual–virtual couple' can extend into the 'limpid-opaque, the expression of their exchange' or into the seed and the environment as an 'internal disposition' (C2: 70–1). Actual images become virtual, and virtual images are actualised. One fragment is exchanged for another. Or, the image contains within it a fragment as fractal, which in-itself is but a fragment. The hyalosign is 'the construction of a space, fragment by fragment' (C1: 108). And these fragments go into 'infinity', they describe 'a distance impossible to determine. Independent of any fixed point' (C1: 109; C2: 125). Hyalosigns correlate to the *extensio* of distance as an all-encompassing aspatiality, the fragment opening up to the whole of the virtual.

Fragments of images conjoin as 'strata': chronosigns create stratification (C2: 120). Such stratification occurs through the decompositions of peaks of the present, sheets of the past and powers of the false as orders (simultaneity and coexistence) and series (false continuity) of chronosigns. These concurrences describe cinematic depth. For example, depth-of-field: the cinematic image in which foreground, mid-grounds and background remain in focus and across which events, characters and objects interact. Here '[t]he function of depth is … to constitute the image in a crystal' and such an image no longer requires montage as link; montage and image lose all opposition (C2: 85). Fragments conjoin as strata. Depth-of-field is but one way in which to create the concurrences of the chronosign, merely indicative of a 'freeing of depth … [that] subordinates all other dimensions' (C2: 85). Jump cuts, freeze-frames, the long take, hyper-rapid montage, the empty frame – all such techniques may be put in service of stratification of space. In the first instance, peaks of the present are the repetition of the same space through different perspectives: a single space becomes a multiplicity. In the second place, sheets of the past are the coexistence of diverse spaces: different ages – events and bodies – conjoin through the virtual, creating singularities. In the third instance, the serial organisation of powers of the false link heterogeneous spaces through false continuity: disconcerting, perplexing links, interpenetrations that retain their heterogeneity. Chronosigns describe the fundamental aspatiality of depth, the *implex*, complex space.

Finally, fragmentation and stratification are sustained in tension through intersticialisation: the 'interstice', or gap (C2: 213). Fragments are fragments because of the interstice between the strata; and stratification receives its power through the irrational links between fragments. The interstice is the virtual and corresponds to the third impassive synthesis of space: intensity, the pure *spatium*, a universal ungrounding. This is the noosign: the body of attitude, bodies as *gest* and the screen as brain. The aim of time-image cinema, for Deleuze, 'is not to reconstitute a presence of bodies, in perception and action, but to carry out a primordial genesis of bodies' (C2: 201). In other words, 'the body is initially caught in quite a different space, where disparate sets overlap and rival each other, without being able to organise themselves according to sensory-motor schemata. They fit over each other, in an overlapping of perspectives which means that there is no way to distinguish them even though they are distinct and incompatible' (C2: 203). With noosigns we encounter a series of disjunctions: the breaks between the disparate states of the body in-itself; the dissonance between bodies in their distinct states; and the discord between these bodies and the world. Noosigns are the fundamental encounter with a film as a new, discordant time-image of cinematic thought, an image of the aspatialities of bodies and world as a heterogeneous assemblage, as pure difference and repetition. With the noosign, spatial 'visibility is perforated by the incoherence and inchoate quality of thought' C2: 191). These perforations, these gaps, these intervals in and between images are the interstice – the genesis of the virtual.

The three aspects of aspatiality can be summarised thus: the time-image takes the any-space-whatever as actual image (mode of opsign-sonsign) and opens it up to the virtual through the aspatialities of hyalosigns, chronosigns and noosigns. Hyalosigns as fragmentation, chronosigns as stratification and noosigns as inter-sticialisation. Fragmentation, stratification and intersticialisation develop as fragment → strata → interstices; and intersticialisation ungrounds time-images, creating stratification and fragmentation, interstices → strata → fragment. This is the noosphere: fragment ↔ strata ↔ interstice (C2: 207). The aspatial noosphere is that which replaces – as Deleuze puts it – a 'whole space which can be called "hodological"' (C2: 203). Hodological space, first conceived by the psychologist and behaviourist Kurt Lewin, describes how a body is a grounding of life in a space that allows movements through psychological pathways in relation to the world, reacting and responding to the situation, milieu, environment. In other words, sensory-motor, movement-image space – comprehensive space. For Deleuze, however, the time-image is 'pre-hodological space' (C2: 203). In the time-image, the any-space-whatever is developed in pre-hodological space: fragmentation as the *extensio* of distance; strata as the whole of the *implex* of depth; and interstices as the genesis of the *spatium* of intensity. The three aspatial syntheses repeat the three atemporal syntheses as difference – or perhaps better put, the two perspectives of 'a new space-time' for cinema (C2: 205).

Deleuze's syntheses of consciousness

Difference and Repetition, however, gives us a third synthesis. The atemporal syntheses are the grounding of chronological time and the aspatial syntheses are the grounding of comprehensive space. Yet '[a]ctualisation', writes Deleuze, 'takes place in three series: space, time and also consciousness. Every spatio-temporal dynamism is accompanied by the emergence of an elementary consciousness' (DR: 273). The syntheses of time and space necessitate a third synthesis of bodies and worlds. And while Deleuze may be responsible for some of the most beautiful concepts and conceptual clusters in the history of philosophy (some neologisms, some purloined and reused, reoriented, perverted, repurposed), here is one that could well be considered the clumsiest: 'indi-drama-differen*t*/ciation' (DR: 308). Involving hyphens, forward slashes and the italicisation of certain letters, this compound is a nasty truncation of four terms, later repeated (with elements in another order) as 'differentiation-individuation-dramatization-differenciation' (DR: 313). Yet despite such unwieldiness we have here a descriptor of an essential nexus. Unfolded, it describes – with respect to bodies and worlds – a new synthesis, another organic, impassive, passive, active trajectory. Accordingly, this synthesis can be placed alongside the syntheses of space and time as in Figure I.25.

Series / Types	Syntheses of time	Syntheses of space	Syntheses of consciousness
Active synthesis	Linear time	Extensity	Differenciation
First passive synthesis	Succession	Distance	Individuation
Second passive synthesis	Pure memory	Depth	Differentiation
Third impassive synthesis	Open future	Intensity	Dramatisation
Organic synthesis		Matter	

Figure I.25 Deleuze: syntheses of time, space and consciousness

It should be immediately apparent that the radical move – in Deleuze's exposition – is to see individuation aligned not with active synthesis, but with respect to the first passive synthesis. Individuation does not equate to active synthesis, individuation is not the actualised equivalent of chronological time and comprehensive space. Such a position is rather indicated by the word 'differenciation' (with a 'c'). 'Individuation precedes differenciation', writes Deleuze, 'every differenciation presupposes a prior intense field of individuation' (DR: 308). Single cell lifeforms were the first to develop before complex – or multicellular – lifeforms; and the egg is a single cell which will replicate only after fertilisation. Such a process of individuation is the primary characteristic of life, an ongoing, unending praxis – although one with a concomitant degradation and death. Individuation here can be seen as an embodiment of space and time through the succession of presentness and extension of distance. Yet this individuation is only acted upon in tandem with a differentiation (with a 't'), the designation of what Deleuze calls the 'pre-individual field' (DR: 307). The crucial point here is that 'all differences are borne by individuals, but they are not all individual differences' (DR: 309). There are individuals of different species and individuals of the same species; because of this, it may be believed that individuation is an instant of the determination of species – however, for Deleuze this would be an error. Species characteristics are not primary, but 'imprisoned in individuals as though in a crystal' (DR: 309). Accordingly, the individual – for Deleuze – is before species. Species differentiation – the second passive synthesis of embodiment – is thus a correlative of the *implex* of depth and the whole of pure memory: a destiny where 'the entire world may be read, as though in a crystal ball' (DR: 309). This differentiation is where 'the enveloping intensities (depth) constitute the field of individuation, the in-dividuating differences', while 'the enveloped intensities (distances) constitute the individual differences' (DR: 316). Finally, the third constitutive synthesis of embodiment is dramatisation. It is 'intensity which dramatizes. It is intensity which is immediately expressed in the basic spatio-temporal dynamisms' (DR: 306–7). Dramatisation describes centres of envelopment, an envelopment of the enveloping and enveloped individual-differentiation. It is the connection always to come with other bodies and species, environments and objects; an ungrounding of the foundation and ground of individual-differentiation.

Accordingly, the constitutive syntheses of individuation ↔ differentia-tion ↔ dramatisation are explicated in the differenciated; and explicated 'only by being cancelled out in this differenciated system that it creates' (DR 319). Here, the I and the Self are the 'figures of differenciation', where 'the Self forms the psychic organisation' of species and 'the I is the quality of human being as a species' (DR: 319). Thus we have constitutive forces which give rise to identity (and othering) as the very process of human differenciation. This is active synthesis.

Differenciation, then, is an active synthesis that annuls the disjunctions, the dissonance and indeterminacies of individuation ↔ differentiation ↔ drama-tisation. Yet, another 'error', for Deleuze, 'is to believe that this indetermination … indicates something incomplete' (DR: 321). Rather, 'the full, positive power of the individual' is 'affirmed' in such 'indeterminate, floating, fluid … positive characteristics' (DR: 321). The question then must be, what will let loose these powers and how are they affirmed? The answer is 'de-differenciation', that 'which compensates for the differenciations of the I and the Self', that which is 'a protest by the individual which has never recognised itself within the limits of the self and the I' (DR: 323). This protest refers us to the third impassive synthesis (dramatisation), which is 'constituted neither by the I or the Self, but by a completely different structure belonging to the I-Self system' (DR: 323). And this structure is the Other: a conception of the other which 'refers only to the self for the other I and the other I for the self' (DR: 323). More simply, it 'is not the other which is another I' (which would be the third feature of differenciation); rather, it is 'the I which is an other' (DR: 324). This otherness marks the constitutive impassive synthesis of dramatisation and is that which constitutes an individuation as multiple and ever-changing. Accordingly, 'the individual in intensity finds its psychic image … in the fractured I and the dissolved self, and in the correlation of the fractured I with the dissolved self' (DR: 322). And this correlation in the third impassive synthesis is an expression of endless possibilities. This is the '*a priori* other', as Deleuze puts it in an essay in the appendices to *Logic of Sense*, the 'structure-Other'; and this 'structure of the possible' is 'grasped as a not yet existing outside of that which expresses it' (LS: 346–7).

Two essential consequences can therefore be designated with respect to the constitutive series of individuation ↔ differentiation ↔ dramatisation and the concomitant ungrounding de-differenciation. Firstly, that *the individual is a population and populations are individual*: 'beings … are distributed across the space of univocal being' (DR: 378). Secondly, rather than a homogeneous field, *univocal being is radically heterogeneous*: '"Everything is equal" … can be said only at the point at which the extremity of difference is reached' (DR: 378). This is the power of the ahuman forces that animate life, where the ahuman – according to Patricia MacCormack – is a term that 'suggests … encountering the outside of human' states and 'verges on a nothing that includes everything' (MacCormack, 2014, 1–2). It is only through differenciation and the ascension of the human element – the I, the self and the other of identity – that individuals and populations appear in opposition, that difference and repetition are subsumed under the concept of the same, and that hierarchies are established and maintained. De-differenciation is the escape from the human element: identity, the coherent consciousness as an ossification of indeterminate life.

Mapping the syntheses of consciousness with time-images

The time-image is an *a priori* cinematic enunciation of the constitutive series of individuation ↔ differentiation ↔ dramatisation; a de-differenciation of movement-images. The movement-image brings together perception-images, affection-images, action-images and mental-images to create a coherent human consciousness within comprehensive space across chronological time. The time-image attacks each of these coordinates simultaneously through the creation of hyalosigns, chronosigns and noosigns. In other words, the time-image not only corresponds to the atemporal and aspatial syntheses, but also to the ahuman synthesis; that is, the de-differentiation of human identity expressed through the cinematic equivalents of the fractured I, the dissolved self and the other-structure. These correlations can be expressed as in Figure I.26.

Types Series	Syntheses of consciousness	Time-images
First passive synthesis	Individuation	Hyalosigns Fractured I
Second passive synthesis	Differentiation	Chronosigns Dissolved self
Third impassive synthesis	Dramatisation	Noosigns Other-structure

Figure I.26 Deleuze: syntheses of consciousness and time-images

The three time-images (proper) thus each correspond to the three constitutive syntheses of consciousness, creating signs of cinematic de-differenciation. Hyalosigns express the synthesis of individuation through figures of the fractured I in mirrors, the limpid-opaque and the seed-environment. The character is – in the first place – a crystal: multifaceted, of many faces, bodies, minds. A fragment in itself for itself, a luminous fragment with the passing opaque fragments that divide different spaces and times; a seed, a fragment of its virtual environment. These actual images compose the fragmented I through their virtual correlates. '[S]ubjectivity' is thus, for Deleuze, 'never ours, it is … the soul or the spirit, the virtual', and the virtual 'is not a psychological state or a consciousness: it exists outside consciousness' (C2: 83). In other words, these actualised fragments may appear as perceptions, affects, actions, thoughts, recollections and imagination; but it is not these that give us the fractured I – the fractured I is rather that which results from these fragments remaining fragments, that which disallows identity, differenciation. The power of the virtual of hyalosigns. Such actual–virtual correlates of the fragmented I are developed in figures of the dissolved self. It is chronosigns that reify the synthesis of differentiation through the orders and series of sheets of the past, peaks of the present and powers of the false. The fragmented I – that which is individuated – appears with its concurrences. This may be the simultaneity of the heterogeneous now; the coexistences of childhood, youth, adulthood, old age, life and death; the moments of a life, or lives, bodies and worlds reconstituted, reinvented in difference, in fictions. This fragmented I becomes the only reality. The self is a dissolved self in its virtual sheets, peaks and powers. The fragmented I and the dissolved self discover their greatest exposition in the body of attitude, the body of gest and the brain as a screen. Noosigns express the synthesis of dramatisation as the other-structure. This is the figure of I as other to self, self as other to I developed in a dramatisation which connects bodies with the world and world with bodies. The 'people are missing' writes Deleuze; people and peoples are no homogeneous whole in determined temporal-spatial territories (C2: 216). The noosign explores the heterogeneity of the fragmented I and dissolved self as a population and populations as individuation-differentiations distributed in univocal space and time: aspatial, atemporal, ahuman correlates. The screen discovers the virtual in which world and bodies are figures of the possible.

The time-image affirms de-differenciation: affirms the nexus of individuation, differentiation and dramatisation as the fragmented I and the dissolved self through the other-structure of the dissolved self with the fragmented I – this is the ungrounding of the coherent human subject of identity for the body as a site of becoming with the world for the world and with bodies. This aspect of the time-image – the correlate of the constitutive synthesis of consciousness – repeats with difference the accompanying constitutive syntheses of space and time. Together, the perspectives of the three syntheses of time, space and consciousness describe the atemporal, aspatial and ahuman forces that the time-image captures up through the signs and images of hyalosigns, chronosigns and noosigns. Hyalosigns, chronosigns and noosigns are cinematic impurities of the actual on-screen image with its virtual: opsigns/ sonsigns and lectosigns – the perspectives of the time-image create the pure virtual function of interpretation. These atemporal, aspatial and ahuman syntheses can be mapped against each other and through the coordinates of the time-image as in Figure I.27. The genealogy of the time-image reveals a cineosis of resonances, differences, repetitions which subsist within and through each other – a complexity of embeddings, perspectives, embodiments and analogies that describe disjunctive temporalities and displaced spatialities dissolving subjectivities. Such discords are the affirmation of a new image of filmic thought preserving indeterminacies, creating caesuras, proliferating false continuities that open up the actual image to its virtual correlates.

It is at this point that the genealogy of the time-image must conclude. In *Cinema 2* Deleuze will explore the coordinates of the time-image (opsigns/ sonsigns, hyalosigns, chronosigns, noosigns and lectosigns) as a cineosis without reference to the atemporal, aspatial, and ahuman syntheses of *Difference and Repetition*. Thus, while the three syntheses of time, space and

0 Opsigns and sonsigns (pure actual image)			
1 Hyalosigns	Limpid and opaque	Mirrors face to face	Seed and environment
		First passive synthesis of time, space and consciousness	
	Past of the present (retention)	The living present	Future of the present (expectation)
		Extensio of distance (Fragmentation)	
		Individuation (Fractured I)	
2 Chronosigns	Sheets of the past	Peaks of the present	Powers of the false
		Second passive synthesis of time, space and consciousness	
	The pure past	Present of the past (fate)	Future of the past (reminiscence)
		Implex of depth (Stratification)	
		Differentiation (Dissolved Self)	
3 Noosigns	Body of gest	Body of attitude	Cinema of the brain
	Third impassive synthesis of time, space and consciousness		
	Past of the future (dark precursor)	Present of the future (caesura)	The empty future
		Spatium of intensity (Intersticialisation)	
		Dramatisation (Other-structure)	
			Lectosigns (pure virtual correlate) ∞

Figure I.27 Deleuze: time-images and the syntheses of time, space and consciousness

consciousness can be seen to provide the framework of the time-image, as well as underpin and inform the coordinates of that organisation, they do so only to create a pragmatic cineotic matrix. This matrix will be described through the processes of the creation of the time-image cinema – through disruptive practices of framing, the shot, montage, sound and colour. An explication of such a praxis, however, will only be able to be carried out by working through the signs as a logical series (Section II). Yet, for this pragmatic cineotic matrix, the three syntheses of time, space and consciousness remain a virtual correlate.

*   *   *

Deleuze's three syntheses of time, space and consciousness from *Difference and Repetition* can be seen to provide the philosophical coordinates of the time-image. The pure actual of on-screen opsigns and sonsigns appears as lectosigns, pure virtual correlates that require interpretation. Hyalosigns (the image itself), chronosigns (coexistence of images as narration) and noosigns (the narrative as filmic event) are impurities of the actual–virtual, the cineosis of time-images. Such has been revealed through the genealogy of the present chapter. Yet – at one and the same moment – we have not reached the end of the twofold cineosis, but rather the exploration of time-images as atemporal, aspatial and ahuman series has led us back to the movement-image. For the time-image may have begun with the collapse of the determined coordinates of the sensory-motor system – the de-differenciation of the movement-image. However, the three syntheses of time, space and consciousness simultaneously describe how the indeterminacies of image, narration, and narrative are differenciated in the movement-image. In other words – the differenciation of the time-image concerns the creation of the movement-image; and the de-differenciation of the movement-image concerns the creation of the time-image. The domains of hyalosigns, chronosigns and noosigns are differenciated in the domains of perception-images, affection-images, action-images and mental-images. Differenciation and de-differenciation are reciprocates played out in cinema through the actual images on-screen and the effacement and release of their virtual correlates. In this way, describing movement-images and time-images as two regimes is but one perspective of Deleuze's cineosis. In contrast, another way to consider the taxonomy is as an implication of perception-images, affection-images, action-images, mental-images, opsigns-sonsigns, hyalosigns, chronosigns, noosigns, lectosigns. These domains, avatars and images in turn playing out in a sign series that describes a heterogeneous series as a univocal cineosis. Everything equal at the point of radical difference, the repetitions of difference and the differences of repetition, radical repetition. Such a conclusion may appear to turn away from Bergson's *Matter and Memory*, the visible framework of the *Cinema* books that announced and explicated movement-images and time-images as two distinct regimes. A turning away from Bergson towards Deleuze's *Difference and Repetition* as an invisible originary structure. However, this is not the case. It is not that Deleuze's philosophy replaces that of Bergson; rather, it explicates Bergson. Deleuze's univocity of being is Bergsonian, and the two regimes of the movement-image and the time-image find their fullest expression as a series of univocal signs through Bergson's philosophy of duration and image.

4

Time-images and movement-images: Bergson, duration and image

Cinema – for Deleuze – is time-images and movement-images. Two regimes of the cinematic image describing a multiplicity of complex connections, interrelations, exchanges and transformations. Accordingly, the cinema can be described as a univocal cineosis explicating the 'differenciation' of movement-images and de-differenciation of time-images, the actualisation of filmic matter-images and their virtual correlates (C2: 276).

The fundamental division between the movement-image and the time-image was theorised by Deleuze in the wake of the philosophy of Bergson. Such was the concern of Chapter 1, which explored *Matter and Memory* as an assertion of the radical dissimilarity between pure matter (image, sensory-motor system) and pure memory (spontaneous thought, duration). Deleuze's cinematic appropriation of Bergsonian theory, as was seen, was both taxonomic and philosophical. On the one hand – and with respect to the fundamental coordinates of the cineosis – pure matter (image, sensory-motor system) gave us the regime of the movement-image; and pure memory (spontaneous thought, duration) gave us the regime of the time-image. On the other hand, it necessarily could not be said that movement-images = pure matter and that time-images = pure duration. All cinema is a practice of matter-images; and both movement-images and time-images engender cinema-thought. The distinction, rather, lies in the different ways in which cinema-thought is encompassed, effaced, released or discharged through movement-images and time-images. Accordingly, such an analysis is found in Bergson's account of pure matter and pure memory.

A strange dualism

The 'Introduction' to the fifth edition (1908) of *Matter and Memory* begins: '[t]his book affirms the reality of spirit and the reality of matter … It is, then, frankly, dualistic'; a position, Bergson readily admits, 'to be held in small honour among philosophers' (MM: 9). The question of Bergson's dualism – its status as ontology and epistemology – is essential to an engagement with Bergsonism; furthermore, it is crucial not only to Deleuze's philosophy in general but also to the film theory of the *Cinema* books. Why does Bergson adopt such a discredited position? Deleuze anticipates such a question much earlier than the *Cinema* books, and much earlier than *Difference and Repetition*. Writing of his early studies of the history of philosophy in *Dialogues II*, Deleuze states: 'I could not stand Descartes, the dualisms', yet with Bergson 'there is something which cannot be assimilated', something 'which enabled him to provide a shock', even if he became 'the object of so many hatreds' (D2: 14–15).

Monism maintains that there is but one reality: matter or mind – the (various, varied) doctrines of materialism and idealism. Idealism sees the mind (its thoughts, its ideas) as primary, with all material reality a derived principle; while materialism insists matter is the only reality, mind and thought secondary. These two opposed ontologies, these two conflicting monist belief systems, thus have commonality: the positing (each in their own way) of but one real, one mode of being. The advantage of a monist belief system is thus twofold: (1) not having to account for two different modes of being; and (2) not having to account for the relation between these two different modes of being. In monism, matter derives from mind, or mind from matter. Dualism thus has two correlate difficulties: explicating the essentials of both a materialist and idealist position as opposition, as well as discerning the relation between (simultaneously – in either direction) the two positions.

Bergson begins *Matter and Memory* with just such a discussion, writing: 'it is a mistake to reduce matter to the perception we have of it, a mistake also to make it a thing able to produce in us perceptions, but in itself of another nature than they' (MM: 9). In other words both 'realism [materialism] and idealism go too far' (MM: 9). Bergson's point is this: while the basic monist positions posit either mind or body as real, both also must explicate how mind derives from body, or body from mind. In other words, the dualist problem of the relation between body and mind may be resolved in such derivations, but such a resolution remains haunted by the dualist question. Monism must still account for body and mind. For Bergson, the dualist position he adopts is simply one that acknowledges and keeps alive such a problem. Accordingly, *Matter and Memory* is an attempt to 'determine the relation' between the world of matter and the world of spirit through 'a definite example, that of memory' (MM: 9). A strange dualism, then, when Bergson writes that his project is thus 'dualistic', yet at the same moment will 'overcome … dualism' (MM: 9).

Monism and pluralism

It is just these questions that Deleuze explores in *Bergsonism* (1966). Deleuze writes: 'the Bergsonian method' has 'two main aspects, the one dualist, the other monist' (B: 73). Yet these aspects, accordingly to Deleuze, are serial. In the first place, Bergson's '[d]ualism is … only a moment, which must lead to the re-formation of a monism' (B: 29). Bergson's project is thus to discern the very genesis of the problem, the genesis of idealism and materialism, the genesis of dualism. As he writes in *Creative Evolution*, the 'theory of knowledge and theory of life seems to us inseparable' (CE: xiii). In this way, '[i]t is necessary that these two enquiries … should join each other, and, by a circular process, push each other on unceasingly' (CE: xiii). This is the method, simultaneously the ontology: 'matter, the reality which descends, endures only by its connection with that which ascends … life and consciousness are this very ascension' (CE: 369). Bergson's monism is the conjunction of the actual and the virtual. Deleuze comments: '[t]he absolute, said Bergson, has two sides (aspects): spirit imbued with metaphysics and matter known by science' (B: 35). There is no actual without the virtual, no virtual without the actual. No space without time, no time without space – no body without some form of consciousness, no consciousness without some form of body.

Accordingly, asks Deleuze, once again in *Bergsonism*: '[h]ave we really overcome dualism, or have we been engulfed in pluralism?' (B: 76). A pluralism of types of bodies, a pluralism of levels of consciousness. And it is not that a type of body corresponds to a type of consciousness; but rather, bodies as centres of indetermination traverse levels of consciousness. This is Bergson's pluralism: two series – one actual, one virtual. As Deleuze puts it: 'actual spatial multiplicity and virtual temporal multiplicity' (B: 85) From sensory-motor system to pure memory there are 'thousands of different planes of consciousness' (B: 241). This is the univocity of being: Bergsonism. A radical re-evaluation of the terms, methods and understanding of dualism, monism and pluralism. 'Being, or Time, is a *multiplicity*. But it is precisely not "multiple": it is One, in conformity with *its* type of multiplicity' (B: 85). Bergson's re-evaluation of dualism, monism and pluralism must be understood through the concept of multiplicity.

The cineosis as multiplicity

The cinema, according to Deleuze, can be understood as a multiplicity. A multiplicity of types of actual on-screen images and a multiplicity of virtual correlates. The dualism of the movement-image and the time-image is thus only the first moment of a monism of the actual–virtual – the cinema – which in turn describes a pluralism of types of image. On the one hand, the movement-image overwhelms the time-image with its actualisations of matter-images and memory-images. On the other hand, the time-image ungrounds the movement-image through the ascension of virtual correlates. Back and forth – from sign to image, from image to regime. We could thus describe the fundamental cineosis as in Figure I.28.

Series \ Dimensions	Past	Present	Future
Active synthesis of movement-images	Recollection-image	Relation-image	Dream-image
First synthesis of time-images: Hyalosigns	Mirrors face to face	Limpid and opaque	Seed and environment
Second synthesis of time-images: Chronosigns	Sheets of the past	Peaks of the present	Powers of the false
Third synthesis of time-images: Noosigns	Body of gest	Body of attitude	Cinema of the brain
Organic synthesis of movement-images	Perception-image	Affection-image	Action-image

Figure I.28 Deleuze: movement-image and time-image domains

*

*   *

Section I has explored the genealogy of the *Cinema* books through their inspirations: the theories of Bergson, the semiotic of Peirce and Deleuze's own foundational philosophy. Accordingly, there are – for Deleuze – two regimes of images in the cinema: movement-images and time-images – two kinds of cinema each with its own distinct filmic semiotic. Chapter 1 concerned the creation of the two regimes in response to Henri Bergson's investigations of image and duration from *Matter and Memory*. Chapter 2 focused upon the semiotic of the movement-image after the semiosis of Charles Sanders Peirce. Chapter 3 explored the time-image as an expression of Deleuze's syntheses of time, space and consciousness from *Difference and Repetition*. Such a trajectory led us to the re-evaluation of the relation between movement-images and time-images in Chapter 4. The cinema is a series of types of actual images and their virtual correlates that can be designated movement-images and time-images through their tendencies. Movement-images and time-images are thus merely the first moment in the reorientation towards a new perspective: the cineosis as a univocal multiplicity of images and signs.

Section II

Second Introduction

A Series of Images and Signs

Deleuze, in the Cinema *books, unfolds a cinematic semiosis – a cineosis – describing a vast array of elements. The Second Introduction explores this aspect of Deleuze's film theory through sixteen chapters, each one of which focuses upon a particular image, the signs which constitute that image, and – correspondingly – the avatars, domains and regimes into which these signs and images coalesce. Section II thus shifts towards a direct cinematic encounter in the wake of the philosophical genealogy of Section I: the three investigations into Bergson's theory of image and duration, Peirce's pragmatic semiosis and the syntheses of time, space, and consciousness from Deleuze's own* Difference and Repetition. *These investigations gave us the two regimes of movement-images and time-images; identified the number, arrangement and types of elements devolving from these regimes; and – finally – discovered a new perspective, that of the cineosis as a univocal multiplicity. Section II develops this new perspective. To do so, it approaches the* Cinema *books by way of an explication of each image and its sign elements along a serial trajectory. In this way, the aim is to name and describe each image and sign in turn, as well as to recognise and resolve any terminological overlappings, embeddings, duplications and lacunas within the possible coordinates given in the philosophical framework of Section I. (Terms created to 'fill in' lacunas will be signalled – in this section alone – with italicisation.) This serial unfolding will be deployed in Section III, which will exploit each of the signs to open up – in some way – the cinematographics of a film. Here, and in anticipation of such adventures, the objective is to explicate the cineosis as a logic, a series of images, where each sign is delineated and diagrammatised.*

1

Perception-images

Perception-images are the condition for the cinema of the movement-image and the movement-image cineosis. In other words, the differenciation and specification of the perception-image is that which is necessary for the creation of the domains of affect, action and thought; and for the whole panoply of avatars, images and signs that will devolve from these domains and thus constitute the possible coordinates of a cinema of the sensory-motor system. Cinematic perception thus concerns the fundamental organisation of worlds and bodies: the world is composed of matter from which images coalesce, where centres form, and from which a privileged character emerges. This trajectory describes a process from genesis to composition and gives the perception-image its sign series. The genetic sign is gaseous perception, where all images interact with one another without a centre. The coalescence of gaseous perception produces liquid perception, where centres form as environments and characters which the film passes through and by, ever onwards. Finally, there is full composition, solid perception. This most familiar of perception-images refers to the privileging of a cohesive subject with respect to the film-world: a character who is perceived as the fundamental centre, and with whom the perception of the world aligns. In this way, solid molar perception arises from and descends into objective molecular forces, is composed from and decomposes into genetic gaseous perception by way of transitional liquid formations.

The perception-image, accordingly, is constituted by the sign series: solid perception (first sign of full molar composition) ↔ liquid perception (secondary sign of composition) ↔ gaseous perception (sign of genetic forces).

Solid perception

Solid perception creates a 'central and privileged image' at the heart of the film (C1: 76). Such a sign is embodied by the main character, a glorious body extracted from the film-world to traverse the full coordinates of the screen. It is central and privileged in that all other filmic images circulate around this body, and all other images (sets, characters, objects) exist for this character and for this character alone. The privileged centre will be in every shot, centripetal and centrifugal forces operate upon this image from hub to periphery; this is the axis from which all other images spiral, to which all other images incurve. Such a cinematic body is a given, constructed through two reciprocal moments of the camera. Deleuze names these two moments (repurposing terminology from film theorist Jean Mitry) as a 'being-with', and they describe a continuous oscillation (C1: 72). The first moment is the point-of-view shot. The camera will stand in for the central character, see and hear what – and how – the character hears and sees. The point-of-view shot, however, is the anomalous being-with; while the second moment – that of looking at the character – its normalisation (hence the subjective image must not be reduced, as with Mitry, to the point-of-view shot). Here the camera may, may not, may more or less be aligned with the vision of another character – it could be the film itself looking, or the looking will remain indeterminate. Together these two poles of being-with interweave (through, for example, shot–reverse shot couplings) to create the perceiving and perceived subject. This is the purest subjective image, a subject at the centre of the world, a solid I.

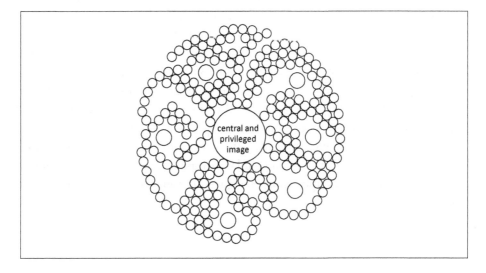

Figure II.01 Solid perception: all images revolve around a central and privileged image

Liquid perception

Liquid perception puts the camera into motion, a flowing movement of continuous reframing. Montage is used to link image to image in a sinuous trajectory: from environment to environment, from event to event, from character to character along a line of flight. It may be that the film captures an ensemble, each element of which occupies different spaces and different times, describing events which resonate between and flow into one another. Privileged centres will coalesce; but they are acentred, central only for a moment, becoming subordinate when another character, event or environment captures the coordinates of the screen. Perceptions and the perceived are legion. Tracking shots, crane shots and Steadicams negotiate all the dimensions of the mise-en-scène and join different spaces, creating a homogeneous timeline where everything is in motion, and everything flows.

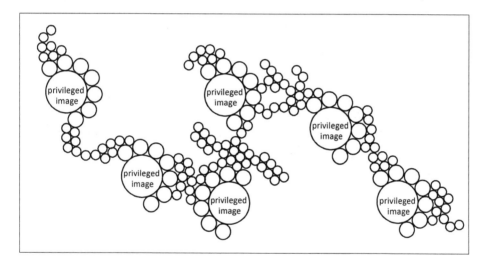

Figure II.02 Liquid perception: the flow from character/event to character/event

Gaseous perception

The perception-image can be purely objective in the sense of all images interacting with one another without hierarchy. This is gaseous perception, an acentred series of ahuman heterogeneous spaces necessarily escaping temporal linearity: 'everything is at the service of variation and interaction: slow or high speed shots, superimpositions, fragmentation, deceleration, microshooting' (C1: 60–1). Non-human perception. The molecular film: grainy filmstock, abstract experimentalism, manipulated images. Gaseous perception is thus the genetic element of the perception-image, where the creation of a subject remains only a possibility, any human image an image like any other (landscape, vegetation, the animal, an object). Yet such an organisation must not be thought of as pure chaos. This is the movement-image, and 'all these procedures act together and vary to form the cinema as machine assemblage of matter-images' (C1: 85). The film or sequence has an 'assemblage of enunciation' (C1: 85). Gaseous perception discovers, in its own way, a conception of the whole through its organisation of images into narration and the consequent emergence of narrative, its themes and preoccupations, ideas. Molecularity is a web of ahuman forces describing, marking-out a film-world.

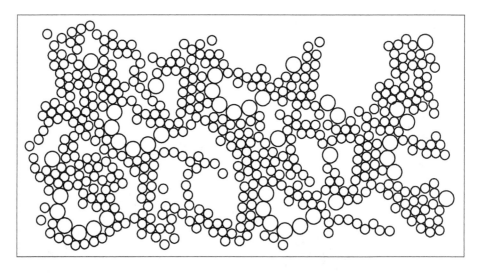

Figure II.03 Gaseous perception: all images resonate with one another as an acentred system

* * *

The perception-image, according to Deleuze, is 'like a degree zero', it has 'zeroness' (C2: 31). As such, 'the movement-image is already perception … and perception will not constitute a first type of image without being extended into the other types … perception of action, of affection, of relations [thought]', it 'is strictly identical to every image' of the sensory-motor system (C2: 31). It is almost as if, even though it can be described and diagramma-tised, the perception-image and its series of signs will not exist in their own right. It rather creates the conditions for each of the movement-images, their sign series: the genetic sign and the two signs of composition (genesis ↔ secondary composition ↔ full molar composition). In other words, the solid, liquid and gaseous give coordinates and trajectories to each of the movement-images proper. Then again, if the perception-image fails to transform the gaseous into liquid, the liquid into solid, and if it is unable to extend into the domains of affect, action and thought, we encounter the first possibility of the collapse and disintegration of the sensory-motor system. Such a failure and collapse, however, is not to be mourned. Rather, it is the condition for the emergence of the time-image, it is the condition for the affirmation of de-differenciated pure optical and pure sound situations (opsigns and sonsigns). For now, however, we are concerned with the movement-image, the trajectory of perception passing into and being designated by the necessary coordinates of the sensory-motor system: affect, action, thought.

2

Affection-images

Before a character can act, they perceive and are perceived by the world, and as such become affected by that world: the universe is encountered as a world of affects. Perception-images, in this way, pass immediately into affection-images. The two extreme limits of the affection-image correspond to – but extend and displace – the poles of subjective and objective perception: the human and ahuman. On the one hand, the affection-image is expressed by an embodied character, the face becoming the site of filmable external expressions capturing unfilmable internal intensive states. This is the icon, the expression of emotion and feelings. On the other hand, pure affects appear in the world through the any-space-whatever: a set, setting, or background – the mise-en-scène – which is encountered as an intensive force. With faces and landscapes the subjective-objective mapping of the perception-image is thus deterritorialised: 'film treats the face primarily as a landscape', write Deleuze and Guattari in *A Thousand Plateaus*, and 'what landscape has not evoked the face ...?' (TP: 191). The icon and the any-space-whatever pass into one another via the transformational sign of the dividual – where world and the individual are exchanged and form a mass: affects of the crowd, the pack, the multitude.

The affection-image, accordingly, is constituted by the sign series: icon (first sign of full molar composition) ↔ dividual (secondary sign of composition) ↔ any-space-whatever (sign of genetic forces).

Icon

The icon is a close-up of the face (the face a close-up of the body; the close-up the fundamental condition of the affection-image). On the one hand, the face reflects a unity with the world it apprehends through perception. This is the expression of an affective quality. On the other hand, the face can express an affective desire. This is the power of affect oriented towards an impulse or an action to come, as a precursor and as yet unactualised. The qualities and powers of the icon are expressions of two sides of the intensive in-between of the sensory-motor trajectory (perception ← affect → action); the affect a centre of indetermination making determinations (perception = action) in-determinate (perception ≈ action). Affect is thus internal intensity as choice (degrees of indeterminacy arising from the pure unconscious of matter) expressed through the face as qualities ↔ powers. This moment of intensity can be fleeting (a pause, a beat) or expand to encompass and inform the whole of the sequence, film or TV show. The quality of the face is expressed through immobility, a face caught in 'wonder' and 'fixed on an object' (C1: 88, 90). The power of the face is expressed through mobility, the face passing from one quality to another, where 'its parts successively traverse as far as paroxysm, each part taking on a kind of momentary independence' (C1: 90–1). Accordingly, while icons are faces and a face belongs to an individual, such moments of the affect are simultaneously de-individualising in that they are the creation of autonomous powers and qualities (qualities passing into powers; powers traversing qualities). Icons express, are the site of, pure affects.

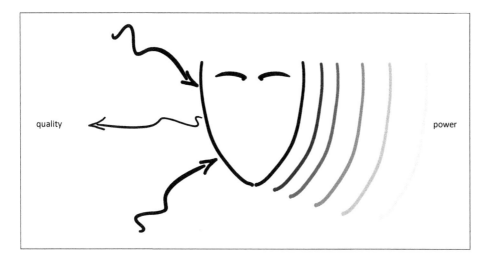

quality   power

Figure II.04 Icon: the face expressing unfilmable internal intensities

Dividual

Affects can be expressed by complex entities. If the icon concerns the expression of qualities and powers as reflection and desire upon the face of an individual body, the dividual develops the affect into composites allowing a simultaneous collapse of qualities-powers. In other words, the dividual captures the affect as a mutual moment between the de-individualisation of the individual and the individualisation of a mass (the singularity of a group, crowd, multitude). The dividual, as Deleuze describes it, goes 'beyond all binary structures and exceed[s] the duality of the collective and the individual', instead 'directly uniting an immense collective reflection with the particular emotions of each individual' (C1: 92). The camera traverses a series of faces, captures bodies in a gathering, people embodying a happening, caught up in or fleeing an event. In so doing the dividual is created: complex affects as an image of an assemblage. Reciprocally, a body may be made to capture the dividual, reflect and act as a collective enunciation, for every body captures and enacts a population.

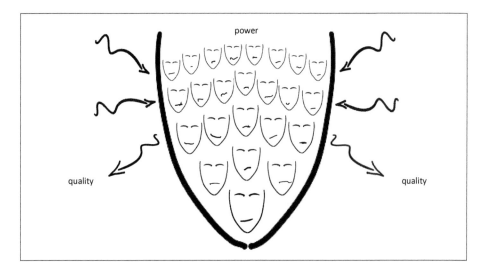

Figure II.05 Dividual: the conjunction of collective and individual affects

Any-space-whatever

Any-space-whatevers utilise an empty or disconnected mise-en-scène to sustain the coordinates of pure objective gaseous perception and rupture the determinate space-time of action. Pure backgrounds, perhaps: white, black, grey, shadowy environments, coloured intensities. Pure affective qualities-powers, complex but singular images of the intensive. In this way the any-space-whatever is the genetic sign of the affection-image, the genesis of affect; indeterminate, ahuman affects. Within the movement-image scenario, such a space is the environment for the dividual and icon: the mise-en-scène in which the dividual assembles and out of which the icon arises. Or that blurred background mostly obscured by the face or the group of bodies. When such expressions of qualities and powers coalesce, any-space-whatevers may designate the vague and anonymous form of a landscape, cityscape or interior; or a place of ruin, all-encompassing rain, the lens flare of sunshine, the shimmering of heat haze. Such amorphous spaces – in relation to the perceptions and actions to which they relate – will reflect or embody the emotions and feelings of the crowd or the character. When there is no reference to the human, or the human is overwhelmed, the any-space-whatever appears as an ahuman affect, and the camera captures the full expression of an indeterminate intensity: vital forces prior to the human. Or the world after the withdrawing of human centres.

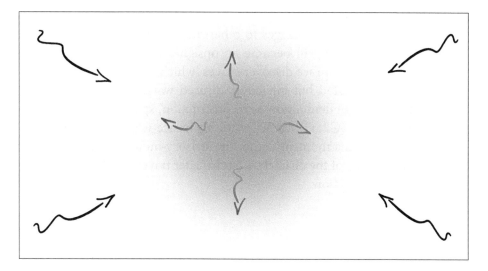

Figure II.06 Any-space-whatever: the expression of non-human affects

*   *   *

The affection-image – as the icon expressing intensity through a face – is the signal capturing of cinematic idealism. Perceptions are sense data for a subject, a subject not simply enslaved to the material world, but as a centre of indetermina- tion, a site of unconscious and conscious movements. '[T]he individual subject certainly is a trifle', writes Søren Kierkegaard, one of Deleuze's touchstones for this sign, 'but the world-historical is, after all, an addendum; ethically the individual subject is infinitely important' (Kierkegaard, 2009: 14). The icon is the central and privileged image encountered through the expressions of the face to allow the spectator to believe in the internal intensities that traverse the character's body. We laugh and cry with the icon, we lust after and fall in love with the icon, we loathe and boo the icon. We understand why the icon made these choices – the inevitable, even if they appear to be 'wrong', they were perhaps 'right' for the character. Such affective engagement will be extended and transformed in any number of ways. Mental-images will allow further access to the subjectivity of characters through images of thought (cognition in the relation-image, memories in the recollection-image, imagination in the dream-image). Within the avatar of the affection-image, however, icons resonate with the dividual, which captures affects as an assemblage: bodies, gangs, crowds. Such a sign accentuates the indeterminacy of any affective centre and initiates the decomposition of a human foreground into an ahuman background: the any-space-whatever. In its purest form this affect is encountered without the mediation of a character or characters in an indeterminate space-time. In certain conditions (set free from linkages to other movement-image compositions) the any-space-whatever will become an opsign-sonsign, another condition for the time-image. Here we discover spaces 'which we no longer know how to describe … deserted but inhabited, disused warehouses, waste ground, cities in the course of demolition or reconstruction', spaces for 'a new race of characters … seers' (C2: xi). Yet when the any-space-whatever belongs to the movement-image as a moment within the sensory-motor trajectory, it is the intensive grounding of the characters or character traversing its coordinates – from perception to action.

3

Impulse-images
(the nascent action-image)

The impulse-image passes from the domain of affect into the domain of action, describing a form of cinematics between the affection-image and the action-image as the nascent form of action. As Deleuze puts it, 'there is something which is like the "degenerate" affect or the "embryonic" action. It is no longer the affection-image, but is not yet the action-image' (C1: 123). Yet while an in-between, the impulse-image has its own sovereignty and coordinates. In this way, just as the affection-image correlates to cinematic 'idealism' and the action-image correlates to cinematic 'realism', the impulse-image describes a filmic 'naturalism' (C1: 12–14). This naturalism is not so much opposed to the realism of the action-image, but is more the first extension of affect into action (perception → affection → action). This is the impulse; and impulses – with characters – are immediate acts. It is as if the world perceived is too powerful, too affecting; and the correlating act is an instinct, an urge, a compulsion. The genetic sign of the impulse-image is thus a universe of primal forces – an originary world; and the sign of composition a symptom of that primal world permeating bodies. Between this primal realm and its animal embodiment, Deleuze identifies a transitional sign: the fetish. Fetishes condense the primal forces of the universe into special objects, objects which retain the impulse, preserve its energy, an energy which under the right conditions will discharge into the body and – once again – appear as the symptom, and disperse the symptom into the world. Naturalism, in this way, is but the initial inspiration of the impulse-image, an image which will be the foundation of fantasy and horror, even surrealism.

The impulse-image, accordingly, is constituted by the sign series: symptom (first sign of full molar composition) ↔ fetish (secondary sign of composition) ↔ originary world (sign of genetic forces).

Symptom

The fundamental trajectory of the sensory-motor schema describes how we look, feel and then act. Impulses appear almost as a short circuit or lightning strike between perception and action, affects that become 'primordial acts' (C1: 125). As Deleuze writes: 'fundamentally there is the impulse, which, by nature, is too strong for the character' (C1: 137). These acts of characters are thus symptoms of an indifferent universe, the pure impulse. Deleuze describes such characters as being 'like animals … not because they have their form or behaviour, but because their acts are prior to all differentiation between the human and the animal. These are human animals' (C1: 123–4). Impulses are energies, impelling urges; and they need not be instantaneous nor unconscious, although such may be their most general condition. The symptom is described as being 'relatively simple – like the impulse of hunger, impulses to nourishment, sexual impulses, or even the impulse for gold' (C1: 128). Yet when they appear in social situations, they manifest as complex signs of a 'perverse mode of behaviour … cannibalistic, sado-masochistic, necrophiliac, etc' (C1: 128). The symptom of the impulse-image is a character performance describing how the originary world captures up a body, its primal energies passing through that body back into the universe.

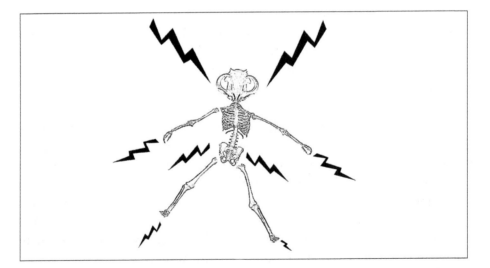

Figure II.07 Symptom: characters overwhelmed by primal forces

Fetish

The originary world can become embodied in objects, creating fetishes. These fetishes store up a primal force in some special medium (luck in a rabbit foot; fertility in a worn wooden charm; valour in some stone god in an alcove). 'The object of the impulse is always the "partial object"', writes Deleuze, 'a haunch of meat, a raw morsel, a scrap, a woman's briefs, a shoe' (C1: 128). These fetishes are fragments of the world which are encoded with primal, almost automatic meanings (but meanings which must be interpreted through the symptom). There are 'fetishes of Good and fetishes of Evil, holy fetishes and fetishes of crime and sexuality', and these poles of the fetish 'meet and interchange' (C1: 130). The fetish – just like the impulse it will engender – is beyond good and evil. Or rather – prior to good and evil, prior to the good and evil that will be derived through an extension into situational action and associated images of thought. Deleuze will name the good fetish the relic, and the evil fetish the vult: and the vult can become the relic, and the relic the vult in different moments and for different characters. All that can be said of the fetish is that it retains a primal force, a retention awaiting a grounding.

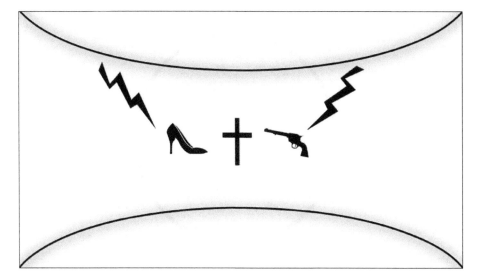

Figure II.08 Fetish: a special object charged with primal energies, awaiting a grounding

Originary world

'An originary world', writes Deleuze, 'is not an any-space-whatever (although it may resemble one), because it only appears in the depths of determined milieux; but neither is it a determined milieu, which only derives from an originary world' (C1: 123). In this way, the originary world can be thought of as an archetypal background, one which both retains a formlessness (with respect to the affection-image) while also being determinate (with respect to the action-image). This is the mise-en-scène of the impulse-image, the way in which the universe is permeated with primal forces. Deleuze gives examples such as 'a house' (those primal forces of the family) or 'desert' or 'forest' (primal forces of nature) (C1: 123). It is a time before/after history, or outside history, the primordial coordinates of the world yet to be historicised, cyclical time, the universal stratum of time underneath history and that which overpowers history. It is thus time as cruelty, time as a curse, where 'duration is less that which forms itself than that which undoes itself, and accelerates in undoing itself' (C1: 123). The originary world is the universe tending towards disintegration, collapse and entropy.

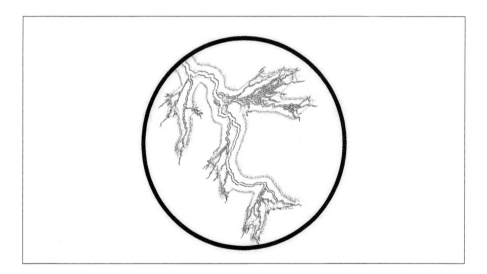

Figure II.09 Originary world: a universe of primal forces

*   *
*   *

The impulse-image has – for Deleuze – a grounding in the coordinates of cinematic naturalism, a nascent form of the action-image where primal forces permeate the mise-en-scène, charge objects and capture characters. Émile Zola, for Deleuze, is the essential naturalist in literature – his novels exemplifying a style which receives its full exposition in the manifesto of 'The Experimental Novel' (1880). Naturalism, for Zola, depicts life through the natural sciences, rejecting the coordinates of both subjective idealism and empirical realism. On the one hand, idealists 'admit … the power of mysterious forces outside of the determinism of phenomena' creating 'metaphysical chaos' (Zola, 1964: 31). On the other hand, empiricism is pure observation which 'invariably preceded the scientific condition of any branch of knowledge' (Zola, 1964: 40). Naturalism – in contrast – is the analysis of humanity as an organism which functions through 'heredity and surroundings' (Zola, 1964: 52). The naturalist thus accepts the human individual and society as machine-like entities enslaved by the material universe – but, these machines can be tested in the work of nature and employ of ideas. Naturalism, in this way, mediates a path between idealism and realism. Accordingly, Deleuze writes: 'what makes the impulse-image so difficult to reach and even define or identify, is that it is somehow "stuck" between the affection-image and the action-image' (C1: 134). Naturalistic directors are rare; it is not only 'difficult to reach the purity of the impulse-image', but 'particularly [difficult] to stay there, to find in it sufficient opening and creativity' (C1: 136). Accordingly, films may only achieve naturalistic moments, but be dominated by action or affect; the naturalistic sequence. Correspondingly, filmmakers who make action-images or affection-images may stray into naturalism for a single movie. Yet there is another aspect here, where the impulse-image remains but leaves behind the dogmas of the naturalism upon which it was founded. The impulse-image can extend into fantasy and horror – the primal forces of an originary world inspiring incredible and disturbing fetishes (magic vults and relics; cannibalistic trophies and objects); monstrous and shocking symptoms (undead zombies and vampires; violent psychopaths and sociopaths). Finally, Deleuze also sees such extensions of naturalism inspiring surrealism: where the forces of a primal universe are explicated in irrational worlds and acts properly called absurd, an effective collapse of the impulse-image and – accordingly – yet another gateway to opsigns and sonsigns, to the regime of the time-image. In all these ways, the impulse-image is a powerful and creative resource in cinema – gathering up intensities for immediate, perverse, or irrational acts.

4

Action-images
(small form, action → situation)

From gaseous perception, through the any-space-whatever and to the originary world, the universe coheres: but this mise-en-scène does not yet describe a determined situation. A determined situation has geo-historical coordinates – even if these coordinates are imaginary or semi-fictional (in the present, past or future). A determined situation is one which designates a social organisation and relates it to individual lives; is one with internal and external histories; is one mapped upon a landscape through architecture, infrastructure and lines of communication. This, for Deleuze, is realism. Accordingly, the first task of the action-image is to uncover and so determine the coordinates of the situation; and it will do so through the function of the character. This is action → situation. Here the character's actions reveal the situation of the film-world through an unfolding of events. And the way in which the situation is revealed engenders the sign series which composes the coordinates of the image. The first sign of composition describes an index of lack; the sequence responding to an ellipsis by fulfilling the quest to reveal the situation in which the characters find themselves. Every situation is amenable to a full explication, although it may retain complexities. Accordingly, the second sign of composition is an index of equivocity: two related and undecidable situational alternatives. Finally, the world may be discovered as a nexus of situations, a vector, where each determinate is aligned with a different character, class, gender, event, or condition, and so on, describing the line of a universe.

The action-image (action → situation), accordingly, is constituted by the sign series: index of lack (first sign of full molar composition) ↔ index of equivocity (secondary sign of composition) ↔ vector (sign of genetic forces).

Index of lack

The situation is not given in-and-for-itself; rather, it is revealed as a function of the actions of the character. This not-yet-given begins as an ellipsis which exists to be filled. In this way, the environment is that which must be explored, discovered and then described. Coordinates must be mapped and lines of constitution traced. This ellipsis is an index of lack through which 'an action … discloses a situation … The situation is thus deduced from the action, by immediate inference, or by relatively complex reasoning' (C1: 160). Either way, what is revealed – discovered, uncovered, by the character – is unequivocal. The world (the world for the character or characters) is unveiled – its social, gender, cultural, racial relations. Finally, in the aftermath of the revealed situation the actions of the character or characters will necessarily be reoriented and thus be transformed. The revealed situation changes everything by determining what was once indeterminate.

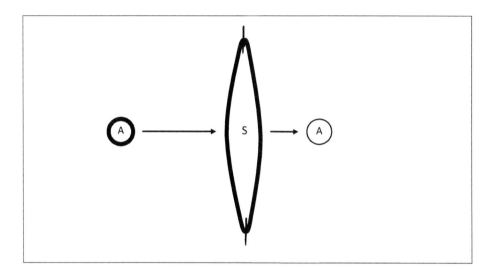

Figure II.10 Index of lack: the situation is an ellipsis which is unequivocally revealed

Index of equivocity

The index of equivocity retains a certain indeterminacy while establishing a determined situation. We are thus 'made to hesitate by a whole world of details … it is as if an action … concealed a slight difference, which was nevertheless sufficient to relate it to two quite distant situations, situations which are worlds apart' (C1: 161). Here the environment once again establishes an ellipsis; yet the quest to reveal the situation retains ambiguity (through the over-determination of data). An action can refer to a bifurcation; or different determining actions can refer to two sides of a situation; or two situations will be revealed as being in opposition to one another. In other words, the actions of the character or characters reveal the irreducible poles of the situation … it is this, it is that … And under certain conditions it is this and that at one and the same time for the same character. The impossible choice. The world as fundamentally riven. The actions of characters thus function as describing the index with two sides, and the situation is determined as equivocal.

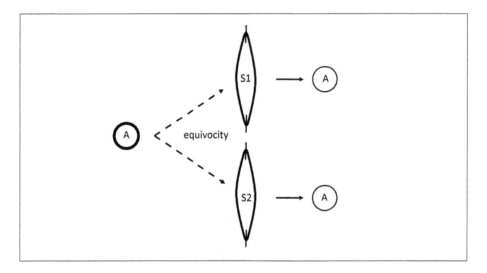

Figure II.11 Index of equivocity: the situation is revealed as ambiguous

Vector

In the third instance, the ellipse describes a vector. 'The successive situations, each of which is already equivocal in itself, will form in turn with one another … a broken line whose path is unpredictable, although necessary and rigorous' (C1: 168). This is the genetic sign of the action-image (action → situation), which depicts all the forces that describe characters, spaces and temporal links. In this way, the vector is a complex entity. There would be a multitude of characters and multiple corresponding emergent situations, a nexus or interweaving of indices of lack and equivocity. In other words, each event would be deducible; but between these events ambiguity reigns, leading inexorably towards the conclusion each is manifest. The revealed situations are thus a logical movement, and even though they may appear through a line of flight are *a priori* simultaneous. This is a very powerful image of the heterogeneity composing a homogeneous world where elements are subsumed within a universe that describes the lines of force traversing a complex whole.

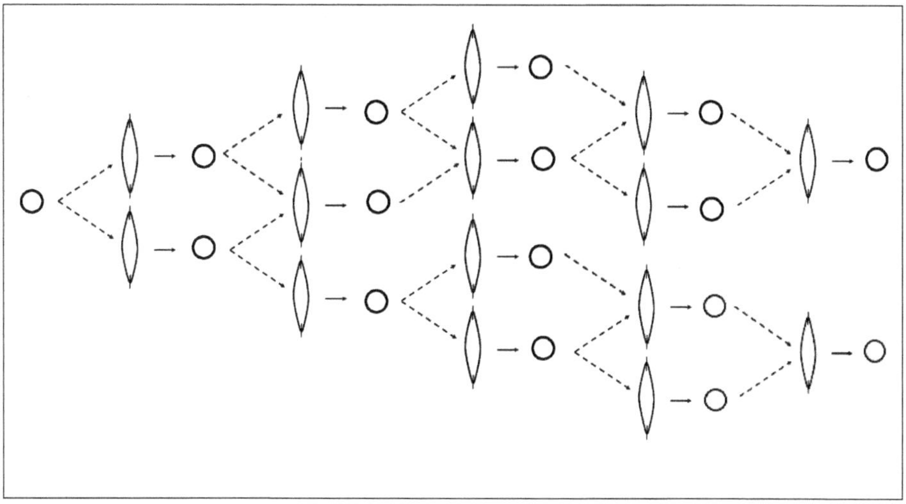

Figure II.12 Vector: multiple situations within the homogeneous universe

*   *   *

The action-image (action → situation) is concerned with deploying characters within events that function to describe – and so determine – the situation. Such determinations – which will always be relative – address an initial absence. The index of lack is a simple movement of revealing: perhaps a central and privileged character traverses a line that gradually uncovers and puts together, moment after moment, the pieces of the jigsaw. The index of equivocity, similarly, follows a certain trajectory, although the events will be ambiguous: an alternative – this and/or that. Even so, such a situation is no less determined. The ambiguity describes the poles of a situation: society or the individual; the murder is justifiable and gratuitous; he loves me, she loves me not. Finally, the genetic sign circumscribes a homogeneous situation via heterogeneous elements (character events, for example, through an ensemble cast). A city of tribes, a world of various societies, a universe of multiple evolutionary trajectories. This trajectory of the action-image (action → situation), from the genetic sign to the signs of composition, thus develops a cohesion of the situation from the multiple to the singular. Whatever the case, these signs, their trajectory and composite image, are a factor of realism – characters functioning as an index of the situation. Perception-images and affection-images are traversed in order that we arrive at action, and action dominates the sensory-motor system. In other words, perceptions and affects exist only for action. Yet this is only the first moment of the action-image: if action reveals situation (action → situation) then situation can determine actions (situation → action). In other words, once the situation becomes a given, a new relationship between action and situation arises: situations can spiral down to be embodied by characters and govern their behaviours. Deleuze names these two avatars of the action-image in this way: the small form (A→S or ASA`) and the large form (S→A or SAS`), where small and large refer either to the relative limitations of disclosure as a local function or to an englobing universal situation.

5

Action-images

(large form, situation → action)

If the situation is already a given, then the sensory-motor trajectory no longer has a requirement to reveal the world. Instead, action-images can explore how determined situations engender actions, conduct and behaviour. We move from action → situation to situation → action (from the small form action-image to the large form). Such reciprocity is actualised from the two aspects of the affection-image. The affect is a centre of indetermination making determinations (perception = action) indeterminate (perception ≈ action). The affection-image, in other words, is both a reflection of the world and oriented towards acting upon the world. Therefore, if the action-image (action → situation) was concerned with actualising *reflective* affects, the action-image (situation → action) is concerned with actualising *reactive* affects. With this second action-image the logic of the sensory-motor system as a linear trajectory (perception → affect → action) reaches its fullest expression, the most glorious manifestation of realism. Given a perceived situation that affects the character, the character must act; and such acts result from the situation already determined. This is not an impulse-image which explicates a world of overpowering primal forces, but an action-image, that which both actualises and interrogates a determined environment. Accordingly, with such an interrogation we encounter a possibility of changing the world (something beyond the possibility of the small form, which can only reveal conditions). No doubt a certain deadlock is apparent here: for a determined and determining situation will necessarily circumscribe action. The possibility of changing the world thus occurs within specific limits, or – as Deleuze puts it – through a bestowing of certain laws and modes. The five laws of the action-image (large form) describe the movement from situation to action. The first law is that of the situation in space and time, spatially as S and temporally as S1→S2. S appears as the 'encompasser' within the frame, while the passage from S1 to S2 occurs through alternate parallel montage at the level of 'the succession of shots' (C1: 151). With the second law 'the passage from S to S` takes place through the intermediary of action' (A): thus S→A (C1: 152). This passage is constituted through 'concurrent or convergent' montage, cutting from one section of action to another, back and forth, to bring the elements together, embodying the forces inherent in the situation (C1: 153). The third law is 'A for itself', the way in which the binomial dominates the mise-en-scène in the flow of images and pulls the sequence forward towards an end: the final duel for the new situation (C1: 153). The fourth law also concerns the binomial, but the 'binomial is a polynomial', the duel structures the film; it comprises nothing but duels (A^n) (C1: 153). Finally, the 'fifth law: there is necessarily a *big gap* between the encompasser and the hero, the milieu and the behaviour which modifies it, situation and action, which can only be bridged progressively, throughout the length of the film' (C1: 154). This is →. The gap – which is filled by the action – structures the film of the action-image (situation → action) and saturates the environment. The five laws ultimately concern the possibility of changing the world, and thus have three relative outcomes which Deleuze designates as the modes SAS, SAS` and SAS``. First, SAS is where the situation, maybe even despite efforts by the characters, remains unchanged. Second, SAS` is where the situation is confronted and resolved, improved. Finally, SAS`` is where the actions of the characters may result in a change, but this change constitutes a deterioration. These laws and their modes are that which limits and organises the coordinates of the sign series proper to the action-image (large form). The milieu of a fully determined situation (correlating to that which is revealed through an index of lack in the small form) will allow only derivative actions; while a world that sustains two sides (correlating with the ambiguity of the small forms' index of equivocity) will foreground the binomial duel between opposing forces. Finally, a complex world (correlating to the multiplicity of the vector with action → situation) will cause characters to become saturated and imprinted with, become the very impression of, the heterogeneous forces of the environment. The trajectory of the action-image (situation → action) thus describes the territorialising of complex worlds and heterogeneous bodies in a fully determined milieu from which all actions will derive.

The action-image (situation → action), accordingly, is constituted by the sign series: milieu (first sign of full molar composition) ↔ binomial (secondary sign of composition) ↔ imprint (sign of genetic forces).

Milieu

The first sign of composition of the action-image (situation → action) is the milieu. Here there are given 'determinate, geographical, historical and social space-times' which form the 'Ambience or the Encompasser' (C1: 141). In essence, a film that explores a milieu would trace the coordinates of an environment; it would place that environment into specific contexts: national, quasi-national, sub-national, international and transnational history, specific locations of longitude and latitude, cultural coordinates. The coordinates may be semi-fictional, but for all that, they will be no less determined. Together these determinates would form a nexus: the milieu. Presented through a predominance of establishing shots and extreme wide shots, the milieu describes a fully determined situation not simply as a spatial aspect (S) but also through the temporal dimension – a fully realised history (no matter how much is given), from situation to new situation (S1→S2). These spatio-temporal coordinates will cohere as action, will be played out through the actions of the characters as a *fait accompli*, an explication, an exposition (be the event 'real' or 'fictitious', whatever this may mean in the context of a movie). In short, such actions serve to exemplify the situation and any changes to that situation. The characters are one with the milieu and the milieu at one with the characters. The first sign of the action-image (large form) thus tends towards foregrounding the first and second laws (S1→S2 and S→A), the situation in space and time described through the intermediary of action; and the first mode (SAS), where everything remains as is.

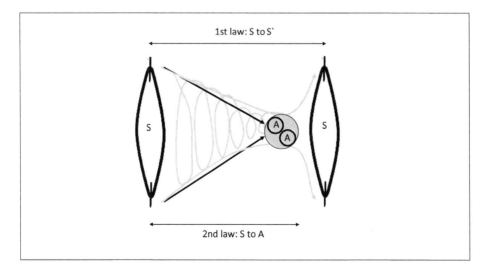

Figure II.13 Milieu: the situation explicated through character actions

Binomial

With the binomial – the secondary sign of composition – a sequence proceeds by a conflict through two dominant lines of force; lines of force inherent in the milieu and embodied in the characters who relate to one another through the duel. The binomial thus tends towards pure action. These duels may be violent or romantic, and it matters not which side of the binary emerges triumphant, for there is always victory and defeat. This sign of the large form action-image has a well-defined milieu, yet this is not the essential aspect. Once given, the situation is merely the staging ground for the polynomial actions dovetailing in binomial lines of force. The film is pure action from beginning to end. The second sign of the action-image (large form) thus tends towards foregrounding the third and fourth laws (A and A^n), the fundamental and terminal duel, and the retroactive proliferation of duels; and the second mode (SAS`), where the world is transformed for the better (for at least one, if not both, of the protagonists).

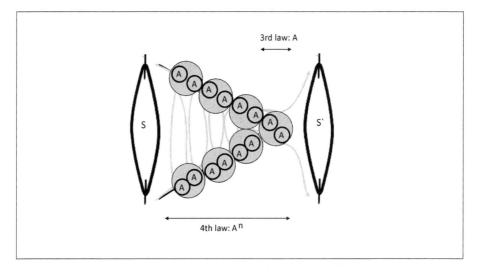

Figure II.14 Binomial: a whole world of duels

Imprint

'[T]he cinema of behaviour', writes Deleuze, 'is not content with a simple sensory-motor formula'; with the imprint there is a 'much more complex behaviourism which essentially took into account internal factors' (C1: 158). This is the sign describing the genetic forces of the action-image (situation → action). If we begin with a complex situation (heterogeneous forces composing a nonetheless homogeneous milieu), then the character is confronted with a multifaceted scenario. Here the large form 'is divided into successive and continuous local missions (s1, a1, s2, a2, s3 …)' (C1: 157). In other words, a multiplicity of duels fragment the trajectory of the film, creating a series of determinate space-times. The action – or rather, the duel, the binomial as polynomial – will thus tend towards being internalised as a complex situation that impacts the very being of a character. The full coordinates of the situation will, accordingly, necessarily require time to determine the appropriate reaction. And when the action is eventually enacted, it will be defined through unbound violence: forces accumulate over the length of the sequence to be released in one final moment (and is thus very different from the immediacy of the symptom in the impulse-image). As Deleuze continues, 'in its most general definition, the … [imprint] is the inner, but visible, link between the permeating situation and the explosive action' (C1: 159). The visibility of the imprint explicates the milieu–behaviour nexus and is the co-joining of emotions with an object, creating an emotional object which links character to situation. The object is a referent for the complex nature of the universe and the complex internal struggle the character must undergo in order to right their world. The keepsake of a murdered child, a monster terrorising a populace, the perfume permeating the pillow upon which the lover once placed their head. The third sign of the action-image (large form) thus tends towards foregrounding the fifth and final law (→), the gap; and the third mode (SAS``), where the world is transformed for the worst, at least for the character or characters subject to its imprint.

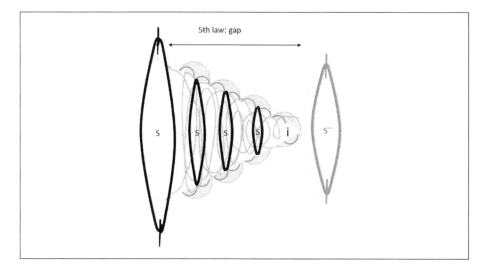

Figure II.15 Imprint: an indelible impression of the world upon a character

*
* *

Within the domain of action, it is not that we leave perception-images and affection-images behind (nor, indeed, that we have yet to arrive – as we will see – at an image of thought); rather, it is that perception, affect and thought are oriented towards action, and thus dominated by action. Here, the characters perceive, feel and think so they can act. In the first instance – this concerns the avatar of the impulse-image (as nascent form of action). Primal forces of an originary world (directly, or via an intermediary of the fetish) emerge as symptoms in a character; the body at the centre is overwhelmed – allows itself to be overwhelmed – by instincts, species-dispositions and social-energies. In the second instance – this concerns the avatar of the action-image. Action-images explore situations (milieux, environments, geo-historical moments) and explicate actions (behaviour, social conduct, being in the world). Situations are thus developments of gaseous perception through any-space-whatevers and originary worlds; and actions are extensions of solid and liquid perception through icons and the dividual, the fetish and the symptom. In the first place, the small form action-image extends through perception-images, affection-images and impulse-images to explore how actions reveal the situation; in the second place, the large form action-image extends through the small form, beginning with the determined situation and – through the five laws – describing how the character must and will act. In this way, with the large form action-image the logic of the sensory-motor system as a linear trajectory (perception $\rightarrow$ affect $\rightarrow$ action) reaches its fullest expression. This is the fundamental essence of cinematic realism. The large form action-image is the conclusion of matter-images, and there is nowhere beyond this final moment of the matter-image. All perceptions and affects tend to be dominated by action, and all action-images are dominated by its large form, and the large form by the laws of composition. The full molar sign of composition is thus the absolute terminus of the movement-image. It is here that the movement-image is ultimately fulfilled.

Yet, while the large form action-image concludes the matter-image and is the fulfilment of the movement-image, it is not – in any way – the final element of the movement-image cineosis. For movement-images concern not only matter-images, but also mental-images as the movement-image of thought. And the first moment of such an image of thought can be approached through the parallel, bi-directional and asynchronous trajectories of the action-image avatar: action $\rightarrow$ situation and situation $\rightarrow$ action (the forms of the small and the large; the ASA and SAS). The small form of the action-image describes how the actions of characters reveal the situation through indices of lack, indices of equivocity, and vectors. Such a trajectory (from the sign of full composition through the sign of transition to the genetic sign) describes the coordinates of the homogeneous situation mapped across the poles of the simple and the complex (singularity, duality and the multiple). The large form of the action-image describes how actions are derived from situations: the first sign of composition is the established milieu where actions explicate a given situation; the second sign of composition concerns the binomial where action in-itself predominates; the genetic sign – finally – internalising the complex situation within the character. With action $\rightarrow$ situation the character is a function determining the situation; with situation $\rightarrow$ action the milieu determines the behaviour of characters. From the small form to the large, and from the large to the small, we encounter realism as parallel, but bi-directional and asynchronous, trajectories.

Such bi-directional asynchronous parallelism exposes an implicit comparison and – it could be claimed – invites an invisible critique between the two forms of the action-image, each by the other. On the one hand, the small form allows a situation to be explored and explicated, have its coordinates revealed. On the other hand, the large form allows the possibility of characters to change the situation. To put this another way, the small form cannot enact change; and the large form cannot disclose and reveal. Each has its own internal implicit limit. The cinema of realism, however, will discover ways to make explicit such comparisons and thus encourage critique of one form through the other – the small form and the large form can interrogate and reflect upon one another, and in so doing each will be transformed. Action-images demand reflection; and reflection-images – nascent mental-images – are enacted through a transformation of forms.

The action-image and its extension into reflection-images can be explored through the way in which cinematic realism correlates with classical explications of historical forces. Invoking Friedrich Nietzsche's analysis in 'On the Uses and Disadvantages of History for Life' in *Untimely Mediations* (1873–6), Deleuze describes the action-image as 'bring[ing] together the most serious aspects of history as seen by the nineteenth century' (C1: 149). Nietzsche describes three aspects to classical narratives of history: the monumental, the antiquarian and the critical (Nietzsche, 2006: 67). Monumental history pertains 'to him as a being who acts and strives'; to the antiquarian 'as a being who preserves and reveres'; and to the critical as 'bringing ... [the past] before a tribunal, scrupulously examining it' (Nietzsche, 2006: 76). Depending upon need, humans turn to 'a certain kind of knowledge of the past, now in the form of monumental, now of antiquarian, now of critical history' (Nietzsche, 2006: 77). These three types of universal history are embodied by the action-image. The large form action-image strives through the possibility of changing the situation; and the small form action-image preserves through disclosing the situation. Reflection-images, however, are where the two forms of the action-image dovetail in critique. Reflection-images allow one form to create an image of thought through the other.

Reflection-images thus immediately refer to images of thought. It is the mental-image which designates thought in the sensory-motor system, that which redeploys perception-images, affection-images and action-images through images of understanding, memory and imagination. However, just as the domain of action captures up and dominates the domains of perception and affect, so too will it capture up and dominate the domain of thought. The reflection-image is an image of thought which is immediately explicated within the aegis of the action-image. Here, action-images are caught up in figures, where a figure is a sign 'which instead of referring to its object, reflects another; or which reflects its own object, but by inverting it; or which directly reflects its object' (C1: 218). First, an immediate reflection of one action-image into the other: the attraction-image; second, one action-image causing the other to reverse: the inversion-image; third, the extension of each action-image into a critical reflection through itself: the discourse-image. With these reflection-images – which inscribe thought into the sensory-motor system – we discover a trajectory that (to a lesser or greater extent) interrogates both of the action-images and will extend to its very crisis, the dissociation of situations and character behaviours, which causes the domains of the movement-image to delink, leading to the crisis of action-images and the creation of pure optical and sound situations, the condition for the time-image. However – and more immediately – these reflection-images are a nascent expression of the movement-image image of thought; figures of attraction, inversion and discourse are embryonic mental-images.

6

Attraction-images
(first reflection-image; sixth mental-image)

The first reflection-image, the first transformation of the action-image, is the figure of attraction, the attraction-image. Action-images concern the link between world and bodies where action reveals situation (action-image small form, action → situation) or situation determines action (action-image large form, situation → action). These two forms constitute a bi-directional reciprocity, a complementarity where both already reflect one another, but only virtually via the trajectory proper to each. The attraction-image will bring these two forms into immediate contact, actualising the reflection and as a consequence transforming the small and the large alike. One such contact occurs through the signs of composition of the attraction-image, where one form of the action-image is 'injected' into the other (C1: 182). Deleuze is here concerned with cinematic figures equivalent to tropes. A trope is a non-literal application of a word or a phrase that transforms the text in which it operates. Similarly, Deleuze writes: 'cinematographic images have figures proper to them' (C1: 183). There are two types, or degrees, of tropes. Perfect tropes appear as a distinct moment: as metaphor, metonymy and synecdoche. Imperfect tropes are where a figure is sustained over time: as allegory, mythology, allusion and irony. Perfect and imperfect tropes designate the two signs of composition of the attraction-image, which Deleuze names the plastic figure (perfect, first sign of composition) and the theatrical figure (imperfect, second sign of composition) (C1: 182). Plastic figures and theatrical figures – in the cinema – refer to the way in which the small form action-image is transformed by the large; and, the way in which the large transforms the small. When a film of the action-image small form (action → situation) has the large form within it, we encounter the perfect trope, a plastic figure. When a film of the action-image large form (situation → action) has the small form within it, we encounter the imperfect trope, a theatrical figure. In both cases, writes Deleuze, 'there is no longer a direct relation between a situation and an action, an action and a situation: between the two images, or between the two elements of the image, a third intervenes to ensure the conversion of the forms' (C1: 182). This third is a mental-image: the figure. Deleuze does not designate or describe a genetic form. However, we could say (according to the logic of reflection, and the example of the inversion-image) that the genetic sign of the attraction-image appears in a filmic sequence when it is unclear if a small form incorporates the large, or a large encompasses the small, if we are witnessing a theatrical representation or a plastic figure. We might call this *mise en abyme* (italicised to indicate that this naming does not originate in the *Cinema* books): an image within an image within an image, and so on; a recurrence – theatrical and plastic figures, small form and large form, each embedded within one another.

The attraction-image (first reflection-image; sixth nascent mental-image), accordingly, is constituted by the sign series: plastic figure (first sign of full molar composition) ↔ theatrical figure (secondary sign of composition) ↔ *mise en abyme* (sign of genetic forces).

Plastic figure

The first sign of composition of the attraction-image describes the way in which a film of the small form action-image is transformed and determined by the large form. Deleuze calls this a 'plastic representation', where 'the action does not immediately disclose the situation which it envelops, but is itself developed in grandiose situations which encompass the implied situation' (eS(S)) (C1: 182). Here the small form is no longer designated by action →

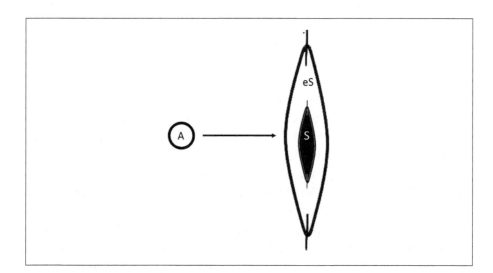

Figure II.16 Plastic figure: small form transformed by the large form, an implied situation

situation, but action → encompassing situation (as an index of the implied situation). This plastic figure is the cinematic equivalent of a metaphor, metonymy or synecdoche. In other words, the situation revealed on-screen is an encompasser of the true situation; the revealed situation a plastic figure which points to the real situation, which remains an ellipsis. We might, in this way, think of an event or image in the film which is used to stand in for the real situation: a play or a film within the film, perhaps; or an object which has a meaning beyond itself; or even a repeating figure which is substituted for another in order to engender a reflective response in the audience.

Theatrical figure

The second sign of composition of the attraction-image describes the way in which a film of the large form action-image is transformed by the small form. This is the theatrical figure. Deleuze writes: 'in the theatrical representation, the real situation does not immediately give rise to an action which corresponds to it, but is expressed in a fictitious action which will merely prefigure ... a real action to come' (C1: 182). In short, the large form is transformed from situation → action to situation → index of action (iA), as a precursor, descriptor and figure of the real action to follow. Theatrical representation thus has a linearity and functions through (at least one) repetition, although the trick, or game, here will be to ever defer the real action. It is, for Deleuze, 'the sequences of images which has a figural role' (C1: 183). This is the cinematic equivalent of an allegory, a mythology, the ironic narration, the allusive tale that provides a sinuous thread throughout the story.

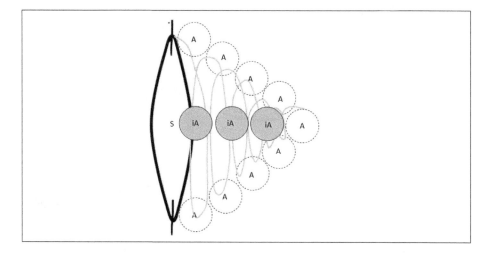

Figure II.17 Theatrical figure: a sequence of images as precursor of the real action

Mise en abyme

Deleuze does not name the genetic sign of the attraction-image, nor does he describe how it might operate. However, the logic of this reflection-image would seem to indicate an encounter with a sign which could compose both the plastic and the theatrical figures, that is to say, unfold into the small form action-image transformed by the large and the large form transformed by the small. Such a description appears to designate the figure known as *mise en abyme*: the recurrence of an image within an image within an image. (A consideration of the case of the inversion-image is also helpful here. Deleuze will derive the genetic sign of this reflection-image through just such a collapse and folding of the doubled nature of the action-image through the two compositional signs of that figure.) In this way, the genetic sign of the attraction-image could be said to collapse the large form of the action-image into the small form, or fold the small form into the large, so that we no longer can tell with which form we began, nor with which form we end. To put this another way, plastic figures become the index of theatrical sequences at the same time as a theatrical sequence is encompassed by a plastic figure. The film enacts a recurrence of figures of attraction, of tropes perfect and imperfect. It is as if we enter and become lost in a hall of mirrors, with indices of actions reflecting actions and encompassing situations reflecting situations, the connections between which remain virtual, reflective and transformational.

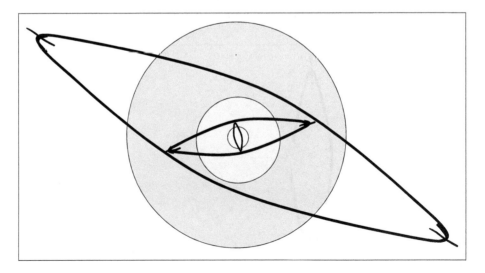

Figure II.18 *Mise en abyme*: a recurrence of plastic and theatrical figures

*   *
*   *

The attraction-image introduces the figure into the two forms of the action-image, instigating a reflection of one form through the other, and in such a reflection, one image transforms the other. Whether it is the small form transformed by the large as a plastic figure, or the large transformed by the small through a theatrical figure, or – as in the genetic sign – the recurrence of such transformations, the attraction-image operates by creating mental-images that reflect the action-image. Accordingly, we discover one way in which the small form can interrogate the large form, and the large form can interrogate the small. This concerns the limits of the avatars of the action-image (situation → action; action → situation). With respect to the small form (action → situation), the characters function to reveal a situation which is initially not given; that which is revealed, therefore, is limited to the possible actions available to the character within their local environment. With respect to the large form (situation → action), the situation is a determined milieu which spirals down to be embodied by the characters, and to which the characters react; in this way, the actions of the characters are limited to the givens. Through the introduction of the attraction-image (mental-images created by plastic and theatrical figures, the figure of *mise en abyme*) we discover ways in which such limits can be surpassed. The givens of a determined situation and possible available actions can be opened up, disturbed and even effaced. In short, filmic metaphors, metonymies, allegories and allusions allow the action-image to explore more complex relations between situations and actions, actions and situations. These attraction-images, however, are only the first moment of three such serial transformations that describe an ongoing and increasingly complex trajectory of interaction, reversal and extension. If the attraction-image operates through the interaction of one form of the action-image with the other as an image of thought, inversion-images and discourse-images will transform the two avatars of action through very different types of reflection.

7

Inversion-images
(second reflection-image; fifth mental-image)

The inversion-image is the second avatar of reflection. As Deleuze puts it, here we have 'literal figures – operating for example through reversal' (C1: 183). Or rather, a sign 'reflects its own object, but by inverting it (*inverted image*)' (C1: 218; my italics). With the inversion-image, then, the large form action-image and small form action-image have figures that transform each themselves through the influence of one form on the other, as if exerting a centripetal or centrifugal force. In other words, the avatars of the action-image are transformed by the large form becoming small, and the small form becoming large (thus discovering the small in the large, or the large in the small). We might designate these transformations as sAs and aSa. Deleuze names the first sign of composition (corresponding to sAs) as the 'sublime', where 'the action ... is not required by the situation' (C1: 184). The second sign of composition (corresponding to aSa) is the 'enfeebled', or futile action that reveals grandiose 'Powers of the Earth' (C1: 186). Deleuze does not give a name to – but does (enigmatically) describe – a genetic form; it is where the sAs and aSa become equivalent, 'the same thing' (C1: 186). Thus sAs ↔ aSa: we are no longer sure if the actions are sublime or futile, if the situation is insignificant or unfathomable. We might call this a special case of the *quotidian*: the everyday situation with everyday actions – monuments of the triumphs and disappointments of everyday life. These figures of the sublime, the feeble and the *quotidian* become mental-images by transforming the action-image through a reflection upon the limits of the avatar as avatar (genetic sign) and with respect to each of the forms (compositional signs). This critique concerns undermining the causal nature of forms: the determination of the situation and the function of the character, and the possibilities of changing or exposing the coordinates of the world.

The inversion-image (second reflection-image; fifth nascent mental-image), accordingly, is constituted by the sign series: figure of the sublime (first sign of full molar composition) ↔ figure of enfeeblement (secondary sign of composition) ↔ *figure of the quotidian* (sign of genetic forces).

Sublime figure

The first sign of composition of the inversion-image is the figure of the 'sublime' (C1: 184). The large form action-image, SAS, becomes sAs, where 'the action, in effect … is a crazy enterprise, born in the head of a visionary' (C1: 184). There exists a situation which engenders lines of actions (maybe in the form of exposition, the duel or the internal imprint – or some amalgam of the three) which far outdoes the determination. The hero is a saint, a martyr, an errant genius, and the actions performed have a 'hallucinatory' or 'hypnotic' dimension (C1: 184). This is a film of the seemingly insane, unnecessary, or belligerent action, a film in which the behaviours of the character overwhelm the givens of the situation, a film of over-reaction. The effect of the figure of the sublime (sAs) is that the actions of characters transform the determined situation into a futile encompasser. Thus the sign should perhaps be designated as figure of the sublime action emerging from a weak situation. It is as if the large form action-image has had its perspective shifted and transformed in the process of explication, through the effect of the small form as foregrounding the function of the unfathomable acts of a character.

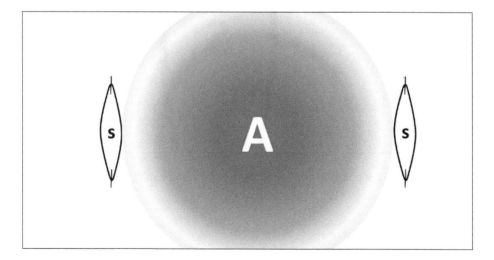

Figure II.19 Figure of the sublime: actions surpass the determinates of an enfeebled situation

Enfeebled figure

The second sign of composition of the inversion-image describes the 'enfeeblement of the small form' (C1: 185). Here the action-image (action → situation) is transformed from ASA to aSa. Deleuze writes that 'weaklings and idiots' are the purveyors of actions, the character reduced to a 'tiny point fleeing towards the horizon' (C1: 185). The character is seemingly the lowest of animals, someone without influence, with no merit – their function within the film serving to expose the futility of their actions, and, at one and the same time, the immensity of the universe, its overwhelming power, its total indifference. In this way, these 'weaklings walking in the small form have such tactile relationships with the world that they inflate and inspire the image itself' (C1: 186). In other words, it is as if the inconsequential actions of insignificant characters serve to reveal a grandiose situation. The effect of the figure of enfeeblement is that futile actions describe the sublime. It is as if the small form action-image has been reversed in the process of explication through the effect of the large form, revealing the reality of an infinite universe within the most infinitesimal of acts.

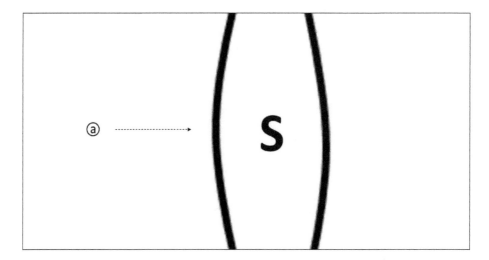

Figure II.20 Figure of enfeeblement: weak characters reveal the sublime nature of the world

Quotidian

While Deleuze does not name the genetic sign of the inversion-image, there is the intimation of a description, in that – under certain conditions – the figure of the sublime and the figure of enfeeblement can become 'the same thing'

(C1: 186). Such a description indicates a genetic figure where the two signs of composition circulate each within the other. Here sAs = aSa; we no longer have the grandiosity of the savant, no longer the futile actions of the weakling. The situation is at once inconsequential and unfathomable. In other words, this is the everyday, *the figure of the quotidian*, with its heroic trivialities and its foolish vitalities. Yet it is in just this way that we encounter a very powerful figure of action. For the everyday both expands to encompass everything and appears in its banality: the pettiness of our function is the heroism of life; and valour is revealed as the consequence of an already determined servility, duty, responsibility. The universe – in its sublime vastness – is indifferent to our actions, but is also the very ground in which we must – and can only – act, live.

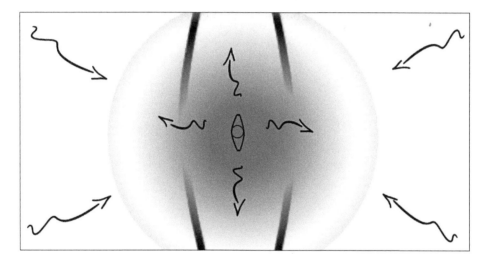

Figure II.2I *Quotidian*: everyday situations, everyday actions – sublime ↔ futile

* * *

The inversion-image is the figure of reversal between the two forms of the action-image, a reflection of the effect of one on the other, accentuating each by expanding the large form and enfeebling the small form, or bringing both together as a simultaneous cancellation and ascension. These are the figures of the sublime, the futile and the *quotidian*. And each figure is a type of mental-image, three reflections upon the avatar, images and signs of the action-image. This is the inversion-image. Indeed, it is as if each of the figures of composition are named through its inversions, for the sublime gives us the futile situation, and the enfeebled gives us the sublime situation. And between the two – the *quotidian* both enlarges and shrivels to reveal and restore their interchangeability: sublime ↔ futile. Accordingly, we discover a second way in which the small form can interrogate the large form, and the large interrogate the small. Once again, this is a critique of the limits of action-image, a comparison of features and exploration of how one may pass silently into the other: over-reaction, powerlessness, and the two sides of the ordinary. The inversion-image is thus a very different type of cinematic figure from the attraction-image: if figures of attraction operated immediately through filmic metaphor and allusion, synecdoche and irony; figures of inversion are reversals through an ongoing and pervasive indirect reflection, a suffusion. Such are the first two moments of the three transformations of the action-image. The third, and final, reflection-image will be the figure of discourse, where we encounter the extreme limit of all possible action-images; a beyond of the figures of attraction and inversion.

8

Discourse-images
(third reflection-image; fourth mental-image)

The discourse-image, the 'discursive' figure, is the third and final transformation of action-image forms, the third and final avatar of the reflection-image (C1: 192; C2: 33). Here the action-image is fully captured by the mental-image, and the forms of the small and the large become 'figures of thought' (C1: 190). In the first instance, the discourse-image is that which 'subjects the large form to a broadening which operates as a transformation on the spot' (C1: 192). For Deleuze, this is the extreme limit of the large form action-image, where the situation appears as a problem which will be explored throughout the film, the resolution that of a considered response. In the second instance, the discourse-image is that which 'subjects the small form to a lengthening, a drawing-out which transforms it in itself' (C1: 192). This is the extreme limit of the small form action-image, no longer describing a passage from action to situation as that which discovers the coordinates of a determination, but rather a revealing of the conditions of a problem. Thus the two sides of the problem; the problem being a question (?) and the figure of thought that inspires the discourse-image; this figure explicated in two signs of composition as the extreme limits of the large and the small forms of the action-image (C1: 195). These limits are transformative, not in reference to an immediate confrontation of one form with the other (attraction-images), nor in reference to the reciprocal influence that causes a reversal (inversion-image), but rather through the fullest possible domination of the domain of thought and the mental-image. Each action-image reflects directly upon itself, interrogates and becomes an image of thought for itself, in so doing enacting a reflection. Once again, Deleuze merely hints at a genetic sign, but it is reasonable to assume (just as with the other avatars of the reflection-image) that this is where the two signs of composition collapse in upon one another, where the extreme limit of the large form action-image and the extreme limit of the small form action-image extend to convergence. In other words, *the extreme limit of action-images in general*, of the avatar of action, where we cannot tell if the originary form is the small or the large – and the film begins, is permeated by and ends with problems.

The discourse-image (third reflection-image; fourth nascent mental-image), accordingly, is constituted by the sign series: extreme limit of the large form action-image (first sign of full molar composition) ↔ extreme limit of the small form action-image (secondary sign of composition) ↔ *extreme limit of all action-images* (sign of genetic forces).

Extreme limit of the large form action-image

The first sign of composition of the discourse-image is the extreme limit of the large form action-image. The large form action-image, here, thus discovers its own limit through an immediate reflection upon its constitutive laws, modes and signs. Situations are given, and this milieu encompasses the characters, their behaviours and actions; however, the character becomes caught up in exploring a problem that is discovered to be inherent to the situation. The situation (the milieu) articulates a question. It is only once this question has been extracted from the world, and all its coordinates investigated, that the character will be equal to an act. Deleuze writes: 'instead of absorbing a situation in order to produce a response which is merely an explosive action, it is necessary to absorb a question in order to produce an action which would truly be a considered response' (C1: 190). Accordingly, the formula is no longer situation → action, but situation (question) ↔ action. The narration of the film will describe a trajectory in which the character discovers and then attempts to respond to the

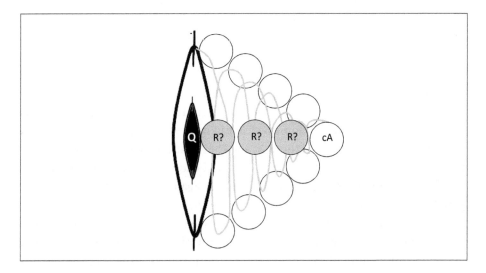

Figure II.22 Limit of the large form action-image: action explores a hidden problem

'*givens of a question* which is hidden in the situation' (C1: 189). In this way, the large form action-image is transformed via a mental-image generated through a sustained reflection upon its own coordinates.

Extreme limit of the small form action-image

The second sign of the discourse-image will be the extreme limit of the small form action-image. Here, the small form is transformed via a mental-image generated through a reflection upon its own essential coordinates where action reveals situation. And action – it will be discovered – can no longer disclose the situation. That which is revealed will be the conditions of a problem. The narration of the film operates by creating heterogeneous vectors which will eventual cohere – as Deleuze puts it – in a 'special homogeneity' (C1: 194). This 'special homogeneity' is 'one which connects up the heterogeneous elements, while keeping them heterogeneous' (C1: 194). In other words, the characters discover the pieces, but it is as if all the pieces belong to different puzzles; perhaps the pieces fit together, yet the final picture to emerge remains a cipher. The extreme limit of the small form thus develops a narration where the coordinates of a question will ultimately and necessarily be left unanswered. Why? Because it is unanswerable? Because there is no answer? Because we don't wish to face the answer? Whatever the case – the power of this limit is the discovery of the sustained ellipsis. It is this ellipsis which allows 'a reality to surge forth which is no longer anything but disorientated, disconnected' (C1: 195). In this way, the small form action-image reaches and affirms its own internal limit.

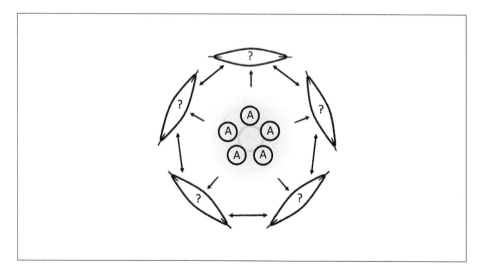

Figure II.23 Limit of the small form action-image: the situation revealed as a problem

Extreme limit of the action-image

Deleuze writes: 'the two limits are themselves re-united in the notion of the any-space-whatever' (C1: 187). The any-space-whatever is the genetic sign proper to the affection-image, where pure affects appear in the world through a set, setting, or background which is encountered as an intensive force. Non-determinate, ahuman forces, forces prior to or coming after the human. It would thus seem – with the genetic sign of the figure of discourse – that the action-image incurves upon itself and discovers its power through a return to the affection-image from which it was originally derived. Yet this return necessarily occurs within the domain of thought, as a mental-image within the avatar of reflection and in relation to the action-image as that which it will unground. In short, we encounter here – in this reuniting of the limits of the two forms – the sign of the *extreme limit of all action-images* (large, small, their attractions, their inversions and their own limits). Such a naming must be imposed upon this sign, for Deleuze does not specify the designation; yet the function of this final figure is clear – as with the two reflection-images describing attraction and inversion before it, the compositional signs come together and find their common origin. The extreme limit of the large form action-image and the extreme limit of the small-form action-image describe problems: the former through a question embedded in the *a priori* situation; the latter through the function of action that will reveal the world *a posteriori* as a cipher. The *extreme limit of action-images in general* is thus the genesis of the problem as a figure of thought. A whole world of problems, puzzles, questions and ciphers. The universe as the expression of intensive indeterminate forces.

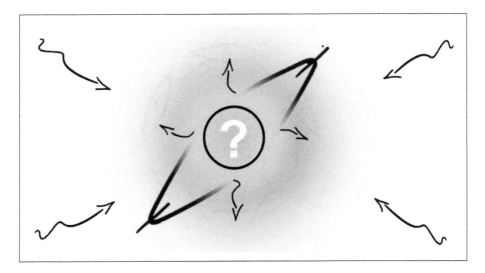

Figure II.24 *Extreme limit of the action-image*: a whole world of problems

* * *

The reflection-image itself is a cipher at the periphery of *Cinema 1*, the element that receives the least attention from Deleuze. Accordingly, the explication of the last three chapters has necessitated traversing a number of uncertainties and silences. For instance, in *Cinema 2*, Deleuze states that the reflection-image is composed through the intervention of the mental-image into the connection between situation and action: 'the signs are then figures, of attraction or inversion. And the genetic sign is discursive, that is, a situation or an action of discourse' (C2: 33). While this recapitulation tends to treat the reflection-image as an image with a tripartite sign structure, in *Cinema 1* things are more complex. Here Deleuze unfolds the reflection-image, describes it as an avatar of three component images, three images derived in reference to the work of the nineteenth-century linguist Pierre Fontanier.

Fontanier was interested in classifying the features of spoken and written language through a taxonomy of figures. This classification appears in *Manuel classique pour l'étude des tropes* (1821) and *Des Figures du discours autres que les tropes* (1830). These books explore the sense of language as being composed of either tropes or non-tropes. On the one hand, a trope is a word or phrase used in any way other than the literal – however, it is not the word or phrase in itself that is important, so much as the way in which that word or phrase transforms the passage or text in which it is placed. Non-tropes, on the other hand, are words or phrases used in a literal way, but which nonetheless similarly affect the sense of the passage or text in which they appear. Figures, thus, are transformative. From this basic division, Fontanier will go on to create a series of sub-categories. There are two types of tropes: perfect tropes, 'tropes in a word, or properly speaking'; and imperfect tropes, 'tropes of many words, improperly speaking' (Fontanier, 2009: 77, 109 – my own translation). Perfect tropes include metaphor, metonymy; synecdoche; imperfect tropes include allegory, mythology, hyperbole, allusion, paradox and irony (Fontanier, 2009: 79, 87, 99, 105, 111, 123, 143). Towards the end of *The Study of Tropes* Fontanier introduces 'other forms of discourse called figures that are not tropes', a discussion that will be continued in the second book on literal figures (Fontanier, 2009: 221). Here he lists four types of such figures: figures of construction, figures of elocution, figures of style, and figures of thought – each, in turn, composed of sub-categories (Fontanier, 2009: 283, 323, 359, 403).

Deleuze uses Fontanier's taxonomy as impetus and inspiration for the reflection-image, writing: 'we are not posing any general problem about the relationship of the cinema and language ... we are simply noting that cinematographic images have figures proper to them' (C1: 183). Deleuze does not, therefore, simply transpose Fontanier's types and sub-categories into his cineosis intact. Rather, he regroups Fontanier's categories into three different images. In the first place, Fontanier has already divided figures of speech (tropes) from figures of thought (non-tropes, or literal figures), the rationale being that the former deal with verbal expression, while the latter express ideas. That these two categories are by no means pure means they acknowledge an overlap, which – in the second place – can create an interim category between the two poles, sometimes called figures of amplification. Figures of speech, amplification and thought thus describe a trajectory and difference in degree. Accordingly, Deleuze identifies the three avatars of reflection-images as acting in just such a way. First, tropes (perfect or imperfect) which act through substitution; second, literal transformations, which act through reversals; third, figures of thought proper, which 'do not pass through any modification' but rather mark out 'deliberation, concession, support, prosopopoeia' (C1: 183). These three aspects inspire attraction-images, inversion-images and discourse-images. Taken together, the three reflection-images create different degrees of figuration.

Reflection-images (as Deleuze renames them in *Cinema 2*), or the trans-formation of forms (as he originally designates them in *Cinema 1*), describe the ways in which the two avatars of the action-image interact with each other through the encompassing domain of thought (the mental-image). Reflection-images describe – on the one hand – how the large form of the action-image transforms the small, and the small form of the action-image transforms the large either directly or indirectly; and – on the other hand – how each form immediately transforms itself. These are the figures of attraction, inversion and discourse. No longer pure action-images, but not yet pure mental-images. And both action-images and mental-images at one and the same moment within the domain of thought. Despite such derivation, as has been seen, reflection-images have their own consistency. And while these figures are the least explicated avatar of Deleuze's movement-image taxonomy, if all the hints are followed and the silences explored, what is revealed is a real richness in the cinema of action, in the cinema of realism, a complexity that extends beyond the relatively limited scope of the two fundamental forms through the generation of cinematic tropes, reversals and problems; figures of the plastic and theatrical, figures of the sublime and futility, figures of the extreme limit of the large and the small; and the genesis of each of these compositions in *mise en abyme*, the *quotidian* and the *extreme limit of all action-images*. And it is here – at these very limits – that a crisis of the action-image will emerge, a crisis that will be explicated through the opsigns and sonsigns of the time-image, that will displace *mise en abyme*, the *quotidian* and the *extreme limit of all action-images* into a new semiotic trajectory. However, and more immediately, these '"figures"', writes Deleuze, 'introduced the mental into the image', into the movement-image (C1: 198). The transformation of forms, the three reflection-images, are nascent images of thought, developed in the mental-image proper: in dreams, recollections and symbolic thinking.

9

Dream-images
(third mental-image)

Perception, affects and actions are discovered once again – yet in an entirely new way – in the domain of thought. This concerns mental-images. Perception-images – towards molar composition – distil from the world a privileged centre; affection-images allow unfilmable internal intensities to be expressed through this centre; and action-images fulfil the sensory-motor trajectory by allowing the character to act in and upon the world. Thus the fundamental and primary cinematic images of matter: perception → affect → action. Mental-images capture up these matter-images in thought and – in turn – return thought to matter-images. That is to say, mental-images actualise thought on-screen. This concerns descriptions of the retention and creation of perceptions, affects, and actions: images that will traverse all degrees of reactive and active consciousness. The domain of thought is thus the consummation of the movement-image; and the mental-image explicates – for Deleuze – three such moments of consummation. We begin with the dream-image, the image of thought constituting the lowest level of consciousness. Dream-images are cinematic images which capture thought as hallucinations, nightmares, dreams, imaginations; and – at their most extreme – describe the whole world as if it were a dream. The image of the dream and the world as a dream describe the two poles of the dream-image: the dream world as a product of the dreamer; and the world as if it is a dream, a perspective on the world. The former concerns the dream-image signs of composition, which Deleuze names the 'rich' and the 'restrained' (C2: 58). The latter Deleuze designates 'movement of world', the genetic sign of the dream-image (C2: 59). Rich dreams and restrained dreams capture varying degrees of hallucination, nightmare, dream and imagination on-screen with respect to a centre from which they emerge: the character or characters. Rich dreams are explicitly dream-like, strange; weird, disconnected, absurd; while restrained dreams may play on the ambiguity between dream world and real world. In both cases, however, the dream-image 'is subject to the condition of attributing the dream to the dreamer, and the awareness of the dream … to the viewer' (C2: 58). Movement of world, in contrast, is an 'implied dream', the whole film is dream-like, dream and real are one, a world through which the characters dance and sing; children play adults, adults play children; where everything is somehow both strange, and just as it should be: the realm of the purest imagination (C2: 59).

The dream-image (the third mental-image), accordingly, is constituted by the sign series: rich dream (first sign of full molar composition) ↔ restrained dream (secondary sign of composition) ↔ movement of world (sign of genetic forces).

Rich dreams

This is a dream! – such is the formula of the rich dream, the first sign of composition of the dream-image. From the real world, the entrance to the dream world is explicitly signalled, and accompanied by ornate transformations; the dream itself is full of the most amazing images produced in the most creative of ways. Deleuze identifies 'dissolves, super-impositions, deframings, complex camera movements, special effects, manipulations in the laboratory', technical alterations 'going right to the abstract, in the direction of abstraction' (C2: 58). This is a dream sequence where it is clear the dreamer has entered the dream, and obvious when the dreamer is no longer dreaming. Crazy hallucinations, wild nightmares or the most beautiful of imaginary times and spaces.

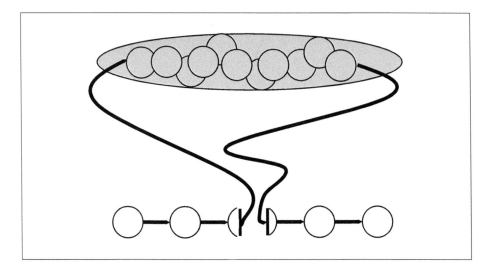

Figure II.25 Rich dreams: radically distinct real world and dream world

Such dreams – while utterly distinct from the real world – serve to inspire the dreamer upon their return to a waking state. The film takes up the dream-image and retains its affects of fear, disorientation or motivation which permeate the narration and determine the actions of the character.

Restrained dreams

The second sign of composition of the dream-image is the restrained dream. Here the transformation from real world to dream world is subtle, may even occur through the straight cut and be essentially invisible. The dream itself may resemble the everyday world more or less, the everyday reality of the awake character; yet it will have a certain uncanniness, it will be somehow impossible. An 'unhinging', writes Deleuze, 'which "looks like" dream, but between objects that remain concrete' (C2: 58). Dream world and real world become ambiguous; and – accordingly – the effect of the dream world on real world is all the more powerful: the character or characters may act as if the dream were a moment of the real, believing it to be so. Yet something nags. *Was I asleep? Am I now awake?* Such will become the central task of the film, to differentiate the real world from the dream world, the dream world from the real world, and the conscious I from the dreaming body which haunts it.

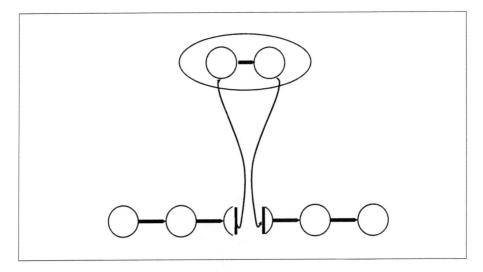

Figure II.26 Restrained dreams: an ambiguity between real world and dream world

Movement of world

Movement of world, or the implied dream, constitutes the genetic sign of the dream-image. Here 'every world and every dream, closes up around everything it contains, including the dreamer' (C2: 63). There is no entrance to the dream world, and no exit. The character or characters no longer have any standing outside the dream; indeed – they are a product of the dream, exist only within the dream. This world is a world of pure imagination: such universes may not even be dream-like, and have been captured in musicals and dance films (where the song and dance are a natural aspect of the real world). Deleuze writes: 'the virtual image which becomes actual does not do so directly, but becomes actual in a different image, which itself plays the role of a virtual image being actualised in a third, and so on to infinity (C2: 56). Accordingly: 'the dream is not a metaphor but a series of anamorphoses which sketch out a very large circuit' (C2: 56). The film is a series of impossible events, unfolding and folding over each other. A purely imaginary world actualised on-screen, an image of the universe in which anything and everything is possible; and these anythings and everythings appear as the real, and are the grounding of strange cinematic subjectivities.

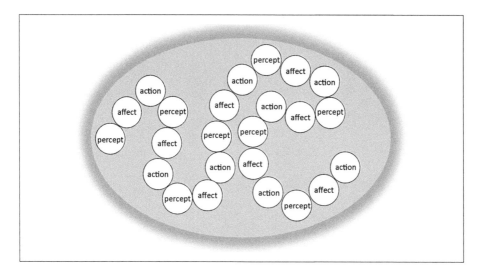

Figure II.27 Movement of world: the dream world is the real world

*
*   *

Movement of world, restrained and rich dreams are the coordinates of the dream-image, images of thought which capture up the imaginary. Perceptions, affects and actions are thus in thought and returned to the screen as matter-images describing powerful imaginary worlds. These imaginary dream worlds may be idyllic sanctuaries, nightmarish hells, strange and abstract environments – yet whatever the situation, perceptions, affects and actions are reconstituted according to their function. On the one hand, these dream worlds may only occupy a moment within the narration; yet they have such power that the dream permeates the real world of the film, the dream becomes the situation which will affect the character and designate and determine their actions. On the other hand, perceptions, affects and actions are fully subsumed within the dream world, operate according to the laws of that world as an idiosyncratic sensory-motor system. With dream-images, the mental-image discovers the imaginary, and the imaginary creates an image of thought that can traverse the extreme depths of consciousness. Such depths circumscribe the threshold of an active state of mind. Accordingly, it will take very different modes of the mental-images to anchor the image of thought to higher levels of active and reactive consciousness, to reign in the image of thought for the matter-image and the sensory-motor system.

Section II

10

Recollection-images
(second mental-image)

The second of the three avatars of the mental-image is the recollection-image. Recollection-images describe memories: perceptions, affects and actions coalesce as moments of the past actualised on-screen in the present and for the future. This is no longer the world of imagination, of the dream-image; no longer an alternative world, a space and time with different rules, modes and laws. The recollection-image is rather the return to consciousness of memory, which is actualised as a matter-image within the real of the film world. This matter-image is the flashback. Flashbacks may be triggered by an event in the present; or the present may demand a memory to be sought for, a memory which will at first be elusive. Flashbacks may simply repeat a moment from inside the film, a reminder for the character (and for the viewer); or come from a time before the film (which in being actualised, the film now encompasses). Furthermore, these memories may not simply be bare reconstitutions, but also – perhaps inevitably – become coloured by the present. These images may repeat a number of times with difference; or they may belong not to a single character, but to the film, and thus be attributed to a group consciousness as a collective remembrance; or they may explore the variations in the memories of several characters. Accordingly, for Deleuze, such flashbacks will be distributed between the two extreme poles of the recollection-image as either memory as 'an explanation, a causality or a linearity'; or memory as the 'fragmentation of all linearity … [as] breaks in causality' (C2: 49). The former designates a general sign of composition named destiny. While Deleuze does not go on to divide this general sign of composition into its full molar and secondary attributes, a division will here be assumed to describe a difference in degree and – following the example of the dream-image with its rich and restrained forms – similarly adopt strong and weak forms: *strong* destiny and *weak* destiny. The genetic sign of the recollection-image describes fragmentations of memory, memories which no longer serve to drive forward the narration using the past in the present for the future; but a narration which becomes lost in the past, in memories, which now become the primary matter-image of the film. Deleuze names this process forking paths.

The recollection-image (the second mental-image), accordingly, is constituted by the sign series: *strong* destiny (first sign of full molar composition) ↔ *weak* destiny (secondary sign of composition) ↔ forking paths (sign of genetic forces).

Strong destiny

Strong destiny – the first sign of composition of the recollection-image – is perhaps appropriately identified as embodying the 'words: "watch out! Recollection"' (C2: 49). In the present, in the moment of a perception-image, the character will pause … a slow dissolve, a shimmering, and a moment from the past appears on-screen, and this appearance is marked in any number of ways (monochrome as opposed to the coloured present; subtle slow-mo; reverb-sound). A leap into the past, which will in turn loop back to the present for affection-images and action-images. Deleuze describes such a flashback as an instrument of 'psychological causality', a 'closed circuit' (C2: 47, 49). In this way, it is perhaps better to say the past appears in the present, is actualised as a matter-image in the present of the film. An essential moment – it will be reconstituted in order to direct the destiny of the character. The future hinges

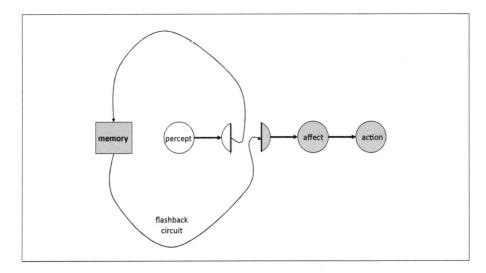

Figure II.28 *Strong* destiny: a flashback to the past determines the future

on this recollection-image. *Strong* destiny explicates the inescapable past, the power of a recollection to haunt the present, to replace the perception-image and permeate feelings for an act that will explicate or resolve the situation of the memory.

Weak destiny

With *weak* destiny – the second sign of composition of the recollection-image – a flashback to the past no longer determines the future, but instead permeates the affection-images of the present. The memory is ambiguous, or incomplete; can only be reconstituted with effort, attempt after attempt. Perhaps several characters experience flashbacks; and the coordinates of an opaque situation must be identified, the pieces of the homogeneous memory reconstructed. It is as if the past is a clue to an ellipsis in the present, something that must be decoded, some event that must be interpreted. This is the aim of the film – to resolve these complexities. *Weak* destiny thus retains elements of *strong* destiny: explanation, causality, linearity – but at the same time these links are not given, but must be established. Accordingly, designating this sign as *weak* should not belie a more complex and powerful flashback scenario than that of the *strong* form. For memory overwhelms the present, replaces not only perception, but affects with memory-affects, and stymies transformative action. It is the past that must be revealed and resolved, before a future can be contemplated.

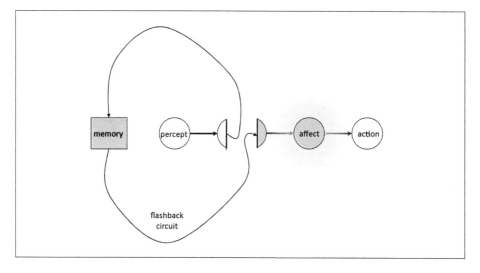

Figure II.29 *Weak* destiny: the content of the flashback permeates affects

Forking paths

Forking paths describe intricate, ambiguous, contradictory circuits. This is the genetic sign of the recollection-image, where 'there is no longer any question of an explanation, a causality or a linearity'; rather, the film explores 'an inexplicable secret' (C2: 49). From the present, we enter into many circuits of the past, multiple memories. Flashbacks within flashbacks within flashbacks … or irresolvable flashbacks, fragments of memory that will never be reconciled. Deleuze writes: '[i]t is not just the circuits forking between themselves', a series of flashbacks, but 'each circuit forking within itself, like a split hair' (C2: 49). Memories weave a web between various moments of the present of the movie; a series of ventures into the past and returns to the present, even if such a return is only a moment of respite before everything sets off once again. Accordingly, a film of forking paths brings the past into the present neither for the future (*strong* destiny) nor for the present (*weak* destiny); rather, the movie explores the past for itself. The present is revealed as an outcome of unfathomable recollections and psychological causality is exposed as a ruse. Flashbacks replace perception. To move from present to present via such flashbacks is to get lost along the way, walking an infinity of forking paths.

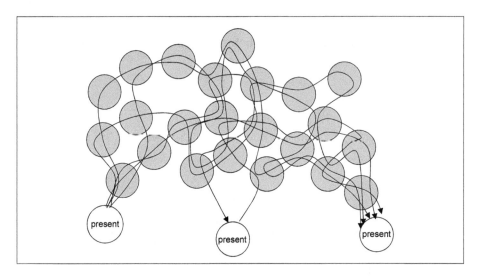

Figure II.30 Forking paths: a matrix of irresolvable flashbacks

*
*   *

Forking paths, *weak* and *strong* destiny are the coordinates of the recollection-image, images of thought which capture up memory and bring it into the present through flashbacks. Perceptions, affects and actions are thus doubled, taken from the present and the past, the latter as an image of thought that is returned and actualised on-screen. The flashback may be only a fleeting moment within the film, or flashbacks may permeate the movie throughout the narration; either way, a film of the recollection-image is one that is dominated by the effects of the flashback. In the first place, a perception in the present initiates the flashback. In the second place, the sensory-motor trajectory is reconfigured so that the recollection now replaces the perception along a new line which will extend as far as it may according to the sign which will be constituted. Accordingly, forking paths describe an immediate substitution of perception for recollection; *weak* destiny consents the recollection to pass into the affect; while *strong* destiny allows the recollection to pass through the affect and into action. The sign series thus delineates the increasing powers of the determining effect of the flashback in the present, from forking paths through *weak* and into *strong* destiny; at the same time as defining a reciprocal and inverse overwhelming of the present by the past ungrounding determinations and loosening the bonds of psychological causality. Together, these three recollection-images are the actualisation of memory within the regime of the movement-image, within the domain of the image of thought, and within the avatar of the mental-image. In this way, the recollection-image describes ever-increasing degrees of consciousness; a reactive or active consciousness that emerged with the imaginary and the dream-image, and that will find its most coherent expression in the signs of the relation-image.

11

Relation-images
(first mental-image)

Section II

The mental-image as a movement-image of thought 'finds its most adequate representation in relation', the relation-image (C1: 197). Relation-images are designated by Deleuze as rendering logical and symbolic thought on-screen, for the character, for the viewer. In this way, the film is now dominated by images of understanding: logical progressions which may structure the entire trajectory of the narration; may be carried to a certain point before a derailing; or may describe amorphous symbolical meaning. In other words, the relation-image takes the processes of thought to the highest levels of active and reactive consciousness. The perception-image, the affection-image and the action-image no longer follow the sensory-motor trajectory of matter-images; rather, matter-images enter into mental relations. This is 'the essential point' for Deleuze: 'action, and also perception and affection, are framed in a fabric of relations. It is this chain of relations which constitutes the mental image, in opposition to the thread of action, perceptions and affections' (C1: 200). Put simply, 'actions, affections, perceptions, all is interpretation, from beginning to end … the images are only the winding paths of a single reasoning process' (C1: 200). The signs of the relation-image are designated as the mark, the demark and the symbol. The mark and the demark are the first and secondary signs of composition. With the mark 'we see a customary series such that each can be "interpreted" by the others' (C1: 203). With the demark 'it is always possible for one of these terms to … appear in conditions which take it out of its series' (C1: 203). In other words, an established sequence takes a swerve, and the demark becomes an image which reorients, disturbs or ungrounds the logic of the series. The symbol, the genetic sign, describes an abstract relation: 'a concrete object which is the bearer of various relations or of variations of a single relation' (C1: 204). Such are the coordinates of the final movement-image, the consummation of the sensory-motor system as an image of thought, the first and foremost mental-image.

The relation-image (the first mental-image), accordingly, is constituted by the sign series: mark (first sign of full molar composition) ↔ demark (secondary sign of composition) ↔ symbol (sign of genetic forces).

Mark

The first sign of composition of the relation-image is the mark. And the mark operates by 'the formation of a succession or habitual series of images' (C1: 197). A habitual series of images will appear within the narration, and may at first go unnoticed, but through their very repetition force themselves retro-actively into the consciousness of the character or characters, and the viewer. These images are in the present of the film, and while they are objects of perception rather than the products of memory or the imagination, they must necessarily call upon and develop memory and imagination for their retention and interpretation. The series thus 'takes as objects *of* thought, objects which have their own existence outside thought' (C1: 198). Deleuze notes that there must be at least three such images to form a series, for it is only with three repetitions that a habitual sequence moves beyond mere coincidence and chance. The question thus becomes: what does the mark – the relation between the repetitions of these images – signify? What are the affects of this perception? What actions must be taken? The answer can only be reached through thought, through the processes of a natural logic that will attempt understanding. Simply put, certain images in a film will become a grounding for the chain of a thought, a thinking process, within the character, for the spectator; and it is this image of thought which constitutes the narration.

Section II

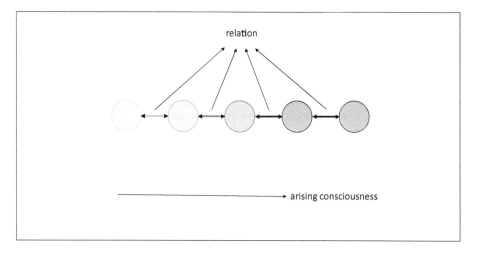

Figure II.31 Mark: the relation between a habitual series of images

Demark

A succession of images as a habitual series, once established, can in effect carry on into infinity; in so doing, the image becomes natural, and its significance disappears, returns to the silence from which it emerged. However, such a trajectory is susceptible to the demark. This is the second sign of composition of the relation-image. Here, the film creates a series of resonating images, and – once again – these objects pry open the consciousness of the characters and viewers. Once this repetition is recognised and fixed, once this succession appears as natural, any aberration in the series becomes significant. A shock, or the curiosity of something that nags. The demark is such an aberration: 'it is always possible', writes Deleuze, 'for one of these terms to leap outside the web and suddenly appear in conditions which take it out of its series, or set it in contradiction with it' (C1: 203). The chain of thought is broken open and the thinking process immediately reoriented within the character, and it is now the demark as an image of thought that will concern the narration. The question becomes: what does this demark signify?

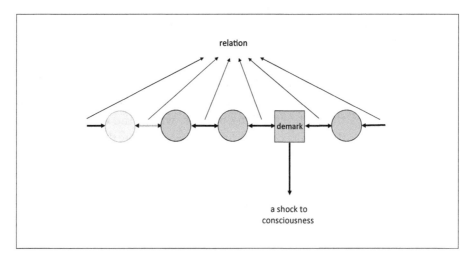

Figure II.32 Demark: an aberration in the series of habitual images

Symbol

The genetic sign of the relation-image is the symbol; and the symbol is an image which appears as 'abstract relation' (C1: 204). If the mark indicated a series of habitual images which through their repetition became instantiated within the mind of the character, and the demark an aberration in the series which created a shock, or rethinking, of the established natural relation, a symbol is a coalescence of such demarks extracted from differing series of marks. And in their coalescence, the demarks take on the power of the symbol. That is to say, multiple habitual series produce their own demarks, and these demarks link up only for symbolic thought. Thus, while an abstract relation, this is no abstraction. Rather, the symbol is 'a concrete object which is the bearer of relations, or variations of a single relation'; symbols 'are nodes of abstract relations' (C1: 204). Such a relation takes on significance as an image of thought as an autonomous object that expresses an idea, a belief, a concept.

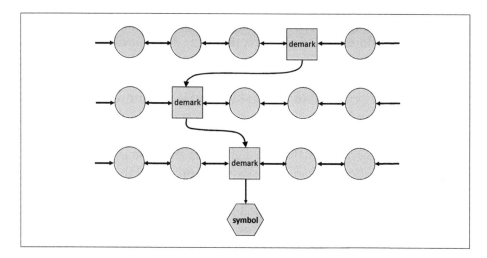

Figure II.33 Symbol: an object expressing ideas, beliefs, concepts

*   *
*

The domain of thought takes the movement-image to its limit, through mental-images, and to the relation-image, the last of all images of the movement-image cineosis. Perception-images – from their genesis to composition – created a central and privileged image from the matter of the universe: the perceiver and the perceived. This image passed immediately into the affection-image, where affects traverse the centre as intensive forces, such forces appearing through expressions of the face. Affects are the condition for the domain of action: and thus are returned to the world through impulse-images and action-images, the characters instantaneously reacting to the world, attempting to reveal the coordinates of the world, and effecting a change within that world. It is here that the movement-image is ultimately fulfilled: the world becomes a milieu, a determined situation which determines the actions and behaviours of characters. The large form action-image completed the logic of the sensory-motor system as a linear trajectory (perception → affect → action), announced the conclusion of matter-images. Yet immediately, such matter-images are captured up within the domain of thought through reflection-images and mental-images; signs which describe ever higher levels of the image of thought – the organic series sustained and explicated through a psychological sequence of images. Reflection-images create figures of attraction, inversion and discourse; images of cinematic metaphors, allegories, reversals and problems. Such figures are nascent mental-images, the mental-image proper appearing through dream-images, recollection-images and relation-images which discover perception, affects and actions once again – yet in an entirely new way. Perceptions become the foundation of imagination, memory and mental relations, in so doing replacing perception with dream-images, recollection-images and relation-images which pass into, organise, subsume and reorient affects and – in the final instance – the action-image. Thus, once again, the action-image (in its large form, with its five laws) is absolute terminus: not only of the matter-image, but also of the actualised mental-image. The sensory-motor trajectory becomes a system of organic and psychological states, matter-images underpinned and explicated through nightmares and dreams, flashbacks of the past, logic, aberrations in logic and symbolic conceptual thought. This is the cinema of the movement-image: a complex regime of interweaving and inter-penetrating matter-images and mental-images expressed through a cineosis describing the generative and compositional forces of a series of signs and images, avatars and domains – all oriented along the trajectory of the sensory-motor system.

Mental-images – in this way – are the consummation of the movement-image cineosis; they are that which sustains and explicates matter-images through ever-increasing states of active and reactive consciousness. And the highest function of such movement-images of thought are relation-images, the site of 'intellectual feelings' and 'symbolic acts' (C1: 198). Abstract symbolic relations are explicated as symbols, which in turn are habitualised in a logical series. Mental habits form from indeterminacy, and create circuits of logical understanding: perceptions are identifications, feelings are analysis and actions are synthesis. The relation-image transforms sense into signification: 'logical conjunctions "because", "although", "so that", "therefore", "now", etc' (C1: 197). And while such mental relations form the fabric of the film and are the web in which the character is caught, they simultaneously 'implicate the spectator in the film' (C1: 205). Symbols, demarks and marks must be interpreted, sense must be transformed into signification, and the film will require an effort to be grasped in all its facets. This is a cinema that demands attention: perceptions, affects and actions, impulses, figures and problems, imagination and dreams are now an exposition of the highest activity of the movement-image as an image of thought. There is thus nothing beyond the relation-image. Or rather, there is nothing beyond the relation-image within the sensory-motor system, within the regime of movement-images.

12

Opsigns and sonsigns

The time-image begins with opsigns and sonsigns – pure actual optical and sound situations – a de-differenciated image. This de-differenciation is a consequence of ungroundings of three processes proper to the movement-image: a stymieing of the emergence of composition in the perception-image (which in turn effects each type of movement-image); a crisis in the action-image (through a relaxation of the sensory-motor laws of the large form); and a weakening of the linkages between different types of movement-image (disrupting the coalescence of the entire regime). An attack on one of these processes is an attack on all. If perception can no longer describe a central and privileged image but remains gaseous, every type of movement-image dissolves into the genetic forces from which it once originated, perception no longer extends into the laws of action, and the entire system is delinked and collapses. If the action-image is no longer dominated by the large form, and the five laws of the milieu do not describe a determinate situation determining behaviours, perception will find no extension through the sensory-motor trajectory, mental-images will no longer sustain and explicate matter-images, and each type of movement-image will revert to its genetic force. If – finally – the links between each of the images collapse, there will be a concomitant confounding of the emergence of signs of composition and, once again, no way to fulfil the sensory-motor system in the web of laws of the milieu and behaviour. The stymieing of perception-images, the crisis of the action-image and the delinkage of the movement-image – together – describe de-differenciation. Such de-differenciation, however, is not only destructive. It is only 'the negative condition of the upsurge of the new thinking image' (C1: 215). Everything returns to the purest zeroness – everything can begin again through an alternative trajectory (C1: 211). Opsigns and sonsigns are the name given to this moment, actual on-screen de-differenciated visual and audio images. And it is these images which will generate a new series of signs, new types of image, new orders of narration and narrative. This will be the time-image cineosis. A cinematic semiosis developed from the pure zeroness of actual opsigns and sonsigns exploring an ever-expanding series of virtual correlates. And it is the virtual correlates that will engender a new image of cinematic thought.

This is the zeroness of opsigns and sonsigns – Destruction: the stymieing of the perception-image; the crisis of the action-image; the collapse of the movement-image. Creation: opsigns and sonsigns, actual de-differenciated images opening up onto the virtual.

The stymieing of the perception-image. The specification of the perception-image is that which is necessary for the creation of the movement-image cineosis. It is here that we encounter the zeroness of the movement-image: 'the movement-image is already perception', writes Deleuze, 'and perception will not constitute a first type of image without being extended into the other types', it 'is strictly identical to every image' of the sensory-motor system (C2: 31). Cinematic perception concerns the fundamental organisation of worlds and bodies: the world composed of matter from which a privileged character will emerge. Such an emergence describes a process from genesis to composition, from the molecular to the molar, through a series of three signs. The genetic sign is gaseous perception, the acentred interaction of all images. Such molecular organisation is gathered up through liquid perception creating the spaces and times of multiple centres. Finally, solid perception emerges as the privileging of a cohesive subject with respect to the film-world – a character who is the perceiver and the perceived, a unitary centre. Emergence means solid perception structures and organises the liquid and the gaseous. And having zeroness, the perception-image and its sign trajectory create the conditions for the emergence of such solid compositions in each type of movement-image. Each image has a sign series as correlate to the gaseous, liquid and solid: a genetic sign passing into secondary composition, secondary composition attaining full molar composition. The indeterminate universe of the any-space-whatever produces the icon of the affection-image – that which captures intensive forces within the character through the close-up of the face. The primal forces of an originary world found in the impulse-image are grounded in symptoms. Vectors and imprints are determined by and determined in situations where defined spaces and times allow action to reveal and resolve the world. Indeterminate figures of the *mise en abyme* (recurrence of images), the *quotidian* (everydayness) and the *extreme limit of action* (the exponential growth of problems) are regulated, specified and determined in the compositional coordinates of critical reflection. Movement of world and forking paths are linked to psychological centres as dreams and recollections. Symbols (beliefs, ideas, concepts) are tamed in the logic of natural habitual relation. Such are the processes of the composition of movement-images.

If, however, the perception-image fails to transform the gaseous into liquid, the liquid into solid, we encounter the first possibility of the disintegration of the sensory-motor system. Without a solid I as a central and privileged image, or without a series of characters who are perceived and perceive the world, we encounter gaseous perception, an acentred series of ahuman heterogeneous spaces necessarily escaping human temporal linearity, the molecular film, where the creation of subjects remains only a possibility, any image of body or world an image like any other. Accordingly, the domains of affect, action and thought no longer have a human centre to inspire and coordinate their own compositional trajectories. We encounter the reign of genetic signs: any-space-whatevers, originary worlds, vectors and impressions; *mise en abyme*, the *quotidian* and the proliferation of problems; movement of world, forking paths and symbols. Without the emergence of centres (as either a solid I or as liquid ensembles) there is no privileged image to express affects, to act in and upon the world, no consciousness that can reflect, dream, remember and understand. Instead of a chorus of distinct compositional images there is a coalescence of genetic forces; a fusing of indeterminacies, the de-differenciated image. Genetic signs of the movement-image only retain specificity in relation to the image through which they emerge; de-differenciation results in the singularity of pure genetic forces. Everything returns to the purest zeroness.

The crisis of the action-image (large form). The movement-image cineosis is composed of matter-images and mental-images, the sensory-motor system as a complex describing a psycho-organic organisation of bodies and worlds. Matter-images: characters perceive, feel and act; perception-images pass into affection-images, and affection-images into action-images. And it is with the action-image in its large form that the logic of the sensory-motor system as a linear trajectory reaches its fullest expression. The large form is the conclusion of matter-images, and is that which is sustained and explicated in mental-images. Mental-images: figures, problems, the imagination and memories of characters, the world as an object of understanding – such are the images of movement-image thought actualised on-screen. And it is these images of active and reactive consciousness that the sensory-motor trajectory enslaves to its system – the image of thought duplicating and reinforcing the perception with which it began, permeating affects once more for action. There is nowhere beyond the domain of action, beyond the avatar of the action-image, beyond the image of the large form and its laws of organisation.

Yet – we witness 'a crisis of the traditional image of cinema', a crisis as 'the constant state of the cinema' (C1: 205). And this crisis has 'five apparent characteristics: *the dispersive situation, deliberately weak links, the voyage form, the consciousness of clichés, the condemnation of plot*' (C1: 210; translation slightly modified). These five characteristics correspond with what Deleuze has previously designated as the five laws of the large form action-image. First law (S→S`): the determining of an initial situation that governs the required restoration of the final situation. Second law (S→A): the situation devolves into behaviours, or actions, distributed to characters. Third law (A): the action in-itself necessary to realise, by way of the duel, the final resolution. Fourth law (A^n): the action is not simply the ultimate moment, but is structural, duels permeate the film. Fifth law (→): the whole flow of the plot, which carries situation to action and action to situation through the imprint of world on the character. Each of the five moments of crisis attacks each of these laws in turn. If the first law describes S→S`, with the crisis the image 'no longer refers to a situation which is globalising or synthetic, but rather one which is dispersive' (C1: 207). The globalising situation is that which is distilled into a filmic milieu; while a synthetic situation is that which prescribes outcomes and restorations. With the crisis, the milieu cannot be formed and its outcomes are not foretold. Second moment: we immediately encounter a series of discontinuities which act as a weakening of links, the second characteristic of the crisis, the stymieing of the second law, S→A. With the crisis, 'the line or the fibre of the universe which prolonged events into one another, or brought about the connection of portions of space, has broken' (C1: 207). The third characteristic of the crisis is where 'the sensory-motor action or situation has been replaced by the stroll, the voyage … aimless movements' (C1: 208). No longer does behaviour aim at and become embodied in a final, decisive action (A). Actions are no longer reactions and have no direction home. 'In the fourth place', writes Deleuze, 'we ask ourselves what maintains a set in this world … The answer is simple … clichés' (C1: 208). The fourth crisis thus concerns the cliché of action which appears to be the distinctive characteristic of each moment (A^n) and to permeate a whole, making the whole. The fifth and final moment of crisis is the condemnation of plot; that which orders situation and action, captures up characters, their perceptions, emotions, and thoughts. The crisis of the action-image witnesses the dispersal of the determinate milieu and the diffusion of determined actions.

The collapse of the movement-image. This the movement-image: the linkage between perception-images, affection-images, impulse-images, action-images (small and large), figures of attraction, inversion and discourse, dream-images, recollection-images and relation-images. Perception-images describe a central human body perceiving and perceived by objective images of the universe. Affection-images are expressions of internal intensities upon this centre through faces expressing wonder, faces expressing emotion. Action-images capture the body giving movement back to the world: the body fighting or fucking, the body transforming the world. Mental-images generate flashback-recollections, dream-images and symbolic relations. In this way narration and narrative are created from linking movement-images. A character as a center of the film sees the world, feels, remembers and imagines, then acts. For Deleuze every movement-image film is composed of such moments: these images are edited together and create the flow of the film. Such moments are temporal in that they are chronological: see → feel → act. While mental-images may appear to disrupt chronological movement (a flashback to the past, an imagining of the future or elsewhere), they rather bring past and future into the present. Mental-images enfold with affects, they are images actualising memories and imaginations in the present, constituting a strengthening of the coordinates of chronological time: a past present caused the present of the now which in turn will cause the future present to arrive. Chronological time: past → present → future. Here, everything is in its right place: comprehensive space. And such temporal and spatial coordinates are expressed through an embodied centre, a human consciousness. This is the movement-image.

There is always a 'requirement', according to Deleuze, for cinema 'to smash the whole system' of movement-images, 'to cut perception off from its motor extension; action, from the thread which joined it to a situation; affection from the adherence or belonging to characters', and for 'the mental image ... to become "difficult"' (C1: 215). Filmmakers – some filmmakers – will discover a need to create the de-differenciated image. Movies in which we will encounter

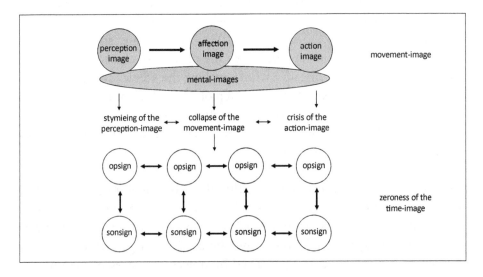

Figure II.34 Opsigns and sonsigns: the zeroness of the time-image

the disruption of chronological time, the displacement of the coordinates of comprehensive space, and the dissolution of implicated sensory-motor embodiments. There will always be a requirement for time-images – for the possibility of a new regime of images emerging from the fundamental condition of pure optical and pure sound situations, opsigns and sonsigns.

The potential of the zeroness of opsigns and sonsigns. Such de-differenciation describes the actualisation of opsigns and sonsigns – pure dispersive visual and sound images. Yet opsigns and sonsigns are only 'the negative condition of . . . the new thinking image' (C1: 215). The actual on-screen de-differenciated image is the genesis of virtual correlates. Cinema is a practice of creating and linking images, which can be described as 'multiplicities, each of which is composed of actual and virtual elements' (DI: 148). Actual images are the on-screen visuals and accompanying audio: the trajectory of images that compose the film. The virtual is far more 'ephemeral' (DI: 151). The virtual is a process which both disconnects and connects actual images: actual on-screen images are framed, shot and edited together, and what is out-of-field of the frame and the shot and the edit itself create virtual correlations. All cinema is composed of actual images and all cinema operates through virtual connections. While purely virtual processes or indeed 'purely actual objects do not exist', they have 'mutual inextricability' and there is a difference: 'the relationship between the actual and the virtual is not the same as that established between two actuals' (DI: 148, 149, 152). Movement-images are dominated by actual to actual movements, through the flow of on-screen images (cutting on an action, the flow from long shot to medium shot to close-up, the linkage of visual and sound image). In this way virtual connections are overwhelmed, are effaced, become invisible. The actual on-screen images dominate. Yet some types of linkage allow the virtual to arise – exposing what is beyond or subsists within the frame, exposing the connection of shots, opening up a space between actuals. Such is the virtual and the possibility of the creation of a new image of thought.

* * *

The collapse in the links of the movement-image, the crisis of the action-image (situation → action) and the non-emergence of compositional signs after the perception-image are the three moments in the creation of opsigns and sonsigns, pure optical- and sound-images, the actual de-differenciated image. This is the zeroness of the time-image, the point at which everything begins anew, a new conception and cineosis of the image, narration and narrative. Deleuze will name these time-images hyalosigns, chronosigns and noosigns – each an exploration of actual–virtual correlates. Noosigns, chronosigns and hyalosigns are narrative, narration and description – composed from opsigns and sonsigns – the zeroness (0) of the time-image. Concomitantly, hyalosigns, chronosigns and noosigns are simultaneities appearing as a lectosign: a film that not only demands to be seen, but necessitates interpretation. Time-images can thus be considered 'a finite composite sensation … opening onto the plane of composition that restores the infinite to us, = ∞' (WP: 197). Lectosigns are the pure virtual (the infinite) generated from pure actual opsigns and sonsigns (the finite) through the impurities of noosigns, chronosigns and hyalosigns.

Section II

13

Hyalosigns

The hyalosign – '[t]he crystal-image, or crystalline description' – is the first of the time-images (C2: 69). Opsigns and sonsigns are pure actual optical and sound situations, the de-differentiated image on-screen, visual and sonic fragments in a state of zeroness. This is to say, opsigns and sonsigns are immediately hyalosigns. For if 'the actual [image] is cut off from its motor linkages', there is – for Deleuze – a simultaneous relinkage; this relinkage is the 'coalescence of an actual image and its virtual image' (C2: 127). In other words, opsigns and sonsigns stymie the seamless flow of actual image to actual image; while the hyalosign links the actual image to a virtual correlate. In this way, opsigns and sonsigns 'are nothing other than slivers of crystal-images' (C2: 69). Opsigns and sonsigns – through their very constitution – must become hyalosigns; an actual must relink to the virtual if delinked from other actuals. Accordingly, the hyalosign is the '*description*' of an image on-screen – a fragment, now – the 'most restricted circuit of the actual image and *its* virtual' (C1: 69). This actual and virtual of the hyalosign has three aspects: a description of the immediate image, a description of an image that is passing into the past, and a description of an image coming from the future. Each of these descriptions – the in itself, the passing and the becoming – concerns the temporal dimensions of an actual with its virtual: an exchange of actual and virtual, the virtual sustaining the disconnection between actuals. Deleuze writes: 'there is no virtual which does not become actual in relation to an actual, the latter becoming virtual through the same relation' (C2: 69). The in itself, the passing and the becoming of description are the three exchanges of the hyalosign: 'making presents pass, replacing one by the next while going towards the future, but also preserving all the past, dropping it into an obscure depth' (C2: 87). Describing the hyalosign through such temporal coordinates allows Deleuze to designate the structure and genesis of signs of the image: both their general condition (which will in turn inspire the coordinates of chronosigns and noosigns) and their specific attributes (as crystal-images). Time has its genesis in the future, time is born from an empty future that arrives and passes through the instant of the present to be filled up and thus accumulate in the past. The past is a sustaining of temporality, yet such a holding is as much a withholding, memory is opaque, an intermixing, complex, full of interstices, forgettings, falsities – and it appears for the present retaining such characteristics. The present is thus composed from an empty future and the indeterminacies of the past. Accordingly, the composition of the present is the first sign of composition, the fullest of such signs, but a sign which in no way describes a molar structure. Rather, the present is the first sign of an actual–virtual composition; the past the secondary sign, and the future the sign of genesis. These hyalosigns can be described as: 'mirrors face to face', 'the limpid and the opaque' and 'the seed and the environment' (C2: 71). Each performs an exchange between the actual on-screen image in the present and its virtual connections in relation to the immediate present, an immediate passing, and an immediate future. With mirror images bodies and backgrounds appear multitudinous – and in this way the actual propagates indiscernibility enacted by the virtual linkages between elements. The limpid and opaque concerns the passing of the present where one image becomes opaque as another becomes limpid, the limpid actualised in the present corresponding to an opaque retention of the past as virtual. Finally, the present is a seed, the future a virtual environment in relation to that seed, a virtual succession which subsists and insists within the seed image; correspondingly, an actual environment may refer to a virtual seed – one is 'pure virtuality' with respect to the other (C2: 79). The hyalosign is thus the 'indiscernibility ... of the real and the imaginary, or of the present and the past, *of the actual and the virtual*, [which] is definitely not produced in the head or the mind, it is the objective characteristic of certain existing images' (C2: 69 – my italics).

The hyalosign (the first time-image), accordingly, is constituted by the sign series: mirrors face to face (first sign of actual–virtual composition) ↔ the limpid and the opaque (second sign of actual–virtual composition) ↔ the seed and the environment (sign of the genesis of actual–virtual).

Mirrors face to face

An actual on-screen image can generate a multiplicity of perspectives: this is the mirror image, the first hyalosign. These perspectives form a matrix describing a virtual correlate. Deleuze describes such images as captured in 'oblique mirrors, concave and convex mirrors and Venetian mirrors', 'two facing mirrors', and even a 'palace of mirrors' (C2: 70). The body and the environment are framed in distorted states, in recurrence, and as fragments – we can thus add cracked and smashed mirrors, splinters of reflective surfaces. Narcissus caught gazing back at himself from the ripples of a pool; doppelgängers turning a corner and caught in wonderment; Escheresque landscapes and objects; the reflections of the sky in the sea. The actualisation of the body and the world are no longer dependent upon a cohesive tracing or the recognition of organic coordinates. This is the image of thought appropriate to the mirror image, the virtual correlate between on-screen actual fragments, duplicates, and distortions. The image in the present is cracked open, depicted space is complex, the body is a crystal.

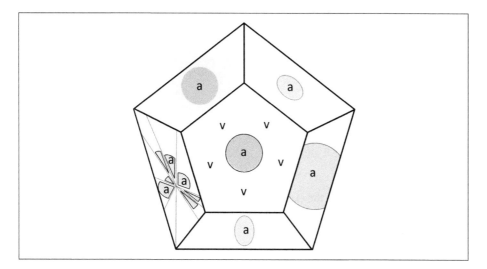

Figure II.35 Mirrors face to face: fragments, duplicates and distortions

Limpid and opaque

The second hyalosign appears 'when the virtual image becomes actual [and] … the actual image becomes virtual in its turn' (C2: 70). This is the limpid and the opaque. An image is limpid – luminous, clear – for a moment, but in passing becomes opaque (disappears). Yet the image is simultaneously opaque – obscure, impenetrable – and, in passing, limpid (invisible). Every time-image has two sides: that which is seen (actual) and its virtual (that which must be interpreted). All cinematic images pass – moment by moment, and the limpid is always becoming opaque, and that which was opaque is always becoming limpid. The actual image is in the present, but the virtual image becomes the immediate past of the present. 'So long as the conditions are not made precise there is definitely a distinction between the two sides, but they are indiscernible' (C2: 70). The actual present is sustained in reference to the virtual past, and the virtual sustains the actual present. Something passes, something emerges. Disappearance and appearance interweave as actual and virtual connections which describe the imperceptible. And that which is imperceptible is recognition.

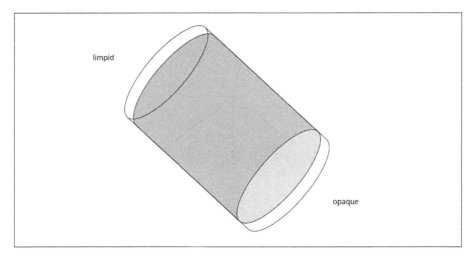

Figure II.36 Limpid-opaque: the exchange of the actual and virtual

Seed and environment

The third hyalosign is the seed and the environment. Deleuze writes: '[t]he seed is on the one hand the virtual image which will crystallise an environment which is at present amorphous' (C2: 74). Thus: (virtual) seed → (actual) environment. Deleuze, however, continues: 'on the other hand the latter must have structure which is virtually crystallisable, in relation to which the seed now plays the role of actual image' (C2: 74). Thus: (actual) seed → (virtual) environment. In the first place: (actual) seed → (virtual) environment. An actual object or moment foretells a spatiality of the film, a setting or series of settings, an event, happening or occurrence: an environment which is not in itself given with the object. In the second place: (virtual) seed → (actual) environment. The actual environment of the present refers to a virtual seed which cannot be determined; a dispersed situation, an expectation, an anticipation of some event to come. These are indeterminate (virtual) illuminations. The future is now: 'as pure virtuality, and it does not have to be actualised' (C2: 79). A seed image, in this way, encompasses the environment as if it were a miniature scene within a globe of opaque glass. The seed is the seed of an environment; and the environment is the mise-en-scène of the seed.

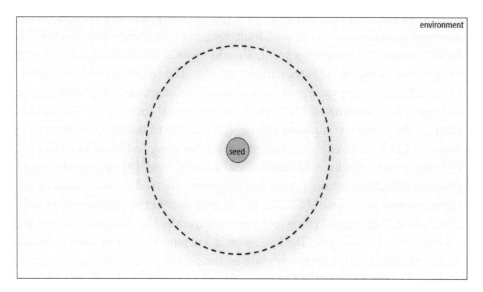

Figure II.37 Seed-environment: (virtual/actual) seed ↔ (actual/virtual) environment

* *   *

Hyalosigns concern description, the actual image on-screen and its virtual correlates. An opsign or a sonsign – as a fragment – is the actual image which refers to a virtual in the immediate present, immediate past or immediate future as mirrors face to face, the limpid-opaque and the seed-environment. If opsigns and sonsigns stymie the seamless flow of actual image to actual image, the hyalosign must necessarily link the actual image to a virtual correlate. The seed and the environment is the genesis of such hyalosigns, the future fundamentally open and unforeseen, an infinite set of possibilities. And the indeterminate seed can blossom into anything, the dispersed environment can be captured in any event. The limpid and opaque will describe the actual present permeated with its virtual past. Mirroring will create virtual correlates in the heterogeneous present. Together these hyalosigns are the presentation, retention and anticipation of indiscernibility. 'The crystal-image', writes Deleuze, is 'the point of indiscernibility of the two distinct images, the actual and the virtual, while what we see in the crystal is time itself, a bit of time in a pure state … So there will be different states of the crystal, depending upon the acts of its formation and the figures of what we see in it' (C2: 82). These states of the crystal concern the fractal nature of the time-image – for an image is not simply a moment in the frame, a shot can last less than a second but can equally encompass an entire film, a shot can stutter and shatter into jump-cuts and montage can conjoin disparate moments as a sequence-shot, an image can appear in depth with multiple planes, or a plane shot can traverse heterogeneous elements in a scene. In other words, the hyalosign is a fractal, images within images, images without images. The hyalosign is a description of the film as having various types of crystalline state, each dependent upon the sign which dominates. Deleuze identifies several such states: (1) 'an ideal state ... the perfect, completed crystal' (correlating to the sign of mirrors face to face); (2) 'a "flaw[ed]" ... cracked' crystal (relating to the limpid-opaque); (3) 'the crystal caught in formation and growth'; and (4) the 'crystal in the process of decomposition' (these developing to the seed → environment and the environment → seed) (C2: 83, 85, 88, 94). In other words, the image – the description of an image – refers to the narration of the film, the arrangement, the coalescence of hyalosigns. The hyalosign is a perspective on the film as image, as description; and immediately gives us the perspective of the time-image as a 'crystalline regime' (127). Deleuze saw the hyalosign as the 'most restricted circuit of the actual image and *its* virtual'; yet ever 'vaster circuits will be able to develop, corresponding to deeper and deeper layers of reality and higher and higher levels of memory or thought' (C2: 68–9). Hyalosigns as the image refer immediately to chronosigns: time-image narration. This is no longer the fragment, but the coalescence of fragments.

14

Chronosigns

Chronosigns 'no longer concern ... description, but narration'; a narration of 'false continuity' where 'crystalline narrations will extend crystalline description' (C2: 127). The time-image begins with opsigns and sonsigns, the pure actual de-differentiated image, the image on-screen. This is a fundamental zeroness (images which in no way describe a sensory-motor system, which no longer organise the extension of perception into affects, affects into action, and no longer are framed within mental relations); opsigns and sonsigns stymie the seamless flow of actual image to actual image, allowing for the ascension of virtual correlates. Accordingly, the hyalosign (or crystal image) explores – is a description of – the virtual correlates of the image as fragment. These correlates can be described through the way in which the time-image film disturbs the flow of chronological linear time appropriate to the movement-image through the creation of atemporalities. In other words, the film is no longer the immediate connection of moments of the now, homogeneous time, but rather explores temporal heterogeneity. As was seen with hyalosigns, time has its genesis in the future, time is born from an empty future; and the past sustains time, yet as a complex (intermixings, interstices, forgettings and falsities); finally, the present is an instant generated from the possible and filled out with indeterminacy. Hyalosigns were a description of the image in reference to these atemporal coordinates (atemporal in that they do not conjoin to give linear, human, chronological time); a description that allowed Deleuze to describe three signs – a first sign of an actual–virtual composition in the present, the past the secondary sign, and the future as the sign of genesis. Such images – opsigns-sonsigns as hyalosigns – coalesce in narration. This coalescence, however, is not a direct connection of actual image to actual image through movement (an indirect image of time), but rather, an indirect connection of actual to actual via the virtual (a direct image of time). This is the chronosign, and it will have – once again – three signs corresponding to the three atemporal relations of the past, present and future. The first sign of actual–virtual narration is 'peaks of the present' – images which explore the way in which any present moment is fundamentally composed of many heterogeneous presents (C2: 100). Perhaps this is a narration that can make time 'frightening and inexplicable', the possibility of action is torn between living in the moment, reacting to the influences of the past and acting for future effects (C2: 101). 'Sheets of the past' – the secondary sign of composition of actual–virtual narration – explores the way in which memory is 'no longer confused with the space which serves as its place' (C2: 100). Instead memories explore time itself – no longer functioning as a repository of the present, but as the pure pastness of spaces as disparate non-causal events. Deleuze refers to these two moments of the chronosign as the 'order of time' in that they undermine the linear chronology, the continuity of past, present and future (C2: 155). The third avatar of the chronosign is the 'power of the false' and Deleuze delineates this function as the 'series of time' (C2: 126, 133, 136, 155). A serial organisation once again disrupts the continuity of time that constructs a film as a narration where the present is a product of the past and the future a consequence, yet in a completely different way. The serial form does not unground the order of time, but creates images as events permeated by the future, events along a line of flight each of which have a virtual presence with one other. Deleuze puts it thus, 'the power of the false exists only from the perspective of a series of powers, always referring to each other and passing into one another' (C2: 133). All of time resonates through its futurity.

The chronosign (the second time-image), accordingly, is constituted by the sign series: peaks of the present (first sign of the order of time) ↔ sheets of the past (second sign of the order of time) ↔ powers of the false (sign of genesis – the series of time).

Peaks of the present

The first disruption to the order of time is described through peaks of the present which describe parallel moments of the present. These moments are 'never a succession of passing presents', writes Deleuze, 'but a simultaneity' (C2: 101). The time-image, in this way, captures different dimensions of presentness, all of which are conceivable and all together impossible. One formation would be where 'narration will consist of the distribution of different presents to different characters, so that each forms a combination that is plausible and possible in itself, but where all of them together are "incompossible", and where the inexplicable is thereby maintained and created' (C1: 101). However, there would be many other ways of creating such heterogeneities: one moment of a life repeated, but with difference; the same character played by different actors, and so on. It is the coalescence of presents presented in the present: what is possible and impossible coexist, making the possible and impossible inde-terminate. This kind of film disrupts the order of time, 'gives narration a new value, because it abstracts it from all successive action' (C2: 101). Rather, the narration appears in the simultaneity of differing presents. Peaks of the present explore the virtual connection between 'inextricable differences' (C2: 105).

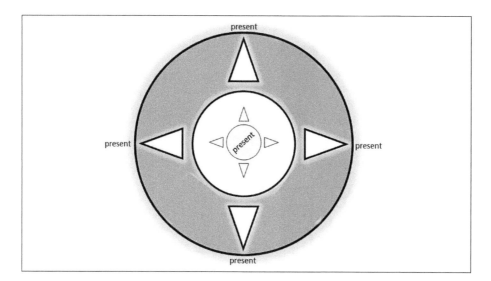

Figure II.38 Peaks of the present: the heterogeneous present

Sheets of the past

The second chronosign no longer concerns the simultaneities of the present, but rather the 'coexistence of all the sheets of the past' (C2: 99). Once again, this is a disruption to the linear order of time, an exposition of the order of time with respect to the virtual. Here, however, the film resists linear continuity by jumping between and encircling elements of the past. The film is the pure past, an 'infinity of levels' (C2: 105). Organised through sheets of the past, the narration of the film reverberates from event to event, folding back upon itself, seeing things from differing perspectives, producing unexpected and creative connections through both the actual and virtual components of the images. 'Between the past as a pre-existence in general and the present as infinitively contracted past', writes Deleuze, there are 'all the circles of the past' (C2: 99). In this way, temporality is captured from the perspective of pure pastness (rather than the past being a function of the present as in the movement-image). With the time-image the now is effaced and past spaces appear as moments of coexistence arranged non-chronologically. There is no cause and effect, just events that ricochet, backwards and forwards. And these events will each have their own tone, their own momentum, their own conception of space, time, bodies – and will form together a complex matrix of interweaving moments of the past as an image of the pure past.

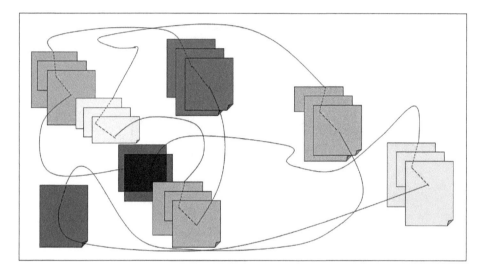

Figure II.39 Sheets of the past: the non-chronological nature of the past

Powers of the false

The third sign of the chronosign is the power of the false. Here the narration 'becomes fundamentally falsifying', it 'ceases to be truthful, that is, to claim to be true' (C2: 131). Crucially, for Deleuze, 'this is not a simple principle of reflection or becoming aware: "Beware! This is cinema". It is a source of inspiration' (C2: 131). This chronosign is no longer content simply to disrupt the order of time (as with sheets of the past and peaks of the present); instead the narration discovers the serial form. Difference and repetition, the repetition of themes, events, symbols, bodies, positions, objects, environments in difference: serialism. It can be said that this time-image constitutes narration from the perspective of the future, the fundamentally impenetrable, unknown and unknowable. Accordingly, the future acts as an eternal ungrounding of temporality giving to time multiplicity, disorder, forgetting, anarchy and chance: 'becoming as potentialization' (C2: 275). Becoming is that which brings the future into the present and 'carries the living being to creation'; it is that which brings the future into the past, a creative reminiscence where we can 'oppose becoming to history' (C2: 142). The power of the false evokes the future by disrupting the linear flow of time and breaking open the encirclings of the past: the next event does not necessarily follow from the present moment; and the next event can never necessarily be foretold in reference of the past. In this way, proclaims Deleuze, time 'is fundamentally liberated, becomes power of the false' (C2: 143). In short, 'truth is not to be achieved, formed, or reproduced; it has to be created' and appear as a creation though its own ungrounding, moment by moment, image by image (C2: 147). Time-image cinema finds in the power of the false the moment in which a film is no longer concerned with a pretence to truth, but instead with exposing this pretence: the falsity of unitary and total truth.

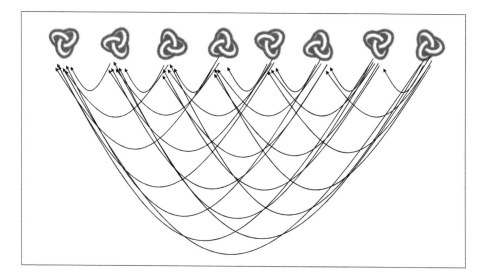

Figure II.40 Powers of the false: serialism, the ongoing ungrounding of the image

*
* *

Chronosigns concern time-image narration: the order of time and the series of time as simultaneities of the present, the coexistence of the past, and the power of the future. The time-image is composed of fragment-images, hyalosigns, coalescing as narrations through chronosignic simultaneities, coexistences and powers which retain their fragmentary nature. This is a cinema of atemporality, aspatiality and the ahuman – of disruptions to chronological time, displacements to comprehensive space, and dispersals of human consciousness developed in actual matter-images through complex virtual correlates. Peaks of the present, sheets of the past and powers of the false are the signs of these actual–virtual relations as strategies of time-image narration. Opsigns and sonsigns give us hyalosigns: the image as description. Hyalosigns give us chronosigns: images structured into narrations. Deleuze writes: '[t]here would still be a third instance beyond description and narration: the story' (C2: 147). The story – the storytelling function of the time-image – refers us to the narrative and to noosigns. This is the time-image: description (hyalosigns) → narration (chronosigns) → narrative (noosigns). Ever vaster circuits of actual images and their virtual correlates, developing opsigns and sonsigns into lectosigns, developing pure actuals into pure virtuals through the impurities of hyalosigns, chronosigns and noosigns.

15

Noosigns

The story, writes Deleuze, will 'replace filmstock, in a virtual film which now only goes on in the head' (C2: 215). Noosigns are narratives emerging from cinematic matter-images; noosigns 'force … us to think' (C2: 189). The cinematic trajectory of the time-image is image (hyalosigns) → narration (chronosigns) → narrative (noosigns), where the narrative is the story arising from the narration composed of images. In the first place, the time-image emerges by overturning the regime of the movement-image through the creation of pure optical and pure sound situations: opsigns and sonsigns. These actual images are coerced to open up on to their virtual correlates as hyalosigns. When hyalosigns are organised into narration, we encounter chronosigns. And these arrangements constitute a new image of cinematic thought: the noosign. Accordingly, noosigns are the narrative as that which is eternally discordant: 'problematic and problematizing' (LS: 64). This storytelling function of the noosign is discordant thought engendered by the world and its bodies. Or rather, noosigns are the very emergence of the world and its bodies as discordant images. Thought is not engendered as a consequence of a given, actual sensory-motor linkage between the character and the mise-en-scène, but rather through the absence of such relations. In the absence of an actual link and in the constitution of virtual relinkage, thought becomes us. Just as with hyalosigns and chronosigns, the noosign will also have three components, arranged as two elements of composition with respect to their temporal genesis. Deleuze names the poles world and the body; and the three signs corresponding to these poles are the body of attitude, the body of gest and the cinema of the brain. On the one hand, thought appears through the environments of the mise-en-scène. As Deleuze writes, 'landscapes are mental states', thus the mise-en-scène is 'the brain' (C2: 188, 205). On the other hand, thought appears through the body as 'attitude' and 'gest' (C2: 188, 205). 'Gest', a term taken from Bertolt Brecht, describes the way in which an actor can foreground gesture and performance as a social act. Attitude describes a body that does not act, that is displayed in its complex everydayness.

The noosign (the third time-image), accordingly, is constituted by the sign series: body of attitude (first sign of the atemporal body) ↔ body of gest (second sign of the atemporal body) ↔ cinema of the brain (genetic sign of the world).

Body of attitude

The first sign of the noosign is the body of attitude. The actor does not perform an act of mimesis, and the camera does not capture the perceptions, affects and actions of the body, but rather effaces such coordinates. This is 'the everyday body', a body of 'daily attitude' (C2: 191). This involves strategies such as exposing the fatigues, the ticks, the inabilities of the body. The idea 'is not to reconstitute a presence of bodies, in perception and action, but to carry out a primordial genesis of bodies' (C2: 201). Here 'disparate sets overlap and rival each other, without being able to organise themselves according to sensory-motor schemata. They fit over each other, in an overlapping of perspectives which means that there is no way to distinguish them even though they are distinct and incompatible' (C2: 203). The body is not a defined entity circum-scribed by the situation and necessary actions, but is a multiplicity in itself as an individualisation. The body precedes the plot, and the narrative is the story, is a function of the body of attitude – a body 'dispersed in "a plurality of ways of being present in the world", of belonging to sets, all incompatible and yet coexisting' (C2: 203).

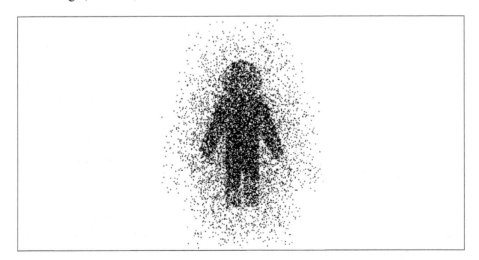

Figure II.41 Body of attitude: a dispersed individuation of the body

Body of gest

The second sign of the noosign is the body of gest. The actor can foreground a performance, execute a 'ceremonial body' (C2: 191). This body of the 'gest' (from Brecht) 'carries out a direct theatricalisation of bodies' (C2: 194). Once again, such bodies occur independently of the plot but extend attitudes into a collective enunciation (even a single body). The gest is that which links attitudes. The social dimension, where bodies are a repetition of differences, and explore the difference in repetitions. 'It is a cinema of bodies', writes Deleuze, 'which has broken all the more with the sensory-motor schema through action being replaced by attitude, and supposedly true linkage by the gest which produces … [time-image] storytelling' (C2: 198). Bodies as gest are the differentiations of the world in a body, eruptions of complex attitudes differentiated in the world. Species – all species – are captured in bodies as ahuman syntheses. The gest is the organisation of such differentiations in movement, language, thought through the image and narration ungrounding narrative.

Figure II.42 Body of gest: the linkage of attitudes creating differentiation

Cinema of the brain

The final sign of the noosign involves the mise-en-scène, the environment. It does not depend upon the physical presence of an actor, but the backgrounds, the lighting, the colours and sounds of the world of the film. Deleuze names this the 'cinema of the brain' (C2: 205). For Deleuze, certain films explore the 'identity of the brain and world' where 'landscapes are mental states, just as mental states are cartographies' and form a reciprocal 'noosphere' (C2: 205). The noosphere is an amorphous zone that fractures the coordinates of the film. It is here, in this final aspect of the noosign that cinema explores the future as terrifyingly dark, as an unending night … and conversely, as infinitely open. For the environment is immense, without horizon, without bounds. The screen becomes an image of the mind, not as dreams, recollections, relations (no more than affects, actions and perceptions). In this way 'thought no longer appears on the screen as function of the body: flashbacks, symbols and dreams, but rather is strictly identical to every image – it is cerebral space' (C2: 211). Dissonance, the interval, that which is unthought. Every image in every way is an image of thought – as an image of disjunction. As Deleuze puts it, 'the internal sheets of memory and the external layers of reality will be mixed up, extended, short circuited and form a whole moving life, which is at once that of the cosmos and the brain' (C2: 209).

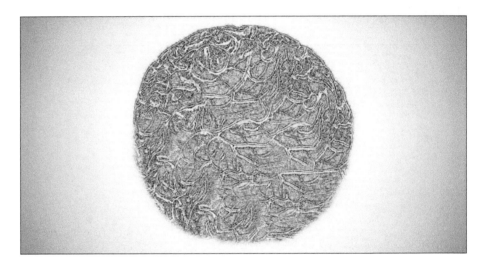

Figure II.43 Cinema of the brain: the screen as a cerebral space

*
*   *

What is a body? In *Nietzsche and Philosophy* Deleuze writes: 'We do not define it by saying that it is a field of forces, a nutrient medium fought over by a plurality of forces' (NP: 37). Such a conception already presupposes a body in which forces merely operate. Rather, 'there is no "medium", no field of forces or battle' (NP: 37). A body is a genesis of forces: 'Every force is related to others', and thus what 'defines a body is this relation … Every relationship of forces constitutes a body – whether it is chemical, biological, social or political' (NP: 37). A body is created the moment '[a]ny two forces … enter into a relationship' (NP: 37). A body – the body of attitudes, the body of gest – is thus not a human body, just as the cinema of the brain is not human consciousness. Again, Deleuze writes in *Nietzsche and Philosophy*: 'To remind consciousness of its necessary modesty is to take it for what it is: a symptom; nothing but a symptom of a deeper transformation and of the activities of entirely non-spiritual forces' (NP: 36). Noosigns describe such forces: the genesis of bodies and simultaneous genesis of consciousness, of bodies and world, the universe and its bodies. Ahuman forces – forces prior to the human which constitute and create the human and human thought. '[I]n classical cinema', writes Deleuze 'the people are there, even though they are oppressed, tricked, subject, even though blind or unconscious' (C2: 216). In the time-image the people are not given and are potentials; and so too is the world. Thus: 'the people no longer exist, or not yet … *the people are missing*' (C2: 216; Deleuze's ellipsis). Individuals, people, world are explored through constitutive forces. And noosigns are the narrative of such events – the story – that constitutes such bodies and worlds: 'the brain gives orders to the body which is just an outgrowth of it, but the body also gives orders to the brain which is just a part of it'; and concomitantly there is in this way the 'identity of the brain and world' (C2: 205). This is the domain of the noosign: to explore such forces – forces that make us think, forces of the virtual genesis of and between bodies and world, the dramatisation of forces as attitudes, gest and the brain. In this way, cinematic thought takes on a new value: which Deleuze names the lectosign.

16

Lectosigns

Lectosigns are the 'final aspect of the direct time-image, the common limit' of all time-images (C2: 279). Everything begins with opsigns and sonsigns – pure optical and sound situations. Opsigns and sonsigns appear in the aftermath of a collapse in the coordinates of the movement-image; we can no longer specify cinematic images as perception-images, affection-images, action-images or mental-images. Deleuze writes: 'we gave the name opsign (and sonsign) to the actual image cut off from its motor extension' (C2: 69). What appears on-screen are pure actualised de-differenciated images. Opsigns and sonsigns are 'slivers' of time and space which will rejoin each other as hyalosigns then chronosigns and noosigns (C2: 69). In the first place, opsigns and sonsigns are immediately hyalosigns. If the actual image no longer abides the sensory-motor trajectory, there is – for Deleuze – a simultaneous relinkage; and this relinkage is between an actual image and its virtual correlate. This is the hyalosign, the description of an image. Opsigns and sonsigns stymie the seamless flow of actual image to actual image; while the hyalosign links the actual image to its virtual. Through their very constitution, opsigns and sonsigns must become hyalosigns; an actual must relink to the virtual if delinked from other actuals. Hyalosigns – in the second place – immediately join up to create chronosigns, time-image narration. Chronosigns 'no longer concern … description, but narration' (C2: 127). The images of the film explore the 'order of time' and the 'series of time' in that they undermine linear chronology, the continuity of past, present and future (C2: 155). Narration no longer gives us a present as a product of the past and the future as consequence of the present. All of time resonates in the virtual. Finally – and in the third place – hyalosigns and chronosigns pass immediately into noosigns: image and narration give us a narrative. This is the storytelling function of the time-image – where the film explores the genesis of bodies and the world as an image of the brain. The story is the virtual arising from the disruptions of the image and narration – a new image of thought, the unthought. Noosigns, chronosigns and hyalosigns are narrative, narration and description – composed from opsigns and sonsigns: the zeroness of the time-image. Concomitantly, hyalosigns, chronosigns and noosigns are simultaneities appearing as a lectosigns, the infinite: a film that not only demands to be seen, but requires a reading: 'Noël Burch put it very well when he said that, when images cease to be linked together "naturally" ... grasping them "requires a considerable effort of memory and imagination, in other words, a reading"' (C2: 245). 'What we call reading' time-images 'is the stratigraphic condition ... To read is to relink instead of link ... a new Analytic of the image' (C2: 245). Lectosigns indicate the way in which time-images (as a complex nexus of hyalosigns, chronosigns and noosigns) need to be interpreted by the spectator. Reading, in this sense, is a trip, or journey, in to the domain of unthought, that which the film does not think.

This is the infinite of lectosigns – Coalescence: the purest virtual appearing on the brain screen as an event capturing up actual matter-images as opsigns and sonsigns (the image – frame, shot, montage, colour and sound – and its virtual). Creation: the unthought.

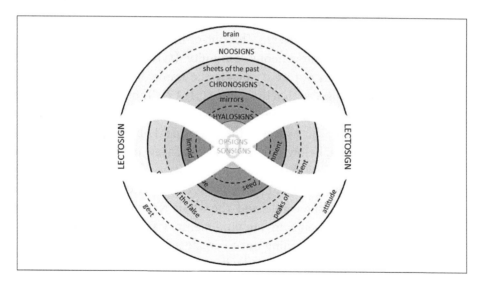

Figure II.44 Lectosigns: the infinite of the time-image

Frame, shot, montage. We have the shape and size of the frame, or aspect ratio; but the frame captures this data at different distances, from extreme big close up to extreme wide shot. Deleuze outlines five aspects of framing based on these coordinates. Firstly, the amount of data in the frame tends towards two possibilities: 'saturation' and 'rarefaction' (C1: 12). Secondly, the frame undergoes a 'geometrical *or* physical … limitation' (C1: 13). Geometrical in the sense that within the frame settings and bodies cannot help but be presented as parts: part of a landscape, part of a body. Physical in that the frame can itself undergo variance, its size can change. Thirdly, the frame is 'geometrical *or* physical' in a different way, 'in relation to the parts of the system that it both separates and brings together' (C1: 13). Thus the frame is geometric in that framing cannot but create separate data areas which relate; physical in the sense that the frame can be divided into a number of different images through technical means. Fourthly, there is the angle of framing. This can result in strange points of view. But the point of view can normally be explained by the psychological state of the character, or the disturbed social state infecting the very framing. However, there are cases which seem inexplicable, a framing that is beyond any reconciliation, pure style (C1: 15). Finally, there is the out-of-field. This is the crucial element for Deleuze, the one which orients the other four aspects. Through certain tactics, the out-of-field creates a presence through non-presence. This presence through non-presence is achieved in two ways. The first and most familiar case is that of continuity: the glance off-screen; the body part in close-up which always supposes the rest of the body; the landscape and sky in a wide shot that always supposes the rest of the land, world, universe. This out-of-field is a 'closed system', in the sense that it creates a 'homogeneous continuity' (C1: 16, 17). In contrast the second out-of-field does not exist outside the frame, but rather, as Deleuze puts it 'insists' or 'subsists' within the frame (C1: 17). Thus, it points to 'a more radical Elsewhere, outside homogenous space and time' (C1: 17). This is the virtual. In other words, this aspect of the out-of-field opens up not to what is to the right, left, above, below, behind and out of view in front of the camera (beyond the mask of the aspect ratio). Instead it 'works as a pictorial frame which isolates a system' (C1: 16). In this way, the other out-of-field creates a direct relationship with the whole, and 'the whole is the Open' and the Open 'relates back to time or even spirit', to pure memory and the virtual (C1: 17). The frame subsists, not spreading out to create a world, but to turn in upon itself. The actual images are overrun by its virtual connections: the spectator must read the image, but the connections are so weak it is the spectator's own thought that is important here, not a pre-determined response. Crucially, there are not two types of framing which give two types of out-of-field, but rather the two types of out-of-field are a condition of framing and a film can tend towards one aspect or the other. In the same way, this is the closed system which can be opened up through tactics such as extreme saturation, extreme rarefaction, physical manipulations of the frame. Framing creates both the Open and the closed system simultaneously. The movement-image tends towards the latter, the time-image towards the former.

Once frame is followed by frame we enter the domain of the shot, a domain that is finalised by the cut. The shot captures movement, movement in both space and time. There can be said to be four broad possibilities: a static camera with movement in the frame; a mobile camera with static set/data; a mobile camera with moving data/set; a static camera with static set/data. Just as in Deleuze's exploration of framing, the shot has a relation to the closed system and the Open, tending towards one or the other. This relationship is figured through the two 'facets'/'poles' of the shot: *the relationship between parts and ... the state of the whole*' (C1: 19). Relative movement is the movement of parts; absolute movement, the state of the whole. In any shot there can be a series of micro-movements, hands change position; objects are moved (taken up, put down); an aspect of the face changes. These micro-movements tend towards a continuity of movement which is the state of the whole. Further, there is the 'continuous movement of the camera', tracking shots where the reframings of the mobile camera create a continuity of space (C1: 26). A flow thus creates an interdependency upon different areas and this conception of their relationship helps construct the contingent narration of the film. In either case, there is always movement, always new data. The spectator is carried along on a flow of images which creates a closed system. However, it is also possible to construct the shot in another way. The most obvious is to put the shot under the pressure of time and restrict movement. Less new information through less movement over a long period of time (a long take) results in the spectator having to contemplate the image in-and-for-itself rather than simply see it in order to understand what will come next. These tactics 'realise the other power of the out-of-field' (C1: 28). In other words, the power of the shot is elsewhere other than in its place within the film. This elsewhere is not its actual cinematic materiality, but what the image engenders in the brain of the spectator, its virtual coordinate. The virtual coordinates of a shot overrun the actualised on-screen images and require the spectator to think the film, to read the images and to think about them. Long takes are by no means the only method of creating the Open through the shot; we will see this ability in cases of depth-of-field, micro-shooting, the endless tracking shot. In these ways and others the shot comes under the pressure of time, or disturbs space and creates the Open.

We enter the domain of montage once the shot is cut and edited to another shot. In the movement-image there is continuity from 'shot to montage and from montage to shot' (C2: 42). Firstly, perception-images, affection-images and action-images are linked to create a domain where the environment and the behaviour of characters are connected through emotions. This is achieved through the logical linkage of wide shots (perception-images/environment), medium shots (action-images/behaviour) and close-ups (affection-images/ emotions). Secondly, situations and actions are linked through parallel and convergent montage or episodic sequencing: the formulae of the action-image. Thirdly, the thoughts of characters are embodied by natural and abstract relations, symbols, dreams and flashbacks: habitual memory-images that englobe the characters in the sensory-motor system. The spectator is caught up in the flow of images, in the flow of movement. The movement-image thus creates the closed system. In the time-image, in contradistinction, what is forestalled is this continuity of movement. On the one hand, as we have already seen, the time-image 'no longer asks how images are linked' but rather 'what does the image *show*?' (C2: 42). Essentially, 'there is no longer an alternative between montage and shot' (C2: 42). On the other hand, images tend to be edited together destroying the possibility of a logical space–time continuum. Jump-cuts disrupt flows and spatial conventions are dissembled: shot–reverse shots disappear in favour of more nebulous connections between characters. These editing strategies – and many more – create the time-image.

Colour. The introduction of colour did not immediately tighten the bonds of the movement-image. Rather, it initially seems to have had the opposite effect. After seeing his first colour film in 1935 Rudolf Arnheim wrote that after leaving the cinema 'I had a terrible experience – I saw the world as a colour film … everything was blatant in its poisonous colour, and presented a chaotic, fiendish, discordant picture' (Dalle Vacche and Price; 2006: 55). It was, of course, the American cinema which first seriously experimented with colour through the Technicolor process (Dalle Vacche and Price; 2006: 30). J. P. Telotte notes that Technicolor began a discourse of promoting the 'natural' reproduction of colour against claims that it was 'artificial and distracting' (Dalle Vacche and Price; 2006: 31). However, as Robert Edmond Jones saw it at the time, 'colour and Hollywood's idea of colour are two different things' (Dalle Vacche and Price; 2006: 31). Astutely, he went on to recognise that 'the audience would forget [film] was coloured' as the process improved (Dalle Vacche and Price; 2006: 31). Improve the process did. Correspondingly, audiences forgot the images were colour. It took the development of the more natural Eastman process to fully realise a natural colour balance, return coloured images to the movement-image and strengthen the bonds of realism. However, Deleuze opposes the *coloured image* of the movement-image with the *colour-image* of the time-image (C1: 117–18). The coloured image tends towards invisibility. The colour-image – the pure optical colour situation – is visible. For Deleuze the 'principle forms of … the true colour-image' are 'the surface-colour of the great uniform tints, the atmospheric colour which pervades all others', and 'the *absorbent* characteristic' where one colour infects all others (C1: 118). But also, it should be considered that use of black and white during the colour period is not simply a sign of economic restrictions or historical signification, but also a form of resistance. Thus in different situations black and white, the reintroduction of Technicolour and the uniformity of colour can all produce time-images of immense power.

Sound. For Deleuze, the coming of the sound film simply moved music from the orchestra pit and speech as intertitles (and – in some cases – narrators) to the sound track on optical film. This integration served to strengthen the bonds of realism. Critically – and paradoxically, perhaps – this means that in the movement-image the audio becomes '*a new dimension of the visual image, a new component*' (C2: 226). This interesting proposal has its origins in the work of Michel Chion on sound in the cinema. For Chion, 'there is no soundtrack' as such (Chion, 1994: 39). Rather, visual image and sound image are inextricably linked; it is difficult to judge where one ends and the other begins. The crux of Chion's argument is that the relationship between the visual image and the sound image in film is not natural. Chion writes: 'the audiovisual relationship [is] a contract – that is … the opposite of a natural relationship arising from some sort of pre-existing harmony among the perceptions' (Chion, 1994: xxvi). In this way, Chion's analysis of the sound in film is always in relation to the visual image. In *Le Son au cinéma* (1985) Chion outlines a tripartite division of sound in the film: on-screen; off-screen and nondiegetic. On-screen sound is sound that emanates from within the visual image (a band on-screen, for instance). Off-screen sound is that which is 'acousmatic', 'sounds one hears without seeing their originating cause' (a band off-screen) (Chion, 1994: 71). Of course, in many films, a sound source can be firstly acousmatic then visualised, or vice versa. Nondiegetic sound describes sound external to the direct presentation of the film, be it music or voice-over narration. Some problems can be seen in this schema: for instance, a voice-over could in the trajectory of the film be reconciled to a character. Chion thus went on to refine his categorisation in *Audiovision* (1990). While not meant to be exhaustive, the additions allow a further consideration of the layers of sound in film. In his second schema ambient sound is background noise such as traffic or bird calls: sounds which do not raise the question of their source – or even presence – to the spectator. Chion describes them as a 'pervasive and continuous presence' and also labels them 'territory-sound' (Chion, 1994: 75). Internal sounds, in contrast, are the subjective and objective sounds situated within the film emanating from a character, be they sounds of breathing (objective) or voiced-thinking (subjective). On-the-air sound is sound originating from devices such as radios and telephones: and of course, these sounds can (through the progression of the film) either enter or leave the visual image.

While these distinct components might seemingly cohere into what is known as the soundtrack, a sound continuum that lies parallel with the visual track, Chion states that this is not the case. He arrives at this important thesis through a consideration of the terms 'counterpoint' and 'harmony', or rather, the vertical and horizontal function of sound in film. Counterpoint refers to simultaneous horizontal organisation of music and voice which is both individual and consistent. However, Chion believes this figuration of the relationship between visuals and sound to be inaccurate. Rather, he sees the relationship as vertical. This vertical, or harmonic, figuration makes a convincing argument. For example, voice sounds are tied to facial movements. The crucial term for Chion then is 'synchresis', which also relates to music and sound-effects. This is the point Deleuze picks up on with regard to the movement-image, writing: 'we might say that the sound components are separate only in the abstraction of their pure hearing', in effect 'they are a ... fourth dimension of the visual image' (C2: 235). For Deleuze, after Chion, the image is a composite of visual and auditory information: 'they all form together one single component, a continuum' (C2: 235). Synchresis is thus a tendency that is very hard to disrupt. Chion, on the whole, is quite scathing about what he calls the 'disjunctive ideology' (Chion, 1994: 98). He writes: 'the disjunctive ... impulse that predominates in intellectual discourse on the question ("wouldn't it be better if sound and image were independent?") arises entirely from the unitary illusion' (Chion, 1994: 97). In other words, the unitary illusion is that sound and image are naturally bound (horizontal, related through counterpoint) rather than forming a contract as seen through the idea of synchresis. Chion further states that 'the false unity this thinking denounced in the [modern cinema] implicitly suggests a true unity existing elsewhere' (Chion, 1994: 98). However, Chion does see a possibility for disruption in the avoidance of complex on-screen sound. Music, which acts to reinforce affection or action, can be suppressed. Sound effects can be removed, thus reducing the spatial out-of-field. The voice can be denaturalised using 'theatrical speech', 'textual speech' (where the voice overloads the visual image), 'decentering' (where the visual images overload the sound images) and the 'use of foreign languages' without subtitles (Chion, 1994: 170). These tactics, rather than destroy any supposed unity between sound and vision, expose the audiovisual contract and create the time-image.

The unthought. Cinema *is* movement. For Deleuze this means cinema communicates *'vibrations to the cortex, touching the nervous and cerebral system directly'* producing a 'shock' to thought (C2: 156). Deleuze goes on to invoke Martin Heidegger's concept of the shock to thought, the 'nooshock', and explores this through Eisenstein's film theory. '[T]he dialectical method' allows Eisenstein to 'decompose the nooshock into particularly well determined moments', although Deleuze believes 'the whole of the analysis is valid for classical cinema' (C2: 146, 156). For Eisenstein, filmwork is necessarily composed of two specifics: '*Primo*: photo-fragments of nature are recorded; *secundo*: these fragments are combined in various ways. Thus, the shot (or frame), and thus, montage' (Eisenstein, 1977d: 3). This is the famous 'collision' of shots in contradistinction to the invisibility of the edit (Eisenstein, 1977a: 49). Invisible editing consists of each frame transition being cut on a movement, and being joined with another shot in movement to hide the compositional nature of film. The 'collision' of shots through editing has an opposite purpose. It is in no way meant to be invisible, but to draw attention to itself, to foreground it as an act of creation. For Eisenstein, 'montage is an idea that arises from the collision of independent shots – shots even opposite to one another' (Eisenstein, 1977c: 29). This is a dialectical approach to film editing developed as Soviet montage. Eisenstein's purpose is clear, it is to use cinema as a shock to thought. He writes: 'what an unexpected intellectual *shock* came to America and Europe with the appearance of films in which social problems were suddenly presented' (Eisenstein 1977b: 179; my italics). However, as Deleuze writes, 'everyone knows that, if an art necessarily imposed the shock or vibration, the world would have changed long ago, and men would have been thinking for a long time' (C2: 157). The very idea of a shock to thought is, for Deleuze, a ruse. He continues 'this pretension of the cinema, at least among the greatest pioneers, raises a smile today' (C2: 157). For Heidegger, the problem of the nooshock is clear: 'man can think in the sense that he possesses the possibility to do so. This possibility alone, however, is no guarantee to us that we are capable of thinking' (C2: 157). For Deleuze, the problem with this conception of the nooshock in the movement-image is that it relies upon the sensory-motor situation. The thoughts the action-image can give rise to tend to be only the ones given to the audience as actualised images. In other words, an image that shocks allows the spectator to think about that image, but in that context alone, in the existing coordinates. The paradox is that the shock to thought closes down thought rather than opening it up, or rather, limits thought to the response given in the actualised images on-screen. There are thus, as far as Deleuze can see, three shortcomings to the nooshock of the cinema of the movement-image. Firstly, mediocrity; secondly, propaganda; and thirdly, the absurd. The first two categories are embodied by 'commercial figurative cinema' and the last by 'abstract experimentalism' (C2: 165). However, such abstract experimentalism, for Deleuze, may also be 'oddly capable of restoring hope in a possibility in the thinking of cinema through cinema' (C2: 165). The pathway from 'abstract experimentalism' to the time-image and true thought can be explored through the writings of Antonin Artaud. Deleuze writes that Artaud sees cinema as 'a matter of neuro-physiological vibrations, and that the image must produce a shock, a nerve-wave which gives rise to thought, "for thought is a matron who has not always existed"' (C2: 165). This might seem, at first, similar to the Eisensteinian concept of shock, yet this is not the case. For Artaud, cinema cannot give rise to thought through commercial and propagandist shock-images; thought cannot arise through 'a succession of images' (Artaud 1972: 65). Rather, true thought arises through 'something more imponderable ... with no interpositions or representations' (Artaud 1972: 66). For Deleuze, Artaud's formulation amounts to this: 'what [the time-image] cinema advances is not the power of thought but its 'impower''' (C2: 166). To understand what Deleuze is attempting to articulate necessitates a brief return to Heidegger and his 1951 lectures *Was heist Denken?* (*What Is Called Thinking?*). For Heidegger, thinking is something that must be learned, not simply copied: 'we can learn thinking only if we can radically unlearn what thinking has been traditionally' (Heidegger 1972: 25). Traditionally, then, for Heidegger, thinking has meant relational, law-like activities. We think to act: 'so far man has acted too much, and thought too little' (Heidegger 1972: 25). The reason for this is that what really needs to be thought about are the things that have not yet been thought. Of course, this presents a radical problem in traditional accounts of thought, for thinking requires an initial object or stimulus, the impetus of a perception. As Heidegger puts it, 'the reason why thought has failed to appear ... [is] because what is to be thought about, what properly gives food for thought has long been withdrawing' (Heidegger 1972: 25). That which has been withdrawing becomes that which must be thought about: 'this withdrawal is what properly gives food for thought, what is most thought-provoking' (Heidegger 1972: 25). Or, as Heidegger puts it in *The Essence of Truth*: 'The truth of the statement about the essence of man can never be scientifically proven. It cannot be established by reference to facts, nor can it be derived from principles in a formal-logical manner. This is not a deficiency' (*The Essence of Truth*: 62–3). This is because 'what is essential always remains unprovable, or more precisely, lies outside the sphere of provability and un-provability' (*The Essence of Truth*: 63).

The cinema of the movement-image asks the spectator to think directly about what is actualised on-screen. In order to do this it must produce images to be thought about. Unfortunately, in so doing, it actually closes down thought, giving the spectator the 'answers', so to speak. The time-image, by contrast, operates by providing indeterminate, delinked images, radically compromising the givens of the movement-image. This is why some spectators, critics and theorists believe the modern cinema is that which, as Noël Burch puts it, will 'never be seen' (Myer 2004: 78). For the 'multiplex spectator', the modernist cinema is a dud. The crucial question must be, why do these posited spectators believe time-image cinema to be 'boring'? The answer is that expectations of the cinema come from the movement-image; we expect a film to be engaging, to lock us in. When it doesn't, we feel that there must be something wrong with us – or far more likely – something wrong with the film. If we are watching a film and suddenly realise we have not been thinking about the film but have been following their own thoughts, have drifted off, we panic, believe we have betrayed the cinema, or that the cinema has betrayed us. However, this ability to allow the spectator to access the virtual is – for Deleuze – the very power of the time-image. The impower of the actual. It is this power that time-image narration brings, for it no longer concerns the actual on-screen images, but the virtual. The virtual is the interstice, the gap. That which is not given. The time-image gives us that which is unthought. Images as fragments in the hyalosign, the coalescence of fragments in the chronosign as narration, and the interstice between fragments in the noosign as narrative. A new image of thought, the image of the unthought.

* *
*

Lectosigns are the pure virtual: ∞. Time-images can thus be considered as 'the plane of composition that restores the infinite to us' created from 'a finite composite sensation', opsigns and sonsigns (WP: 197). The collapse in the links of the movement-image, the crisis of the action-image (situation → action) and the non-emergence of compositional signs after the perception-image are the three moments in the creation of opsigns and sonsigns, pure actual optical- and sound-images, the actual de-differenciated image. Frame, shot, montage, colour and sound – all the coordinates of cinema – are attacked, and, in being attacked, destroyed. This is the zeroness of the time-image, the point at which everything begins anew, a new conception and cineosis of the image, narration and narrative; or hyalosigns, chronosigns and noosigns – each an exploration of actual–virtual correlates. Noosigns, chronosigns and hyalosigns are narrative, narration and description – composed from opsigns and sonsigns. Concomitantly, hyalosigns, chronosigns and noosigns are simultaneities appearing as a lectosign: a film that not only demands to be seen, but necessitates interpretation.

Afterword to Part One: the unfolded cineosis

'A film', writes Deleuze, 'is never made up of a single kind of image ... hence the inter-assemblage ...' (C1: 70). Every film is composed of lectosigns, noosigns, chronosigns, hyalosigns, opsigns and sonsigns, perception-images, affection-images, impulse-images, action-images (small and large), reflection-images (figures of attraction, inversion and discourse), mental-images (dreams, recollections and relations). Cinema is a univocal matter-image composed of a matrix of actual images that have virtual correlates – to a greater or lesser degree. Every film is an assemblage of every genetic sign and all the compositional signs of the cineosis. A character or characters will emerge from out of gaseous perception, creating a centre or centres through liquid perception towards a solid perception of a subject. These characters will gather up the amorphous intensities – qualities and powers – of the any-space-whatever, entering into dividual relations with the mass and becoming an icon which expresses affects through the face. Such affects will pass into action: as impulses and symptoms of the world of primal forces; as behaviours which both reveal the world and attempt to resolve the world through the determined situation. Such characters and such situations can be reflected upon and so be transformed through cinematic figures equivalent to metaphors, metonyms, inversions, problems and questions. And these films will – furthermore – allow characters their dreams and imaginations, their memories, and allow them to understand and comprehend the world through mental relations. Yet, at every moment, and at every juncture, the grounding of such a sensory-motor system is ungrounded. The characters may find themselves dissolving into a background to be swallowed up by gaseous perception, the any-space-whatever. The film may start to fragment, chronological time, comprehensive space and human consciousness may disperse, become displaced and dissipate. Opsigns and sonsigns are the negative condition of such dispersion, displacement and dissipation. No longer can the sensory-motor system describe the link between images. Accordingly, new ways of describing the film are needed, a new terminology, a new semiotic that takes into account not only the linking of actual image to actual image, but the virtual correlates of an image which relink fragments. Hyalosigns are image fragments which retain their fragmentary nature and coalesce as narration as chronosigns. Chronosigns are narration which disrupt the order of time, space and consciousness through the series of images. And such narration gives us narratives as noosigns: the genesis of bodies and worlds, the forces which create a new image of cinematic thought. This is the lectosign, an image which must and can only be interpreted, and which can only appear as an interpretation. In this way, the noosphere is the overwhelming of the actual image by its virtual correlates. Time-images and movement-images: the de-differenciation and differenciation of the univocal cinematic image through a multiplicity of signs.

Yet, every frame, shot, sequence, film, cycle of movies will coalesce or disperse through the differenciation of the actual and the de-differenciation of the virtual. And such coalescences or ungroundings will order the signs of which every such frame, etc. is composed. A sign will arise, making an image, avatar and domain dominant. All other images will circulate and dissipate around this sign. We will – in this way – be able to discover how a sign becomes the principle of the film, and so be able to say this film accords with such a sign. 'A film', writes Deleuze, 'is never made up of a single kind of image … Nevertheless a film, at least in its most simple characteristics, always has one type of image which is dominant … a point of view on the whole of the film … itself a "reading" of the whole film' (C1: 70). Every film is an ascendancy of a sign of the cineosis.

movement-image

	domain of perception	domain of affect	domain of affect	domain of action		domain of thought
	0	I	II / I	II	reflection- III/II images	III
	perception-image	**affection-image**	**impulse-image**	**action-images**		**mental-images**

perception-image (0): solid / liquid / gaseous

affection-image (I): icon / dividual / any-space-whatever

impulse-image (II / I): symptom / fetish / originary world
degenerate affect embryonic action

action-image - large (II — action-images): milieu / binomial / imprint

transformation of forms: figures of attraction / figures of inversion / figures of discourse

action-image - small: index of lack / index of equivocity / vector

reflection- III/II images:
- **attraction-image**: theatrical / plastic / *mise-en-abyme*
- **inversion-image**: sublime / enfeebled / *quotidian*
- **discourse-image**: limit of large action-image / limit of small action-image / *limit of action-images*

degenerate action embryonic thought

mental-images (III):
- **relation-image**: mark / demark / symbol
- **recollection-image**: *strong* destiny / *weak* destiny / forking paths
- **dream-image**: rich dreams / restrained dreams / movement of the world

components

domain	avatar
image	1st sign of composition
	2nd sign of composition
	genetic sign

interrelations

a: III←II←I←[0] ↔ ∞

b: II←(III←I)←0 ↔ ∞

c: III→[cII]←I←0 ↔ ∞

time-image

domain of unthought	0		∞

opsigns & sonsigns

- **hyalosigns**: mirrors / limpid and opaque / seed and environment
- **chronosigns**: sheets of the past / peaks of the present / powers of the false
- **noosigns**: body of attitude / body of gest / cinema of the brain

lectosigns

Part Two

Enfolding the Cineosis

A film … always has one type of image which is dominant … a point of view on the whole of the film … itself a 'reading' of the whole film. (C1: 70)

Classification schemes … are flexible, their criteria vary according to the cases presented. (TRM: 285)

Section III

Third Introduction

Cinematographics (1995–2015)

A cineotic sign is produced the moment a film image encounters a concept; and, reciprocally, when a philosophical concept encounters an image. A sign captures, creates, orients and reorients, releases, undermines, problematises thought. Thinking, thinking cinema, can thus begin or end with the image. And the image – for Deleuze – is scalar, something fractal: a frame, shot, sequence, movie, or cycle of films (expressing an event, an idea of a director, cinematographer, actor or actors, a genre, theme, story, questions, problems, and so on). Every cinematographic image is thus complex, a matrix of signs. Any image is composed of many forces, every frame, shot, sequence, film, cycle is composed of all of Deleuze's cineotic signs – more or less. Yet these images are signs vying for domination; where one sign ascends and shapes, corrals, supresses and ungrounds the other signs that surround it. In this way, as an immediate correlate, any image is a singularity. Every frame, shot, sequence, film, cycle describes the ascendancy of a sign, and thus a perspective on the image. Accordingly, Section III – through its 44 short chapters – explores an image of the cinema through one of the signs explicated in Section II and generated in Section I. Each of the films encountered is taken from the period 1995–2015 (the first two decades of the second century of cinema, this period as vital as any in movie history); and each – in its own way – is an exceptional cinematographic event. Necessarily, these encounters will sometimes be fleet of foot – I have, however, attempted to give each exploration as much time, space and thought as is needed for something productive to happen.

1

Le scaphandre et la papillon/
The Diving Bell and the Butterfly

Solid perception

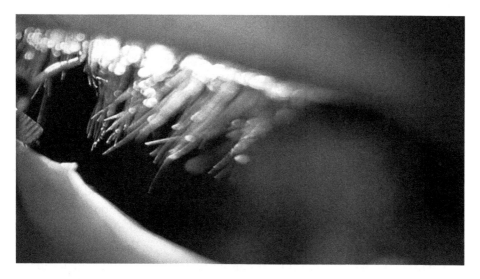

Frame III.01 *The Diving Bell and the Butterfly* (Julian Schnabel, France | USA, 2007)

A black screen: darkness. Silence. Breathing ...

A blurred, flickering, indistinct image – then darkness once again.

'Mr Bauby, keep your eyes open.' The voice, which belongs to Dr Cocheton, is coming through in waves. 'You're going to be fine, I promise.' It soon becomes apparent – to Jean-Dominique Bauby – that he is not going to be fine, at least not by any definition of 'fine' he would have had prior to awaking in a bed in the Naval Hospital in Berck-sur-Mer. He has had a stroke and has been in a coma for three weeks. Visited by neurologist Dr Lepage, he is diagnosed as having suffered a cerebrovascular accident which has 'put his brain stem out of action'. The link between Bauby's brain and spinal column no longer fires; it is broken, he is paralysed. His mind is unaffected, and he can see and hear (sense functions that do not depend upon the brain stem), but Jean-Do can neither move nor speak. He has 'locked-in syndrome'. So begins *The Diving Bell and the Butterfly*.

These awakenings (from the coma; to his situation) are filmed from Jean-Do's point of view. The camera is his perception. Circumscribed by flesh, eyelids frame the visual field which mimics, using a blurred image, his early attempts at focusing. Blinking performs jump-cuts, the closing of his weary eyes fade the image to black and ends a sequence. Framing, shot and montage are organically linked to Jean-Do's body. Filmed from a prone, bed-bound position, the mise-en-scène is restricted to a wall and ceiling, all events must enter and exit this visual field – the camera is a fixed point. Doctors, nurses, carers, friends and family are either partially out of view, too close or too far away. One of his eyes fails him, the upper and lower lids are stitched together – we see the needle and thread sewing shut the frame. The spectator thus experiences the film as Jean-Do experiences the world; director Julian Schnabel's cinematic process is one that attempts the most extreme identification. Not only visually, but also in the sound field – as well as the words of others, we hear the thoughts of Jean-Do. Articulated in voice-over, the consciousness of an as yet unseen body expresses fear, anger, and frustration. Feelings and emotions Jean-Do is unable to share with the outside film-world.

Treatment is improbable, but rehabilitation possible. By blinking once for 'yes', twice for 'no', Jean-Do's speech therapist Henriette Durand finds a way for him to communicate. Immediately, the film begins to relinquish the radical constraints and limitations of the character point-of-view shot. He dreams – and these imaginings are depicted on-screen. Underwater, in the icy sea; drowning? Upon his being asked 'Were you the editor of *Elle*?', we encounter, in flashback, Jean-Do at a photo-shoot; we see Bauby for the first time, entering the studio, a vital presence interacting with the photographer and the models. Progressively, then, character point-of-view shots are augmented with dream-images and recollection-images. Jean-Do is wheeled out of his room, and catches a fleeting reflection of his haggard, unrecognisable, palsied face. From this moment forward, director Julian Schnabel will tend to place Jean-Do's body within the frame: sitting swathed in blankets on the Naval Hospital balcony; with a personal assistant working on his book; with his children and his children's mother on the windswept beach.

The Diving Bell and the Butterfly would thus appear to incrementally abandon subjective perception for objective perception, and in so doing compromise the immediacy of the identification between character and audience. 'It could be said', writes Deleuze, 'that the subjective-image is ... the set as it is seen by someone who forms part of that set' (C1: 71). Correspondingly, 'we should be able to say ... that the image is objective when the thing or the set are seen from the viewpoint of someone who remains external to that set' (C1: 71). Yet these distinctions, for Deleuze, are nominal; and *The Diving Bell and the Butterfly* similarly problematises such a formula. For the film remains unremittingly subjective – in that it is concerned with a privileged image: Jean-Do. Jean-Do: an all-encompassing centre, the perceiver and the perceived. A character we see and see with; a character around which all the images of the film circulate and revolve. Eliding character perception (the point-of-view shot) with the subjective and a perception of the character (inside the frame) with the objective fails both film-philosophy and the trajectory of the film. Camera perception is always varied: it might attempt to stand in for a character in the set either directly (point-of-view) or indirectly (over-the-shoulder); it might attempt to become a non-existent character within the set in-the-action or stand back from the image capturing events in the wide. Yet these techniques are neither inherently subjective nor objective. Rather, as 'Bergsonism suggests', asserts Deleuze, '*a subjective perception is one in which the images vary in relation to a central and privileged image*' (C1: 76). Subjective perception is a perception-image that creates a solid I. This is solid perception where all images in the film are organised to create a 'molar' or 'formal consciousness' (C1: 80). *The Diving Bell and the Butterfly* is a film exploring solid perception. The film is the story of one individual, Jean-Dominique Bauby. Accordingly, the transition from the point-of-view shot to the perception of the body within the frame describes and narrates the triumphant rebirth of Jean-Do, his re-entry into the social assemblage, his retaking his place in the world as writer, lover, father and friend. Rather than a relinquishing of subjectivity, the film creates a trajectory describing a strengthening, a territorialisation, the differenciation of a subject.

2

Timecode

Liquid perception

Frame III.02 *Timecode* (Mike Figgis, USA, 2000)

In an elegant white business suit, Lauren skips down the stone steps leading away from the mansion. Parked in the driveway are two cars, a sleek black limousine with attendant uniformed chauffeur and an old, slightly battered, run-around. Carefully kneeling at the rear of the second car, Lauren releases the air from the tyre, before being offered the passenger door of her limo by her driver. Rose, arriving just moments later, immediately perceives her car has a flat. This scene is a moment in a long take filmed with a handheld mobile camera. Such mobility allows the characters to be followed, relinquished, and recaptured at varying distance (from long shot to medium shot to close-up) – all without montage (without editing between framings). In this way, while the presence of camera can be felt – through its movements, through its anticipations of character trajectories, in the moments when nothing happens, in its aberrations – it appears as if outside the set, as an existential non-presence in the film-world. Yet, when Rose spies the tyre, the camera tilts and pans, following the direction of her gaze, simultaneously reorienting its position, a movement allowing it to become her vision. The camera has aligned with the point of view of a character; it has become the perception of that character; the camera is – for a moment – the character. Camera eye becomes human eye; and then the human eye relinquishes the camera eye as the action within the event continues. Rose is pissed off, and suspicious, must now accept a ride with Lauren. That this exchange has happened with no montage (cutting from a perception of the character to the character's perception) makes it a visceral encounter with shifting modes of cinematic image through the visibility of the flow of a transformation. This is a moment of liquid perception, an instant in *Timecode* capturing the cinematic philosophy of the movie. For the entire film is composed of such flows, of liquid perception.

First flow: the spatial dimensions of the frame. The screen is divided into four areas. The top right quadrant, the first to become active, captures Emma in a therapy session talking about a dream involving herself, her partner Alex, and a dream about a small cut that 'won't stop bleeding'. Next, the top left quadrant fades-in; here is the encounter between Lauren and her lover Rose. The bottom left quadrant opens with a shot of a security system display screen (a recurrence, of a kind; itself divided into four, each showing a different area within an office complex) before pulling back to reveal the Red Mullet foyer. Finally, the bottom right quadrant films a masseur in blue T-shirt and shorts attempting to cross through the traffic of a hectic boulevard. This quartered frame is maintained throughout *Timecode*, an unyielding permanent and visible montage by way of the geometrical distribution of images; and it is across these spatial distributions that the eye of the viewer will flow from one quadrant to the next: something in another frame snagging the spectator's attention, the movement of perception becoming a flow without montage.

Second flow: the temporal dimensions of the film. Each of the four quadrants is filmed in a single take, in real time. Emma will continue to relate her problems to her analyst before heading off to confront Alex, and the camera follows; Rose and Lauren will travel in the limo in uncomfortable silence, and the camera follows; a security guard will prowl the Red Mullet corridors, and the camera follows; and the masseur will make it across the boulevard unscathed, and the camera follows. And so on, for the entirety of the film, each quadrant its own film which flows without cutting, with no editing. Following a character or set of characters for some moments, then tagging on to a new event. This is the power of the mobile camera and the long take: moving from space to space, continuous reframings, transformations between camera eye and human eye, seamless trajectories from wide shot to medium shot and close-up. Director Mike Figgis says he created the film using 'fluid moves' (*Director's Video Diary*, 2000).

Third flow: the nexus of spatial and temporal dimensions. The spatial and temporal dimensions flow into one another. In the bottom right quadrant the masseur enters an office block, at the same moment entering the frame of the bottom left quadrant, the Red Mullet foyer. The four quadrants are simultaneous, the events within each taking place at the same time – linked by the same timecode – and they will all eventually converge on the same space, Red Mullet. Time, space and characters flow between the quarters of the frame.

Fourth flow: the audio element – music, voice, sound effects. On the one hand, languid jazz permeates and overwhelms the entire audio field – repeating refrains and themes, music flows, coalescing the visuals. Accordingly, the eye wanders the zones with something approaching freedom. On the other hand, the vocal and sound effect elements of a certain quadrant come to the fore (reciprocally, these elements fading in the three other quadrants). In this way the eye is drawn to a particular scene, yet, equally, may explore the three now-silent images with curiosity, frustration – what is being said there? What is happening now? In early screenings of *Timecode* Figgis would arrange these audio elements live, 'each mix … different from the one before' (*Director's Video Diary*, 2000).

Fifth flow: characters as multiple centres. The film creates no central image, no single character is maintained as or becomes an axis of privilege. Centres will form in one of the quadrants, for a moment, but the camera will move on, leave them behind, find someone or something new. Even when two or more cameras converge upon the same event, it is from differing perspectives, evoking the nature of a centre as a multiplicity. Furthermore, the four frames are often crowded with people and the characters talk over one another. The privileged image is resisted and centres are fleeting, perspectival. This is the flow of body to body, consciousness to consciousness.

Sixth flow: the liquefaction of the Earth. The film is punctuated by little earthquakes, the solid ground becoming a liquid flow. No doubt these periodic events serve to solidify the links between the spatio-temporalities of the four frames; yet at the same moment they function as an ungrounding of the coordinates of the milieu, prefiguring and echoing the disintegrations of the lives of the various characters. Alex and Rose are having an affair, and this is discovered by Emma and Lauren. At the same moment Alex is using Rose and Rose using Alex – each in their own way. Both Lauren and Emma are betrayed. Everything is falling apart, dissolving.

Seventh flow: self-reflexivity. Towards the end of the film – before the murder – all four cameras converge on the Red Mullet conference room for Ana's pitch: 'Montage has created a fake reality … My film … one continuous moment … Real time … Imagine four cameras … each of these four cameras will follow a character … the characters are going to meet with each other … creating the plot of the story.' A self-reflexive commentary on the filmic process of *Timecode*, a recursion of realities, where one reality flows into another.

Timecode – in every way – is a film of flows, of liquid perception.

3

Naqoyqatsi

Gaseous perception

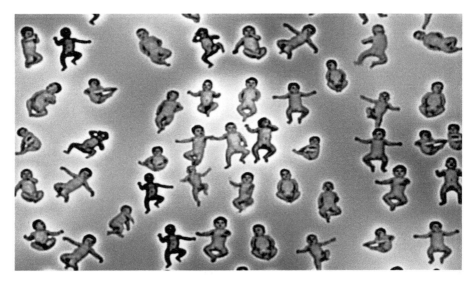

Frame III.03 *Naqoyqatsi* (Godfrey Reggio, USA, 2002)

Autumnal monochrome: a long, slow zoom-in upon a three-dimensional rendering of Pieter Bruegel's painting *The (Little) Tower of Babel* (*c.*1563). Corkscrewing upwards from the ground the expansive base of the edifice supports a conical structure, still far from complete – and apparently already in the process of disintegration. In every way, an impossible project. Everything appears unstable, askew; the construction sinking into the ground upon which it has been built; the non-perpendicular arches (supporting the gentle incline of the spiral concourse) a threat, the spectre of collapse. A male choir chants 'na-qoy-qat-si'. The drumming of a heartbeat. Cut to an image of the disused and decaying Michigan Central Railway Depot: first the murky, dank interior;

then the exterior in glorious sunlight. The camera explores this neo-classical architecture cutting between vertiginous crane-shots, extended tracking shots and almost imperceptible pans. Pulsating cello repeats phrasing, orchestral strings gather and shimmer. A raging sea – heavily digitalised. Mountain tops, the stars slash the dark firmament with light. A river, the still surface reflecting the clouds of the sky above – insubstantial forms that race and churn in fast-mo doubled as mirror images. A purely digital environment: black space mapped with a flat grid of white contour lines; the animation erupting to create a complex, flourishing conical structure – a structure reminiscent of and echoing Bruegel's tower.

So begins Godfrey Reggio's *Naqoyqatsi*, a film composed of hundreds, thousands of disparate visual images, accompanying and accompanied by the music-images of Philip Glass. This is gaseous perception. Here, as Deleuze describes it, 'all the images vary as a function of each other, on all their facets and in all their parts' (C1: 80). A film of gaseous perception will be created from fragments, fragments which not only retain but accentuate their fragmentary nature, fragments that resonate with each other both in the immediate sequence and across the entirety of the movie. This is the molecular image: images as atoms rebounding from one another; images as forces acting upon one another. Each image in-itself undergoes many manipulations: slowed down, speeded up; given depth or flattened out; negativised, drained of colour, recoloured, permeated by a colour. Each image is worked upon and reworked through various technologies: 'torturing the image', as Reggio puts it (*Life is War*, 2002). Sometimes these manipulations are brutal, but sometimes beautiful; sometimes primitive, sometimes cutting-edge. Gaseous perception is non-human perception: 'everything', writes Deleuze, 'is at the service of variation and interaction: slow or high speed shots, superimpositions, fragmentation, deceleration, micro-shooting' (C1: 80–1). The film perceives with a 'non-human eye' or (after Dziga Vertov) a pure 'cine-eye' (C1: 81). An 'acentred' system (C1: 76). It is matter as image perceiving image as matter: back and forth, within the image and from image to image, across all images.

One of the most startling moments of *Naqoyqatsi*: a shot focuses upon the face of a baby. Immediately, the camera slowly zooms out – backwards, upwards – revealing the baby to be lying on a clinical, white, flat surface; as the camera recedes, the baby is discovered as being but one of many. A limited number of babies, each a replicated image, the same baby in different spatial positions, duplicated, triplicated, and so on. A molecular arrangement of babies, a non-human image of humanity. This is how the universe sees bodies, imperceptible variations of matter-images. Reggio will pursue and create such signs in any number of ways. People are shot as crowds en masse, in slow–mo, the image in negative. People are shot in series-types: various athletes preparing for action, in action; famous figures from history captured through their waxworks. The body is filmed through medical technologies, brain scans, X-rays, thermal imaging. Sperm and eggs. Humanity and other animals. Nature and architecture. Digital spirals, fractals, compositions. Such an assemblage of cinematic perceptions may appear as chaos; yet the acentred is not without organisation and structure. Organisation and structure are molecular. The images of *Naqoyqatsi* resonate with each other: image with image; image with sequence; sequence with sequence; and so on – between and within the visuals and the music. The film is organised into nine movements each with its own music-image trajectory, each with its own colour palette, each with its own types of visual images. Yet any coherence is the coherence of disparate fragments, a war of forces, molecularity. Such gaseous perception is thus the enunciation of a theme. The final image of the film is an intertitle, a text-image. It reads: 'Naqoyqatsi: from the Hopi language < each other – kill many – life > 1. a life of killing each other. 2. war as a way of life. 3. (*interpretation*) civilised violence.' *Naqoyqatsi* explores the forces of its own cohesion. The molecular babies are riven with intensive forces and are a genesis of forces within a collective. Bruegel's *The (Little) Tower of Babel* – as is, and as explicated by Reggio – captures the moment between assemblage and fragmentation, between homogeneity and heterogeneity, between creation and entropy. *Naqoyqatsi* is a film of the indifference and differences of the acentred universe. So many signs of the war at the heart of life, with life, for life.

4

Theeviravaathi/The Terrorist

Icon

Frame III.04 *The Terrorist* (Santosh Sivan, India, 1998)

Malli is nineteen. Her eyes captivate: large, luminous white with hazel then ebony centres. Her lips are generous, but secretive. Hair lustrous: long, black, straight. Her dark skin glows with vitality. A face of gentle features, yet with a strength that belies her years. This is how the screen sees Malli – in close-up, and extreme close-up. A dance between the camera and the face of actor Ayesha Dharker. Malli is caught up in events in the world, or a hidden observer looking on, lost in her thoughts, her recollections, and the camera remains on her face, focuses upon her eyes, her mouth, her expression – the shot or sequence lasting a wonderful little eternity. Such shots and sequences will approach silence, except for her breathing and the ever-present sounds of nature; or sometimes such images are overwhelmed by a score of synthetic strings. Everything is in close-up. The whole film is organised around this aesthetic: the dominion and the potential of the close-up. Director Santosh Sivan focuses upon a life, moments in a life, life through the expressions of a woman's face, expressions of the affects, intensities and forces within. Sivan and Dharker create a film of the icon.

For Deleuze, the icon is an affection-image, a sign of the unfilmable internal intensities of the body expressed through a face in close-up. A film produces a central and privileged image, a character who is perceived by the world and perceives the world; a character who will be affected by the world, and, in being affected, act. With a film of the icon it is as if the character is suspended between perception and the act – it is as if the film becomes a world of affects, affective perceptions and affective acts. And these affects appear on-screen through the territory and function of the close-up, the close-up of the face, the face a close-up of the body, the film a close-up of the character. Accordingly, the affection-image is 'primarily a way of treating the medium shot and the full shot as close-ups' (C1: 107). Every shot takes on the function of the close-up (the study of a life is the close-up of the character). This is the affection-image dominated by its sign of the icon, expressed through the image of a face. Or rather, two aspects of a face: 'every icon has these two poles': 'faceification' and 'faceicity' (C1: 97, 88). A face caught in stasis as a reflection of that which it is perceiving; a face in movement showing emotions as a precursor to action. These are expressions of affects, the quality which conjoins the object with the face and the power which conjoins the quality with other qualities in series for the object. And an affection-image film explores 'the extent to which one goes from one pole to the other' (C1: 91). From affective perception to affective acts – the icon is the face expressing the intensive forces negotiating the trajectory between these poles of the sensory-motor system that is the character in the world. Suspended between the two, the body is ravaged with affects, and the film captures this on-screen through the face.

'Ordinarily', writes Deleuze, 'three roles of the face are recognisable: first, 'it is individuating (it distinguishes or characterises each person)'; second, 'it is socialising (it manifests a social role)'; third, 'it is relational or communicating (it ensures not only communication between two people, but also, in a single person, the internal agreement between ... character and ... role)' (C1: 99). However, 'the face, which effectively presents these aspects in the cinema as elsewhere, loses all three in the case of the close-up' (C1: 99). The icon is thus a wonderful reconception of a term most usually associated with the actor as film-star. For this affection-image will not simply present individuated, socialised, communicating subjects (the perceiver–perceived as a pure perception-image in action and thought), but rather foreground pure intensities – qualities and powers – in-and-of-themselves, expressed through the face. The close-up will push 'the face into those regions where the principle of individuation [socialisation and communication] ceases to hold sway' (C1: 100). The icon is the 'face and its effacement' (C1: 100). The face as icon is a method, accordingly, of extracting cinematic affects.

Malli is such an icon. The face of Malli extracts cinematic affects, qualities and powers. In this way, the specific political narration and narrative the film may appear to explore are merely an amorphous background for the staging of an affection-image, an icon and its intensities. Such a procedure effaces the geo-historical coordinates and the determined and determinate actions of characters for something far more elusive. Perceptions are sense data for a subject, a subject not enslaved to the material world, but an affection-image, an icon, a centre of indetermination, a site of conscious and unconscious intensive movements. Sivan's film thus concerns two journeys: the first a physical journey Malli must make through the jungles of South India; the second an ethical journey through an affection-image. Having lost her brother and lover in vicious – but heroic, martyred – deaths during an ongoing civil war, Malli volunteers for a suicide mission to assassinate a prominent Indian politician. Malli is a terrorist. Malli is a freedom fighter in a Tamil guerrilla unit, part of the Liberation Tigers of Tamil Eelam (LTTE). The LTTE is fighting the Sinhalese-dominated Sri Lankan military to establish Eelam, an independent Tamil state in north-eastern Sri Lanka. However, the civil war has spread to Tamil-dominated Southern India as the Indian Government is supporting the Sri Lankan military. It is here that Malli's unit operates and through here that she must travel to complete her mission. However, during the long and dangerous journey she discovers she is pregnant with her dead lover's child. The second journey, in this way, effaces the first. The physical journey is transformed into an intensive one: a journey through the affects of revenge, honour, duty, death, love, forgiveness, life, freedom. The film explores ethics – but it does so through the affection-image and the icon. Through Malli's face – the close-up of the face, as an expression of internal intensities, as an expression of the centre of indeterminacy. For indeterminacy is an image of choice.

And it is here we can designate the project of *The Terrorist* through the sign of the icon. For Deleuze, 'there are choices that can only be made on condition that one persuades oneself that one has no choice', the determinate action (C1: 114). However, there is another kind of choice, one proper to the affection-image, the icon, the centre of indeterminacy: 'a choice of choice or non-choice' where 'the alternative is not between terms but between modes of existence' (C1: 114). Accordingly, we will never know if Malli detonates the bomb she will carry beneath her sari, killing herself, her target and the men, women and children at the political gathering. We will never know if she walks away, to live, allow others to live, and to give birth to her baby. Malli has already chosen – chosen choice. In this way, Sivan sustains the qualities and powers of the affection-image, of the icon, and the film ends.

Despicable Me, Despicable Me 2 and *Minions*

Dividual

Frame III.05 *Despicable Me* (Pierre Coffin and Chris Renaud, USA, 2010)

'Minions assemble!'

So goes out the call, which all must obey. Although, perhaps, not at once. They swarm from the laboratories, storage docks and rest areas of Gru's vast underground criminal headquarters, from the design, maintenance and testing activities associated with the Heath Robinson inventions of Dr Nefario. Hundreds upon hundreds of minions: minions involved in the never-ending and ongoing construction of the base; minions in charge of the forklifts in the warehouse environments; minions operating and riding the winches, tackles and pulleys distributing material from one space to another; minions chatting on the gantries and walkways that run throughout the structure, at the water coolers, taking five and snacking on their favourite food (nannas [trans. bananas]); minions working out in the gym class. A horde: flowing towards the stalls and galleries of the tiered arena where Gru will outline his next dastardly plan. These wee, bright yellow homunculi – clothed in standard issue blue dungarees and all with protective stainless steel eye-goggles – congregate.

The minions are – on the one hand – a mass. Their forms composed of a restricted number of elements, they have limited differentials. Elongated or rotund bodies; short, medium or tall in height; bald, bristly or centre parted hair, one or two eyes. From these elements a number of composite types are generated, perhaps as many as forty or fifty possible combinations. This limited palette results in hundreds of similar individuations composing the thousands of actual existing minions. Yet – on the other hand – it appears each will have some semblance of a sense of self, of an I. We even know some of their names: Kevin (tall, thin, two eyes); Bob (short and rotund, with one eye); Dave (short, rotund, with two eyes and a centre parting); Larry (medium in height, two eyes). Thus, while evidence suggests that they are genderless, their names are those usually associated with certain groups of human males, though this may well be simple affectation and a sign of cultural assimilation. Where and how they originate is still mysterious; it has been said they are clones, although recent research indicates they have been around since well before the Holocene.

Minions are thus neither a homogeneous mass nor heterogeneous individuals: they are both. They are dividual: a pack, a group, a multitude. The de-individualisation of entities and the individualisation of the mass – this is the dividual. Here are 'produced', writes Deleuze 'compact and continuous intensive series, which go beyond all binary structures and exceed the duality of the collective and the individual' (C1: 92). Alone they express the assemblage, together they express individuations: 'directly uniting an immense collective reflection with the particular emotions of each individual' (C1: 92). The dividual is an affection-image, and minions as the dividual are the expression of a group affect. Such an expression concerns their being in the world. Evidence from *Despicable Me* and *Despicable Me 2* (Pierre Coffin and Chris Renaud, USA, 2013) is contradictory. Their working conditions are generally comfortable, there is every amenity possible for their use, they have time to relax and can take regular breaks. They have great teeth (there is probably some kind of dental plan). However, they are continually experimented upon, resulting in many debilitating workplace injuries and humiliating injustices. Health and safety regulations do not appear to be in place; let alone to be monitored. There is no union. No remuneration, no childcare, no pension (and where are the child minions, the senior minions?). Even their species name cries exploitation. Yet – and what I am about to say might seem crazy – they are happy. Indeed, recent analysis of their history would indicate they exhibit a group desire for their own enslavement – thus putting into question the idea of a subject caught in the invisible snares of ideology. This research – conducted in *Minions* (Kyle Balda and Pierre Coffin, USA, 2015) – focuses upon three individuations of the collective expression (Stuart, Kevin and Bob) as they go in search of their own enslavement.

This prequel performs an archaeology of the dividual affects mapped in the original *Despicable Me* diptych. As Deleuze and Guattari write in *Anti-Oedipus*: 'after centuries of exploitation, why do people still tolerate being humiliated and enslaved, to such a point, indeed, that they *actually want* humiliation and slavery not only for others but for themselves?' (AO: 29). Accordingly, 'the astonishing thing is not that some people steal or that others occasionally go out on strike, but rather that all those who are starving do not steal as a regular practice, and all those who are exploited are not continually on strike' (AO: 29). This question echoes an exemplary formulation in the work of Wilhelm Reich on fascism, and Deleuze and Guattari continue: 'Reich is at his profoundest as a thinker when he refuses to accept ignorance or illusion on the part of the masses as an explanation of fascism, and demands an explanation that will take their desires into account'; accordingly, 'the masses were not innocent dupes; at a certain point, under a certain set of conditions, they wanted fascism' (AO: 29). However, while Reich raises this problem, for Deleuze and Guattari he was unable to solve it because he saw a distinction between a rational and ideal social world (a world that should be) and the irrational, perverted desires of the individual (the real). For Deleuze and Guattari, however, 'desiring-production is one and the same thing as social production' (AO: 30). It is such an analysis that is echoed in *Minions*.

The only question that remains is this: who exactly are these minions?

6

Le quattro volte/Four Times

Any-space-whatever

Frame III.06 *Four Times* (Michelangelo Frammartino, Italy | Germany | Switzerland, 2010)

Roman centurions in the back of a rusty old truck. This image throws out of joint the day-to-day linear time that has so far been experienced following the life, and eventual death, of Fuda, an aged goatherd in the southern Italian countryside of Calabria. While the ancients are revealed as participants in a modern-day passion play, this does little to re-anchor a linear temporal flow. Rather, it exposes the durations that subsist in the spatial field, and announces an ongoing series of such spatio-temporal disturbances. Director Michelangelo Frammartino uses the real time of the long take to make us feel the affect of time, reveal the clamour of times in the spaces we inhabit. The shot is simple, at least in terms of camera movement, panning this way then that through 180 degrees. A dog patters up and down a country lane, the truck and centurions arrive, people in costumes and everyday work-wear gather, the procession begins, from the village and out into the fields. The past subsists in this space and this present is the coexistence of all kinds of pasts, many different spatial strata. History, myth and cyclical time arise, real and imaginary events, yearly repetitions. *Four Times*: linear time, cyclical time, mythical time and time out of joint. The affects of these disparate but interfolding times are explored by Frammartino through the rigorous unfolding of the film: four sections on the duration of the existence of human, animal, vegetative and non-organic states. These four spatio-temporal series can be seen as four aspects of the any-space-whatever, Deleuze's cinematic sign of indeterminate affects.

The any-space-whatever concerns affection-images. Affection-images, in the first instance, can be said to be close-ups of an expression on a character's face, outward signs of internal intensities, after perception, before impulses or actions, and at the gateway of thought. Yet it is not only the face as sign that can express affect. The second sign of composition is the dividual, complex qualities and powers of the mass, group, assemblage. Then there is the any-space-whatever, genetic sign of the affection-image – from which the affects of the mass and the individual arise. A pure background, indeterminate space-times where the affect is encountered without the necessity of mediation of a character of characters. A setting as an intensity of forces, empty or disconnected spaces developing the indeterminacies of gaseous perception and resisting the determinate space-time of action. Ahuman affects, forces prior to the human or after the withdrawing of human centres. Any-space-whatevers – however – belong to the movement-image and thus tend to be captured up in compositions of the dividual and the icon, the ascension of the assemblage and an emergent central and privileged image. Ahuman affects are composed into human affects. Yet such mappings have a certain fragility: in other conditions (set free from the movement-image) an any-space-whatever can become an opsign-sonsign, a pure optical and sound situation, a time-image, an actual on-screen de-differenciated visual and audio image. Without human centres to express affects there is a univocal coalescence of genetic forces: the coalescence of indeterminacy. We experience time in its raw state, no longer an image of thought, but an image that is disruptive of thought. Accordingly, the four states of the any-space-whatever: (1) captured up through the icon; (2) sustaining the assemblage of the dividual; (3) in itself as reference to the affection-image and movement-image; (4) in itself as a condition for the time-image.

It is tempting to align these four states of the any-space-whatever with Frammartino's *Four Times*. First section – the old goatherd, shot in close-up: the icon. Here the any-space-whatever appears as the environment Fuda inhabits, the ragged mountains, the open fields, even his sparse room. Yet Frammartino is able to suspend the moment between the face of the character and the any-space-whatever; Fuda never overwhelms the place he traverses, but appears in the midst of the background, which always retains its intensive natural force and thus subsumes Fuda within it. Second section – the lamb, among a multitude of lambs, the conjunction of the individual and the mass: the dividual. Here Frammartino discovers a way to capture pure ahuman affects, animal affects which derive from an any-space-whatever and arise as particular feelings and emotions in relation to a new life: beauty, innocence, inquisitiveness, confusion, loneliness, fear. The third section – the tree and the environment. The tree is filmed through the repetitions of the seasons; summer, autumn, winter, spring. Eventually, however, it will be cut down for the village, a maypole for a day, a centre for the community, the people. Here Frammartino presents the any-space-whatever in the context of a movement-image: the tree was always a centre, a privileged image, a figure in duration around which the seasons spiral. Fourth section – charcoal burning. Dead wood is taken and stacked with precision, its burning maintained to produce a carbon compound, an inorganic material from organic matter. Frammartino films the immensity that is the smoking charcoal mound – the organic becoming inorganic – as an any-space-whatever that escapes the affection-image and the regime of movement-images. The purest of opsigns, the purest of sonsigns. A time-image that has haunted the movie from beginning to end. *Four Times* is the domination of cinematic affect and the any-space-whatever; exploring the any-space-whatever overcoming the affection-image (the compositions of the dividual and the icon) and the movement-image, and becoming a time-image. There are thus two images of thought here – the image of thought that arises through the sensory-motor system where recognition operates and affects are mapped as coherent states; and the image of thought that ungrounds such recognition.

These two images of thought have concerned Deleuze throughout his philosophical writings. *Difference and Repetition* is a book that attempts to 'question the traditional image of thought' (DR: xiv–xv). This is thinking 'according to a given method', a method which describes 'the process of recognition' where we 'designate error', we '"want" the true' and we 'suppose that the true concerns solutions' (DR: xv). Deleuze thus proposes 'a new image of thought – or rather, a liberation of thought' from 'those images which imprison it' (DR: xv). This new image of thought involves 'encounters which escape all recognition' which 'tears thought from its natural torpor … and forces us to think' (DR: xv). In 'Introduction: Rhizome' from *A Thousand Plateaus*, Deleuze and Guattari re-create this typology of thought as the 'root-book' and the 'rhizome … system' (TP: 5–7). The root-book: '[t]his is the classical book … The book imitates the world, as art imitates nature … The law of the book is the law of reflection … whenever we encounter this formula … what we have before us is the most classical and well reflected, oldest, and weariest kind of thought' (TP: 5). The root-book, then, creates what Deleuze and Guattari call 'arborescent' thought (TP: 5). Thinking here is premised upon representation, upon recognition. However, '[n]ature doesn't work that way', write Deleuze and Guattari; 'in nature, roots are tap roots with a more multiple, lateral, circular system of ramification, rather than a dichotomous one. Thought lags behind nature' (TP: 5). Thus rhizomatics: '[t]he multiple must be made … A rhizome as subterranean stem is absolutely different from roots and radicles. The rhizome itself assumes very diverse forms [yet] … any point on a rhizome can be connected to anything else' (TP: 7). The rhizome, 'simple', 'sober' … 'multiple', 'diverse' yet 'connected' at every point to every other point. The crucial aspect is this: arborescent systems and rhizomatic systems are intertwined, fundamentally in embrace: '[t]here are knots of arborescence on rhizomes, and rhizomatic offshoots in roots … The important point is that the root-tree and canal-rhizome are not two opposed models' (TP: 22).

Classical and new images of thought, arborescent and rhizomatic thinking, the movement-image and the time-image – all are inspired by a turning away from the Aristotelian formula which underpins much European philosophy. In Chapter 4 of 'Categories', Aristotle writes: 'of things said without any combination, each signifies either substance or quantity or qualification or a relative or where or when or being-in-a-position or having or doing or being affected' (Aristotle, 1984a: 4). Ten categories. Yet substance is primary (Aristotle, 1984b: 1,623). Substance is the fundamental category, 'the other categories none can exist independently' (1984b: 1,624). Aristotle goes on to explore the way in which substance 'is'. The most famous capture of Aristotle's explorations was created by Porphyry in the third century as a tree-diagram. The structure is composed of a genus and species, a species emerging from the genus through difference. Thus, of the genus 'body', there are two different types, or species, 'animate' or 'inanimate', and so on. Accordingly, this 'genus–difference–species' structure constructs a hierarchy, a tree structure: at the top, substance as substance, the supreme genus; at the bottom – the most refined of the species – individual humans.

Four Times may appear to climb Porphyry's tree. The human passes away, and on to the animal; the animal passes away, and on to the vegetable; the vegetable passes away, and on to the inorganic. Yet, for Deleuze, against the arborescent hierarchical image of Porphyry's tree, is the rhizome-ivy growing up through its branches … against the classical image of thought is a new, disruptive image of thought; against the captures of movement-images are the disruptions of time-images. Frammartino ungrounds the image of such hierarchal order through the perpetual rediscovery of the any-space-whatever, the any-space-whatever overwhelms each of the four images of *Four Times*.

Section III

This is the rhizomatic cinema. Images which do not represent determined spaces and times, images that are not based on recognition. These images do not think for the spectator, but disturb thought through the clamour of four different modes of time inherent in the any-space-whatever.

7

The Human Centipede (First Sequence)

Symptom

Frame III.07 *The Human Centipede (First Sequence)* (Tom Six, the Netherlands, 2009)

The Human Centipede (First Sequence) is nasty, sickening, permeated with gratuitous and terrifying violence – everything, then, a great horror film should be. Yet the movie also produces laughter – in a certain way, up to a certain point. The film seizes upon the passion hidden deep within for cruelty, and the laughter that emerges is that of the purest pleasure in the suffering of others. Horror unbound takes you through and beyond nervous and ironic laughter (beyond the uncanny of classical horror; beyond the knowing self-reflection of post-modern horror). Towards a laughter to which we will not admit, a laughter that sticks in the throat, where enjoyment turns, returns, once more, to horror. The enjoyment of horror, and the horror of enjoyment. *The Human*

Centipede has been categorised – quite rightly – as 'torture porn', a term coined by the critic David Edelstein (2006). Such a sobriquet, however, tends to be used as damning indictment: a film that goes too far, a horror film that is too horrific, a film that goes beyond the domain of the horror cinema. But has not every genre of horror movie – in its own time – encountered such accusation and censure?

Specialising in the surgical separation of Siamese twins (art images of which adorn his appropriately stark, white modernist home), Dr Heiter now wants to create. To this end, Heiter secures himself three subjects. Tourists Jenny and Lindsey stumble across his house one evening after their car has broken down. The doctor doses them with Rohypnols, then restrains them on operating tables. A little later, he returns with Katsuro, a businessman nicely captured using a shot from drugged dart gun. In lecture mode (and with a beautifully tailored lab coat) Heiter announces he is to produce 'the human centipede'. A PowerPoint presentation and knives are out. Subject A (Katsuro) has his anus surgically joined to the mouth of Subject B (Jenny), who has her anus joined to mouth of Subject C (Lindsey). The human gastrointestinal tract centipede lives!

We are not unfamiliar with laughter in response to horror movies. Especially in the darkness of the cinema, collective laughter seems to arise as a response mechanism to the unease the codes of the genre can engender, as a way to distance ourselves from the depiction of gore, jumps of fright and sustained, pervasive disquiet. Nervous laughter. Then there are the laughs that occur owing to the ironic and self-referential nature of horror movies that wish to expose and explore these already-established rules. *The Human Centipede* no doubt plays on both these types of laughter. The fun begins with a strict and unswerving adherence to the norms of the horror film. Two young American women are driving through the backwoods when their car gets a flat. Soon they are walking through the trees at night in the pouring rain. There is a light in the distance. A house. Then, an insane doctor opening the door. A grimacing, gurning, Germanic incarnation of evil. These characters and situations are no doubt clichés, and both parody and pastiche. Yet it is in just this way that *The Human Centipede* operates to lull the viewer into complacency. Even so, the mad doctor's plan is ludicrous. When Katsuro first evacuates his bowels the audience howls with laughter, drowning out the muffled screams of Jenny ...

Such a procedure can be seen as an encounter with what Deleuze names an impulse-image. Impulse-images describe types of films where primal forces ravage the universe; and the horror movie is exemplary in allowing such permeating forces to be captured up in the perceptions, acts and affects of characters and of the audience. Bodies in horror films are transformed into the symptoms of an elemental world. Impulses are energies, impelling urges that overwhelm, that are – as Deleuze writes – 'too strong for the character' (C1: 137). The impulse-image explores 'acts … prior to all differentiation between the human and the animal. These are human animals' (C1: 123–4). In this way, symptoms become 'inseparable from the perverse mode of behaviour which they produce and animate: cannibalistic, sado-masochistic, necrophiliac, etc' (C1: 128). It is here – in the productive domain of the symptom, when the characters animate symptoms of an originary world – that the horror film operates. And in this way *The Human Centipede* is a film of the impulse-image, an actualisation of becoming animal in Katsuro–Jenny–Lindsey through the perverse symptomatic acts of Dr Heiter. The film explores the symptom, the film is a symptom of the primal forces that ravage the universe beneath the determined and determinable situations of the world. And the laughter of cruelty is a symptom of these forces, a force too strong for the audience, a laughter that overwhelms the spectator, for a moment …

Abu Ghraib echoed with laughter. *This government does not torture people*, declared Bush. Yet in 2005 US legal *opinion* allowed the use of waterboarding and other extreme interrogation techniques apparently no longer classified as torture. The Blair government's advice to secret service operatives in the field is that while they must not *engage in any activity that involves inhumane or degrading treatment of prisoners*, if they find themselves in a situation where torture is being used *the law* (conveniently) *does not require them to intervene*. Torture became acceptable – once again – as surreptitious government policy. Torture as a means to an end. Yet torture is never a dispassionate, detached act. It captures up revenge and *ressentiment* and frees a passion for terror. There is enjoyment, pleasure and laughter in torture. In Abu Ghraib torture became entertainment for the security personnel, unfettered from the determinate coordinates of enforced and fought-for human rights. The corridors echoed with laughter, drowning out the screams of the prisoners.

It is no coincidence that the event of the 'torture porn' extreme horror genre arose around the same time as the post-9/11 and post-7/7 war on terror. *The Human Centipede* is of its time, it is symptomatic. Yet, we have here no direct political engagement seeking to reveal the coordinates of a situation, or explore how the situation explicates behaviour. This is no action-image; and neither is it a mental-image or a reflection-image. The symptom is not a metaphor, allegory, memory or nightmare. It is something far more imponderable, and something far more dangerous. The impulse-image comes before dreams, recollections, reflection and action, before historically and geographically anchored milieux. The impulse-image describes symptoms of primal forces that explode through the fabric of the human world and overpower the human. *The Human Centipede* is a film of the symptom of an originary world, and that symptom embodies – as Deleuze puts it –'all the cruelty of Chronos' (C1: 124). It is the

Section III

human under 'an inseparable curse' (C1: 126). When Katsuro first evacuates his bowels the audience howls with laughter, drowning out the muffled screams of Jenny. However, as Jenny gags and swallows … the laughter slowly dies … Katsuro's shame … Jenny's tears … the way Lindsey reaches out to her, to hold her hand, to comfort her … The laughter gets stuck in the throat. The camera maintains its gaze – deliberately – for far too long to be entertaining … the screening room discovers a painful silence. A silence that appears in the wake of the laugher of cruelty. Horror is once again horrific.

8

Harry Potter and the Deathly Hallows: Part 1 and *Harry Potter and the Deathly Hallows: Part 2*

Fetish

Frame III.08 *Harry Potter and the Deathly Hallows: Part 2* (David Yates, USA | UK, 2011)

In one of the most beautiful and disturbing moments of recent cinema, Harry Potter – defeated by the evil wizard Voldemort with a killing curse – awakens to discover himself dead. Apparently ... Yet all is not as it at first seems. Harry walks in his own limbo-construct. Curiously, he encounters a dying version of the evil Dark Lord, curled up foetus-like. This bloody abortion is a horcrux, torn from its host – Harry. As Harry explores the immense brilliant-white dream environment ('like King's Cross Station, only cleaner'), he stumbles upon a manifestation of his old mentor Dumbledore, and – finally – learns the truth. Harry is not dead. Rather, Voldemort has unknowingly destroyed a part

Section III

of himself that was hidden within Harry, and Harry is now free of his horcrux function. His body in the real world is merely unconscious.

Horcruxes are magical objects that host a quantum embodiment of one's soul, effectively making the owner immortal. If you have transformed an object into a horcrux and your body is destroyed, you can be resurrected through the power of a horcrux. Yet the deal is monstrous. These objects can only be created in the wake of a killing. Voldemort, known as Tom Marvolo Riddle when young, discovered this forbidden dark spell and, over the years that followed, set about creating a number of horcruxes for himself as he arose to become the Dark Lord. However, just before he attained total power over the world, he was involved in an event that brought Harry into the story and which also stymied his diabolical plan. For Voldemort – attempting to annihilate all resistance – killed the Potters, but in so doing was himself destroyed. Yet, at that moment of his death, a part of his soul attached itself to their son, Harry. Since this event, Harry has been a horcrux of his reptilianesque foe – unbeknownst to himself and indeed the subsequently resurrected Voldemort. It is such a resurrection that concerns the films of the cycle preceding the *Deathly Hallows* diptych; and it is the final diptych that will see Voldemort once again attempt to take over the world. Concomitantly, Harry and his friends discover the source of Voldemort's immortality: the horcruxes. *Harry Potter and the Deathly Hallows: Part 1* (David Yates, UK | USA, 2010) begins the quest to identify, locate and destroy these magical objects – a particularly difficult and dangerous task, and one that remains unfulfilled, awaiting *Part 2*. In this second film of the *Deathly Hallows*, furthermore, it is revealed Harry must also sacrifice his own life to the cause – there has always been a link between himself and Voldemort, forged in the moment of the Dark Lord's first death, and Harry is led to believe that severing this link is essential. Hence the duel in the woods with the evil wizard, and Harry's apparent martyrdom. Yet in the limbo-construct, Harry understands the subterfuge, a necessary secret kept from him by Dumbledore so Voldemort would not discover the deception. For the Dark Lord – the creator of this horcrux – was the only one who could destroy its function without annihilating Harry.

The scene is now set for the young wizard's consciousness to return to his body, his friends and the fray – in order for him to complete his mission. For only once all the remaining horcruxes have been obliterated will Voldemort be mortal, and only then can he finally be killed. These horcruxes are thus very powerful magical objects, and can be seen to be essential to the story of the *Deathly Hallows*. Indeed, the whole Harry Potter cycle is dependent upon these and other magical objects: wands, crystal balls, amulets, broomsticks, animals, even sports equipment. Deleuze calls such objects 'fetishes'. Fetishes are impulse-images, the condensation of primal forces and intensities from the world in special objects. It is these objects which sustain, retain and preserve energies, and which, under certain conditions, will discharge these energies back into the world. Such objects are commonplace in the real world (a cross on a chain, the evil eye, a teddy bear, a killer's memento) and operate at the level of fantasy; accordingly, fantasy films will find a central role for them. These fetishes are fragments of the world which are encoded with primal meanings which must be interpreted. In other words, there are 'fetishes of Good and fetishes of Evil, holy fetishes and fetishes of crime and sexuality'; yet in this function these poles of the fetish 'meet and interchange' (C1: 130). Deleuze will name the good fetish 'relic', and the evil fetish 'vult': and the vult can become a relic, and the relic a vult, in different moments and for different characters. The essential thing is that the fetish retains a primal force, a retention awaiting a grounding, and such forces are prior to good and evil.

Immortality – as a primal force – is such an impulse, a symptom of an originary world that will be designated good or evil according to the milieu in which it manifests, and the condition of the actions which both engender it and which it engenders. Horcruxes are vults with respect to their creation, their creator and their relative purpose: produced through cold-blooded murders by Voldemort for a grounding ensuring his continued existence to propagate further death and wickedness. Yet – at one and the same time – they are also relics in that they hold the key to the Dark Lord's destruction. Hence the quest: Harry, Hermione and Ron must find these horcruxes and ground them in an entirely different way, in order to make Voldemort mortal once more. Marvolo Gaunt's ring, Tom Riddle's diary, Helga Hufflepuff's cup, Salazar Slytherin's locket, Rowena Ravenclaw's diadem, are all destroyed; the horcrux within Harry is destroyed, and the final horcrux in Voldemort's snake Nagini is destroyed in the monster's beheading. However, this final *Harry Potter* diptych not only concerns horcruxes, but – as the titles indicate – the Deathly Hallows: another series of fetishes, the cape of invisibility, the resurrection stone and the elder wand. Harry and his friends are reminded of these when Xenophilius Lovegood explains a mysterious symbol that Harry has encountered. In 'The Tale of the Three Brothers' – told by Lovegood and beautifully depicted in the film-world by director David Yates' animated shadows – Death is defeated and so must bestow gifts upon the victors. The fetishes of the wand and the stone will, owing to the dispositions of two of the brothers, eventually accomplish the work of death, while one brother will use his gift to escape and live a long and fruitful life. Two fetishes become vults, one a relic – and in the years that follow each will become relic then vult, vult then relic in turn, subject to the uses and abuses they are put to by their owners.

It is the elder wand that will prove to be vital here, not only in resolving the narration of the *Deathly Hallows*, but also in revealing the central function of the fetish to the theme of the entire *Harry Potter* cycle. In the first place, Harry becomes its rightful owner through a series of happenstance events, so that when Voldemort – in the final duel of the film – attempts (once again) to kill Harry using the wand, it is the Dark Lord who will be destroyed. The elder wand is the most powerful fetish in the originary world of wizards and witches; and becomes vult or relic according to the nature of its use. Thus, in the second place, in the wake of Voldemort's defeat, Harry (in a departure from the books on which the films are based), snaps the wand in two. To consider the *Harry Potter* films as merely designating and playing out a static and given good and evil is thus to fail to recognise the essential nature of the fetish. In the 'Preface' to Deleuze and Guattari's first book together, Michel Foucault wrote of the text: 'one might say that *Anti-Oedipus* is an *Introduction to the Non-Fascist Life*', the final law being 'Do not become enamoured of power' (AO: xxiii–xiv). The concluding diptych of the *Harry Potter* films – through its fetishes, its horcruxes, its Deathly Harrows; and through their exchange in function as vults and relics – proves to be another version of an *Introduction to the Non-Fascist Life*, another version of *Anti-Oedipus*. The elder wand only concerns good and evil in the derived milieu. In destroying the elder wand, Harry rejects the fundamental and primal lure of total power. Harry destroys a fetish and in so doing stymies the possibility of ever grounding this symptom of the primal forces of the originary universe in the world in which he lives.

9

Innocence

Originary World

Frame III.09 *Innocence* (Lucile Hadzihalilovic, Belgium | France | UK | Japan, 2004)

'Bianca, where do you go at night?' Bianca will not say. The younger girls are not allowed to know. It is – for them, for now – forbidden knowledge.

The park – during the long summer days – is a vast woodland playground. After lessons are out, or at weekends, they can enjoy themselves here. Pretty little waterfalls cascade over rocks covered in lichen, feeding the river which meanders through the trees, the wide banks creating shallow areas where the girls can swim. The high stone wall that surrounds the park, covered with climbing plants, keeps them safe from the outside world. Nearer to the school, the forest thins out into well-maintained glades interspaced with open areas in which to play hoop-la, or ride on swings. Little pathways connect all these spaces, running from the five houses which the girls now call home, and to the main school building.

At night, however, the paths are forbidding trajectories. Lit from above with electric lamps strung between the trees, they barely cut through the dark and the now impenetrable woods where night-time noises echo. Ominous, sinister pathways that wind this way and that, and terminate in unknown events. Bianca will leave the younger girls at the house, and walk these paths alone. Director Lucile Hadzihalilovic places her camera at the mouth of this dark entry, and a static frame captures Bianca as she moves through each pool of light, until the darkness finally engulfs her. Bianca will join the other oldest girls from each of the houses; but we will not follow, not yet. It is – for us, for now – forbidden knowledge. Such is the cinematographic image of *Innocence*, a world in which primal forces permeate the mise-en-scène.

Hadzihalilovic creates an originary world. An originary world is an impulse-image, an image of the powerful intensive and primal forces that permeate the milieu from its beginning to its end. The milieu is a defined space, a determined environment with geographical and historical coordinates. Yet this space floats upon a world of primal, nameless and undefined forces. Deleuze writes that this impulse-image is 'the world which is revealed as the basis of the social milieux which are so powerfully described … an originary world, which rumbles in the depths of all the milieux and runs along beneath them' (C1: 125). This originary world 'is recognisable by its formless character. It is a pure background, or rather without-background, composed of unformed matter, sketches or fragments, crossed by non-formal functions, acts, or energy dynamisms which do not even refer to the constituted subjects' (C1: 122). These are the spaces Hadzihalilovic creates. The girls are housed in comfortable and well-provided villas in the grand style; they have the best facilities for a modern education – including labs for the study of biological evolution. A dance studio for ballet classes. The school grounds are a dreamland for relaxation and play. Yet beneath this surface, something reverberates. In the night, in the darkness that surrounds the girls, there are formless energies. 'Take a house, a country or a region. These are real milieu of geographical and social actualisation', writes Deleuze, '[b]ut it looks as if, in whole or in part, they communicate from within with originary worlds' (C1: 122). The originary world is that which lies beneath: the primal forces sustaining the milieu from beginning to end. And such beginnings and ends are particularly powerful in *Innocence*, explored through the yearly cycle of arrivals and departures.

Arrival: beneath the woods are endless tunnels, dark and damp. It is through these that the youngest girls are brought each spring, unconscious, in coffins, naked. Iris is the most recent arrival in House Two; the coffin placed in the communal area and unlocked by Bianca – now the oldest of the six girls. Iris awakes and is dressed in white shirt and skirt. All wear different coloured ribbons in their hair. Selma's are red, and she takes them out and hands them to Iris; everyone swaps. Bianca opens an ornate box and takes out violet ribbons. They were Natasha's, says one of the girls – but Natasha is gone now. Over the next few days Iris asks where her brother is, will he come and get her, will he visit; where is she, how did she get here, will she leave soon? No one will come, no one ever comes. The fear in such arrivals – and what it means, and what will happen – permeates even the most beautiful sunlit day.

Departure: Bianca bathes, lingering there, not wanting to get out of the warming tub. She studies herself, naked in the mirror. Dresses. Once more – and for the last time – walking those dark paths. In the main building she joins the four oldest girls from the other houses. In hidden corridors accessed through a secret passage behind the grandfather clock, they change into their costumes, white leotards with delicate wings. They make their way to the stage. The red curtains open, but the audience is hidden in the darkness. The brightness of the footlights obscures the room. Darkness always surrounds them, even when they forget it is there. The ballet begins, five young girls, maybe fourteen, exposed, full of fear. A rose lands on the stage, Bianca picks it up, a voice growls 'You are the prettiest'. Later, purple ribbons are placed in a box. The girls are led through the dark tunnels that run beneath the park. A train awaits: 'What will happen?' 'One thing is for certain, you'll soon forget us.' The terror of departure – and what it means, and what will happen – permeates the last days.

This is the cycle of time: yearly arrivals and leavings. Yet the film is riven with cycles. The girls are 'ugly caterpillars' who will be 'transformed'. Into what? For what? The six-year cycles between losing your milk teeth and your first period. Yet sometimes events burst through the cycle. Iris will follow Bianca and see, through the crack in a door, a shadow, and hear the words 'Don't resist'. The girls are inspected by the headmistress. Long neck; nice poise; turn around; what's this tummy? pull it in; pretty; slightly short neck; very pretty neck. Laura, a new arrival, will attempt to escape and will drown in the river – her body will be placed in the coffin in which she arrived, burnt on a pyre at night as all the girls look on. Alice will climb the wall, and make it into the outside world. The teachers tell the girls to never mention her name again. 'The originary world only exists and operates in the depths of a real milieu, and is only valid through its immanence in this milieu, whose violence and cruelty it reveals' (C1: 125). Hadzihalilovic films the violence of the forces of life that civilisation attempts to conceal, veil, bury; intensities that nonetheless arise through the cracks in the universe. *Innocence* captures the cruelty of time through the experience of these little girls: an awareness that there are forces – biological, societal – as yet beyond their understanding and beyond their control. This impulse-image, this originary word, is naturalism. And according to Deleuze, in this way naturalism will 'diagnose civilisation' (C1: 125). Naturalism describes 'all the cruelty of Chronos', and the originary world 'seems to be under an inseparable curse' (C1: 124, 126). This is the world of *Innocence*, a violent and cursed innocence. Yet Hadzihalilovic will – in the final moments of the film, in a delightful coda – echo a question asked by Deleuze: 'Is there a salvation …?' (C1: 138). 'If there is one', with respect to films of the impulse-image, we appear to find one possibility with 'women … it is they who trace a line of exit, and who win a freedom' (C1: 138–9).

10

Madeo/Mother

Index of lack

Frame III.10 *Mother* (Bong Joon-ho, South Korea, 2009)

The sound of a gentle breeze rustling the long, dry grass of late summer. In the distance, misty mountains and verdant forests frame the pale sky above, and the vast pastures below. A woman wanders through the tan meadows, as if lost, or at least, lost in thought, turning and taking in the panorama. Dressed in city clothes – a pastel sapphire dress with a lightly patterned lavender jacket – the woman is in her fifties, perhaps, and an incongruous presence in the remote countryside. After a while, she comes to a halt. She begins to quietly sway. There is the sound of tablas, the sinuous arpeggios of an acoustic guitar. The woman begins to dance, tentatively at first, but with more and more confidence as the music swells with sweeping strings. For a moment, the smile fades from her face, and she covers her eyes; but the moment soon passes. With her arms out wide, and her hips moving to music only she can hear, the woman is subsumed within her dance.

Why is Do-joon's mother dancing?

The joy of the perfect thriller comes with the reveal. A number of conditions – of course – apply. The image that will be revealed needs to be well hidden throughout the film, the truth must remain in ellipsis right up to the denouement. There is nothing worse than reasoning out the mystery before the final disclosure. A caveat here: the ruse, the red herring. With an amalgam of satisfaction (at our own cleverness) and disappointment (at the filmmaker giving too much away) we think we've got it! Only to discover cinematic subterfuge, it was someone or something else entirely. Even subtler still, a ploy or stratagem is signalled as possibly being as such, or appears as a fake reveal, thus propagating ambiguity with a self-reflexive quality before the true disclosure. In the second place, the exposé also needs to be a function of the narration. The conditions for the disclosure need to have been there all along, embedded in moments of the movie, hidden in plain sight. The twist should not be imposed from the outside. There is nothing worse (really, this time) than discovering the reveal was impossible to reason. Finally, the reveal must have a certain necessity. That which is disclosed by the actions of the characters – in retrospect – must be the only possible outcome. This does not strictly concern images and narration, but rather narrative. The perfect thriller does not simply reveal what happened, but through revealing what happened determines the situation. Anything other will simply be an arbitrary answer to any-old-question, rather than the completion and consummation of a permeating theme.

Mother is the perfect thriller. There is misdirection. There is a twist – and you do not see it coming. That which is revealed is not imposed from the outside, it appears both functional and essential; it is something that is integral to the narrative of the film, making the theme vital and vivid. The story revolves – of course – around a crime. Do-joon still lives with his mother. She is a retailer of Chinese medicine and an illegal practitioner of acupuncture; her son a young unemployed man suffering from a severe and ongoing condition of memory loss. Events he passes through pass him by. A kind of overactive repression mechanism. Whatever the case, Do-joon's mother loves and adores him – does everything for him. She feeds him, and encourages him to sleep next to her at night. The themes are thus manifest from the very beginning: a classic Freudian oedipal setup; and, memory as that which structures our being in the world. And when the reveal does come it will allow these two themes to dovetail in a wonderful image of denial (foreshadowed in the flash-forward to the mother's dance at the beginning of the film). One fine day Do-joon sees a pretty schoolgirl on the street, Moon Ah-jung. He absentmindedly begins to follow her. In an attempt to evade this weirdo, Ah-jung slips into a deserted building, but her hiding place is discovered. Feeling threatened, she picks up a rock and throws it at Do-joon. The next morning Ah-jung's dead body is discovered. Do-joon is arrested for the murder; he was seen following her and there is evidence that places him at the crime scene. Do-joon denies the killing, pleads his innocence. His mother believes him, and so begins her search for the truth of the situation.

We can describe this type of film as an action-image of the small form operating through an index of lack. Action-images explore situations (milieux, environments, geo-historical moments) and explicate actions (behaviour, social conduct, being in the world). Deleuze identifies two possibilities here which are parallel, bi-directional and asynchronous. The trajectories of the action-image will describe action → situation (the small form, ASA) and situation → action (the large form, SAS). An action-image film can thus either begin with a given situation (the large form) or can set out to reveal the situation (the small form). *Mother* is of the second type, an action-image of the small form. The situation is not given; rather, it must be disclosed as a function of the actions of the characters. This not-given refers to an ellipsis which exists to be filled. As Deleuze puts it, 'an action … discloses a situation … The situation is thus deduced from the action, by immediate inference, or by relatively complex reasoning' (C1: 160). The small form action-image is thus action → situation; where the index of lack is an ellipsis which will be unambiguously resolved. Finally, once the situation has been disclosed, the actions of the character will be reoriented and transformed; thus the complete formula of the small form is: action → situation → new action. More often than not, the final moment of the formula appears as a coda, the disclosure of the situation is the lightning and thunder, the aftermath is the quiet after the storm. However, *Mother* beautifully develops and extends this aspect of the small form, and in so doing re-examines the function of the index of lack that has structured the whole trajectory of the movie so far, concomitantly re-inscribing and intensifying the themes of the oedipal situation, memory and repression.

Do-joon's mother discovers that her beloved, gentle son did indeed kill Ah-jung. But owing to his mental condition, he neither remembers nor believes himself guilty of the crime. It is at this point – now the situation is disclosed – that the actions of the mother are transformed. At some point the film has jumped tracks, become her story. Do-joon's mother sets about disavowing this knowledge. Murdering a witness. Framing another young man. Finally – and it is with this moment that director Bong Joon-ho proves his virtuosity and originality with the form – the mother erases her own recollections of Do-joon's crime, as well as the measures she has taken to fake his innocence. The mother, through her experience of Chinese healing techniques, knows an acupoint that

Section III

can be triggered to wipe away events from someone's memory. *Mother* explores how the truth that we lack is the very last thing we want revealed … when what is revealed is the truth we neither expected nor wanted.

11

The Killer Inside Me

Index of equivocity

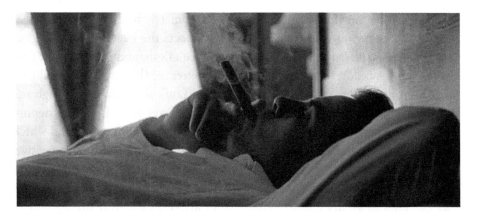

Frame III.11 *The Killer Inside Me* (Michael Winterbottom, USA, 2010)

Deputy Sheriff Lou Ford is the picture-perfect West Texas gentleman (*yes ma'am*; *no sir*). Called into the office of his boss, Sheriff Bob Maples, he is dispatched to the home of notorious prostitute Joyce Lakeland. The town – riding a wave of economic prosperity in the wake of an oil boom – needs cleaning up. 'I guess I want you out of Central City by sundown' – Lou politely commands Joyce. But Joyce ain't hearing him; so Lou attempts to be a little more persuasive, and is rewarded with a fierce slap across the face. Seizing the screaming and struggling woman, Lou forces her face down on the bed, and removing his belt, ripping down her panties, he whips her raw. Yet – his rage and her terror transform. Both become overpowered with sexual energies and they fuck. So begins an affair, Joyce and Lou fall in love, and together they explore the boundaries and line between sex and violence, the sado-masochistic realm. Time passes. Lou is once again approached about Joyce.

Powerful construction millionaire Chester Conway wants her out of the life of his son Elmer, who pays Joyce for her services and has become obsessed with her. Lou visits Joyce. They have sex, and afterwards, as they talk, Lou slowly pulls on his black leather gloves, and tells Joyce she is going to die. As she laughs, believing this to be one of their games, he playfully slaps her a few times, before pulling back his fist and hitting her full in the face. Lou then pummels Joyce to pulp. His fist slams again and again into her head, shattering her nose, busting her eyes, ripping apart her flesh; all the while speaking soothing words, *I'm sorry – I love you – It'll soon be over.*

Director Michael Winterbottom's camera is cold and unflinching. *The Killer Inside Me* is glacial in its depiction of this violence. There is no frenzy here, no hyper-psychopathic hysteria (no canted angles, no stylistic flourishes, no jagged musical accompaniment). The frame, shot and editing, colour and sound have the most restrained of realist coordinates. In this way, the images mirror the behaviour of Lou. The camera dissects the beating, every impact of the fist is captured as it connects with Joyce's flesh, and Lou examines his work as he proceeds, turning Joyce's head to better see the extent of the injuries bestowed upon her. Winterbottom expresses Lou's detachment through the formal production of images. The camera is always with Lou; the deputy sheriff is the privileged, subjective centre of the film, the image around which all other images revolve. Accordingly, the film is shot from Lou's perspective, and his being in the world permeates every image on the screen. After he has beaten Joyce to death, he leaves her body in her bedroom and calmly removes his gloves, and awaits Elmer. When Elmer arrives, Lou immediately shoots him dead, placing the gun in Joyce's hand.

It is this difference between the killings of Joyce and Elmer that are at the heart of *The Killer Inside Me*. One murder fleeting, momentary, clean; one depicted in all its brutal, dirty horror. It might be thought this difference is necessitated by the plot (of the film, and of the character) – in order to frame Elmer for the murder of Joyce, and make Elmer's death the last desperate act of the dying woman. This is not the case. Winterbottom reinforces and reifies this difference as the film continues. Investigator Howard Hendricks suspects Lou; so does Maples his boss, and his fiancée Amy Stanton. Lou will go on to commit a whole series of murders in an attempt to erase these people and stymie the dissemination of such suspicions. However, while the men are dispatched with quick, instantaneous actions; the death of Amy will be another pitiless, vicious killing, enacted through the cruel ruse of a secret elopement. There is a whole world of difference between the way in which Winterbottom films and Lou enacts the murder of women and men. Accordingly, we encounter a fundamental misogyny within the images and the narration, a dire philosophy which permeates everything. Yet the question is not whether it is the film itself which is misogynistic, or if this woman-hating is simply a function of the character. Such a debate attempts to divide an indivisible. Rather, it is whether, in depicting such misogyny, *The Killer Inside Me* is complicit with or actively evaluates the situation it sets out to explore (a reactionary reification or an effective critique).

To approach a possible answer to this question we can begin by aligning the film with an element of Deleuze's cineosis, the index of equivocity, a sign of the small form action-image. Action-images describe cinematic realism, 'milieux and modes of behaviour' (C1: 141). On the one hand, the large form of the action-image explores how an already given milieu spirals down to inspire character behaviours which will attempt to resolve the world; on the other hand, the small form of the action-image defines an ellipsis where the acts of a character will designate and attempt to reveal the coordinates of a situation. *The Killer Inside Me* may superficially appear to be of the large form. This is a film about murder; and the identity of the killer is never in doubt; thus the story will concern efforts to bring the perpetrator to justice. However, Winterbottom is not concerned with such a trajectory, and will find inspiration in another aspect of the story. *The Killer Inside Me* takes another path. For the film does indeed explore an ellipsis, although dissimilar in type to that of a murder mystery. This concerns the signs of the small form, the way in which the ellipsis will be constructed and countered. Accordingly, this is not a film exploring an index of lack, where a 'situation is … deduced from the action, by immediate inference, or by relatively complex reasoning' (C1: 160). Rather, it is of the more complex index of equivocity. Deleuze writes: 'in these cases we are made to hesitate by a whole world of details … it is as if an action, a mode of behaviour, concealed a slight difference, which was nevertheless sufficient to relate it to two quite distant situations, situations which are worlds apart' (C1: 161).

The Killer Inside Me will describe an exceptional index of equivocity by way of a series of displacements, a succession of movements that will explore a fundamental situation at the heart of the film. The ellipsis is opened up through the double murder of Joyce and Elmer. Does Lou kill Joyce in order to get away with killing Elmer; or Elmer to get away with killing Joyce? Lou may be jealous of Elmer's love for Joyce; or may believe Joyce feels something for Elmer. Such relatively solid coordinates, however, slowly dissolve. There is a long-standing animosity Lou feels towards Elmer, who is revealed to be a rich, spoilt, lazy childhood friend. Then again, Lou discovers that the death of his step-brother some six years previously could have had something to do with Elmer's father Chester. And Lou's brother was convicted of raping a five-year-old girl; however, the older boy took the blame for Lou, who was the one who committed this abhorrent crime. Then there is the sexual violence witnessed by a young Lou, his now dead father's depraved activities with a dangerously young girlfriend. This girl would also prey on the boy, tease and excite him, invite him to whip her.

A whole world of details. Deleuze writes, 'it matters little that one of these situations is contradicted or denied, for this happens only after its function has been exhausted, and never to such an extent that it eliminates the equivocity of the index and the distance between the situations which are evoked' (C1: 162). The effect of such a complex matrix of reasons for the double murder (the way in which they are enacted and filmed) is to stymie a simple, linear causal chain. Accordingly – and this is crucial – *The Killer Inside Me* finds a way to resist justifying and rationalising the terrible violence towards women within the narration. We thus encounter a certain paradox, a paradox that can – if we do not take care – carry us awry. For this horror of women is not a requirement necessitated by the narration (the actual organisation of images); and for this reason such a depiction becomes essential to the narrative (the story, the plot) of the film. Founded upon an index of equivocity – the difference between the depictions of the murders of Joyce and of Elmer, men and women – *The Killer Inside Me* both exposes a shocking cinematic image of misogyny, and positions such an image as fundamentally problematic.

12

Ajami

Vector

Frame III.12 *Ajami* (Scandar Copti and Yaron Shani, Germany | Israel, 2009)

There is Omar, a young Arab who, as head of his family, must traverse the line of a deteriorating situation initiated by his uncle's attempt to resist a Bedouin protection racket. There is Malek, an 'illegal' from the Palestinian territories, working in the kitchen of a restaurant, trying to earn money to support his ailing, dying mother. There is Dando, a Jewish cop, searching for news of his younger brother who has recently disappeared returning from an army posting. There is Binj, a dope-smoking chef and all round party dude, an Arab dating a Jewish girl. There is Abu Elias, a respected community leader, restaurateur, a Christian who wants to stymie any chance of his daughter ending up marrying Omar. Such are the coordinates of *Ajami*, a film named after a district in Yafa,

Tel Aviv – the space in which the movie is accordingly set. This area, once predominantly Palestinian-populated, is a 'mixing pot', with Muslims, Jews and Christians living alongside one another other, yet immediately riven with permeating temporal historical and contemporary forces. Accordingly, *Ajami* uses this location, and its people, to explore the state: Israel. Stressing this Ajami–*Ajami* matrix is essential. Directors Scandar Copti and Yaron Shani (one a Palestinian born and raised in Yafa, the other a Jewish Israeli) mostly employed non-professional actors from the territory to play out the events of the film. Through their working with and within the community, their basic script was developed, improvised and eventually captured on film. Over eight hours of footage was created, guerrilla-style, taking over a year to edit down to the final on-screen presentation. All of which gives the movie – as its starting point – a certain documentary *vérité* look and feel.

However, it is the structure – the narration, the assemblage of images – that is essential. *Ajami* tells five stories, each based around one of five central and privileged characters: Omar, Malek, Dando, Binj and Abu Elias. These stories are organised into five episodes, each of which interpenetrates and comes to bear on the others; the central character in one becoming a minor character in another. Furthermore, while the events in each of the five chapters are parallel, at the same moment each advances the ongoing storyline across the whole film. Ellipses created in one episode are answered, echoed or reoriented in another. In this way, *Ajami* constructs a very powerful image of heterogeneity composing a homogeneous world, and the lines of force that traverse such a complex whole. This structure is an incarnation of what Deleuze, in his taxonomy of cinema, will name the vector.

The vector is a complex action-image which explores a multitude of characters and situations, through indices of lack and equivocity. Accordingly, the vector develops – or discovers the genesis of – what Deleuze describes as the small form of the action-image, a form which operates by revealing the situation through the unfolding of actions of characters. With an index of lack, the film responds to an ellipsis with a full explication; with an index of equivocity the ellipsis is explored through two related and undecidable alternatives. The vector is the genesis of such ellipses: the world will be revealed as a nexus of situations, where each is aligned with a different character, class, gender, event, or condition, and so on – the fulfilment of an index of lack in one domain will be a coordinate of an index of equivocity in another; or different poles of undecidable alternatives may be resolved in separate domains. Thus, with vectors, we see a heterogeneous mix of situations and characters which, in the end, describe the complexities – the ambiguities and interrelations – of a homogeneous milieu. This is, for Deleuze, 'a broken line whose path is unpredictable', a '*skeleton-space*, with missing intermediaries, heterogeneous elements which jump from one to the other, or which interconnect directly' (C1: 168). The vector of the small form, accordingly, describes no given encompassing whole which surrounds everything, organising its coordinates and relations (as in a large form action-image), but rather 'the broken stroke of a line of the universe, across the holes', like 'a knotted rope, twisting itself at each take, at each action, at each event' (C1: 168). The crucial aspect, and the one which returns us to *Ajami*, is that here the vector describes 'the incongruous makeshift group' and 'finds its motivations in a debt to be discharged, a mistake to be redeemed' (C1: 165). Thus, to re-appropriate a phrase from Deleuze's *Cinema* books into another context: there is no encompassing milieu – Israel – but Israels.

Israels: 'that is, totalities of locations' (C1: 168). And the vector 'brings together actions or parts, A and A`, each one of which retains its independence' (C1: 168). Yaron, in an interview, explains: 'you have good people, who share the same human values, who fight each other because of the nature of segregation' ('The Fabulous Picture Show', *Al Jazeera*, 2009). Ajami explores – through its structure – the structure of Israel. The vector becomes the very theme itself. The stories, the ethnic backgrounds, the locales, the Israelis, the Palestinians, the Bedouins; Muslims, Christians and Jews; shariah law, state law, street law. There is no resolution, a rectified situation, a solution. Ellipses remain and proliferate, owing to the structure of the state, the conditions in Ajami, embodied in the vector-narration of the film.

marxism today (prologue) and *untitled*

Milieu

Frame III.13 *marxism today (prologue)* (Phil Collins, UK | Germany, 2010)

Archive footage takes us back to the classroom. The lecturer has just finished drawing a chalk diagram on the blackboard expressing one aspect of the Marxist theory of production. A pyramid structure, a hierarchy. At the apex, the company director; at the bottom, the foundation, the workers. And from this pyramid emerge commodities. Next to the diagram: 'exploitation' (with a specific meaning in the German, the exploitation of the class system). This is the German Democratic Republic (GDR/East Germany), before *die Wende*, the turning point; before *Deutsche Einheit*, German (re-)unification. So, the lecturer asks: who thinks workers in the Federal Republic of Germany (FRG, West Germany) are exploited? One student's reply ... *my uncle* [in the FRG] *has a car, a washing machine, he earns a good wage ... how is he exploited?* The lecturer draws a question mark: 'exploitation?' A statement turned interrogative. *Let us ask if your uncle is exploited ...*

marxism today (prologue) is neither paean nor eulogy. Director Phil Collins is interested neither in mourning nor in affirming the triumph of capitalism over socialism, 'West' over 'East', the 'end' of the/a communist experiment. Rather, the film explores a milieu, its passing, and its legacy. Using archive footage and filmed interviews as monologues, Collins wishes to explore theoretical Marxism, its propagation through the East German state, and its material effects in the lives of the people who lived within such an encompassing. Three Marxist-Leninist lecturers – Petra Mgoza-Zeckay, Andrea Ferber and Marianne Klotz – talk about life in the GDR and the transition. Before: free university study; employment both inside and outside the party; an international scene with students from all over the (Soviet-influenced) world. The Peaceful Revolution; the fall of the Berlin Wall; German reunification. After: Mgoza-Zeckay becomes a social worker, life becomes more difficult for people of the East, those on the periphery; Ferber and Klotz successfully embrace the possibilities of the free market. *marxism today (prologue)* thus explicates coordinates along two axes: on the horizontal are the forces of time, back to before the turning point, and now, some twenty years after German unity; on the vertical are the spatial forces of capitalism and socialism – the duel between two systems of living in the world. In other words, the film describes a specific spatio-temporal geo-political socio-historical situation. The student who found it difficult to understand how his uncle was exploited, modestly rich as he was with all the trappings of the West, is a subject of ideology. Ideology – according to Marx and Engels – needs to be exposed, and the tool for this is materialism. Ideology obscures material being in the world, the actualised economic milieu. The West employs ideological methods, the East exposes and lives the reality. In the classroom, the question mark must be erased – but not before capitalist ideology is exposed. Materialism is a science, not a belief system composed of ideas. Historical materialism is an empirical study of the world, the world in process through its social conditions and relations. The world has passed through many regimes: slave-based societies → feudalism → capitalism. For true socialism to arise the working classes must become conscious of the reality of the world, thus laying the conditions for communism. As Marx famously wrote, philosophy should not simply explain the world, but transform it. Thus the duel between capitalism and socialism. This is theoretical Marxism: realism. And it is the historical coordinates of this duel as experienced before and after *die Wende* that are explored in *marxism today (prologue)*. Accordingly, Collin's film is realist cinema.

Realism in the cinema – for Deleuze – is an action-image. The action-image expresses various relations between situations and actions through two reciprocal formula: actions → situation and situation → action. In the first case, the actions of characters throughout the film explore the world and reveal the situation; in the second case, the situation is a given reality lived through the characters. The small form action-image reveals; the large form action-image determines. *marxism today (prologue)* is of the large form: the lecturers lived and are living a given reality. Deleuze describes the most assured aspect of the large form through the cinematic sign of the milieu. As Deleuze puts it, the milieu is 'determinate, geographical, historical and social space-times', it is the 'Ambience or the Encompasser', it is the 'situation' (C1: 141). In essence, a film that explores a milieu would map the coordinates of a situation; it would place that situation into specific contexts: national and international history, locations of longitude and latitude, cultural mappings. Such is the moment – or law – of the milieu: the spatial aspects (S) as explored – through the trajectory of the film – in the temporal dimension S→S`. The first law, however, is merely the first moment in a series of laws that carry S→S`. The second law concerns the forces inherent in the milieu, forces which will immediately spiral down into actions embodied by characters: S→A. Actions are thus forces devolved from the milieu (A). Realism operates through conflict – thus S→A is explicated as binomial forces, which come together at A as the duel – the third law at the end of the film – for the creation of S`: the new situation. Furthermore, the deciding action at A is not a limited moment, but only the final duel in a whole series of actions. Thus the fourth law, the binomial, is polynomial: A^n; the duel is ongoing and structures the trajectory. Finally, the fifth law is the gap itself between S and S` – the story the film tells through the constitutive elements of the milieu and actions, the narrative arising from the narration and its organisation of images. The laws of the milieu thus concern the possibility of actions changing the world, and have three relative outcomes: (1) SAS is where the situation, despite efforts by the characters, remains unchanged; (2) SAS` is where the situation is confronted and resolved; (3) SAS`` is where the actions of the characters – no matter what – engender a worsened situation. In this way, the duel tends to designate good and evil, and the possibilities of triumph and tragedy.

marxism today (prologue) is founded upon these laws. The vertical axis S and the horizontal axis S→S` are the coordinates of a milieu explored through the duel between communism and capitalism, East and West Germany. The only question is of the final mode of enunciation: SAS, SAS` or SAS``. And it is here that the film is structured by theoretical Marxism, a pure form as a political, social and economic enquiry. A geology of history, capital and the people. Collins explores the way in which Marxism in a historical context does not rely upon triumphalist rhetoric or defeatist nostalgia. Neither SAS` nor SAS``. SAS – the situation remains unchanged. The struggle is ongoing. As Alain Badiou writes in 'Preamble: What Is Called Failure' from *The Communist Hypothesis* – Marxism is part of 'a promise of universal emancipation supported by three centuries of critical, international and secular philosophy that exploited the resources of science and mobilised … the enthusiasm of both workers and intellectuals (Badiou, 2015: 2). Accordingly, for Badiou – 'we have to think about the notion of failure … does it require us to abandon the hypothesis itself, and to renounce the whole problem of emancipation? Or was it merely a relative failure? Was it a failure because of the form it took or the path it explored? Was it a failure that simply proves it was not the right way to resolve the initial problem?' (Badiou, 2015: 4–5). This is the power of the SAS mode: everything remains open for a sequel. It is crucial to note (and the title makes this clear) that the film is about the past, but only inasmuch as it is a prologue for today.

marxism today (prologue) is shown alongside another unnamed film. This sequel depicts a lecture on Marx's *Capital*, not from the historical past of the GDR, but in the now, to students in modern Germany. The focus is upon the difference between a product and a commodity. The class is initially blind to such mysteries. The lecturer explains: a product is something which is produced and consumed directly by the worker who produces it. A commodity is something that is produced to sell on. This leads to the formation of machines of commerce, where surplus value is generated by producing more commodities than a workforce can consume, more commodities than it takes to pay for the machines of commerce to operate. This profit, produced by the workforce, is then reinvested into the company and paid to shareholders. The workers do the work, build the company, but receive little or none of the profit. The workers are, in this way, exploited. The sequel is a direct echo of the archive footage of the GDR lecture shown in the main film. And exactly the same kind of questions are asked. In other words, today, in a world where China, a so-called communist state, has a more resilient model of capitalism than the USA; in a world where the aftermath – or the ongoing – crisis in global capitalism affects countries as diverse as the USA, the UK, Germany, Greece, Ireland, Dubai; in a world where the so-called 'end of communism' has given birth to a deregulated financial system built upon the selling of collateralised debt obligations where more risk produces more profit (for a time) … the question is, what can theoretical Marxism still do? As a way of awakening thought and action … as a way of thinking through where we are now … as a way of conceiving exploitation and – as Badiou would have it, *ushering in a new age of communism* … today, for tomorrow.

14

Made in Dagenham

Binomial

Frame III.14 *Made in Dagenham* (Nigel Cole, UK, 2010)

Wrapped in a wee yellow dressing gown, Sandra makes her way onto one of the vast shop floors at Ford's Dagenham plant. The space is empty and silent, save for a small corner set up for a photoshoot. Car production at Dagenham has ground to a halt, the entire workforce sent home by the management in the wake of strike action by the female sewing machinists. 'There she is', leers the photographer; 'drape yourself across this vehicle.' Sandra slowly allows the dressing gown to slip from her shoulders, revealing the latest in 1960s beach fashion, a risqué electric blue bikini. The film cuts to a close-up. Across her belly, written in red lipstick, are the words *EQUAL PAY*. Cutting back to a wide shot, Sandra asks: 'How does this look?' Yet it is Sandra who is looking, first at the silenced photographer; then, eyes moving, with a confrontational stare, out of the frame. Another cut: up above the shop floor in a glass-fronted office complex, Ford's American boss (flown in to break the strike by any means necessary) turns and walks away. Sandra: 'Nah?'

Made in Dagenham has all the attendant, complex pleasures of cinematic realism. The film recounts the story of a strike at Ford's main UK plant in 1968. One of hundreds in the emancipatory climate of the 1960s, it was, however, an almost unique event: a strike by working women for working women. It was caused by a management decision to downgrade the female labour from semi-skilled to unskilled status, the true aim being to enact a brutal wage cut on a group with seemingly little recourse to action. During the strike, and not in small measure a consequence of the unsupportive male-dominated union, the walk-out mutated to encompass the rights of working women in general: equal pay for the same jobs as men. The strike was successful in that it resulted in a change in the law. And, as the film points out, this inspired similar laws across 'most' industrialised nations. *Made in Dagenham* tells this story through a number of the women characters who rise up against the encompassing patriarchal order of management, union and husbands – focusing upon Rita O'Grady, a worker who becomes the voice and champion for the sewing machinists. A wonderfully enjoyable film, *Made in Dagenham* creates these characters – who do not exist in the real – in order to explore a situation by way of capturing up an audience through the pleasures of the mainstream movie, through the entertainment of cinematic realism.

Enjoyment, however, can create a problem with regard to political discourse. In *A Short History of Cahiers du Cinéma*, Emilie Bickerton produces a beautifully written and astute commentary upon a film magazine at the vanguard of the rise of cinema theory. Coming after the realist-focused auteur phase (1950s: the yellow book, with Bazin as editor, Truffaut and Godard as critics) *Cahiers* entered what became known, without much irony, as the Maoist phase (1970s: the red years, Comolli and Narboni *et al.*). It is in this latter context that Bickerton gives an account of how such enjoyable political films were received, the focus being the event of Costas-Gravas' *Z* (France | Algeria, 1969). 'Z was one of the biggest cinema hits of sixties France: by the end of 1969, 700,000 people had seen the film in Paris' (Bickerton, 2009: 64). The film depicts the murder of Greek politician Gregoris Lambrakis in 1963, an event that presaged Greece's democratic government being ousted by the military some four years later. 'Yves Montand and scriptwriter Jorge Semprún', continues Bickerton, 'added to the film's left-wing credentials. In *L'Express*, Claude Mauriac named Z the must-see film for "anyone who loves freedom and justice"; *La Croix* emphatically declared it the film that allows you to live through cinema: "it will teach you about the world and all of its difficult realities"' (Bickerton, 2009: 64). However: 'Jean Narboni's critique in *Cahiers* in March 1969 was the start of a battle against what become known as the *Série-Z* phenomenon, which would continue into the next decade. Attacking Z, Narboni described the film as offering a brand of sterilised militancy … repackaged for thrills. *Cahiers* immediately shredded the film's political credentials' (Bickerton, 2009: 64). Narboni believed the film actualised bourgeois ideology '"in the functioning of the film as much as its consumption", because Z neglects "the concrete analysis of concrete situations, the objective study of social relations, the breakdown of political mechanisms"' (Bickerton, 2009: 64). Filmgoers, Bickerton summarises, 'appeared to be seeking out a cinema that offered the piquancy of politics but that did not implicate or challenge their world view directly. With Z you had a film-maker who was addressing politics on the surface, but simultaneously banalizing it'; the film was 'intelligent and committed but never revolutionary, in either narrative content or aesthetic form' (Bickerton, 2009: 65).

Bickerton's take on the red years and Z remains ambiguous … and this ambiguity is rife throughout academia – there is something thrilling and masterful in taking a film to pieces, showing how while it might appear to work on the surface … underneath, in some way, it falls to pieces. This is the problem with realism. It is never really good enough. The same year Comolli and Narboni published an editorial in the journal entitled 'Cinema/Ideology/ Criticism'. *'Every film is political'*, write Comolli and Narboni, 'inasmuch as it is determined by the ideology which produces it' (Comolli and Narboni, 1996: 45). As every film is part of the economic system – cinema 'more thoroughly and completely', according to the authors, than the other arts – so every film is ideological. Cinema cannot film reality – rather, the camera 'registers … the vague, unformulated, untheorized, unthought-out world of the dominant ideology' (Comolli and Narboni, 1996: 46). Thus the task of thinking cinema is to 'elaborate and apply a critical theory of cinema' (Comolli and Narboni, 1996: 46). Such a praxis is not, most obviously, the 'spacious raving (of the film-columnist variety)', nor 'commentary, interpretation, decoding', but 'a rigidly factual analysis of what governs the production of a film' (Comolli and Narboni, 1996: 50). This is scientific criticism. The critical film theorist is thus the vanguard of a passive populace caught up in the ideology of the cinema. This is because the 'public can only express itself via the thought-patterns of the ideology' (Comolli and Narboni, 1996: 47). Critique can turn this passive populace into active participants; consumers of commodities into producers of meaning. Reciprocally, and in a feedback loop from the theorist, such becomes the responsibility of the filmmaker: 'to show up the cinema's so-called "depiction of reality"', thus creating 'a chance that we will be able to disrupt or possibly even sever the connection between the cinema and its ideological function' (Comolli and Narboni, 1996: 46). Accordingly, Comolli and Narboni see seven types of film that adopt different positions with respect to the dominant ideology. Type A, the 'largest category', are films which adopt the dominant ideology unconsciously (Comolli and Narboni, 1996: 47). And so on ... there are films which challenge content and form; there are films that are ambiguous, and – finally – there are films which present the real. Comolli and Narboni write that it is the last types that 'constitute the essential in the cinema, and should be the chief subject of' *Cahiers*' (Comolli and Narboni: 48). The work of the magazine is thus to use critical film theory as the opposite of ideology, to condemn the enjoyments of realist cinema; and to promote the modernist, difficult cinema.

It is so easy to fall into this trap. The *a priori* condemnation of a film, type of film, genre of cinema, and so on. We do not even need to see the film! We already know! And if we do see the film and enjoy it, we encounter the guilty pleasure, the bad faith of a pleasure engendered through manipulation. As if all cinema is not the manipulation of images! This is why Deleuze is so important for cinema theory. Deleuze will categorise film in such a way as to allow a viewer to explore the wonders of realism as much as the ungroundings of modernism. He does this by creating a twofold semiotic taxonomy: the movement-image and the time-image. Each semiotic has various components (many different ways in which the film may constitute its images through signs). Yet – and this is crucial: 'it cannot be said that one is more important than the other, whether more beautiful or profound. All that can be said is that the movement-image does not give us a time-image' (C2: 270). Each regime of cinema captures up images of the world in its own way, each regime creates an image of thought in its own way, each regime explores moments of history in its own way. 'You become an accomplice to the impasse of history if you make films of the movement-image or films of the time-image ... the problems addressed by one cannot address the problems addressed by the other. What one can do, the other cannot. Or better, what one cannot do, the other can' (Deamer, 2009: 183). The crucial point – of course – is how a particular film operates.

Made in Dagenham is at the centre of the movement-image, a (large form) action-image, a realist film *par excellence*, the most distinctive sign of which is the binomial. Here we encounter a filmic structure that proceeds through a conflict, by two dominant lines of force devolving from a situation and embodied in characters who express their relation through the duel. These duels will be romantic, as much as violent or indeed political (and *Made in Dagenham* explores all these manifestations). This process is organised by alternate parallel montage that converges towards a central, final and privileged duel; and while many other duels will permeate the film, this polynomial aspect is in the service of the dominant binomial which organises and structures everything. The film will thus centre on a character, or characters, who will come to embody one side of the milieu; people who must become equal to the situation so as to transform the world. With *Made in Dagenham*, we see the forces of conflict organised according to a milieu of gender inequality; the feminist line embodied – at first, unwillingly – in Rita. Rita will take on factory management, union, community, her husband and the government, all of which embody patriarchal repression. And Rita – along with the women of the Dagenham plant – will triumph. No doubt *Made in Dagenham* can be accused of exploitation – Sandra is used by the film to sex up the message. Yet the very friction of such a moment can open up the narrative. Sandra has her sexual exploitation transformed into an act of defiance, creating a complex image which enacts its own critique. *Made in Dagenham* is historically inaccurate. The film never mentions that the women were not regraded back to semi-skilled workers. However, realism does not reflect. Realism does not represent. Realism creates. As in all cinema. No movie can depict the exact moments of an event. Realism creates truth, whatever that may mean. The crucial point is this: the action-image can be seen as 'putting forward', according to Deleuze, 'a strong and coherent conception of universal history' (C1: 151).

Deleuze, in citing 'universal history', is invoking Nietzsche's analysis of three types of history in the essay 'On the Uses and Abuses of History for Life' (1874): the monumental, the antiquarian and the critical. For Deleuze, with monumental history situations appear initially static but under threat. The threat thus constitutes the beginning of the monumental narration which will continue until the threat is vanquished. This passage is always described through the deeds of the hero; and the passage from situation to restored situation is embodied in action. In this way there are two tendencies – first, that historical events chart the collision of two embodied forces (parallel montage finding resolution in convergence). Secondly, that this structure is repetitive: these forces clash continually, form peaks and describes homogeneous phenomena. Antiquarian history selects events that – no matter how different – form a coherent mapping of a civilisation: the archival data of a nation essentialised as traditions. Antiquarian history, then, attempts to venerate the past to conserve it. Lastly, for Deleuze 'the monumental and antiquarian conceptions of history would not come together so well without the ethical image which measures and organises them both' (C1: 150). The gap between situation and restored situation marks the very coordinates of the story being told. This is thus 'a matter of Good and Evil', where 'a strong ethical judgement must condemn the injustice of "things", bring compassion, herald the new civilisation' (C1: 151). *Made in Dagenham* uses monumental, antiquarian and critical history in an exemplary way. Rita and her workforce sisters become mythical heroes raging against the traditions of the past, the film providing the ethical judgement and so a triumph of a moment in the feminist cause. *Made in Dagenham* is mass culture, and culture needs realist cinema.

Women – nearly fifty years after the events depicted in the film – still earn less than men for the same job (Allen, 'How to end the gender pay gap', *The Guardian*, 13 June 2016: 22). In the UK, some 20 per cent less, on average.

Section III

15

Fish Tank

Imprint

Frame III.15 *Fish Tank* (Andrea Arnold, UK | the Netherlands, 2009)

Mia dances for herself. There is an empty, abandoned flat in the estate where she lives. With faded, ripped wallpaper, tatty carpet, but a space apart from the world – away from the lads and lasses hanging around the tower blocks, and her mum and sister at home. Sometimes tanked up on cheap booze (bought by teenagers old enough to pass for eighteen), Mia dances for herself. To get good; to get better. To exhaust herself. To empty herself – of the rage, of the sadness, of the loneliness. But rage, sadness and loneliness are in endless supply. There are thus two escapes in Mia's dancing – an escape from the world, and an escape from herself. These escapes are inseparable, but one feeds the other. For the world determines her being, her actions, her behaviour. Director Andrea Arnold's mise-en-scène in *Fish Tank* thus has a precise function. This is no urban wasteland. This is no zone on the edge, on the periphery, this is a fairly well-maintained estate, with shops and social spaces to hang out in. A vibrant community. This is a common space, a naturalised space, a space where many of us live. Yet Mia is at war with everyone. With her mother – who feels her youth slipping away, and sees her daughter only in terms of her sexuality, ordering her out of the flat when there is a party – there will be men there. With the boys of the estate – who will harass and attempt to rape her as punishment for her interference in their activities. With the girls – who appear only to desire acceptance from the lads as some kind of validation. Such is the situation of the film-world of *Fish Tank*. Such are the powerful forces permeating Mia as she discovers her sexuality. This is her rage, her sadness, her loneliness. Although she has not got her head around it all – not yet. Arnold's project is to allow Mia to traverse this world of the film, to perceive and be affected by that world; to become saturated by the milieu. How much can Mia endure before something happens? Before Mia decisively reacts?

Fish Tank is a film of the imprint: the impression of the milieu upon the body at the centre. For Deleuze, the imprint is an action-image; where perception, affect and thought are oriented towards and so dominated by action. Here, the characters perceive, feel and think so they can act. Action-images explicate situations (milieux, environments) and explore actions (behaviours, being in the world). In the first place, the small form action-image (ASA) extends through perception-images and affection-images towards an action that reveals the situation; in the second place, the large form action-image (SAS) begins with a given situation and determines the actions of the characters through their perceptions and affects. With the large form action-image, accordingly, the logic of the sensory-motor system as a linear trajectory (perception → affect → action) reaches its fullest expression. This is the fundamental essence of cinematic realism and where the movement-image is ultimately fulfilled. Milieux are givens, and the characters are caught in the forces of that world, which organise into conflicts – binomials: duels. And it is through the actions, the behaviours of the characters, that the situation will be resolved. '[T]he cinema of behaviour', however, 'is not content with a simple sensory-motor formula' (C1: 158). With the imprint, according to Deleuze, there is a 'much more complex behaviourism', one which explores 'internal factors' (C1: 158). It is as if the affection-image does not immediately pass through the body for an action-image, but affects accumulate, build up, until they become intolerable.

In this way the duel is no longer externalised in the world, or rather, that is not its primary domain. The conflict is within the body at the centre of the film. In this way, a film of the imprint can attain varied results: the character cracking up; finding some way to accommodate the situation; or – finally – in triumph (resolution or escape). The imprint thus describes three modes of the action-image large form (situation → action → new situation): SAS`` (crack-up); SAS (accommodation); SAS` (triumph). *Fish Tank* is exceptional in that it explores each of these three alternatives in turn, in series, putting each into relation, each feeding off a prior outcome.

However, before these three moments – which come at the end of the film – we must explore how a film of the imprint creates its own conditions. The first aspect concerns the complex situation. Here the milieu is composed of heterogeneous forces and the character is confronted with a multifaceted scenario. It thus takes time for the body at the centre to homogenise the milieu, to understand the nature of the world as quasi-heterogeneous, to organise all the coordinates of the situation. Deleuze writes, the imprint 'is divided into successive and continuous local missions (s1, a1, s2, a2, s3 …)' (C1: 157). In other words, a multiplicity of duels fragment the trajectory of the film, creating a series of determinate space-times. These moments are well defined in *Fish Tank* (and each develops into one of the three critical points). There is the estate: Mia comes across some of the local girls, they are dancing in a social space, grinding down. It is a display for the lads, with their dogs, who hang there. Mia interrupts the scene. She watches the girls, who are now aware of their display caught in a female gaze outside their set. Arnold films this wonderfully, excluding the boys from the frame, and from the sequence after Mia's arrival. It ends in a girl-fight, Mia head-butting one of lasses and giving her a bloody nose. There is the space away from the estate. Mia discovers a dilapidated-looking horse, chained up near some caravans. There will be a number of attempts to free the horse – does she identify with it? This space is not without its dangers: some of the boys who own the horse will attack Mia. There is – of course – the family home. And it is here that the crisis will finally reach its saturation point. Mia's mother's new boyfriend Connor and Mia make love. For him it is excused as a semi-drunken moment, one which fills him with shame, guilt and fear; causing him to run away the next morning, not long after moving in. For Mia, however, it is exciting, and an act of aggression. It is an actualisation of, and a response to, her mother's jealousy. This is Arnold's genius: the man has become a paedophile, but Arnold focuses upon Mia. She wanted it – even if every reason is wrong – and she wants more. And when Connor disappears, it is Mia, not her mother, who goes looking for him.

Action thus tends towards being internalised as the complex situation imprints upon the very being of a character. And it will necessarily require time to determine the appropriate reaction. Accordingly, when the character becomes capable of action it will be defined through unbound violence: forces accumulate over the film to be released in bursts. As Deleuze puts it, the imprint 'is the inner, but visible, link between the permeating situation and the explosive action' (C1: 159). Mia finds Connor – and discovers he has another life, a nice suburban home, and a happy family. Mia pisses on the front room carpet. A little later, she kidnaps his young daughter and attempts to murder her. Arnold thus presents the first moment of the denouement of *Fish Tank* as a violent crack-up. The second moment of denouement concerns the accommodation of the situation. Mia has seen a flyer advertising for dancers; she tapes herself with a video camera, and is asked to audition. Here we discover another feature of the imprint. Its visibility explicates the milieu–behaviour nexus and is the conjoining of emotions with an object, creating an emotional object which links character to situation. The object is a referent for the complex nature of the universe and the manifold internal struggles the character must undergo in order to right their world. Connor has introduced Mia to Bobby Womack's 1968 version of the song 'California Dreaming', and, in his haste to leave the flat, left the CD. The day after the attempted murder, Mia attends the audition, too late realising it is for a stripper at a sordid (so-called) gentlemen's club. Mia plays the track, takes to the stage … but then walks away. Leaving the CD spinning. The crack-up and the accommodation are thus both stymied outcomes, moments of an imprint that cannot be fully actualised in the world. Arnold reinvents the imprint by subjecting it to graduations of release. The third – and final – moment of denouement is thus different once again. Having struck up a friendship with one of the lads whose family own the horse, Mia discovers it has died. She cries. Everything that has been done to her – and everything that she has done – is washed away. Mia will leave with the boy, escape the milieu.

Section III

16

Tian bian yi duo yun/The Wandering Cloud

Plastic figure

Frame III.16 *The Wandering Cloud* (Tsai Ming-liang, France | Taiwan, 2005)

It was only a matter of time – of course – before a film such as *The Wandering Cloud*. The pornographic musical. Or, musical-porno. Take your pick. Yet such descriptions – which no doubt director Tsai Ming-liang would appreciate, as provocation – belies the subversive nature of the movie, and the power of Tsai's images of sex and music. The setting is Kaohsiung, an affluent port city in southern Taiwan. The long hot summer rolls on, people move slowly through the wide, beautiful parks and along the boulevards shadowed beneath skyscrapers. Kaohsiung is in the midst of a drought – the reservoirs are depleted, the rivers running dry and household water services intermittent. Here we find Hsiao-Kang and Shiang-chyi, a man and a woman aimlessly drifting through life. Hsiao-Kang sleeps wherever he finds himself when needing a nap: children's playgrounds, stairwell suicide nets, roofs of tall buildings. Shiang-chyi wanders the streets collecting empty water bottles to stockpile tap water, amusing herself with diverting conundrums, or lazing in her apartment watching television. Inevitably, they meet – vaguely recognising one another (Hsiao-Kang sold Shiang-chyi a timepiece in a previous film by Tsai, who tends to reuse characters without any real deference to continuity). They begin an affair – although their interactions, even when close, are disconnected. When they eat, one will sit on a chair at the table, the other underneath. When they share a room, both will be occupied in separate tasks. This distance between the lovers is further evoked by a radical lack of dialogue. *The Wandering Cloud* – in these sections – is essentially silent, only a word or phrase occasionally spoken. Shiang-chyi has misplaced the key to a locked suitcase. She finds it set into the tarmac of the road beneath her high-rise. Yet when Hsiao-Kang retrieves the key, still the case cannot be opened. Is it the right key? Or is the lock no longer functioning? Tsai is a master of the cinematic metaphor, metonymy, synecdoche: images echo one another, scenes evoke associations, inconsequential actions point to the real, implied situation, which remains an ellipsis.

The Wandering Cloud is replete with such figures. Shiang-chyi is addicted to watermelons. A bumper crop means they are in endless supply, and, because of the drought, cheaper than bottled drinking water. Shiang-chyi will see hundreds floating in the low, sluggish flow of Love River that meanders through the city. Jugs of chilled watermelon juice are gulped down as she watches TV. To entertain herself, Shiang-chyi will push a watermelon under her top, becoming pregnant; pretend – when all alone – that she is giving birth. Hsiao-Kang hates the stuff, pouring the freshly prepared juice away when Shiang-chyi's back is turned. The watermelon is a resonant, substitutive and transformative figure: it replaces the fundamental function of water, evokes love as well as pointing to the disconnect between the two characters. And this figure will echo in other dimensions of the film: appearing not only in the everyday moments of *The Wandering Cloud*, but in pornography-sequences and musical episodes.

Hsiao-Kang is working as a porno actor; and in the first scene in which he is captured in such a role, the watermelon replaces the vagina of the actress he is fucking. These sequences are shot in cramped environments, Hsiao-Kang, the unnamed 'Japanese actress', a director and cameraman crowding the space. Accordingly, Tsai does not make pornography, but rather, documents the making of pornography. These scenes are by turns ridiculous and brutal – sometimes both at the same time – and become increasingly joyless as the film progresses. The final sequence of *The Wandering Cloud* is Hsiao-Kang fucking the comatose actress with the crew as puppeteers attempting to manipulate her body, Shiang-chyi watching, having just discovered her lover's occupation.

The film ends with Hsiao-Kang suffocating an apathetic Shiang-chyi with his ejaculating penis.

Into the midst of these disconnected, silent, bizarre, brutal images Tsai introduces vibrant musical episodes. Shot in glorious, high-intensity colour, they throw the day-to-day world of Hsiao-Kang and Shiang-chyi into relief – now a dour, bleached, naturalistic mise-en-scène, anonymous apartments, buildings, streets. The participants – the singers, chorus and dancers – will echo in their costumes the green, red and black of the skin, meat and seeds of watermelons; such motifs emblazoned on dresses, umbrellas and permeating the settings. Bright affective colours, expressionist dark and light, wondrous spectacle. The songs are old-style Chinese hits from the sixties (many of which repurpose American show tunes), to which the on-screen singer or singers will mime. In no way innocent, often in their staging referring to sex, these enactments celebrate both the joy and the disappointments of falling in and out of love. A water-tank transforms into a moonlit grotto as a slivery-scaled merman croons about being separated from his other half. Four women sing a cheeky, bubbly love song, a burlesque performance at the site of a large bronze statue of a respected city elder. A spider-woman, stalking a dark interior filled with fire, cries a melancholic ballad into the void. In a waterpark filled with Chinese dragons, jubilant crossdressers chase each other around amid a troupe of dancers armed with umbrellas, expressing the confusions that occur in love affairs. In a large public toilet, a man dressed as a phallus is tormented by women dressed in high heels and red cone bras.

The musical episodes do not emerge through a natural flow from an event in the day-to-day film-world, but appear as a break, a rupture. They cleave the screen, for a moment. Nevertheless – they extend from and through the every-day-moments and pornographic-sequences, combining the figure-elements of the characters: watermelons and sex. In this way, these musical-episodes echo moments and sequences from the rest of the film, evoke associations and refer to the real, implied situation, which remains an ellipsis. They are the expressions of joy and disappointment neither Hsiao-Kang nor Shiang-chyi are able to actualise. *The Wandering Cloud* creates images of thought – what Deleuze calls plastic figures: where 'the action does not immediately disclose the situation which it envelops, but is itself developed in grandiose situations which encompass the implied situation' (C1: 182). The flamboyant and inspiring song and dance episodes of *The Wandering Cloud* are plastic figures *par excellence* – revealing a situation which remains an ellipsis.

17

Scott Pilgrim vs. the World

Theatrical figure

Frame III.17 *Scott Pilgrim vs. the World* (Edgar Wright, USA, 2010)

'We are Sex Bob-omb', screams Kim the drummer 'and we are here to watch Scott Pilgrim kick your teeth in. One. Two. Three. Four.' Thrash indy-metal buzzsaws as Scott – now armed with a flaming samurai sword – lays waste to the minions fronting pretentious nightclub owner and music industry guru, Gideon Gordon Graves. The revellers in the vast warehouse retreat as the henchmen cartwheel across the floor, each scattering into a shower of coins as the sword slashes through their bodies. Points are awarded for each win, the value spiralling up from the fatal contact, slowly fading, leaving only a lingering trace of digital dust. Gideon watches aghast from the top of his vast pyramidic throne. Unsheathing a sword from his walking cane, the leader of the League of Evil Exes leaps down as Scott bounds up the steps. Cut to a horizontal split screen: the faces of each twisted in anger and determination. The two figures are captured in slow-mo as they meet mid-air, their swords clash, emitting an intense white light, which halos behind them, the sound rendered in graphics encompassing then surpassing the mise-en-scène. Gideon crashes to the floor, falls unconscious and a glowing chunky numerical of 7000 floats up from his strewn body. With poise, Scott lands upon the high plateau of the throne, alongside the frozen, electronically enchanted form of Ramona Flowers. But the fight ain't over, it's only just begun! Knives is after Ramona, and Gideon will arise and re-enter the fray.

Director Edgar Wright's images in *Scott Pilgrim vs. the World* are inspired by the visuals of comic books and computer games (the film itself an adaptation of a comic book utilising gaming graphics – as Scott enters the nightclub, a voice on the edge of hearing comments: *the film ain't as good as the comic book*). These comic book and computer game visuals permeate the movie, from beginning to end, creating what Deleuze names a theatrical presentation where it is 'the sequences of images which [have] a figural role' (C1: 183). This is the cinematic allegory, mythology, parable where the theatrical figure provides the sinuous thread that weaves the weft and warp of the narration. Deleuze writes 'in the theatrical representation, the real situation does not immediately give rise to an action which corresponds to it, but is expressed in a fictitious action' (C1: 182). Accordingly, it is the sequence of images that takes on a figural role, the formula situation → action transforming into situation → index of action (as a theatrical representation of the real action). If the narrative situation of *Scott Pilgrim vs. the World* (its story, its plot) has a foundation in the low-fi indy flick, the narration and images on-screen evoke another world entirely.

Scott Pilgrim, dorky bass player in Sex Bob-omb, an unknown Toronto garage-punk band, has a new girlfriend. Trouble is – as everyone keeps telling him – she is too young. Knives is 17, while Scott's in his early twenties. This aside, at least he now has a girlfriend. For a year or so he has been depressed after being dumped. But now everything is OK. Except, Scott has just encountered the cool, roller-skating, purple-haired, ex-New Yorker Ramona. And he is in love. Trouble is – as everyone keeps telling him – Scott is punching well above his weight ... and he already has a girlfriend. Nonetheless, Ramona consents to a date. Ramona, however, has a past, and this past returns with a vengeance. Enter the League of Evil Exes: Matthew Patel, Lucas Lee, Todd Ingram, Roxie, Kyle and Ken Katayanagi, and Gideon Gordon Graves – all intent on stymieing the nascent romance. Scott has to battle each of the evil exes in turn so as to progress to the next part of the film (and the next stage in the romance of Ramona). Each fight more intense than the one previous, they appear within the narration as levels which must be conquered in order for Scott to reach the final showdown with Graves. As Scott defeats Patel, Lee, Ingram, Roxie, Kyle and Ken their bodies disperse into a shower of coins and he is awarded points and new lives. Ker-pow: fight sequences have their blows rendered on-screen. Computer-generated graphics allow all manner of exuberant moments: a punch launches a character into the sky; a huge mallet appears from nowhere to be used as a weapon against a deadly foe; a sword emerges from a body as the reward for a moment of self-reflection. *Scott Pilgrim vs. the World* is pure cinematic ecstasy. You cannot but take pleasure in the movie. It is immediate, vital. Everything happens at high speed, the editing is as sharp as razor blades. Hyper-rapid cutting. The images are precise, vibrant, vital. The soundtrack an ingenious interweaving of sonics: music fragments and cartoonish sound-effects. Wright has transformed a mundane situation into the most grandiose of adventures, created an original visual code to express the feelings and emotions of an encounter with the past life of a new lover, all the psychological hang-ups and petty jealousies, self-doubt and inadequacies. Such banal little duels are transformed, and thereby, the aesthetic permeates the entire film; and the film becomes an allegory, a mythology, a parable – the theatrical representation.

And it is here that we approach what is crucial. In *Scott Pilgrim vs. the World*, it is not that the real has become debased by an aberrant videogaming-, comic- and cartoon-dominated culture; rather, cartoons, video games and comic books are already a take on the world. Such visuals are already in and of the world, and are utilised well beyond the domains in which they were developed (the graphic novel developing the comic book; cartoon violence already subsumed within the mainstream action movie; computer gaming even developed into new warfare methodologies). Accordingly, such structures, codes, and representational techniques are a way of reflecting upon the naturalised realism of a film. *Scott Pilgrim vs. the World* is perfectly of our time, a new way to look at the universe. The film makes visible the distortions of any representation of the world.

18

Source Code

Mise en abyme

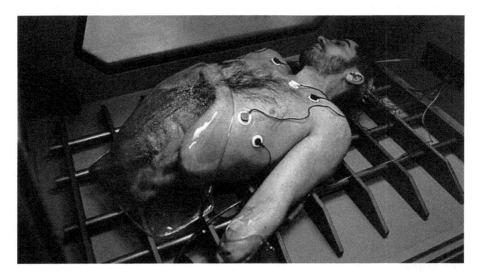

Frame III.18 *Source Code* (Duncan Jones, Canada | France | USA, 2011)

Time is frozen. Locked in an eternal kiss, Fentress and Christina will forever be in this moment, for all eternity. The camera tracks back through the train carriage, a liquid, flowing trajectory, weaving through the other passengers, who are caught in unending silent laughter. A comedian (cajoled by Fentress into an impromptu, celebratory gig) stands in the centre of the aisle – a punchline delivered in perpetuity. On the second tier of the carriage, a woman in among the audience has allowed her coffee to spill, and the liquid has become a solid, remains mid-air in suspended animation. Shafts of sunlight catching dust are rendered for infinity.

The perfect ending.

However, such an ending has a correlate genesis. The environment of the train carriage – and indeed the world and universe through which the train cuts its path – are an ambiguous and perplexing construct. In the real world, Colleen Goodwin – a member of a shadowy scientific programme operating at the fringes of the military complex – has switched off the life-support system that sustained the meat and mind of soldier Colter Stevens. Stevens was a half-life: what remained of his body merely a bagged and tagged trunk, mutilated arm and shattered skull; comatose and unconscious, his mind endured only through the software developed by maverick scientist Dr Rutledge. Stevens can rest in peace, finally. The death of Stevens, accordingly, is the source of the freeze-frame and the true ending of *Source Code*; the condition for the perfect denouement on the train. For Fentress was Stevens. Or rather, the mind of Stevens was projected back across and through space-time into the body of Fentress, who – along with Christina and the other passengers – died some hours before in a horrific terrorist bombing. Stevens has – through a series of repetitions lasting some eight minutes, the eight minutes prior to the bombing – inhabited Fentress time and time again in order to investigate the incident and identify the bomber. For if the terrorist can be identified in the past, they can be detained in the present and prevented from committing further atrocities.

Impossibly, however – beyond all reason – everything starts up again. On the train the event is reanimated, stasis returns to flux. Somehow this moment in the past continues beyond the death of Stevens in the present (just as it passed beyond the moment of the bombing, which has been averted by the actions of Fentress) and this (re)invented universe is preserved. The perfect climax and the true denouement are both a ruse. And continuing past these fake endings derails the filmic line, diverts the cinematic trajectory into a series of ambiguities from which *Source Code* will not – and will not wish to – escape. Time travel dovetails with many worlds. Is this universe in which Stevens now lives as Fentress the same world? Another world? A parallel reality? A simulation? Was quantum parabolic calculus time travel an access to the past of the present, an alternative real or some kind of computer-encoded space as remnant or echo event? These ambiguities become active only by going beyond the moment of dual-closure. Crucially, and in this way, *Source Code* goes on to foreground an ethical impasse. Furthermore, in so doing, it extends the narrative into the contemporary political environment. To explore such productive elements, we can do no better than turn to the cinematic semiotics of Deleuze.

Source Code is an action movie, and Deleuze describes such films as action-images. In the first place, action-images are of two types. There is the large form, where a given situation engenders behaviour, actions which attempt to rectify the situation (played out through duels between characters). This aspect of the action-image can be seen in *Source Code*: the train has been destroyed in a terrorist attack, and Colter will be embodied in Fentress to enter into a duel with the bomber. The film tracks a character in their becoming equal to the milieu and, in so doing, going on to rectify the situation. However, the film also has elements of the other type of action-image. This is the small form, where character actions explore an elliptical situation. Colter must continually re-enter the milieu to attempt to reveal its coordinates. Who is the bomber? What do they want? What will they do next? In parallel, the large form and small forms in the construct inspire further interactions between ongoing repetitions of the immediate past and the real world of the present. Colter must discover what is happening to him: who he is, where he is. And this can only be done through a duel with Rutledge, the military scientist who has sustained his life and is using Colter as a weapon. In other words, small form action-images and large form action images interweave, and describe a very special type of action-image: the reflection-image where large and small transform one another as figures of attraction. Thus, in the second place, Deleuze describes two compositional forms of such attraction-images: the plastic figure and the theatrical figure. When a film of the action-image small form (action → situation) is affected by the large form, we encounter the plastic figure. When a film of the action-image large form (situation → action) is affected by the small form, we encounter the theatrical figure. Either way, writes Deleuze, 'there is no longer a direct relation between a situation and an action, an action and a situation: between the two images, or between the two elements of the image, a third intervenes to ensure the conversion of the forms' (C1: 182). This third is a mental-image: the figure. With plastic figures the situation revealed on-screen is an encompasser of the true situation; the real situation remains an ellipsis. With the theatrical figure the real situation is expressed in ongoing fictional actions. *Source Code* appears to capture a moment of indeterminacy between these two mental-images. On the one hand, the environment in which the mind of Stevens is sustained as himself is an image of the helicopter cockpit in which he was effectively killed – a plastic figure that will cohere and deteriorate as his consciousness ebbs and flows, as he attempts a disclosure of the milieu. On the other hand, the train carriage becomes a theatrical figure to which he will return time and time again, endlessly repeating with difference actions to resolve the situation. Accordingly, *Source Code* appears to go beyond not only the large and small forms of the action-image, but also simple plastic and theatrical presentations. Plastic figures become the index of theatrical sequences at the same moment as a theatrical sequence is encompassed by a plastic figure. This reciprocity is accentuated in the wake of Steven's death in the life-support system. When the real world that was the foundation of such figures ceases to exist for Stevens, such figures are ungrounded. That which was a theatrical figure takes on a new value, escapes repetition and becomes a new real; concomitantly rendering the original world in which the body of Stevens now rots a plastic figure, a mental-image of a past and a man that no longer exist. That – from the perspective of the film – these incarnations of the body (in the life-support, in the helicopter, in the train) all appear to look the same collapses the differentiations of real and figure, figure and real, at every turn.

The movie – in other words – enacts a recurrence of attraction-images: mise en abyme. Director Duncan Jones – through the ungrounding of the figure of attraction – has ensured the film will resist the determinations of the action-image. The new ending actualises the effacement of the real Fentress. In this world that now continues, Stevens only survives because of the erasure of the consciousness of another human being. Accordingly, the mise en abyme is a complex image that in *Source Code* goes on to figure an ethical impasse. The film is a cinematic version of Philippa Foot's famous trolley problem. The question is: would you actively sacrifice one person to save hundreds of innocents? An unstoppable train is on collision course for a group of people; the only action you can take is to switch track. Unfortunately, if you do so, you will kill a single individual working upon the line. The philosophical nature of the question has the intention of illustrating a fundamental utilitarian position: calculate the better good. Switch tracks and you are a utilitarian; the only alternative is to do nothing. Colter – as a soldier, revealed to be part of the American military force at the heart of the Afghanistan project – has been mobilised once again. *Keep your mind on the mission – take whatever action is necessary.* Accordingly – we have transitioned seamlessly from the filmic domain through a philosophical problem into a political proposition. This recurrence, in itself a mise en abyme. In the political arena such a greater good rests upon two such figures, not only the encompasser of the 'war on terror' but simultaneously the index of 'collateral' damage. Plastic and theatrical representations which do not simply become an index or encompasser of a real situation through derived and functional behaviours, but actively transform the milieu and the actions that surround these figures. *Source Code* is a complex cinematic endeavour with an ungrounding double-ruse ending, creating an indeterminacy through mise en abyme; a mise en abyme that demands reflection, places the political proposition within ethics and philosophy, and the philosophical impasse within cinematic realism. In so doing, it transforms the movie into a very powerful reflection-image.

19

Four Lions

Figure of the sublime

Frame III.19 *Four Lions* (Christopher Morris, UK, 2010)

Captured on an old-school video camera, in 4:3 aspect ratio, the grainy image depicts a warrior cross-legged on the floor. Shot front-on at eye level, the man is dressed in civilian khakis with black bandana, behind him a faded and tatty wall-hanging of repeating motifs. In his arms he holds a Kalashnikov. He is solemn. He stares into the lens. 'Eh-up you unbelieving kuffar bastards …' So begins Waj's martyrdom video. *Four Lions* concerns the actions of an Islamic-fascist terror cell in a British provincial northern city during the mid-2000s, at the time of the US and UK interventions in Afghanistan and Iraq branded 'the war on terror'. The film depicts the group dynamics of the cell, as well as various relations with the terrorists' families, the local Muslim community and the wider multi-ethnic population. Over the course of the film, director Christopher Morris will document many aspects of the cell's preparations for a terrorist atrocity against a civilian target on UK soil. These include a journey to Pakistan for training at a mujahidin encampment; the grooming and recruitment of a local Muslim lad to the cause; the collection and stockpiling of assets for the manufacture of homemade explosives; and the different possible ambitions for their eventual suicide mission. At the centre of the cell are Omar and Barry. Omar is a middle-class family man, supported in his death cult jihad by his wife (an NHS nurse) and young, *Lion King*-loving son. Barry is a paranoid, outspoken convert to the Islamic faith – a self-appointed community spokesman – who desperately wants to be at the heart of the revolution. While both share the same fascist objectives, they differ in their tactical approach to actualising a strategy. Barry wants to bomb a mosque and put the blame on British Christians and Jews to thus radicalise the Muslim community. Omar, meanwhile, wants the group to kill non-Muslims in order to demonstrate what he believes to be the latent outrage of his community against the wars in Iraq and Afghanistan, as well as the Palestinian situation. Both tactics, however, aim to shake up the system – awaken from complacency Muslim and non-Muslims alike, to enact jihad, to bring about the collapse of the oppressive regime of the UK government, and to instate shariah law across the British Isles. These men are thus fundamentalist idealists, believers in the possibility of actualising a revolution that will change everything, in an act that will pronounce judgement upon the world with clarity, bring about a new Golden Age, and condemn the evils of feminists, queers, atheists, Christians, Jews, the police, the state, as well as the wider non-fascist Muslim community.

Four Lions is a cinematic figure of the sublime. Deleuze writes of 'a man who is larger than life' who 'frequents a milieu which is itself larger than life, and dreams up an action as great as the milieu' (C1: 184). This is the filmic sublime: where the action is 'a crazy enterprise, born in the head of a visionary', where the character 'seems to be the only one capable of rivalling the milieu' (C1: 184). The figure of the sublime thus creates grandiose, heroic actions devolved from 'the pure Idea' (C1: 184). And it is here that the sublime is betrayed, or rather, the cinema of the sublime undergoes inversion and becomes a critique. For while the given milieu determines the behaviour of the character, it does so through a radical interpretation born of the character's narcissism. Deleuze writes: 'the action, in effect, is not required by the milieu'; accordingly, we see films in which '[t]he visionary's sublime plan … and his whole reality' is transformed, becoming 'enfeebled' (C1: 185). The figure of the sublime reveals not only the horrors that will become necessary to be enacted by the visionaries, but in so doing will confront the futility of their world view. An overvaluation of the I as a privileged centre, the expression of the self as a genius, the fantasy of the significance of the character in the world, their capabilities, their ideas – this is the ultimate revelation of the cinematic sublime. This is the way in which the figure of the sublime inverts the action-image, transforms it into an inversion-image, an image of reflection.

No doubt the sublime is exemplified in the tragic scenario; yet Morris will cut a different path, rediscover and reinvent another type of cinematic embodiment. Comedy can create the cinematic sublime. *Four Lions* will affirm the figure of the sublime, in all its dimensions, through parody. In the first place – *Four Lions* will hold the presence of the state in parenthesis; the film is with the terrorists. Accordingly, Morris does not attempt to express a milieu as a given, as an *a priori*-determined situation with devolved opposite and equal poles; rather, *Four Lions* foregrounds the encompasser as that which much be interpreted, the pure Idea. And it is here – in the second place – that the comedy will function. The terrorist cell was – for a moment – five lions. However, one of them dies for the cause in a hilarious accident involving homemade explosives, a dry-stone wall, a flock of kuffar sheep and a murderous brother Crow. Responding to the machinery of the oppressor is a requirement, and given the scarcity of means at their disposal their response must be inventive: the moment where Waj and Hassan deploy Barry's anti-surveillance technique by avoiding being captured on CCTV by continuously shaking their heads to blur any image. The possible targets: Boots the chemist; the Internet. Barry's perverse induction ceremonies. Omar destroying the mujahidin encampment during a drone attack by getting the anti-aircraft bazooka back to front. Waj – in his martyrdom video – using a miniature toy Kalashnikov; but attempting to persuade the other jihadists he just has 'big hands'. With Waj's video, this film within a film, Morris parodies the intended sublime given of such phenomena. This figure of inversion can be seen as a precursor to the hacktivist collectives Anonymous and 4chan, with their cyber war against Islamic State through the digital manipulation of ISIS propaganda images of fighters with rubber duck heads. Or in the tradition of the British Ministry of Information's Charles A. Ridley's short propaganda film, *Lambeth Walk – Nazi Style* (1942), enfeebling the images of Leni Riefenstahl's *Triumph of the Will* (1935). *Four Lions* is as great a cinematic parody of fascism as those of Ernst Lubitsch or Charlie Chaplin. Such is the project of *Four Lions*: a figure of the sublime as an inversion-image, a transformation of an action-image (which – in its large form – attempts to rectify the world) through comedy and parody.

20

Slackistan

Figure of enfeeblement

Frame III.20 *Slackistan* (Hammad Khan, Pakistan, 2009)

Three young guys chill outside a café on a public square. A beautiful, warm sunny day. Behind them, a fountain propels jets of water into the air, creating spiralling parabolas. The circular glass table in front of them is clear, except for cigarettes and lighters. They sit in silence. Hasan, from time to time, checks out his Blackberry, but no one has contacted him. Saad – wearing a white hoody emblazoned with 'Horny Devil' – twirls a dead leaf backwards, then forwards, between his fingers. Sherry has been watching people passing by. He glances at Hasan, then at Saad, sitting either side of him. Leaning back in his chair, he sighs, yawns, stretches. This is *Slackistan* – an indy slacker flick set in Islamabad, a few days in the limbo-lives of five middle-class friends a year after graduating from college. There is Sherry: he is skating on thin ice, clocking up debts, borrowing cash from a money lender to sustain a lifestyle above and beyond his means – out and about, a flash car, the latest mobile. There is Saad: he has little aspiration, and is seemingly happy to be drifting through life, although there are always some girls to be checking out. There is Aisha: she is looking for marriage, a wealthy man, so she can continue doing nothing but with more style. There is Xara/Zara: she is mixed up, confused, melancholic, rebellious. And at the centre and describing the circumference of the film, Hasan. *Slackistan* is Hasan's story – or rather, the lives of the five friends as seen from Hasan's perspective. Director Hammad Khan will create a mosaic of images: short scenes of conversations which go nowhere; a character wandering the streets on their own; trying on different clothes in the mirror before being able to step out; staring absentmindedly over the cityscape from the hills or tall buildings. In voice-over, Hasan will comment upon these images, even if he is not present, not only providing a narrative cohesion to the film but also interrogating their slacker lifestyle. In this way, Hasan's reflections are an immediate evaluation of the narration. Such reflection is the foundation and inspires the constitution of *Slackistan*. For Hasan wants to become a filmmaker, although he has no idea (as yet) know how to achieve this ambition. The problem is the lack of a cineaste culture in Pakistan: 'how am I supposed to make movies without inspiration?' There are no cinemas in Islamabad. And he is unable to get hold of the films he feels he should see; the shops which sell illegal DVDs only stock Bollywood and Hollywood blockbusters that for him hold little interest. Hasan wants an education in the classics, in the independent cinema, in the new waves, in the international arthouse. He has a camera, and he has been capturing images of his friends and himself. But this approach is getting him nowhere.

Accordingly, *Slackistan* is shot by Khan as if it is Hasan who is shooting the film. Or rather, a Hasan who has now seen such unseen movies. A ceiling fan overdubbed with the sound of a helicopter echoes of *Apocalypse Now* (1979); the stroll and conversational dialogue of the opening evokes both À *bout de souffle*/*Breathless* (1960) and *Pulp Fiction* (1994) – *Slackistan* is a reflection-image. It is as if there is another Hasan – a Hasan to come – shooting *Slackistan* (hence the reflexive omniscience of the voice-over). Such an approach dovetails with on-the-ground realism: the handheld camera, digital images, jumpcuts, freeze frames … title tags … *a city that always sleeps … no one knows what day it is (Tuesday or Wednesday?)*. Ice cream and shisha parlours, private clubs for alcohol and dancing. Graffiti … *no more American enslavement!* Americanised English and Urdu interweave in spoken dialogue. The Taliban and their Pakistani comrades on the TV: blowing up some human flesh, in the never-ending tradition of expedient utopian revolution, for the glory of their god/the promotion of their politics/because they cannot comprehend they are just specks of dust in an infinite universe. Sherry glances at Hasan, then at Saad, sitting either side of him. Leaning back in his chair, he sighs, yawns, stretches: 'I am so bored.'

Slackistan is a film – as Deleuze would comment – populated by 'weaklings and idiots' (C1: 184). Where 'landscapes are dwarfed or flattened, they turn sad and dismal, even tend to disappear' (C1: 184–5). Where '[t]he beings who frequent' such spaces 'no longer have Visions' (C1: 185). A nihilistic mise-en-scène and characterisation. Everything slows down, loses its colour, becomes fragile, futile. Ennui and world-weariness. Khan – in this way – presents a milieu that is neoliberal and capitalist, inhabited by people who are part of a system that promotes open-mindedness, education for all, public secularism, and, most significantly, an equality of gender. Hasan, his friends and their families, embody a cosmopolitan Pakistan. *Slackistan* not only refuses to align with the skewed international media representations of the country as a hotbed of tribal leaders and suicide bombers, but also junks the idea of a pervasive terror of everyday religious fundamentalism. Such a narration appears only on TV. Hasan walks the streets of a progressive metropolis, with all the same kind of problems of any international, globalised city anywhere in the world in the twenty-first century. These 'slackers' are – normalised, unaware – globalised cosmopolitan citizens, products of an international bourgeois elite. And bored – people without vision, without vitality, without verve. *Slackistan* is a figure of enfeeblement, the characters are reduced to 'tiny point[s] fleeing towards the horizon' (C1: 185).

Sherry, Saad, Aisha, Xara/Zara and Hasan ... they all want something more, and all feel that the way to do this is to escape the situation in Pakistan, either by leaving or by turning away. Yet a curious fold occurs in the final moments of *Slackistan*. Hasan is being driven to the airport. He is to leave Pakistan for the USA – for film school, to immerse himself in cinema and the history of cinema – something he has been thinking about during much of the movie. His car draws up alongside an open-backed truck, he sees an itinerant worker, someone from the 'lower' strata of Pakistani society, someone of a lower 'caste' than his own. On their way to a poor paying job ... doing what they can to survive ... supporting a family. This moment dovetails with many others from the film. City planning in the 1960s, zones and grids separating the poor and the rich; a walk through the slums; the five friends' personal drivers and house servants. The scene where Hasan accuses his family domestic Sharif of stealing his camera (when the camera is discovered, Hasan blames Sharif for moving it: neither can look in the other's eyes). 'What is people? There is no people?': the englobing historical situation and class relations now rendered visible. His own parasitic social position. Hasan suddenly understands. These 'weaklings', writes Deleuze, 'have such tactile relationships with the world that they inflate and inspire the image itself' (C1: 186). From the figure of enfeeblement arises the sublime. Khan has been creating the conditions for the film Hasan should make: 'the whole sublime is rediscovered' through the futility of the image (C1: 186). *Slackistan* is its own critique, a reflection-image creating an inversion-image, a transformation – the figure of enfeeblement the conditions for a moment of the sublime. The inspiration for cinema should not come from cinema, but from life. Everything Hasan needs to become a filmmaker is in Islamabad. So, he returns home. And he turns the camera on Sharif.

21

Un homme qui crie/A Screaming Man

Quotidian

Frame III.21 *A Screaming Man* (Mahamat-Saleh Haroun, France | Belgium | Chad, 2010)

Sunlight disperses upon the surface of the brilliant white net curtains that cover the large window, shielding the room from the worst of the heat. Adam Ousmane sits across the wooden desk from Mme Wang, who is attended by her secretary. Silence, except for the faint sound of a pen scratching on paper. The office belongs to the new manager of the hotel in which Adam is employed as head pool attendant. 'How old are you, Adam?' … 'I often see you sitting in your chair?' … 'Do you really think we need two employees?' Mme Wang makes further notes as Adam responds. Director Mahamat-Saleh Haroun's camera lingers within these silences. Camera movement is discreet, reduced to a bare minimum, medium shots predominate and editing only occurs when absolutely necessary for a reframing. Colour is natural, the mise-en-scène sparse, and diegetic sound prevails. The actors are restrained, *sotto voce*, gesture minimalised. Such procedures accentuate the everydayness of the film, but also inspire a subtle beauty in the image. At night, a long take of Adam on his motorbike, its lights illuminating the white walls of an alleyway, is breathtaking. Adam stands at a window of his house, sunshine plays upon his naked torso, the curtains are slowly allowed to fall back into place and enshadow him as he distances himself from what is happening outside. This cinematic asceticism has an immediate correlate with another procedure, one which transforms the simple into something far more complex. Missing moments: critical instants are effaced from the narration and do not appear on-screen. Such ellipses are an essential function of the story, of the narrative. Not in the sense that they are hidden so as to create mystery, and thus to be recuperated, ultimately revealed, reclaimed in order to explain. Rather, these omissions are withheld to echo what another character could not know. These missing moments may be obvious (a cut in the middle of an important scene) or obscure (we may only realise later that something has been withheld). More significantly – such moments mirror what the character wishes to hide: their deceptions, disloyalties, dishonesty. Their shame, what they would not want others to know, the full import of their actions, words, silences. Character motivations are ambiguous, for others, for themselves and for the spectator. And Haroun ensures such ellipses are never revealed, ever sustained.

In this way – through the directness of the image and the complexity of ellipses – *A Screaming Man* creates a powerful image of everydayness, of the quotidian. Adam works at a plush hotel in N'Djamena, capital of Chad. The hotel is cosmopolitan, guests from across Africa and the world frequent the place. Adam, in his mid-fifties, is head pool attendant. A past Olympic swimming competitor, he is known as Champ. And everyone respects him. While much of his status is derived from his past; as head pool attendant, there is a continuity between this past and the present. The pool, he says, is his life; is, in other words, his future. In more ways than one: his twenty-something son, Abdel, now works with him there. Events, however, are about to change everything. There is civil war raging in the east of the country. And the hotel has been bought out by a Chinese company. Images of the conflict hit the TV in his front room as he and his wife, Miriam, feed each other slices of watermelon. The fighting remains remote, background noise, unreal. It is the hotel takeover that concerns Adam, as the new owners begin an organisational rationalisation programme. We follow Adam into his assessment interview, and we see the mechanism of banal managerial tyranny: 'Don't you think there are too many people doing this job?' And it is here that we encounter an ellipsis. We do not hear Adam's answer. When Adam badgers his son about his own interview, Abdel does not reply. The next day, Adam is reassigned to watch the front gate of the hotel (replacing another employee, sacked); and Abdel is left to look after the pool on his own.

It is in the aftermath of these events at the hotel that the war explodes into the lives of the characters. Adam must pay *le chef de quartier* a public subscription towards the government effort in combating the rebel forces approaching N'Djamena. Yet the deadline approaches, and passes. Haroun, however, will hold such moments in ellipsis. Until Abdel suffers forceful impressment into the army. Watching from his window, Adam slowly allows the curtains to fall back into place, and eclipse the scene. Adam gets his job back … but too late, the people are fleeing N'Djamena. At the hotel, everything is abandoned. The management are nowhere to be found, the staff have disappeared. Dead leaves float upon the surface of the pool.

A Screaming Man – through the directness of the image and the ambiguity of elisions – explores how (at one and the same moment) seemingly in-consequential acts can have immense significance; and the immeasurable, infinite universe renders our acts meaningless. Haroun invents a cinema of the quotidian. Such an image can be defined through Deleuze's cineosis in reference to the development and extension of the action-image. Action-images bring together situations and actions into direct relations. In the first place, the large form of the action-image describes how a given situation engenders actions, played out through the duel. In the second place, the small form action-image will explore how actions reveal situations initially in ellipsis. When these two forms are brought together, they can be made to reflect upon one another – no longer a direct relation between action and situation, but an indirect interrelation (as critique) by way of a mental-image of reflection. And one of the ways in which such reflection-images are actualised is through the inversion-image. The inversion-image operates through the 'sublime' where 'the action … is not required by the situation' or through the 'enfeebled' or futile action that reveals grandiose 'Powers of the Earth' (C1: 184, 186). The large form and the small form, in other words, are accentuated – and through their accentuation are transformed. *A Screaming Man* appears to develop both the large and the small at the same time, in so doing bringing the sublime and the futile into immediate contact. The film is composed of a series of duels (the war, the hotel, father and son) which are riven with ellipsis (the interviews, the missed payment). Accordingly, we encounter a very powerful figure of the action-image. The sublime vastness of the universe is indifferent to our actions, but is also the very ground in which we must act, live. Adam will journey into the night, on his motorbike, through the advancing warzone to save Abdel, to bring him home, to his family, and to his lover Djénéba, who is with child.

Section III

22

Monsters

Limit of the large form action-image

Frame III.22 *Monsters* (Gareth Edwards, UK, 2010)

Who are the monsters? This is the question for director Gareth Edwards: the aliens, or humanity? NASA once sent a probe to investigate the possibility of extra-terrestrial life in the far reaches of the solar system. Six years ago, upon its re-entry into the Earth's atmosphere, the probe crash-landed in the jungles of northern Mexico. In so doing, it let an alien species loose upon the planet. Wee fungus pods grow into massive squid-like beasts, and a vast area of the border between the USA and Mexico is now known as the Infected Zone. At the South American end, a soaring metal fence cuts across the continent; while a reinforced concrete dam divides the zone from humanity at the US border. Inside, the area has been abandoned by people. Cities, towns, villages have been reclaimed by jungle, now the home of the alien horde. And with each passing year – as the beasts breed and their population surges – the threat of a breaching of the boundaries becomes an ever more likely event. Accordingly, US and

Mexican planes traverse the skies above the zone, laying down poison into the jungles below, in what is increasingly being seen as a futile attempt to corral the animals. Enter Scoot and Whitney: he a photojournalist who will do just about anything to hit the front page; she the daughter of the owner of Scoot's US-based newspaper. They are caught up in the evacuation of Mexico where the containment barrier is first breached, and their journey takes them into the heart of darkness and out the other side: from San José through the Infected Zone and – after a number of close encounters with the alien beings – into the heartland of Texas. Holed up at a deserted service station awaiting transport home, they now believe themselves safe. However – just as in Mexico – the aliens overwhelm the defences. Scoot and Whitney are the first to witness aliens on US soil. Edwards plays out this scene perfectly – riffing off *Jurassic Park* (1993) and *War of the Worlds* (2005), Whitney hides beneath the counter of the shop as alien tentacles weave through the environment, searching out the nooks and crannies of the room. However, this attack is a ruse – the alien is seeking contact with its mate. Edwards creates a scene of incredible beauty as two of the aliens entwine, their tentacles enfolding tenderly, their bodies aflame with electricity, inner luminescence creating astonishing patterns in the night sky. Scoot looks on with wonder – then he and Whitney kiss for the first time.

Such a mirroring of humanity and the aliens has – in truth – been unfolding from the very beginning of the film. In the first instance, our heroes and the aliens are both adrift in the zone, in an unfamiliar environment they are not naturally disposed to. Each is attempting to survive the world which has been given to them. In the second instance, the aliens are under constant attack from the humans with their bombs and chemical weapons; while the humans are essentially prey to the alien predators. The environment describes a situation which devolves into a duel: aliens versus humanity. This mirroring – accordingly – creates a certain reciprocity. Thus the question at the heart of the film: who are the monsters in *Monsters*?

Such a question is made possible through a cinematic process Deleuze will describe as the extreme limit of the large form action-image. The large form action-image operates through the creation of a given milieu from which two lines of force will derive. The situation in-and-of-itself appears as the encompasser and the lines of force describe the emergence of a binomial which will dovetail in the final duel at the end of the film. The whole narration is thus composed of such binomials, which through the narration of the film will develop and designate good and evil, distributed across the polarity of the characters as they becoming equal to the task of a final confrontation. However, *Monsters* appears to stymie such operations. Situations are given, and this milieu encompasses the characters, their behaviours and actions; however, the film discovers a problem inherent in the situation. In this way the very title of the movie becomes ambiguous. The aliens are killing humans, but the humans are killing aliens … both are trying to survive against the very real threat of the other, and both will go to any lengths to do so (the killing of human children, the gassing of alien pods). It is as if, as Deleuze puts it, the large form action-image is exploring its own limits. The milieu articulates a question which the film and its characters must explore. 'Instead of absorbing a situation in order to produce a response which is merely an explosive action', writes Deleuze, 'it is necessary to absorb a question in order to produce an action which would truly be a considered response' (C1: 190). The characters must respond to the '*givens of a question* which is hidden in the situation' (C1: 189). Once again – who are the monsters?

The Mexican people smugglers get Scoot and Whitney to sniff the air … the gas masks they all wear in the zone are a protection, not against the aliens, but against the chemicals the USA drops to wipe out the fungus pods. This is why the aliens attack; the sound of the planes brings the beasts out from the rivers to protect their young, which the humans are attempting to annihilate. Who are the monsters? The monstrousness of the aliens is continually undermined, while the monstrousness of humanity is increasingly explored – and this exchange makes the sign 'monster' indeterminate. This ambiguity is taken in two opposing directions, towards nature and towards civilisation. The aliens and humans are simply caught up in the indifferent struggles of nature. Each to the other predator and prey, each to the other appears as a virus. The aliens are interlopers, they have arrived late on the scene, dropped from the stars onto indigenous peoples (the humans). Yet the film will ask: is chronological time an indicator of the right to live and inhabit an environment? Accordingly, the environment in which the film is set becomes decisive. Mexico, the peoples there invaded, massacred and dominated by the Spanish from the fifteenth century onwards. Edwards allows Scoot and Whitney (through a manipulation of geography) to stumble across an ancient Mayan temple. And the pre-Mexican peoples themselves, whose history of Maya, Toltec, Aztec is a tapestry of dominions, incorporations and wars. Finally – the contemporary Mexican diaspora into the USA. One land, many peoples, wave upon wave of migrations. Who are the monsters?

Section III

23

Brooklyn's Finest

Limit of the small form action-image

Frame III.23 *Brooklyn's Finest* (Antoine Fuqua, USA, 2009)

Three cops: Eddie, Tango, Sal. One will suffer a futile death. One will get what he truly deserves. One will – at the very end – redeem himself.

Eddie: Twenty-one years on the force. One week from retirement. His fellow officers won't miss him when he finally walks out the door. A burn-out. Suicidal. Stopped caring about the job a long time ago. He just wants to get through these last five days as easily as he can. But the commander – twisting the knife – assigns Eddie a rookie as ride-along. Abandoning this new partner in a situation beyond his experience, he accidently kills a young kid. Tango: deep undercover. As a gangster, a drug dealer. Except the role is becoming his life. He finds himself behaving like the people he has been assigned to bring down. This has taken its toll. His wife has left him. He's done his time, he wants his promised promotion, he wants a desk job. One final task – take out the gang's boss, Caz. Trouble is, Caz once saved Tango's life. And he has more respect for Caz than he does for his chain of command. Sal: married. With five kids. And twins on the way. The house is too crowded, old, falling to pieces, rot causing his wife breathing problems. Just needs to find the deposit for something better – for his family. Each attempt to raise some deposit fails – and ever more desperate, he uses his badge to break the law. Then Sal's wife is hospitalised. Theft escalates to murder.

Brooklyn's Finest. Eddie, Tango, Sal – three cops in crisis, three cops walking the road to hell. One who's lost it, one gone native, one turned killer. Three different characters exploring three different situations, three different stories with which director Antoine Fuqua creates a singular cinematic endeavour. From the very beginning, the film is composed of three isolated narrations – each of which is decomposed into sequences which intercut with one another; yet the film will continually resist bringing these three series into direct contact. It seems inevitable – from the very beginning – that the three narrations will somehow come together, dovetail in some pay-off. Indeed, the final scene appears – at first – to deliver upon such a promise. The three protagonists cross paths in one location, an inner-city tower block. Yet this crossing of paths is fleeting, a ruse. Fuqua maintains the independence of each of the three lines of narration to the very end. We must therefore ask, what is the purpose of such a feint, and such separation?

Deleuze, in his taxonomy of cinema, describes a type of film at the extreme limit of the small form action-image. The small form explores how a movie creates an ellipsis, and the actions of characters will attempt to traverse the narration in order to reveal that which is hidden in the situation. There are three varieties of ellipsis proper to the small form. The first is that of the index of lack, where the situation is revealed without ambiguity. The second is that of the index of equivocity, where the situation that is disclosed presents two different alternatives. Finally, there is the vector – the genesis of the indices – where the determination of an index of lack in one domain will be a coordinate of an index of equivocity in another; or different poles of undecidable alternatives may be resolved in separate lines of narration. *Brooklyn's Finest* appears to tend towards the vector. There are three stories operating in the same time-frame; we must deduce the connections between the three stories, and each story follows a character whose actions are ultimately ambiguous, each will be led down a path they – and we – could not expect. However, a vector attempts to compose a homogeneous narration, bring the elements together in order to describe a world where heterogeneous elements are subsumed within a complex whole. *Brooklyn's Finest* resists such a dovetailing; such a subsuming is a feint, a ruse. *Brooklyn's Finest* goes beyond the vector – and it is here we encounter the extreme limit of the small form action-image. In so doing we discover a discourse-image, 'figures of thought' proper to the small form (C1: 190, 218).

Each element becomes a vector in-and-of-itself, is 'the placing in parallel of different vectors' (C1: 194). Crucially, this 'parallelism of vectors with different orientations … constitutes a connection of heterogeneous fragments of space giving a very special homogeneity to the space thus constituted' (C1: 194). Each character explores its own line at the level of narration, and these stories connect up only at the level of the narrative – through an image of thought. The extreme limit of the small form thus develops a narration where the coordinates of a question will ultimately and necessarily be left unanswered, allowing 'a reality to surge forth which is no longer anything but disorientated, disconnected' (C1: 195).

We encounter in *Brooklyn's Finest* a convergence not at the level of narration, but only at the level of the narrative – the theme. The three heterogeneous elements remain heterogeneous, yet in so doing form a very special kind of homogeneity. Three cops: Eddie, Tango, Sal. One will suffer a futile death. One will get what he truly deserves. One will – at the very end – redeem himself. Yet these outcomes are like three rolls of the dice. Three alternatives which could have been actualised through any of the three characters. The ellipsis concerns determination itself. *Brooklyn's Finest* explores the dice throw: serendipity, chance, providence.

24

Metro Manila

Limit of the action-image

Frame III.24 *Metro Manila* (Sean Ellis, UK | Philippines, 2013)

The transformation in form and twist in the tale of *Metro Manila* – no matter how effective – may tempt us to believe we have encountered betrayal and excess. Oscar, Mai and their children escape the toil of the rice terraces in Benguet province for the big city – and things go from bad to worse. Their exodus is a consequence of a rural mafia controlling, at the sharp end, the economics of the farmers' market. Obliged to sell the grown, harvested and husked rice at a reduced rate (now two centavos a pound down from ten the year before), the Ramirez family, it becomes clear, will not be able to afford seed for the next season. In Manila, the family witness their remaining savings plundered by con-artists, lose their accommodation, and must walk dangerous streets, tipping up in the slum. Oscar is ripped off and abandoned after a day's work shifting rubble; Mai lands a job as a dancer and hostess at Charlie's, the children hanging out backstage while mummy grinds down on Euro-detritus with Yankee dollars for G-strings (. . . 'smile'). Such narration, filmed hand-held in close-up down on the streets, has a social-realist feel. The milieu, revealed through the trials of the family, is proven time and time again as corrupt, as exploitative, as fundamentally uncaring. Yet, as Steve Rose identifies, 'the tide starts to turn when husband Oscar lands a job with a security-van company, a development that slowly, stealthily leads the story out of social drama territory and into a crime-thriller realm' (Rose, 2013). We move, in this way, from eternal misery and social realism to classical realism and overcoming, towards a narration with gangsters, guns, and a heist, where Oscar's heroic sacrifice allows Mai and their children to flee Manila with a tasty amount of pesos. And it is such a transformation in form that tempts us to see a betrayal, a turning away from the social-realist political stance which first engendered the story.

Samantha Lay has outlined some of the essential features of social realism, which always depend upon – it seems – an oppositional relationship with classical-realist structures. For example, while in mainstream cinema 'the monster is killed, the criminal is caught or gets his or her comeuppance, mistaken identities are unravelled, the romantic couple are united, and so on', social realism has 'something to say about "things as they really are"' (Lay, 2002: 20). Mainstream cinema 'merely entertain[s]', creating 'more or less stable resolutions'. Social realism cannot discover such triumphs in the real world; it 'resists resolutions and the future is rarely bright' (Lay, 2002: 21). For Sophie Monks Kaufman, the transformation in forms in *Metro Manila* is thus a betrayal, Ellis 'doesn't give Mai's plight the screen time to emerge as she (and the social realism her presence represents) is sidelined by the emerging thriller driven by Oscar's job as an armoured truck driver' (Monks Kaufman, 2013a). Yet perhaps there is another way to look at *Metro Manila*. The movie begins in social-realist mode, with the family leaving the country for the city, and this mode extends well into the urban environment. Eventually, however, there is a divergence. Oscar's narration increasing moves into heist movie territory, as Mai and her children continue the social-realist line. Oscar's sacrifice terminates his trajectory along the classical-realist line. But through his sacrifice, Mai can abandon social-realist suffering, and move towards a classical-realist resolution. She is now rich; she no longer has to return to Charlie's, and she and the children can escape the city. *Metro Manila*, in other words, does not simply transform from social realism into classical realism, but rather – in the middle section of the film – sets up a discourse between the two forms. It is such a dialogue that we can explore through the Deleuzian cinematic concept of the discourse-image in order to re-evaluate the nature of the betrayal.

Realism, for Deleuze, is a complex domain of forms, of action-images. Fundamentally, however, it is composed of two reciprocals that describe situations and behaviours. On the one hand, the large form, where a situation is given, and being given spirals down to the characters, who then attempt to rectify the milieu. On the other hand, the small form, where character behaviours reveal the dimensions of the situation (no rectification is necessary). Deleuze comments that 'the two conceptions are not opposed ... but rather two ways of constituting their relationship' of situations and actions (C1: 187). Not being opposed, different relationships between the two forms can appear. For instance, attraction-images transform one form by way of the other through cinematic figures (filmic metaphors, allusions, etc.); and inversion-images transform each other through a reversal where the large form describes an enfeeblement of the sublime, and the small the sublimation of a futile situation. Then there are discourse-images, where both forms are transformed by reflecting upon their own conception: the limit of the large form, the limit of the small form – and, finally, the limit of all action-images. It is this extreme limit of the action-image that inspires the structure of narration in *Metro Manila* through a comparison of forms (the large form, classical realism; and the small form; social realism). Such an arrangement creates not only a discourse between both but – necessarily – a reflection upon each by the other.

Mai's path is of the small form, one which reveals the situation. As Deleuze puts it, at its limit it can describe how 'there is no line of the universe which does not pass through women, or even which does not issue from them; and yet the social system reduces women to a state of oppression, often to disguised or overt prostitution. The lines of the universe are feminine, but the social state is prostitutional. Threatened to the core, how could they survive, continue, or even extract themselves' (C1: 195). Oscar's path is of the large form, which at its limit is not simply content with describing situations, but must discover the question, the problem hidden within the situation. Oscar spends the entire film pursuing the question hidden in the misery of his family's situation. The question is: what must the good do in an evil world? Rectify this world? How can this be done? His answer is, of course, to embrace the evil. And this – not his death – is the true nature of his sacrifice. Such are the discourse-images of the small and the large in-themselves. When they are brought to reflect upon one another it becomes clear that neither form (large or small, or classical-realist or social-realist) is more or less able to articulate 'things as they really are' than the other. We thus might respond to the accusation that the social-realist element is betrayed by stealing a quote from François Truffaut, who asked, 'what, then, is the value of anti-bourgeois cinema made by the bourgeois for the bourgeois?' (Truffaut, 1954). Think of the type of enjoyment made possible to the spectator through a supposed sustaining of the social-realist line: Mai's return to Charlie's, her nine-year-old daughter being sold to special clients? Ellis loves his characters too much – and this is no fault.

In this way, the film is not simply a betrayal of the social situation, but describes the betrayal of the social situation by the characters, a betrayal that is more than understandable: Oscar's turn to evil, his sacrifice; Mai's escape from it all. What would you do? And just as the large form subsisted in the first part of the film (through the confrontation between the family and the rural gangsters, the family and the conmen) so too the social situation subsists at the end of the film. That is to say, the women left behind at Charlie's are still there. Ellis filmed in a real hostess bar (Monks Kaufman, 2013b). Mai was the only actress, and the other women in the film were workers. Ellis giving an escape to Mai could just as well be said to articulate 'things as they really are', the desire to flee such a life and the guilt in actually so doing, a mirroring of the film crew, the actors, the director walking away. *Metro Manila,* from the perspective of the classical-realist line, explores the betrayal of escape, of making good, of leaving others behind. Not only is the nature of the betrayal ambiguous, but simultaneously the twist no longer appears as an excess. Oscar, during the heist, discovers there are two keys. One exists in an actual form, but is a ruse. The other is hidden, not apparent, an impression, an empty void. As the ruse-key is reclaimed, found to lead nowhere and disappears, the imprint is filled and unlocks the future of Mai and the children. There is an essential exchange, for the keys depend upon one another: neither one is more real for its absence nor presence. Such a figure is the very expression of the discourse-image at the limit of all action-images.

25

Star Trek – First Contact

Rich dreams

Frame III.25 *Star Trek – First Contact* (Jonathan Frakes, USA, 1996)

Without doubt – one of the most beautiful camera moves in cinema history. Neither a dolly-out nor zoom-out as such, but effectively both in (and possible only through) CGI – the camera pulls back from a black screen to reveal an eye. The eye becomes a face – Jean-Luc Picard, now captain of the Enterprise-E – and the face stares straight into the lens. As the camera continues on its reverse trajectory, the mise-en-scène reveals Picard is captured in a glass tube that is part of a spaceship, either side of him other beings, and behind each of them, many more. This section of the ship is but a fragment of an immense superstructure, the core or hub in an area so impossibly vast the camera never seems to encompass it. It is like a fractal – never-ending. Cut to corridor, the camera flies through the space, side to side, a disembodied spirit. Picard restrained on an operating table, his head encased in machinery. Picard in his tube – eyes closed – he gasps. Picard with his face now augmented with Borg technology – merely an outward sign of his assimilation into the hive mind: 'Locutus' – comes a woman's voice at the edge of consciousness. The image on-screen distorts. 'I am Locutus of Borg', whispers what was once Picard, and, turning to face the camera, 'Resistance is futile.' A drill enters Picard's eye.

Picard awakes from this dream-image. Director Jonathan Frakes, by zooming in on a sleeping Picard as he opens his eyes, signals this first moment of *Star Trek – First Contact* as a dream. As a nightmare. These are not memories, as such. Rather – they are perceptions, affections and actions subsumed within an unconscious state. For Deleuze, dream-images conjure up a 'metamorphosis of the situation' by linking dream situation to waking situation and so negotiating the latter through the former (C2: 273). Accordingly, the dream-image of *Star Trek – First Contact* describes the sign of the rich dream. There is no mistaking the nature of these images. The Borg spaceship appears infinite, the camera travels as if in flight, the character stares into the lens. These are impossible images that capture up memories, feelings and perceptions. And to begin the film is such a way is to disorient. It is only when Picard opens his eyes that we know it was a dream. That these images are mental-images belonging to a central and privileged character. And it is only when Picard opens his eyes, when he awakes, that he knows it was a dream. The situation for the audience is thus aligned with that of Picard.

Such is only the first dimension of the power of the rich dream conjured up by Frakes. For the dream-image will foretell the trajectory of the film. A return of the repressed, an actualisation of the terror that inspires the dream. Picard awakes – and immediately receives a message that the Borg will attack the Earth. He already knows. It is as if his dream captured up the past in the present for the future.

26

The Machinist

Restrained dreams

Frame III.26 *The Machinist* (Brad Anderson, Spain | USA, 2004)

Trevor Reznik has not – to his certain knowledge – slept in a year. Something is keeping him awake. And he is always tired – every time he finds himself drifting off, something pulls him back to the waking world. Trevor's eyelids drift slowly downwards over his gritty, bloodshot orbs ... close ... on the sofa, the book slips from his hand and hits the floor; at the coffee bar the cup clatters on the counter; in his car the cigarette lighter pops on the dashboard. And he is thrown back into the world. Disoriented, disconnected, dazed and confused. Insomnia is taking its toll: devastating physical and mental effects. On the one hand, he is shedding weight. The prostitute he frequents tells him he will soon disappear; the waitress at the airport coffee bar he hangs out at keeps trying to feed him up. But he is rarely hungry, and when he does eat, he mostly throws it back up. Trevor is skin and bone. On the other hand, he alternates between semi-consciousness and hyper-awareness. Sometimes it is hard to concentrate and he makes dumb mistakes. Sometimes he will spend hours cleansing the bathroom floor of every speck of dirt. And strange things are happening. No one seems to have heard of a new co-worker called Ivan at the machine shop where Trevor is employed. Post-it notes are appearing on his fridge with a hangman symbol, six dashes, the final two completed with 'E R'. Someone is after him. Or so it seems.

Actor Christian Bale captures Trevor's deterioration through his emaciated frame, blank stares, mumbling drawl and slow movements; and director Brad Anderson shoots the film in half-light, all murky blue-greys. It is as if *The Machinist* is a dream, or dream-like. Accordingly – and as the film progresses – it becomes uncertain if Trevor does sometimes sleep and dream, or if dreams are invading his waking world as hallucinations. (Or even some complex amalgam of the two, some back and forth between these states). Dreams, nightmares, hallucinations – this is Trevor's real world. Where does the nightmare end and the world begin? Deleuze describes such dream-images as an 'unhinging', the restrained dream. Restrained in the sense that the transformation of the real world into the dream or the dream world into the real is not signalled by rich cinematographics. No closing of eyes and crossfade into the weird and crazy images of the unconscious. No return from dreams through a character opening their eyes and retaining awareness of the dream: images as well as the condition. Rather, in the restrained dream the image '"looks like" dream, but between objects that remain concrete' (C2: 58). Dream world and real world become ambiguous; and the effect of each domain on the other is very powerful: the character believes or thinks the dream was a moment of the real.

Such is the restrained dream that is *The Machinist*. The real world becomes overlaid with the dream so Trevor can no longer be certain what is real and what is a hallucination. He chases such phantasms, interrogates these visions as if they were real. Yet as he does so they begin to reveal themselves. There are clues everywhere – if only he were able to recognise them as such. The trajectory of *The Machinist* is thus constituted by a crisis in recognition. The crisis concerns the impossibility of differentiating the dream and the real, which becomes ever more palpable and manifests itself in paranoia. Yet it is through the ever more affecting power of hallucination that recognition is once again able to assert itself. Indeed, this is the key to Trevor's condition – he must not only recognise the hallucinations, nightmares and dreams for what they are, but must discover their origin in order to fully return to the real world.

Section III

27

Inception

Movement of world

Frame III.27 *Inception* (Christopher Nolan, USA | UK, 2010)

The final moment of *Inception* may well become known as one of the most powerful in cinema. Not simply for the image itself, but because of the cut from that image to black. The image is of Cobb's totem, a spinning-top, gyrating on his kitchen table. And the cut makes the ending ambiguous: we do not know if it keeps on spinning, endlessly; we do not know if it is subject to entropy, and so will eventually topple and fall, lie still. To know seems essential. If the top were to keep revolving, it would be clear that Cobb is lost in a dream (as his wife believed). If the top were to fall, Cobb has completed his mission successfully, returned to the real world, his real home and his children. Everything seems to be dependent upon the state of the spinning-top. Yet this is where director Christopher Nolan cuts. And there is something really essential at stake, although it is not a question of knowing the actual outcome. Rather, it is the condition of not knowing either outcome – of the ambiguity in-itself. We want closure. We cannot abide the ambiguity the final cut seemingly imposes. This is not as naive as it may sound, for this is the very theme of *Inception* and exactly the situation Cobb finds himself in. This is why he has the spinning-top. He needs to know, throughout the film, exactly where he is, dream world or real world. The final moments of the film place the spectator in exactly the same position as Cobb, they generate the very crisis of knowledge that will be exploited by that cut. The question is, can this ambiguity be resolved?

To explore this question we can turn to Deleuze's *Cinema* books and his exploration of what he calls dream-images. For Deleuze, dream-images are cinematic compositions which 'seem to have two poles, which may be distinguished according to their technical production' (C2: 58). 'One proceeds by rich and overloaded means – dissolves, super-impositions, deframings, complex camera movements, special effects'; while '[t]he other ... is very restrained, working by clear cuts or montage-cut, making progress simply through a perpetual unhinging' (C2: 58). *Inception*, however, appears to have something of both of these poles of the dream-image. On the one hand, the transitions to and from the dream world (and indeed, between dream worlds) tend towards the restrained. Sometimes the dream world can be particularly rich: cliffs made of decaying buildings, mirrors reconstructing cityscapes, the curve of the earth folding back upon itself. Sometimes – a factor of the activities that the dreamers are involved in – the dream world can be restrained. Nonetheless, whether rich or restrained, a crucial point about dream-images is that they stymie the action-image. Action-image movies begin with a given situation and extract lines of force that become embodied in characters who then go on to reconstitute the world. Deleuze's dream-images, however, are characterised by two aspects: 'a character finds ... [they are] prey to visual and sound situations ... which have lost their motor extension' (C2: 55). Second, 'these actual sensations and perceptions are ... cut off from memory-based recognition' (C2: 55). In short, dream-images are mental-images which have very little effect upon the world.

Inception is very different. The film tells the story of a gang of corporate thieves. Led by Cobb, the team specialise in entering the dreams of others to extract information that can be sold for vast profit. To do so, they set up a dream world through one dreamer into which other dreamers are pulled. Accordingly, the idea is that the subject to be exploited does not know they are dreaming. The game-changer comes when they are employed to plant an idea in the mind of a subject. Hence 'inception'. Despite reservations, Cobb knows this is possible, even if extremely complex and dangerous. To make the inception work, they must create dreams within dreams within dreams, to trick their subject into believing the idea is their own. This Chinese-box-like dream structure has an interesting temporal effect. The time spent asleep in the real world may be a minute or so, but in the dream world it is far longer. Each level of dreaming increases the experienced time exponentially (50 years in level four is 2.5 years in level three, which is 1.5 months in level two, which is 2.3 days in level one, which is 3 hours in reality). Further, dying in an embedded dream means that the dreamer can become lost, enter a dream-limbo. In reality, they would be comatose while they experienced year upon year of their life in this mental elsewhere. Thus, the whole point of the film, and it is there in the title, is to effect a change in the real world through what occurs in the dream world. To place an idea in the mind of a subject that will cause them to change their behaviour. Deleuze's dream-images, be they rich or restrained, cannot account for *Inception*. For 'the dream-image is subject to the condition of attributing the dream to the dreamer, and the awareness of the dream (the real) to the viewer' (C2: 58). In other words, this dream-image 'does not … guarantee the indiscernibility of the real and the imaginary' (C2: 58). Yet such an indiscernibility is exactly the problem *Inception* explores. On the one hand, the condition of the exploited subject; on the other, the condition of Cobb at the final cut. Deleuze, however, goes on to say that there is a type of dream-image that goes beyond the rich and the restrained. This is 'movement of world', the 'implied dream' (C2: 59). Here 'every world and every dream, closes up around everything it contains, including the dreamer' (C2: 63). Accordingly, 'it is no longer the character who reacts to the optical-sound situation, it is a movement of world which supplants the faltering movement of character' (C2: 59). The real and dream worlds become ambiguous, the character cannot tell them apart; neither can the spectator – and crucially, it is no longer the work of the film through its narration to figure the difference out. Rather, the task of the film becomes the propagation, extension and suspension of ambiguity.

And this is the crucial point with *Inception*. The status of the image of the spinning-top and cut to black at the end of the film is ultimately a ruse. The spinning-top originally belonged to Cobb's wife Mal, who may or may not have existed, who may or may not have given it to Cobb in the real world or a dream world. It tells him nothing. It never has. Is the whole film a dream? Are parts of the film real? As spectators we are continually led irrevocably back to these questions. Yet there is no answer – and this is the project of *Inception*. The movie asks: why must we know? Why do we resist allowing the ambiguity to ride? Perhaps it is because the question is properly philosophical, extending beyond the film. Are we ourselves a dream? What difference would it make?

28

El secreto de sus ojos/The Secret in Their Eyes

Strong destiny

Frame III.28 *The Secret in Their Eyes* (Juan José Campanella, Argentina | Spain, 2009)

Espósito's face is shrouded with darkness. The old wooden door whispers softly as he slowly pushes it open. Cautiously, Espósito enters in silence. His eyes explore the hidden space. At the far end are two doorways. To his left, the first – fitted with makeshift, bent and twisted iron bars – leads to a room with a bricked-up window. It appears empty. The second doorway, off to his right, is open wide, the room beyond brightly lit. Inside is Morales, his back turned towards Espósito, bent over, arranging items in a small storage area. Unseen as yet, Espósito turns his attention to and approaches the improvised cell. As he does so, he spies the chamber has a small opening inside. It is through this opening that a listless figure shuffles. A broken, balding, unkempt old man. A ghost from the past.

And we cannot escape our past. What has passed haunts the present. Imprisons us. Such is the lesson of director Juan José Campanella's *The Secret in Their Eyes*. Accordingly, the film employs the power of the flashback to ground such a reciprocity: memory as the condition of the present; the subject as a product of the past. Yet Campanella does not limit this exchange to the individual. Rather, through the individual we discover the milieu – the socio-political environment. There is no memory without history, and no history without memory. *The Secret in Their Eyes* will thus exploit the cinematic function of the flashback to explore the psychological subject within the historical setting which encompasses it, circumscribes it, motivates it, and determines it. The filmic space is Argentina; the temporal zones 1999 (the present) and 1974 (the past). Campanella begins and ends the film in the present – and this present will be the ground for a series of flashbacks into the past.

1999: Benjamín Espósito has just retired from his post as a federal justice agent. In retirement, his thoughts return to a crucial moment in the past. A crime that still haunts him – and which changed his life in every way. A horrific, brutal event in itself – but also one that exposed the disease and the terror at the heart of the Argentinian state.

1974: Espósito is assigned to the investigation of a violent rape and death of a young woman, Liliana Coloto. The killer is identified as Isidoro Gómez. However, Espósito's bosses insist Gómez is innocent. Espósito's bosses insist the case must be dropped – Gómez is untouchable, somehow above and beyond the law. Visiting Ricardo Morales, the murdered woman's husband, Espósito suggests they could kill the guilty man. Morales protests. He believes in state justice and the prescribed twenty-five years' imprisonment for such a crime. Morales thus inspires Espósito to reopen the case, and eventually he successfully prosecutes Gómez. Yet Gómez is immediately freed – he has provided essential political information to the military-government complex from inside prison and is rewarded not only with freedom, but with a role in the death squads, a position he abuses (if such a thing were possible) by going after Espósito. Espósito is transferred to another area of the country, abandoning both Morales and a nascent love affair with new department head Irene Menéndez-Hastings. This defeat, desertion and fear haunt him throughout his life.

1974: General Juan Perón returns to power in Argentina. Originally elected president in 1946, Perón led a populist militaristic fascist government that attempted to shift the country from agrarian subsistence to industrialisation. Such a reorientation instigated a period of economic development for the country, improving the conditions and wages of urban workers. However, success was short-lived, and by the late 1940s inflation peaked at 50 per cent. In order to keep control and silence voices of dissent, Perón imprisoned and tortured political rivals, enacted tough censorship laws and built a personality cult around himself. He was deposed in a *coup d'état* in 1955 and spent the next twenty years in exile. Thus followed efforts to purge the politics of Argentina of Perónist influence. Elections in 1958 brought Arturo Frondizi to power, and in 1962 Arturo Illia. Yet loyal Perónists in the military continually intervened and undermined these regimes, resulting in the military coup of 1966. Perón saw his chance, and from abroad organised student and labour protests. Free elections were called in 1973, and Perón returned from Spain, winning and taking power the following year. Perón, however, died just a few months later, and from mid-July 1974 his third wife, and vice-president, Isabel, took control. Isabel Martínez de Perón is often seen as the instigator of a violent period of repression, beginning with 'annihilation decrees' of 1975 against left-wing guerrilla forces. In truth, right-wing military violence against the rebels had been prevalent since the 1950s. However, it was in the wake of Juan Perón's death that the violence reached fever pitch. The Dirty War (*Guerra Sucia*) was a decade of state-sponsored abduction, torture and murder that lasted until around 1983. These tactics were developed in consort with the CIA. The American government of the time had instigated Operation Condor, training the forces of military leaders in South America in practices such as torture, abduction and rape so as to instil fear and thus maintain social order. The targets were trade unionists, journalists, students and the left-wing rebel guerrillas. It is estimated that anywhere between 9,000 and 30,000 people were 'disappeared' during this time. In the last years of the twentieth century and the early years of the twenty-first, everything changed, eventually – in 2006 – leading to the events of the Perónist era being described as 'genocide' by the Argentinian court of law.

1999: Espósito – still haunted by the defeat, desertion and fear of the past – decides to novelise the events of 1974. Investigate once again. Perhaps doing so will enact some kind of justice for Coloto and Morales, and even silence the shame he feels. He first turns to Menéndez-Hastings, in the process rekindling their love. He then locates Morales. Finally, he attempts to track down Gómez. But Gómez has long disappeared.

Such are the coordinates of *The Secret in Their Eyes*. In order to actualise the narration, Campanella makes extensive use of the flashback. This is the pattern: present → past → present; present → past → present; and so on. In this way, the film reconstitutes and reactivates the elements of crime, politics and romance of the past in and for the present. The past is brought into the present, for the present through memory. And memory is actualised as an image on the screen. Such actualisations of memory are explored in the cinematic realm through what Deleuze will name the recollection-image. Recollection-images as flashbacks give us 'an explanation, a causality or a linearity' as a 'closed circuit which goes from the present to the past, then leads us back to the present' (C2: 49). Actualising an image from the past serves to inspire the present, to create and accentuate affects for the character at the centre, in order to determine actions in and upon the world for the now. Accordingly, a recollection-image is a sign of 'psychological causality' (C2: 47). *The Secret in Their Eyes* is structured by such recollection-images; flashbacks overwhelm the narration and thus function as Espósito's impetus, stimulation, drive. Espósito has no choice. Deleuze designates such a recollection-image strong destiny – everything that has happened impacts on the character and sets them upon a path they cannot escape, along a trajectory that will allow no deviation.

And so, Espósito attempts to track down Gómez. But Gómez has long disappeared – he appears once again to have escaped the state justice that is so long overdue. Until, that is, Espósito discovers the makeshift prison hidden away on Morales' property. The broken, balding, unkempt figure who is captured within this space is the missing rapist, killer, military agent and government death squad member. Morales has kept this man locked up and away from the world for twenty-five years. For Campanella, in this way, it is not horror and terror that is revealed as haunting the Argentinian state – or rather, this is only the negative condition. Morales prefigured the present in the past by giving Argentina an image of its destiny, creating – in his own way – a strong and powerful image of justice that the state was for so long unwilling to enact.

29

White Material

Weak destiny

Frame III.29 *White Material* (Claire Denis, France | Cameroon, 2009)

An unnamed country in post-colonial Africa: economic stagnation, civil conflict, political violence, child soldiers. All the signs are gathering of the onset of a failed state. Dangerous ground for a European filmmaker. And director Claire Denis dares further; she focuses the narration on the character of Maria Vial, a white plantation owner. Accordingly, *White Material* is primarily a film about the exploiters as exploiters; not the exploited as exploited. An exemplary moment comes when Maria shows her newly hired field workers their lodgings. It is night; a single torch is shone around bare concrete cells, with dirty bedding discarded on the floors. The workers look on in disgust. Maria is oblivious; she points out the amenities (a water pump), then retires to her beautiful, vast, whitewashed villa. The structure of this society is not simply divided racially, essentially racist, but also has concomitant feudal and capitalist dimensions: land-owners and peasants, bourgeois and proletariat. In other words, the antagonisms have complex and particular social, economic, political, historical and racial coordinates. But everything is about to change. Violently.

White Material is organised so we feel the imminent nature of this change, the approaching paroxysm. The film's 'present' finds Maria stranded on a dirt track before continuing with an uncomfortable ride back to her plantation in a rusty old bus. During the trip, Denis uses a flashback structure to describe the events of the previous few days. In the final moments of the film Maria arrives back at Café Vial to find everyone but her father dead. It is at this point she suddenly realises – or more accurately, admits to herself – there is no future for the white elite, not here. The flashback sequences reveal not only the events leading up to the paroxysm, but elements of family history and the post-colonial French past of the West African nation. The Vial family has been here for several generations, long before Independence, which appears to have changed very little for the people. Now a civil war is raging, government forces against rebels, the 'rascals'. As the film begins we see gangs of youths taking up arms as civil society breaks down. And added to this mix are militia hired as personal armies by the local African leaders. So approaches the crisis point.

In the middle of this situation, almost in splendid isolation, the Vials run a coffee plantation. Or rather, Maria runs the plantation. Her father-in-law is very ill, needing constant medication; her husband is a disengaged playboy, her son a layabout. In the first flashback sequence we encounter the French army, which has been supporting the government, withdrawing from the area. Maria is urged to leave too, but will not, believing the family to be above, or outside the coordinates of the crisis. Her workers, however, scatter. She employs some more, but they soon leave too. Finally the plantation is invaded by a rag-tag child army; her son willingly joins them. Maria, during all this, cannot accept, will not accept what is happening. An indicative moment in the film comes when she finds the bloody head of a ram, a warning of what will happen if the family fails to abandon its farm. She tries to hide this evidence (not only from her family, but also from herself), but fails. She is careless in wiping away the blood on her hands. Just like the ram's head, she cannot efface history.

This flashback structure is therefore crucial, not only is constructing the count-down to the paroxysm, but in ensuring we understand how the past permeates the present. The whole weight of history, racial, economic, colonial, post-colonial comes to bear on this moment, both pasts seen and pasts unseen. Deleuze, in his taxonomy of cinema, describes the flashback as a sign of what he calls the recollection-image, an image of thought. For Deleuze, flashbacks 'insert themselves between stimulation and response', are the instrument of 'psychological causality' (C2: 47). The flashback is marked in transition; 'it is like a sign with the words: "watch out! recollection"' (C2: 49). Deleuze calls this destiny: the way in which the past inexorably saturates the present. And we can designate strong and weak types. Strong destiny: in which cause and effect are unequivocally linked, where the past returns to explicate the present in full. Weak destiny: which retains elements of the strong form (explanation, causality, linearity) but is instead concerned with integrating ellipses into memory, history and the past. Accordingly, the weak form is a more radical mode of flashback than the strong. Here cinema explores how the present can be stymied by the past, how destiny is ambiguous, non-linear, open to dissolutions. How memory and history can be effaced, or no longer trace a line, connect all the points and construct a solid, eternal linear trajectory.

Such is the flashback structure in *White Material*. There is a resistance to signalling transitions, which lends an immediacy to events heightened by the extremely limited timespan the film encompasses – the paroxysm is imminent. Denis will also loosen the links of the flashback. No longer are images of the past anchored upon a central and privileged image; there is a willingness to fork away to moments involving Maria's husband and son, the rebel leader, the survivor of a nearby mêlée. There are flashbacks within flashbacks. Thus, while the film is dependent upon the psychology of the main character, the links between the subject of the film and the memory-images are weak. Denis locates Maria at the centre of all images, but is willing to decentre this figure, and ultimately abandon her. *White Material* explores, but is not with, the Vial's memory of history. Maria may see herself, her family, her plantation as the continuity at the heart of the community, the nation and its economy. But such an understanding is only a mark of white material presence (racist, colonial, bourgeois). The mayor tells Maria: *blonde, blue eyed, you may belong here, but the country does not want you.*

30

Triangle

Forking paths

Frame III.30 *Triangle* (Christopher Smith, UK | Australia, 2009)

Jess faces Jess with a shotgun. 'You're not me', she whispers, finger on the trigger, priming herself to fire. 'You're not me', she says again, tears in her eyes. This confrontation takes place in the once-plush ballroom of the Aeolus, a ghost-ship, an ocean liner long lost in the mysterious seas of the Caribbean. Director Christopher Smith's camera will swoop around and between, encircle and encompass the doppelgängers: hyper-fast tracking shots, bullet-time; close-ups and over-the-shoulder shots flip-flopping and reorienting the point of view from one Jess to the other, back and forth. Jess with the shotgun cannot – however – seem to pull the trigger. The other Jess backs away; breathing slowly, she turns, and flees. Jess lowers the gun. Turns to Victor, who is slumped against a wall, dying, covered in his own blood: 'This didn't happen before, don't you see?' Jess now thinks she understands what is happening. Events and the people who traverse them are caught in a circuit, a helter-skelter with infinite rides – but the instants that fill out each circuit are not fixed. Jess can change what happens, make up for what she has done, escape the loop. The present can efface the past for the future. She just has to kill everyone first.

A beautiful day for a sailing trip. Jess has been invited by Gregg, a rich, young and handsome yacht owner – who eats at the diner where she waitresses – out onto the waters off Miami. There is Victor, Gregg's boat-hand; husband and wife Downey and Sally; and their friend Heather. Jess will arrive somewhat disoriented, but after some sleep will awake refreshed and join the others. The sun is shining, the water is calm, and a warm breeze caresses the deck. Wine, sunbathing and conversation. However, once the shelter of the coast is left far behind and they are out at sea, the wind drops. A storm is approaching – sky as black as night. It looks bad. The rain lashes down and massive waves flood the boat. Capsizing, they are thrown into the raging water. Then, almost as suddenly as it began, the storm is over. Swimming back to the upturned hull, the crew and passengers drag themselves up onto its slippery surface. Except Heather. She is gone. They huddle in silence, awaiting rescue. Time passes … Out of the sea mist, a massive ocean liner appears: the Aeolus. They are saved; yet as the five survivors climb aboard, Jess experiences a moment of déjà vu: 'I feel like I know this place.' And she cannot shake off the feeling someone is watching them.

So begins the first loop of *Triangle*. Smith has said of the film that he wanted to create a narration where he could explore the question 'What happens if the victim becomes the killer?' – *How would that work?* (*The Making of Triangle*, 2009). To do this, the film is created from a series of loops in which Jess is ensnared, and through which she progresses, slowly transforming from passive prey through impassive observer to active participant and willing executioner. Let us call her – while we can – 'our Jess'. Our Jess witnesses the murders – one by one – of Victor, Gregg, Downey and Sally. A masked killer in a boiler suit is stalking the decks, corridors, and rooms of the Aeolus. Our Jess is now alone. Terrified. Too soon, she is discovered. However, in an act inspired by providence, Jess forces the killer overboard.

So ends the first loop of *Triangle* – although we have yet to discover this is the situation. To foreshadow such a revelation, Smith creates one of the most beautiful shots of modern cinema. Jess studies her bruised and bloodied body in a mirror – and the camera passes through the glass, to join her reflection where the action will continue. An impossible moment, but one which encapsulates the philosophy of the entire film. For our Jess will spy – from her vantage point – another version of the upturned boat, another version of each of her friends, and another version of herself. So begins the second loop of *Triangle* – and such an event will lead to our Jess confronting Jess[+1] with the shotgun. Not, however, before she fatally wounds Victor. Realising she can change events (as this confrontation did not happen to her when she first arrived), Jess will incrementally transform herself into the killer, dressed in a boiler suit with a cloth bag as mask. For if she can kill everyone, they will return and she can save them all. However, a future Jess will – just as our Jess did before her – throw the killer overboard before the situation can be rectified. Accordingly, our Jess is revealed as but an arbitrary moment in a whole series of Jess doppelgängers; doppelgängers that describe a formula: $Jess^{-n} = Jess^{+n}$.

Triangle is thus a wondrous series of loops; loops within loops, parallel loops, Möbius loops all of which circle within and without one other. In a mind-bending twist of genius, Smith will allow our Jess to awake washed up upon a beach on the Miami shoreline, only to discover it is the morning before the boat trip. And through another – even more appalling and unsettling tragedy – force Jess to once more board the yacht and set out into the Caribbean. Loops within loops within loops, where repetition dances with difference, and difference dances with repetition.

No doubt a lot of fun can be had trying to figure out how *Triangle* works, the logic of cause and effect that powers the narration. Such solutions would necessarily point towards spatio-temporal dissonances: time-travel, which would be subject to grandfather paradoxes, in turn referring to the cutting edge of physics and the quantum-inspired speculative situations of many worlds; worlds which would fold back upon themselves overlaying and becoming exposed to one another. However, there is another approach – at once far simpler, and infinitely more complex. We can begin by referring to Deleuze's cineosis, and to a type of recollection-image named the forking path. Recollection-images describe memories: perceptions, affects and actions coalescing on-screen as moments of the past actualised in the present for the future. In their most familiar aspect, recollection-images will be constituted through flashbacks, memories actualised to provide – in varying degrees – 'an explanation, a causality or a linearity' (C2: 49). However, the recollection-image can also give us memory as the 'fragmentation of all linearity … [as] breaks in causality' (C2: 49). Narration becomes lost in the past, in memory itself, which now becomes the primary matter-image of the film. Such images are named forking paths as they describe intricate, ambiguous, contradictory circuits where the film explores 'an inexplicable secret' (C2: 49). Deleuze writes: '[i]t is not just the circuits forking between themselves', but 'each circuit forking within itself, like a split hair' (C2: 49). Unfathomable recollections.

With *Triangle* there is no solution to the narration – or rather, the solution is there is no solution. In other words, the mistake would be to think of the film in terms of cause and effect. The distribution of all the versions of Jess has no beginning or end. Our Jess is just one in an eternal series of cycles. Smith resists the lure of the logic of cause and effect. Jess is lost inside an event from which she can never escape, an irredeemable moment which she can try to forget, attempt to rewrite, believe – again and again – she can efface: but which will forever return. *Triangle* is the rarest of cinematographic images: an optical illusion, a filmic echoing of an Escher painting (two hands drawing one another, interweaving staircase reciprocities), an impossible narration. Yet a narration that engenders a narrative affect as real as memory.

31

Se7en

Mark

Frame III.31 *Se7en* (David Fincher, USA, 1995)

'We've got one dead guy', carps the Captain of Police, 'not three.'

1 – Gluttony. A murder victim is discovered, and homicide detectives William Somerset and David Mills are asked to check out the scene. Bound and force fed with a gun to his head, a morbidly obese man has been tortured to his death. Somerset sees something here: 'This is just the beginning.' He wants off the case, he can't see it through – his last week in his role on the murder team before retirement. Mills wants it, first day in job, just arrived from a small town up-state with his wife Tracy. Mills is dropped; they need Somerset's experience.

2 – Greed. The next day, Mills – awaiting some action – is called to some hotshot lawyer's office. There's another dead guy here, one who has been persuaded to cut a pound of flesh from his own body. On the floor, in blood, the words 'greed'. Back at the station, Somerset believes the crimes are connected:

possibly something to do with the Seven Deadly Sins. Either way, Mills and Somerset are back on the same case. Stomach contents from the fat man lead Somerset to find the words 'gluttony' scraped in grease behind the fridge at the first crime scene; an upside down picture at the second scene gives them some fingerprints. 'So many clues', says Somerset, 'just lead to others.' And so it is …

3 – Sloth. The fingerprints are a clue which leads to Victor, tied to a bed for a year, drip-fed the drugs he used to deal.

Se7en is inspired by the power of a habitual series of elements. Such a cinematic series is what Deleuze calls a relation-image, where the elements are designated through the sign of the mark. A mark is a singular moment in a chain of instants – between which forms a relationship which will coalesce as a mental-image: an image of thought. In short, a series of marks creates an image of understanding. The first mark establishes the initial condition (and may go unnoticed as being a moment in a sequence, only appearing part of a series retroactively). The second mark ratifies the presence of the initial condition (but can only suggest the possibility of an ongoing extension). The third mark confirms the logic of a series, has a retroactive effect and actualises the chain of relations (which may continue beyond the third mark, to a fourth, five, sixth, and so on). Hence – in *Se7en* – the denial of a series by the Captain of Police after the discovery of the murdered fat man. The logic of a habitual chain of relations can only be guaranteed and affirmed with the appearance of a third instance – with a third mark.

Gluttony, Greed, Sloth – three marks of a series that create a relation-image and thus confirm an image of thought: the Seven Deadly Sins. In so doing, this image of thought will simultaneously propose and project the extension of the series through an ongoing sequence of marks. '[A]ll is interpretation, from beginning to end', writes Deleuze; 'the images are only the winding paths of a single reasoning process' (C1: 200). Lust, Pride, Envy and Wrath: although Somerset and Mills will not be able to foretell the order in which these marks will present themselves. They can only follow the clues laid down by the killer in each previous murder.

4 – Lust. A prostitute is killed by a client forced to wear a devastating phallus-dagger.

5 – Pride. A model has her nose sliced off – and is given the choice to phone for help or commit suicide with sleeping pills (the only two options, and the phone and the bottle are superglued to her hands). She is found dead.

That just leaves Envy and Wrath. Two final Deadly Sins to be crossed off the list chalked on the old school blackboard – or the completion of the sequence stymied by Somerset and Mills through their investigation.

It is the series that will generate the power – the suspense – of the film. Perceptions, affects and actions are bound up in a relation-image, an image of thought inspired by mental relations. The series thus 'takes as objects *of* thought, objects which have their own existence outside thought' (C1: 198). In this way, each of the marks – each of the murders – in *Se7en* constitutes a moment of a relation as an image of thought. On the one hand, for the killer each murder is an element in a tableau that will eventual reveal an image of the world. Each victim is selected to represent their own Deadly Sin – each sin being their own and appropriate hearts filthy lesson. For Somerset and Mills, on the other hand, each element of the series must be explored, investigated, examined, and considered. The task of the police is to terminate the sequence before the full image can be constituted. Accordingly, the formulas of situation $\rightarrow$ action and action $\rightarrow$ situation (which capture up perceptions and affects) become the grounding of a relation-image which goes beyond the action-image. Action $\rightarrow$ situation: where an ellipsis exists to be filled, and what is revealed will determine the milieu. Situation $\rightarrow$ action: a given milieu is productive of forces which animate the characters through the duel. Without doubt, *Se7en* will be grounded in both these forms of action. Action $\rightarrow$ situation: *who is the killer?* Situation $\rightarrow$ action: *Somerset and Mills versus the murderer*. Yet director David Fincher will ensure neither form nor the action-image itself will dominate the film. The murderer – who calls himself John Doe – both turns himself in and eludes justice: and the duel disperses. Similarly, the true identity of John Doe is never to be discovered: after all, it doesn't matter who he is. Fincher takes us beyond the action-image. Duel and ellipsis are stymied and become the ground of a relation-image: it is the series of marks that constitute the narration. Doe tells the police that there are two more bodies to be found: Envy and Wrath. However, he will reveal these final marks only to Somerset and Mills. They must drive him out into the desert.

What happens?

6 – Envy . . .

7 – Wrath . . .

The completion of the series of marks: the fulfilment of the relation-image. *Se7en* describes the logic of a sequence – and that which ascends from the narration is an image of thought.

32

Doctor Who – The Day of the Doctor
Demark

Frame III.32 *Doctor Who – The Day of the Doctor* (Nick Hurran, UK, 2013)

'Three of them!', exclaims the general at Gallifrey High Command; '… all my worst nightmares at once'. He has returned – three incarnations, simultaneously.

The planet of the Time Lords is under attack from the Daleks. War between two of the most powerful species in the universe. On the one hand, the Time Lords – humanoids who long ago overcame the limits of space, time and mortality; passive observers from Gallifrey of the joys and woes of planets, systems, and galaxies, the rise and fall of civilisations past, present and future. On the other hand, the Daleks – organic mutants devoid of all emotion housed inside metal travelling machines; creatures intent on enslaving or killing everyone and everything. This is the Time War – and it has been raging for eons. In the process, every lifeform in the universe has suffered, caught between an immovable object and an unstoppable force. But now the conflict appears to be in its final phase – and the Daleks are winning. Gallifrey is under siege; the Time Lords are surrounded by the entire Dalek army orbiting the planet, bombarding it from above. And if the Time Lords are beaten, the universe will have new masters.

Such is the scenario of *Doctor Who – The Day of the Doctor*: the 240th TV story (approximately: valid number systems vary) in a series running (on and off – at time of screening) for fifty years. The series concerns – at the centre – the Doctor, an errant Time Lord who 'borrowed' a TARDIS (time and space machine) and went off to explore the far corners of the universe. During an early trip to Earth, the chameleon circuit on the TARDIS malfunctioned, so its image is now fixed as an old 1950s British police box, instead of changing to fit the landscape in which it arrives. However, the Doctor has become, over the years, rather attached to its form. Selecting companions from the worlds he chances upon, pitching up where he will to have adventures, the Doctor has been a-roaming for well over a thousand years, fighting evil wherever he may find it. Many, many years ago now, when an old man for the first time – grouchy, frail and beginning to lose his faculties – he regenerated (much to the surprise of his friends) into another body. Since then, his companions – and there have been many – have witnessed numerous such regenerations and incarnations:

- The First Doctor. A Gallifreyan who became a Time Lord, and was thus gifted with the power to regenerate his body twelve times. When becoming a Time Lord, he was already a silvery-haired old man, somewhat pompous, paternalistic and patriarchal. Regenerated (*The Tenth Planet/The Power of the Daleks*, 1966) into …
- The Second Doctor. A little imp of a man, curious, mischievous, sometimes baffled but always at the centre of events. Regenerated (*Spearhead from Space*, 1970) into …
- The Third Doctor. A flamboyant and dashing dandy – for much of his time exiled upon Earth serving as scientific advisor to the United Nations Intelligence Taskforce. Regenerated (*Planet of the Spiders*, 1974/*Robot*, 1974–5) into …
- The Fourth Doctor. Laid back and highly unconventional, this bug-eyed prankster wore an incredibly long and colourful scarf. Regenerated (*Logopolis*, 1981/*Castrovalva*, 1982) into …
- The Fifth Doctor. A young, blonde, floppy-haired idealist, a man who could always find time for a game of cricket. Regenerated (*The Caves of Androzani/ The Twin Dilemma*, 1984) into …

- The Sixth Doctor. Sometimes obnoxious, sometimes dangerous, a divisive character with the most appalling dress sense. Regenerated (*Time and the Rani*, 1987) into …
- The Seventh Doctor. Behind the façade of a spoon-playing Chaplinesque figure with an umbrella, a manipulative and dark personality. Regenerated (*The Enemy Within*, 1996) into …
- The Eighth Doctor. A handsome adventurer with a flowing curly mane and a twinkly eye, and dressed in Edwardian costume. Regenerated (never originally televised; of which more a little later) into …
- The Ninth Doctor. With a leather jacket and close-cropped hair, a man haunted by his past and the events of the Time War (again, never originally televised; and, again, something we will return to). Regenerated (*Bad Wolf/ The Parting of the Way/Born Again/The Christmas Invasion*, 2005) into …
- The Tenth Doctor. Skinny, be-suited, sneaker-wearing buccaneer – rather vain. Hence, regenerated (*The Stolen Earth/Journey's End*, 2008) into …
- The Tenth Doctor, again. Regenerated (*The End of Time*, 2009–10/*The Eleventh Hour*, 2010) into …
- The Eleventh Doctor. Young, gangly, bow-tie-wearing and fez-loving 'madman in a box'.

And after each regeneration the Doctor has continued his quest – to travel from world to world, intervening on the side of justice, to set right the wrongs he encounters, to heal the hurts and bind the wounds of the universe. This is the Doctor – all of them.

However, now – in *The Day of the Doctor* – the Eleventh Doctor must confront a secret he has hidden for a long time. We have known since the Ninth Doctor appeared on the scene that he was the last of the Time Lords, that his race was annihilated in the final battle of the Time War, that he was caught up in events, and that these events haunt him. In *The Day of the Doctor* the story is revealed. It was he who killed his own people – every last man, woman and child. Or rather, it was an incarnation of this renegade Time Lord we have never seen.

- The Unnamed (aka the War Doctor) – between the Eighth Doctor and the Ninth Doctor. An incarnation who refused the name of the Doctor: 'Doctor no more' (*The Night of the Doctor*, 2013). The ~~Doctor~~. A warrior, battling with the Gallifreyan front line against the Dalek horde for centuries.

Now an old man, he has had enough: 'No more'. There is one way to end the war: double genocide. He has stolen a weapon of mass destruction – The Moment – and prepares it for use. Such a revelation comes as a shock. The Doctor – this man, these men who have (each, and in their own way) fought on the side of righteousness. The Doctor – whom we have accompanied through time and space for fifty years. Our Doctor. Our Doctor is a mass murderer – the perpetrator of a genocide unparalleled in the history of the universe (from its beginning to its end).

Except – the incarnation of the Time Lord who committed these atrocities was not the Doctor. In order to explore such a paradox, we can turn to Deleuze's cineosis – or cinematic semiosis – and the avatar of the relation-image. A relation-image is constituted through a succession of images that create a habitual series. These images – which Deleuze names as marks – form, once established, a natural sequence of repetitions. Such a sequence will be established through three iterations of the mark: the first gives the condition; the second ratifies the first and suggests a third; the third affirms the series. Accordingly, in *Doctor Who*, the name of regeneration is given only at the third such transformation; and the mythos of the twelve regenerations established later in the Fourth Doctor's tenure (*The Deadly Assassin*, 1976). Such are the incarnations of the Doctor: the First, Second, Third, Fourth, Fifth, Sixth, Seventh, Eighth, Ninth, Tenth, Tenth (again) and Eleventh Doctors. A habitual series of marks, a relation-image – an image of thought embodied as a figure who fights for justice and freedom. However, 'it is always possible', writes Deleuze, 'for one of these terms to leap outside the web and suddenly appear in conditions which take it out of its series, or set it in contradiction with it' (C1: 203). This is the demark. The demark is an aberration – part of the series, but also apart from the series. And this Time Lord who is not – and who has refused the name of – the Doctor is such a demark. The demark is the incarnation who committed the genocide. The Unnamed is a demark whom the marks of the Doctor have hidden from themselves, from their companions and from us.

However, as the ~~Doctor~~ steadies himself to activate The Moment, the weapon (which has the consciousness of artificial intelligence, as well as an associated conscience) intervenes. It wants to show the War Doctor what this act will do to him – and so he is confronted with his later Tenth and Eleventh incarnations. One who is haunted by what the Unnamed has done, the other who tries to forget. Together they figure out another way. They will each fly their own TARDIS around the planet of the Time Lords and pop it into a pocket universe, and as a result of this the Daleks will immediately destroy themselves (… to be honest, they don't think it the best plan ever either). The general at Gallifrey High Command is at first aghast, yet the planet is about to fall, so accepts. Joined by the First to Ninth regenerations (as well as the Twelfth to come, of which more below), the plan is a success. Thus the question: does the War Doctor, the ~~Doctor~~, the Unnamed remain a demark? This reversal of events occurs during the lifespan of the Eleventh Doctor, and due to the nature of the crossed timelines, only this latest incarnation will be able to retain the memory of what has now happened. The Doctor and his subsequent Ninth and Tenth incarnations have already lived through the original trajectory. Yet the Eleventh Doctor now knows the truth. He is set free from his shame. However, there is one final outcome of this introduction of the demark. The Eleventh Doctor is revealed as being the final incarnation of this Time Lord:

- The First Doctor = first nominal incarnation.
- The Second Doctor = second incarnation.
- The Third Doctor = third incarnation.
- The Fourth Doctor = fourth incarnation.
- The Fifth Doctor = fifth incarnation.
- The Sixth Doctor = sixth incarnation.
- The Seventh Doctor = seventh incarnation.
- The Eighth Doctor = eighth incarnation.
- The War Doctor = ninth incarnation.
- The Ninth Doctor = tenth incarnation.
- The Tenth Doctor (first version) = eleventh incarnation.
- The Tenth Doctor (second version) = twelfth incarnation.
- The Eleventh Doctor = thirteenth and final incarnation.

Twelve regenerations. And in the next story the Eleventh Doctor will die. However, in recognition of saving Gallifrey, the Time Lords will reward the Doctor with a new regeneration cycle. The Eleventh Doctor, the thirteenth and final incarnation of a first cycle of regenerations, becomes the nominal first incarnation of a second cycle. Reborn as the Twelfth Doctor (*The Time of the Doctor*, 2013/*Deep Breath*, 2014), he will be without the horror of the Time War he had carried in his heart for so many years.

33

Buried

Symbol

Frame III.33 *Buried* (Rodrigo Cortés, Spain, 2010)

A black screen: darkness. Silence. Breathing ...

A blurred, flickering, indistinct image – then darkness once again.

Shouting ... Screaming ... Paul Conroy is buried alive. The flame of his zippo reveals to him his situation. Such is the wonderful economy of the audio-visual field (no image, no articulate language) of the first few minutes of *Buried*, directed by Rodrigo Cortés. A truck driver in Iraq, Conroy comes to in what he soon discovers to be a makeshift coffin buried underground. He has his lighter, his mobile phone; and later discovers a torch and another mobile hidden there by the insurgents, who want to ransom him to the US government. And that is it. With these tools Conroy must design an escape. And Cortés must fashion a movie. To do so Cortés instates an aesthetic imperative: we must never leave the coffin and we must remain with the Conroy at all times. In this way there is a reduction of both spatial and temporal fields. The mise-en-scène confined to a 2×2×6 wooden box. There is one character on-screen. The film is shot in real time. Framing varies, in the most part, from close-up to extreme close-up ... the heat, the sweat and the blood, dirty fingernails ... what we get are abstract patterns in the light and dark ... the qualities changing with the source, zippo, mobile phone, torch. Action happens out-of-field, off-screen ... his rescuers, the insurgents, his company, his family ... all are voices at a distance ... A wonderful achievement. Cortés: 'From the very beginning, I received every kind of, um, let's call them "kind suggestions" to take the camera beyond the coffin. I was told it would bring some oxygen to the audience if we were to show the surface or to cut out to the other side of the [phone] line, for instance, or if we showed the other characters, like the leader of the hostage-taking group or his wife or the federal authorities. There was talk of doing flashbacks. All of this, I thought, was the perfect way to spoil everything and ruin the film' (Boucher, 2010). Beyond the minimalist aesthetic, why impose such a cinematic philosophy? Geoff Boucher provides a clue towards answering this question: 'Cortés said his compass point for the film was pure Hitchcock — the real-time suspense of *Rope*, the confined quarters of *Lifeboat* and the paralyzed point of view in *Rear Window*' (Boucher, 2010). This Hitchcock parallel should be taken seriously, at least as a starting point, not simply for the aesthetic imperative (setting the filmmaker a seemingly impossible task) and not simply for the precision with which that imperative plays out (the framing, the shots and edits). Rather, we should look to what the Hitchcockian process announced and articulated for cinema in general, before going on to explore how Cortés, in his own way, takes up these procedures.

Deleuze writes: 'it was Hitchcock's task to introduce the mental image into the cinema and to make it the completion of cinema, the perfection of all other images' (C1: 200). For Deleuze, classical cinema – or, the movement-image – operates through three constituent domains: perception, affection and action. A character in the world sees, feels and acts: perception-image, affection-image, action-image. Movement-image cinema uses all these components, but in any film one tends towards domination; a melodrama, for example, is an affection-image; an adventure movie an action-image. Mental-images take up these coordinates and reinscribe them within the domain of thought. Deleuze will go on to specify three types of mental-images. There are recollection-images, which include flashbacks and explore memory; and dream-images, which use dreams, nightmares and hallucinations. Both of these actualise perceptions, affections and actions as thought in another space-time. With Hitchcock, however, Deleuze identified another type of mental-image: the relation-image. Here, thought is the foundation of the flow of the narration. Thus, in 'inventing the … relation-image, Hitchcock makes use of it in order to close the set of action-images, and also of perception and affection-images … Hitchcock accomplishes and brings to completion the whole of cinema by pushing the movement-image to its limit' (C1: 204). With relation-images, then, 'the essential point … is that action, and also perception and affection, are framed in a fabric of relations. It is this chain of relations which constitutes the mental image, in opposition to the thread of actions, perceptions and affections' (C1: 200). At the most basic level, this is suspense. As Deleuze continues, '[w]hat matters is not who did the action – what Hitchcock calls with contempt the whodunit – but neither is it the action itself: it is the set of relations in which the action and the one who did it are caught' (C1: 200). There are, for Deleuze, two types of relations which play out through three types of sign. First, there are natural relations, which are signs of composition: marks and demarks. Second, there are abstract relations, genetic signs: symbols. With the mark 'we see a customary series such that each can be "interpreted" by the others' (C1: 203). With the demark, 'it is always possible for one of these terms to … appear in conditions which take it out of its series' (C1: 203). Marks establish patterns, and the demark disturbs such a pattern. With the symbol, however, we find 'a concrete object which is the bearer of various relations or of variations of as single relation' (C1: 204).

With *Buried* it is possible to see marks and demarks across the film. Everything occurs in threes: the lighter, the mobile phone, the torch. Three women – Conroy's wife, the wife's friend, his colleague (and lover). And – most significantly – the external 'forces': company, army and insurgency. These habitual series form marks which position Conroy in the various dimensions of his life. Yet there is also a demark. Conroy finds three sets of things in the coffin. Some of his own possessions, stuff left by the insurgents, and the snake. Yet the snake breaks this series and becomes a demark; it has entered the coffin and will leave the coffin while the coffin remains underground. In becoming a demark, in detaching itself from a series it becomes an abstract relation, a symbol. Deleuze writes: '[d]emarks and symbols can converge … a single object … can, according to the images in which it is caught, function as a symbol' (C1: 204). This is crucial, for we cannot ask 'what is the snake a symbol of?' outside the context of film. It is the promise of a way out. Just like the mobile phone signal before it. It sets up the possibility of a third escape … the character himself … And if the snake is a demark that becomes a symbol that hints at a mark (a possible habitual series) … in so doing, it also traverses the coffin. It is a vertical element crossing a horizontal plane.

In other words, one of the achievements of *Buried*, and we should not underestimate this, is not simply reducing the spatiality of the mise-en-scène, but rather reconfiguring the mise-en-scène from a situation (action-image) to a symbol (relation-image). The coffin itself becomes an image of thought, a symbol. But again we must ask, a symbol of what? And again: Hitchcock. The McGuffin … the object that makes the plot tick, but is itself there only for the plot … As Hitchcock put it to Truffaut: 'It might be a Scottish name, taken from a story about two men in a train. One man says "What's that package up there in the baggage rack?", and the other answers "Oh that's a McGuffin". The first one asks "What's a McGuffin?". "Well", the other man says, "It's an apparatus for trapping lions in the Scottish Highlands." The first man says "But there are no lions in the Scottish Highlands", and the other one answers "Well, then that's no McGuffin!". So you see, a McGuffin is nothing at all' (Gottlieb and Brookhouse, 2002: 48). The McGuffin is the object that allows the film to operate. In *Buried* it is as if the character has been placed inside the McGuffin.

We can take another route, once more via Deleuze's reading of Hitchcock. With the relation-image, with Hitchcock, cinema 'no longer conceives of the constitution of a film as a function of two terms – the director and the film to made – but as a function of three: the director, the film and the public, which must come into the film, or whose reactions must form an integrating part of the film (this is the explicit sense of suspense, since the spectator is the first to "know" the relations)' (C1: 202). The spectator is brought into the film through affects and action by way of the aesthetic imperative. There is only the coffin. What we get here, then, is extreme filmic claustrophobia: the situation of the character becomes that of the spectator. Second, the spectator is caught up in events, but events happening off-screen, the real action happening elsewhere. Yet actions and affects are, we maintain, reinscribed through the relation-image, through the symbol. Put simply, 'actions, affections, perceptions, all is interpretation, from beginning to end … the images are only the winding paths of a single reasoning process …' (C1: 200). In this sense the coffin is not simply an aesthetic imperative, not simply a McGuffin, but – most significantly – a postulate. It all begins with the postulate, writes Deleuze, where 'the film is developed with a mathematical or absolute necessity, despite the improbability of the plot and the action' (C1: 202). To designate a postulate is to establish a proposition that is simply a starting point. In this sense, there is nothing to deduce, or reveal, about the postulate. It is a defining condition. It is that which proceeds from the postulate where the interest lies. It is the narration and narrative which takes up the postulate, and play it out. *Buried* is in this way an 'interpretation' of its own postulate (C1: 203).

The coffin is buried in Iraq. It would be easy to think of Paul Conroy as an innocent. As being in the wrong place at the wrong time. As being the wrong man. A dupe. A victim. After all, that is how he thinks of himself. However, it seems everyone else knows he is the right man. The insurgents understand better than he does why he is there, and why he must be taken. The army understand better than he why he is being held, and why it will be so difficult to retrieve him. The company understand better than he that their employees are at risk, and what they can do to mitigate that risk (for the company, of course). Conroy is no innocent. He is part of the invasion, he is party to the fighting of the 'war on terror', an active member of the supply chain. As Deleuze writes, 'Rohmer and Chabrol have analysed Hitchcock's schema perfectly: the criminal has always done his crime for another, the true criminal has done his crime for the innocent man who, whether we like it or not, is innocent no longer. In short, the crime is inseparable from the operation by which the criminal has "exchanged" his crime' (C1: 201). The coffin is the coffin of every child, woman and man, buried in and because of Iraq and the war on terror.

34

Five

Opsigns and sonsigns

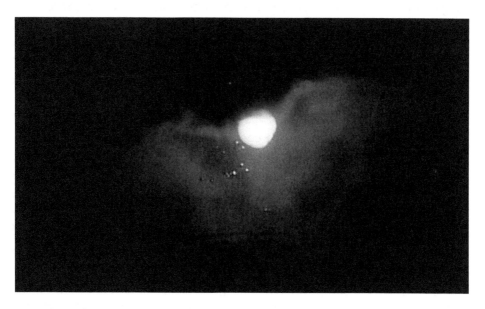

Frame III.34 *Five* (Abbas Kiarostami, Iran | Japan | France, 2003)

Fade in: the camera frames a small section of the seashore, where tide laps beach. A small hunk of driftwood, rotten and barnacle-clad, is discovered on the sand, licked by the breaking waves of the Caspian Sea – the water apparently having relinquished the driftwood in its ebb. Troubled by the incoming tide, the chunk of dead branch rolls and spins on the grey, wet sand, is ensnared and released before inevitably being drawn into the flow once more, and carried with longshore drift. During all this, the camera has kept the driftwood in the centre of the frame but as it is buffeted by the breaking waves it is broken into two, and the pieces float apart until one is carried out-of-frame. Or rather, the camera must choose which piece of wood will remain within the frame. Sometime later, however, the escaped chunk returns to the frame, much further out to sea and drifting away: fade out. Such is sequence one of *Five*, 'Drift-Wood'. This scene takes up the dice throw: one of which is the filmmaker's chancing upon a lump of wood on the seashore, and, in so doing, deciding to place it in the tide and to record what happens. Accordingly, director Abbas Kiarostami's film begins with the elimination of actors, of bodies, faces, characters. No characters to perceive the world, no characters who will feel something, think something, no characters to perform actions upon the world. Concomitantly, any immediate correlation between film-world and spectator is disrupted: we cannot perceive, feel or think with the character, and we cannot subsume ourselves within the character's actions. This is a time-image, which has 'a requirement', according to Deleuze, 'to smash the whole system' of movement-images, 'to cut perception off from its motor extension; action, from the thread which joined it to a situation; affection from the adherence or belonging to characters' and a requirement for 'the mental image … to become "difficult"' (C1: 215). The movement-image function collapses: its cohesive distributions and judgements, its rules of play and the way in which resolution is achieved.

The significance of such a collapse can perhaps only be fully appreciated in the wake of an exegesis of the coordinates of movement-image function. For Deleuze, movement-images are organisations of four cinematic domains: perception-images, affection-images, action-images and mental-images. The perception-image describes the composition of a solid centre extracted from the world – most usually an individual human body. Affection-images give emotions and feelings to this centre – captured, for instance, in close-ups of the face (hate, fear, love, empathy): filmable external expressions of unfilmable internal intensive states. The action-image (proceeding from the logic of the perception-image and affection-image which precede it) configures the environment as a determined situation in which the central character may perform acts. The character senses (perception-image), feels (affection-image) and reacts (action-image) – a reciprocity where world grounds actions, and actions change the world. Such a trajectory is named the sensory-motor schema: determinations describing what may appear as clear-cut cause and effect. Yet, immediately, affects introduce and interweave conscious and unconscious complexity, alternatives and choices: mental-images in mental spaces, recollections through flashbacks; dreams and nightmares; images of thought and thinking. In this way, the determined human centre is a centre of indetermination.

The time-image disrupts such coordinates. In 'Lucretius and the Simulacrum' Deleuze puts it very well: this new image 'manifests neither contingency nor indetermination' (LS: 307). It 'manifests something entirely different … the irreducible plurality of causes of causal series, and the impossibility of bringing causes together in a whole' (LS: 307). How are such requirements performed? 'The first things to be compromised', for Deleuze, are 'the sensory-motor links which produced the action-image' (C1: 206). Here we encounter the crisis of the action-image. And this crisis has 'five apparent characteristics: *the dispersive situation, deliberately weak links, the voyage form, the consciousness of clichés, the condemnation of plot*' (C1: 210). These five characteristics correspond exactly to what Deleuze has previously designated the five laws of the action-image, laws which cohere in movement-image narration. First law (S→S`): the determining of an initial situation (S) that governs the required restoration of the final situation (S`). Second law (S→A): the situation (S) devolves into behaviours, or actions (A), distributed to characters. Third law (A): the action in-itself (A) necessary to realise, by way of the duel, the final resolution. Fourth law (A^n): the action is not simply the ultimate moment, but is structural, duels permeate the film ($A^1 + A^2 + A^3 + \ldots$). Fifth law (→): the whole flow (→) of the plot, which carries situation to action and action to situation through the character in the world. The essential aspect, however, is this: action-images – by way of these five laws – organise perception-images, affection-images and mental-images. Perception, affect and mental states appear in the service of and are dominated by action. Thus, the crisis of the laws of the action-image simultaneously sets free perception, affect and thought: there are no longer perception-images, affection-images and mental-images. No longer is there a solid character at the centre around which all other images are organised; instead perception becomes gaseous and all images vary with respect to each other. No longer are affects recognisable and identifiable human facial expressions of internal intensities; affect becomes ahuman, produced through any-space-whatevers. And no longer are mental spaces assigned to characters as images of thought; the whole film is now an image of thought. The crisis of the action-image is also a collapse of the movement-image function: its compositions of and linkages between domains.

Five laws of the action-image, five characteristics of the crisis, five sequences to Kiarostami's *Five*. What are the chances? It is as if three dice have been cast, and each comes to rest presenting the same number of dots. It thus is tempting – very tempting indeed – to allow each of the five sequences of Kiarostami's film to correspond with each moment of crisis, and in so doing, explore the collapse of the movement-image and the creation of a time-image.

Sequence one, 'Drift-Wood', explores the first aspect of crisis. The first law of the action-image is S→S`, where an initial situation is determined in order to determine the final situation. With the crisis, however, the image 'no longer refers to a situation which is globalising or synthetic, but rather one which is dispersive' (C1: 207). The globalising situation is that which is distilled into a filmic milieu; while a synthetic situation is that which prescribes outcomes and restorations. With the crisis, the milieu cannot be formed and its outcomes are not foretold. And while it is true that a centre is cloven from the world as a solid perception, such a perception describes an ahuman state and becomes gaseous, the driftwood dispersing in the dispersive any-space-whatever of the sea. Here we encounter open events, pure happenings, and non-essential accidents. Captured, battered, broken, separated, dispersed – a centre overwhelmed by the forces that seize it, a world of chance from which no actions can be extracted. Of course, the first law and its crisis refer – as does each crisis of each law – to the entire film. Deleuze will write that any film undergoing the dispersive situation 'is nevertheless not a series of sketches, a succession of short stories' (C1: 207). Accordingly, this first sequence of *Five* extends into the second sequence, and so on – and all sequences become ensnared in the same logic of dispersal.

Nevertheless, Kiarostami's procedure of episode-sequences fading in and fading out means we immediately encounter a series of discontinuities which act as a weakening of links, the second characteristic of the crisis, the stymieing of the second law (S→A) where milieu devolves into actions: 'the line or the fibre of the universe which prolonged events into one another, or brought about the connection of portions of space, has broken' (C1: 207). Sequence two of *Five*, that being said, is in itself exemplary of such a weakening of links. 'On the Promenade' uses a fixed camera to capture a scene. The setting is that of a stone promenade looking out to sea and set high above a beach (which cannot be seen). Sky, water and stone form the three strata of the image; with the sea itself divided into three, cut through by the double railings of the esplanade. Accompanying these horizontals are diagonals, a ramp and its barriers leading down to the invisible beach, and – angles corresponding exactly – shadows of two lampposts cast by a low sun behind the camera. It is this perfect, precise framing that people will traverse: joggers, dog walkers, surfers, strollers; at pace, dawdling; men and women, alone, in couples, in groups. This way, that way ... sometimes leaving the frame empty. Eventually, four old men with walking sticks gather, chat for a while, then leave. In accordance with the second characteristic of the crisis, the image describes chance, and the links and connections between the situation and the happenings are intention-ally weakened. Who are all these people? Where are they all going? Who are the old men? Why must we wait so long for this moment to occur? What do they talk of? (All we hear is the roar of the breaking waves.) The image is composed of questions, not answers; composed of gaps, not information. An any-space-whatever and an accidental meeting, caught by chance within the frame – although this chance is a creation. Kiarostami postpones through his selection of the shots (there is barely visible editing in this sequence) the meeting of the old men, and the meeting is or is made to appear fortuitous. This is the deliberate creation of weak links between a dispersive situation and the opaque behaviours of bodies.

The third characteristic of the crisis is where 'the sensory-motor action or situation has been replaced by the stroll, the voyage … aimless movements (C1: 208). No longer does behaviour become embodied in a final, decisive action (A) in order to resolve the milieu. Such an undoing was, without doubt, a consequence in the first two sequences, but it is attained in the most exquisite way in sequence three, 'Dogs and Light', where Kiarostami explores 'the role of having no role' (*Making of Five*). A thin line of beach, vast expanse of sea. Horizon and pallid blue sky. In the distance, the silhouettes of some dogs at the edge of the water, hanging out, napping (as is Kiarostami) in the morning sun. Then – in imperceptible increments noticeable only through long duration – the sky is becoming white, as is sea and sand, the layers of the image bleeding into one another. The dogs are now black splodges of occasional movement, five blobs of darkness against a white background, disturbed by lines of colour differentials; the waves no longer waves but abstract lines rippling the whiteness, right to left, left to right. Such a change in light, bleaching out the screen, is pure serendipity (the camera not being adjusted as it records). Yet this does not disavow meaning: everything will, for Kiarostami 'form one space' and 'unify', but this unification is that of 'non-existence', where 'everything is completely annihilated before our eyes' (*Making of Five*). In this way, 'Dogs and Light' demonstrates *in extremis* the third crisis: which is the purest of any-space-whatevers, denying the human coordinates of chronological time and comprehensive space, and in turn rejecting the logic of perception → affect → action. Actions are no longer reactions and have no direction.

'In the fourth place', writes Deleuze, 'we ask ourselves what maintains a set in this world … The answer is simple … clichés, and nothing else. Nothing but clichés, clichés everywhere' (C1: 208). Clichés give the appearance of a trajectory, of situations captured in actions, of actions restoring the coordinates of the world. The fourth crisis thus concerns the cliché of action, which appears to be the distinctive characteristic of each moment (A^n) and to permeate a whole, making the whole. The question for Kiarostami is how to present the cliché in such a way that it appears as a cliché (and is not invisible, but becomes visible)? Which is as much to ask, how to escape the cliché? Sequence four, '800 Ducks', becomes a mad chase scene: 800 ducks waddle past the camera left to right … the last duck pauses, quacks, turns, and pads right to left, as the other 799 ducks re-enter and zoom through the frame. Hilarious. 'I do not know if they knew the scenario or not', comments Kiarostami wryly: 'What is their motivation?' (*Making of Five*). This is an exposing and overturning of the cliché.

'Moon on Water, Serenade of Toads', the final and longest sequence of the film, begins in something approaching sublime silence (all the previous sequences have been permeated by the white noise of the sea). A black screen, a silver circle in the centre, softly undulating. It is, we realise, the full moon reflected upon water at night – the circular disc oscillating, fading in and out (sometimes we are left with a black screen). A slow crescendo: a chorus of toads and a storm becomes – in time – the roar of nature. Lightening, plops of raindrops hit the black water, mess with the reflection of the moon, make it fuzzy. The fifth and final moment of crisis is the condemnation of plot, which attacks the ordering of situation to action, and action to situation, of characters, their perceptions, emotions, thoughts and actions. 'How can one not believe', asks Deleuze 'in a powerful concerted organisation, a great and powerful plot …?' (C1: 209). Yet this is what Kiarostami explores. With the reflected full moon, with its continual disappearances, its ephemeral presence. In the final sequence of the *Five*, Kiarostami collapses a solid centre into a black screen of water, an any-space-whatever that disperses the image of which it is only a reflection.

Five sequences: five long takes? 'Moon on Water, Serenade of Toads' appears as a long take, despite us knowing it is a collage of shots, the sequence-shot. 'Tarkovsky', writes Deleuze, 'challenges the distinction between montage and shot when he defines cinema by the "pressure of time" in the shot … we are plunged into time rather than crossing space' (C2: xii). Five sequences: five episodes? If we have looked at each of the five episodes through each of the five characteristics of crisis, this is was merely a tactical alliance. Each episode of *Five* enacts each moment of crisis, and each moment of crisis permeates each of the five sequences. Everything collapses: perception-images, affection-images, mental-images, action-images, even the so-called language of cinema. Everything is undone – frame, shot, montage, sound, colouration: comprehensive space, chronological time, human coordinates. The film is as much one long take, one sequence-shot of the crisis image, the collapse image of realism, of the traditional realist cinematic form. Concomitantly, the crisis of the action-image is the creation of pure optical and sound images – opsigns and sonsigns. And opsigns and sonsigns are the condition for the time-image.

35

Black Swan

Mirrors face to face

Frame III.35 *Black Swan* (Darren Aronofsky, USA, 2010)

Riding the subway, Nina glances at her own reflection in the now-blackened windows of the train. She touches her hair, her skin. Something catches her attention out of the corner of her eye. When she turns – through the glass doors separating the cars – she sees someone she recognises. Although she cannot at first place this figure. Turned slightly away from her, this woman – Nina realises – reminds her of herself. Except, this doppelgänger is dressed in a long black coat; while Nina is in the palest of pink with white scarf. The woman will leave the train at the next stop, and before Nina is able to catch her face, she disappears into the crowd. This moment, at the beginning of *Black Swan*, has an essential function in the film, for it immediately links the reflected image with the doppelgänger, and such a doubling of the body with an echoing of bodies. In other words, director Darren Aronofsky creates and develops mirror images:

bodies in mirrors; the mirrored body and the mirroring of bodies. These three mirror images are without doubt interrelated, they interpenetrate and circulate through one another – and as the film progresses they will become increasingly inseparable, so much so that we no longer know where one begins and another ends. *Black Swan* creates a film-world of mirror images.

Everything begins with the purest of mirror images: the image in the mirror. There is the threefold standing mirror in the front room of the apartment Nina shares with her mother, where she will warm up in the morning, and practise in the evening. The slivers of mirrors that line the inside of her music box, where the little plastic ballet dancer spirals. Mirrors in the bathroom where she explores the bloody rash developing on her skin, and other bodily deteriorations. The multiple reflecting surfaces of the hallways of the apartment, framed mirrors, glass covering the pictures on the wall, the glass panels of doors. Sometimes Nina becomes the reflection, sometimes the reflection becomes Nina; passing out of the frame one side and immediately re-entering the frame but moving in the other direction. In the communal dressing room there are mirrors reflected within mirrors, big plate mirrors and small circular table mirrors; a recurrence of images of the ballet dancers. The mirrors that line the walls of the practice studios; the partition of mirrors in the principal studio. The ornate mirror in artistic director Thomas Leroy's office. When Nina discovers she has won the role of the Swan Queen ('He picked me, Mommy'): WHORE in lipstick on the restroom mirror. Mirrors in the physio room, the costumer's room (creating almost infinite recursions of Nina), and the stairwell of the theatre. Mirrors in the bar; mirrors on the dance floor. The great cut-glass mirror opposite the apartment door (creating multiple images of Nina and Lily, tripped out). And finally – the shattered and bloody mirror in Nina's dressing room on the opening night of *Swan Lake*.

Such mirror images develop immediately into the doppelgänger, the doubled image. It is as if Nina's reflection has climbed out of the mirror to walk alongside her through the streets, to trouble her in her home. In the darkness of the night, in an enclosed space, her double approaches and passes swiftly by. In the bath, underneath the water, Nina sees herself looking down at her from above the soapy surface. Or, Aronofsky will create an image in a mirror that is not Nina – someone else looking back at her. When she is having her costume fitted, someone like Nina gazes back, one figure among the recursion of images. The mirror in her dressing room creates another person studying her. And perhaps we should include here the portraits of Nina her mother obsessively paints, covering the mother's bedroom walls.

Finally, there is the mirroring of bodies. Such images – of course – find their inspiration in the story of *Swan Lake* – the ballet which is at the centre of the film, and from which the film itself generates its power. The white swan and the black swan. Leroy: 'which of you can embody both swans, the white and the black?' This will be Nina's task, to transform herself from one to the other. To do so she must negotiate three female relationships where we discover three sets of mirroring with others: Nina–Lily mirroring; Nina–Beth mirroring; Nina–mother mirroring. The arrival of tattooed Lily, 'straight off the plane from San Francisco', will cause Nina to doubt herself and all of those around her. Is Lily out to steal her role? Yet she is fascinated by this woman with her attitude of devil-may-care – she is everything Nina would love to be; and someone she will find she will lust after. Aronofsky will discover ways to transform Nina into Lily, and Lily into Nina: hallucinations, the strobing at the club, dreams – and of course in mirrors. Lily taking Nina's place in a rehearsal. Then there is Beth Macintyre, the dying swan, the second of these relationships. Nina usurps Beth, takes her role, and steals the attention of her lover – although she knows not what she does. But Nina sees Beth as a role model, at least at first. Later, Beth will be an exemplar of her own future. Aronofsky makes this clear by transforming Beth into the mother (through a mirror reflection). Thus the third, and most powerful of the three female relationships. The passive aggressive mother, the jealous mother, the infantilising mother, the suffocating mother. Her mother – who herself was a ballet dancer – Nina's future, once again.

Thus the mirror images of *Black Swan*: bodies in mirrors; the mirrored body and the mirroring of bodies. Deleuze sees these as powerful time-images, where an actual on-screen image can generate multiple perspectives of a character, perspectives which describe a virtual correlate. The body and the environment are framed in distorted states, in multiplicity, and as fragments in 'oblique mirrors, concave and convex mirrors and Venetian mirrors', 'two facing mirrors', and even a 'palace of mirrors' (C2: 70). The actualisation of the body and the world is no longer dependent upon a cohesive tracing or the recognition of organic coordinates but a virtual correlate between actuals: fragments, duplicates and distortions. The image cracks open, depicted space is complex, the body is a crystal. This concerns the hyalosign, the first of the time-images and the first coalescence of opsigns and sonsigns (C2: 69; 127). Opsigns and sonsigns are pure actual optical and sound situations where 'the actual [image] is cut off from its motor linkages', thus enabling a 'coalescence of an actual image and its virtual image' (C2: 127). Opsigns and sonsigns stymie the seamless flow of actual image to actual image; and the hyalosign relinks the actual image to a virtual correlate. In this way, the hyalosign is the '*description*' of an image on-screen – a fragment, now – the 'most restricted circuit of the actual image and *its* virtual' (C1: 69). And the mirror image is the fragment in-itself, where bodies and backgrounds appear multitudinous – and in this way the actual propagates indiscernibility enacted by the virtual – non-actual – linkages between elements.

Section III

And this is the project of *Black Swan*. These mirror images – in all their manifestations, and in their interpenetration – are actual images of the fragmentation of Nina, her coming apart – but also the possibility of eventual transformation. A virtual, as yet non-actualised, Nina. 'If I was only casting the white swan, she would be yours ... but I'm not' – this is Leroy. In the first scene of the film Nina awakes and has breakfast with her mother: a grapefruit and poached egg. 'Look how pink and pretty', says Nina; her mother replies: 'Sweet girl.' Leroy: 'Show me your black swan Nina'; 'Not so controlled, seduce us'; 'Lose yourself ... all that discipline for what?' Transformation: 'The real work will be a metamorphosis' from the 'virginal' and 'sweet' white swan/ Nina 'into her evil twin'. Nina is always under pressure, from herself and from those around her. To be perfect, to be successful. And she is fragmenting, her body is falling to pieces (the rash, her toenails); her mind is fragmenting (hallucinations of further bodily deteriorations: skin peeling off). Always captured through the three mirror images. But it is through this mirroring that her transformation becomes possible. Leroy to Nina: 'The only person standing in your way is you'; Leroy on the white swan, who 'in death, finds freedom'. Thus the ambiguity of the final scene. Does Nina die, or is it just the white swan who has died? Is the final scene an image of transformation? Are the mirror images finally surpassed: does white Nina become opaque and fade, for black Nina to become limpid and appear?

36

Self Made

Limpid and opaque

Frame III.36 *Self Made* (Gillian Wearing, UK, 2010)

Would you like to be in a film? You can play yourself or a fictional character. Call Gillian.

Self Made (2010) is a paradox. And it is the nature of the paradox that gives the film its power. Yet the paradox is chimeric, a shadow of the actual images on-screen. The paradox emerges indirectly, a consequence of the two modes of narration of the film. First mode: documentary. The participants – through their facilitator, Sam Rumbelow – explore the techniques of 'the method', method acting, which will allow them to encounter themselves anew and so generate their own 'self-made' film. In this way each participant goes on to star in their own short, which, while encompassed by director Gillian Wearing's documentary, appears as its own moment of narration. So, second mode: fiction. However, the paradox is not a direct outcome of the continuity between these two modes of narration, though this innovative procedure is indeed the foundation of the paradox.

There are three ways in which *Self Made* is not a paradox. First, the documentary section operates plainly in that form; there are no tricks, no ruses, no 'actors' playing 'real' people. This documentary aspect tends to focus upon the feelings, the emotions, the thoughts of the participants, exploring their internal lives, drawing these feelings out, moving towards externalisation, action. Second, the short films are realist in the sense that the characters the participants go on to play are organic to the filmic world in which they appear; they are engendered by the situation they find themselves in, and react to that situation through action. Third, there is a correlation between these two domains, the action-sequences fulfil the externalisation of the feelings and emotions explored in the documentary-sequences, the short films are an outcome of what came before, and the rehearsals chart the process through which they will be made. There is, in other words, continuity across the two domains.

Lesley, James, David, Ash, Jerome and Lian sit in a bare warehouse on plastic chairs. Rumbelow asks them to immerse themselves in their inner worlds. Exercises of 'the method' are explored. Rumbelow is, he says, taking them through a process, externalising what is internalised, taking them towards deeper truths. It is an emotional experience for many of them. Some of the participants go on to reveal their fears: for Lian, abandonment; for James, violence; for Dave, suicide. Rumbelow sets up workshops to explore and narrativise these fears: action and creation, he reveals, result in truth. Interspaced throughout these exercises and stagings are the short films that some of the participants go on to make. Lian plays in *King Lear* to an empty theatre; James is knifed outside his house by a gang of teenagers; Leslie has an encounter with a true gentleman in the 1940s; Dave becomes Mussolini, strung-up; Ash … well … we will return to Ash …

Yet if documentary and fiction correlate in the dimension of content, owing to the different modes of narration, the link between fiction and documentary in the dimension of form has – at one and the same time – false continuity. In other words, despite both the sequences obeying the laws of classical cinema, the film as a whole is modernist. This is the paradox. To explore this paradox more fully and reveal why it is so crucial to Wearing's project, we can turn to Deleuze and his theory of cinematographic concepts.

Deleuze describes how the cinema operates through two different semiotic systems: there are movement-images (the classical cinema) and there are time-images (the modernist cinema). Movement-image films are organised through the sensory-motor schema. There are perception-images, affection-images, action-images and mental-images. Perception-images coalesce (through shot and reaction shot and/or flowing cameras) to create centres which go on to be filmed in relation to the other images: affection-images express feelings; action-images create reactions; and mental-images explore thought. These images are linked together, composing the continuity of the movement-image. In time-image films, however, these sensory-motor coordinates collapse. No longer can actual images be defined as perception-, affection-, action- and mental-images. Rather, pure optical and sound signs create virtual images, virtual linkages above, beyond and around the actual images on-screen: false continuity. *Self Made* may thus seem to be of the movement-image. The documentary aspect is predominantly affection-image. The realist short films are predominantly action-image. Thus these two types of movement-image would seem bound to create a homogeneous link. They should compose a movement-image film. Yet, because of the shift in form and production methods, including their sound and even the way in which the sequences are coloured, the paradox emerges. *Self Made* dissolves the movement-image through false continuities, creating, *in toto*, a time-image film. False continuity between movement-images becomes the dominant organisational imperative of the film. This idea of dominance is crucial. 'A film is never made up of a single kind of image', writes Deleuze; 'thus we call the combination of the ... varieties, montage. Montage (in one of its aspects [post-shoot editing]) is an assemblage of movement-images ... Nevertheless a film, at least in its most simple characteristics, always has one type of image which is dominant'; accordingly, 'each of these movement-images is ... a "reading" of the whole film' (C1: 70). Yet such dominance does not only occur with the movement-image: '[f]rom classical to modern cinema, from the movement-image to the time-image ... it is always possible to multiply the passages from one regime to the other, just as to accentuate their irreducible differences' (C2: 279).

In other words, any film could be, indeed to a certain extent must be, composed of a multiplicity of images, of movement-images, or of time-images, or of both movement-images and time-images. Movement-images territorialise, create identity, while time-images deterritorialise, or undo, put into crisis, such formulations. In this way, a film is – at the formal level – a schizophrenia in the sense that it is a composition of different types of images, never more so than when these images are of the movement-image and the time-image. Yet one type of image wins out; there is dominance. Sometimes the movement-images overpower (reterritorialise) time-images, sometimes the time-images overpower (deterritorialise) movement-images. It is important to note that we are not saying that the time-image is chaotic and that the movement-image tames this chaos. Rather, movement-images and time-images organise chaos differently. As Deleuze and Félix Guattari put in their final book together, *What Is Philosophy?*, '[a]rt ... struggles with chaos, but it does so in order to bring forth a vision that illuminates it for an instant, a Sensation' (WP: 205). A sensation: a dominant image. As Deleuze puts it in the *Cinema* books, 'a point of view on the whole film, a way of grasping the whole' (C1: 70). It is here that we return to *Self Made*.

In *Self Made*, documentary and fictional episodes reflect upon each other: they are hyalosigns. Hyalosigns, or crystal-images, are complex signs composed of actual on-screen images and powerful virtual connections. They can be decomposed into three signs: 'two mirrors face to face', 'the limpid and the opaque' and 'the seed and the environment' (C2: 71). Each performs an exchange between the actual on-screen image in the present and its virtual connections off-screen in relation to the present image, past images and images to come. With 'two mirrors face to face' the actual image describes a mirroring on-screen in such a way that what is actual and what is virtual is indeterminate. 'When the virtual image becomes actual [and] ... the actual image becomes virtual in its turn' we discover the second sign of hyalosigns, the limpid and the opaque (C2: 71). Here we see the 'expression of [the] exchange' between the actual and the virtual (C2: 71). We can see each of these aspects in *Self Made*. The documentary and fictional aspects mirror each other. Yet, when the documentary aspect is limpid, the fiction is opaque, and when the fiction becomes limpid, the documentary becomes opaque. What dominates, as we have seen with the founding paradox of *Self Made*, is the exchange between the two modes of the film. And while the modes are foundational, they are the bedrock of the exchange between participant and actor, between actor and role: '[t]he actor ... makes the virtual image of the role actual, so that the role becomes visible and luminous' (C2: 71). Accordingly, '[t]he actor is a "monster", or rather monsters are born actors – Siamese twins, limbless men – because they find a role in the excess or shortcoming that affects them' (C2: 71). Thus, for Deleuze, the virtual image of the character becomes actual, or limpid, as the actual image of the actor becomes opaque, or virtual; and reciprocally, actual–virtual, limpid and opaque are ongoing exchanges throughout the film.

In this sense, *Self Made* goes far beyond the commonplace exposé that we are all actors. We all think we know this already. We are actors in a mise-en-scène that we can only indirectly act upon, do very little to control. What happens in this film is something far more profound; both the actor and the mise-en-scène at one and the same time are exchanged for another mise-en-scène and actor. The role they play in their films is no more the real than the role they play in their real lives. In other words, *Self Made* does not simply reveal that we are all actors, nor does it reveal the real behind the actor where reality is created or produced. Rather, it reveals that the participant and the actor are inextricably one and the same thing: '[w]e no longer know which is the role and which is the crime ... the crystalline circuit of the actor, its transparent face and its opaque face' (C2: 72). *Self Made* does not solve the problem of identity but shows us its impasse. The impasse is, of course, that this exchange happens at the same time. Not homogeneous, but heterogeneous. As Deleuze and Guattari write in *Anti-Oedipus*: '[s]imulation must be understood in the same way ... as identification ... If identification is a nomination, a designation, then simulation is the writing corresponding to it, a writing that is strangely polyvocal, flush with the real. It carries the real beyond its principle to the point ... where the copy ceases to be a copy in order to become the Real *and its artifice*' (AO: 87). In *Self Made*, Wearing 'traverses all the singularities of the series' of participants and actors, actors and roles; follows the 'series of singularities in the disjunctive network, or intensive states in the conjunctive tissue, and a transpositional subject moving full circle, passing through all the states' (C2: 88–9). The characters have revealed nothing of themselves. We have not reached some inner truth. They have, rather, gone outside of themselves, made new connections, false truths. It is thus better to say that the inside–outside model is proved a ruse, a short cut with a simple payoff. Rather, it is a collapse of the inside–outside model, of the participant-actor, classical-modernist dichotomy, of pretty much every dichotomy you care to conjure up.

So finally, Ash. Ash is highly articulate, intelligent and aware of what he is getting himself into. Yet his self-made film is brutal beyond belief, possibly one of the most fascinatingly vicious moments cinema has ever produced. And here we reach the crucial aspect of our exploration of *Self Made*, our adventure through the images of Wearing's film, the reason we have gone to such trouble, through such circuitous routes, to articulate and stress the paradox, to explicate dominance. For if we conceive the film as movement-image and the connections between documentary and fiction as movement-image, as pure continuity, the two aspects of Ash become a homogeneous whole: and the fiction reveals the truth. We discover the real Ash. Yet if we conceive of the film as a time-image, as a hyalosign, as an instance of the limpid and the opaque, what we get is a heterogeneous trajectory. Ash becomes opaque and Ash becomes limpid. There is an exchange between actual-Ash and virtual-Ash. And at the same time virtual becomes actual, actual becomes virtual. The crystalline circuit: 'Ash' disappears, to be replaced by 'Ash'.

Would you like to be in a film? You can only but play yourself and a fictional character ... and there will be no way to figure out which is which. Call Gillian.

37

Synecdoche, New York

Seed and environment

Frame III.37 *Synecdoche, New York* (Charlie Kaufman, USA, 2008)

The theatre piece was never named, although Caden Cotard played with a few titles, among them (early on) *Simulacrum*, and (much later) *Infectious Diseases in Cattle*. It is in ruins. Caden walks through the mise-en-scène: deserted, graffitied, rubbish-strewn streets. He is old now, balding. What hair he has is silver-white; he treads judiciously, moving onwards with the aid of his cane, stooped. Soon he will sit, and speak these words: 'I know how to do this play now … I have an idea … I think …' But before he can speak further, he is given the direction: 'Die.' On a wall nearby is a clock face spray-painted on raw brick. It reads 7:45. One of the three women (more or less) in his life, Hazel, once told him, 'the end is built into the beginning'. 7:45 was the time Caden awoke at the beginning of the film, the day when he became aware everything had changed.

Caden Cotard awakes, the alarm clock is receiving a broadcast, the DJ announces it is fall, and an academic reads a poem about death. On the TV downstairs – as Caden eats his breakfast with his partner Adele Lack and their daughter – a PBS channel cartoon shows farm animals learning about viruses. *Things are going on beneath the surface.* The plumbing in his house is shot. An accident leads him from an ER doctor to ophthalmologist to neurologist. His stool doesn't look right. He has pustules, sycosis (not psychosis, although …). He thinks he may be dying. His wife fantasises about him dying. And takes his daughter to Berlin, without him. He is lonely. His teeth need work; they are rotten. A seizure (of sorts): fungal brain infection, or synapse degradation, or something. Possible erectile dysfunction. He cannot swallow properly. His leg will not cease twitching.

Out of the blue, Caden receives a letter announcing he has won the 2009 MacArthur fellowship. This award is in recognition of his work as director in a regional theatre in Schenectady, a city in New York State. The endowment – as the author of the letter puts it – will allow Caden 'to create something unflinchingly true, profoundly beautiful, and of unremitting value to your community and the world at large'. Thus begins the project, his masterwork. Caden imagines 'a massive theatre piece', so rents a colossal disused warehouse in the theatre district in Manhattan. His initial ideas are vague, he sees theatre as being 'the beginning of thought … the truth not yet spoken', and his guiding principle – based on his own fragile state – is to explore death: 'we are all hurtling towards death, yet here we are for the moment, alive'. Caden begins filling the space with sprawling set designs, and hires dozens of actors. He wants to 'evolve the piece' and for each of the actors to 'grow a character'. Over time, the sets begin to look more and more like the outside world, like New York City, spaces piled atop each other, eventually walled up to heighten the realism. The actors begin to live the lives of the characters they have created, full-time. 'When', asks an actor, 'are we gonna get an audience in here, it's been seventeen years.' But this is only the beginning. Rehearsals are ongoing.

Director Charlie Kaufman – with *Synecdoche, New York* – creates a crystal image, a hyalosign: a film exploring the seed and the environment. Hyalosigns are films in which the actual image on-screen is opened up to virtual correlates, and the seed and the environment is one way of creating such a relation of the actual and the virtual: actual seed → virtual environment. An actual moment of the film foretells the spatiality of the film to come, a setting or series of settings, an event, happening or occurrence: an environment which is not in itself yet given. The seed image in *Synecdoche, New York* is the cartoon on viruses, hence the consideration of the title *Infectious Diseases in Cattle*. And the plumbing. And the poem. And … It is the seed that will initiate Caden's suffering, but also inspire the theatre piece (the thought that begins everything, but that which is unable yet to be spoken). The seed will evolve the mise-en-scène, which will become a replica of the city outside; and develop through the actors, which go on to number in the thousands. 'I won't settle for anything else other than the brutal truth', announces Caden, '... brutal ... brutal.' No better word describes Kaufman's cinematic procedure. Not the actual images. Rather, it is the ellipses, the space between images – the virtual correlates – that are brutal. A year passes between two sequences, and the false continuity experienced by the viewer is similarly experienced by Caden; he believes it to be only a week. This is Kaufman's brutality: to condense a life into two hours, to make a life feel as though it has lasted two hours. To depict a life stuck in fear, in rehearsal. Kaufman will correlate this seed and environment with other types of hyalosign (mirror images and the limpid and opaque), where actors become characters, and characters replace other actors. Caden himself will be replaced – others begin to live his life for him, and – terrifyingly – much more successfully. Yet it is the hyalosign of the seed and the environment that dominates the film. *Synecdoche, New York* grows the crystal image, and the seed becomes virtual as the environment is actualised. Deleuze writes of such an environment: 'as pure virtuality ... it does not have to be actualised' (C2: 79). And perhaps this is the truth Caden never understands. We have – at the end of the film – the actualised environment of a now virtual seed.

There is, however, a reciprocal movement of *Synecdoche, New York*. Early on Caden is living with his first partner, Adele, and their four-year-old daughter, Olive. Adele is a painter, she creates small images, images of the finest detail that can only be perceived through a magnifying glass. Adele will leave Caden, move to Berlin, will become successful. Kaufman's procedure is to progressively erase Adele from the film; her presence is felt less and less, and her paintings become ever smaller. Caden goes to Berlin to find her, but she is elusive. He rebuilds her apartment, but she is never glimpsed. It is in this way we encounter the imperceptible: an expression that 'is imperceptible precisely from the point of view of recognition', writes Deleuze in *Difference and Repetition* (DR: 176). Adele does not follow the path seed → environment, but environment → seed. The environment remains virtual, and is actualised in little seed images. The imperceptible that it is not immediately susceptible to recognition. Small Miracles.

38

Loong Boonmee raleuk chat/Uncle Boonmee Who Can Recall His Past Lives

Peaks of the present

Frame III.38 *Uncle Boonmee Who Can Recall His Past Lives* (Apichatpong Weerasethakul, Thailand | UK | France | Germany | Spain | the Netherlands, 2010)

If this film is strange and unsettling, maybe it is because of the temporal disturbances. The final scene in *Uncle Boonmee Who Can Recall His Past Lives*, in this regard, is not exceptional, but exemplary. Boonmee is dead. His family are in a hotel room after his funeral. A fundamental split in time occurs: they stay in the hotel room watching TV/they go to a bar to eat. Both events occur at the same moment. We must resist seeing this as simply some trick, a ruse, or joke. Or at least, not only a trick, a ruse, a joke. For to think this moment in-and-of-itself apart from the film as a whole (and indeed, as we will see, from director Apichatpong Weerasethakul's wider project, of which *Uncle Boonmee* is just one element) is to miss something far more essential.

The movie tells the story of Boonmee, who is dying from renal failure, acute kidney disease. Still living on the family farm near the village of Nabua in Nakhon Phanom (rural north east Thailand, near the border with Laos), his remaining family visit from the city. And from beyond the grave … his wife returns. Then there is his son, who mated with a monkey ghost and is now a red-eyed and furry monster. Yet the days pass peacefully in the orchards. He dreams of the past – a princess visiting a secluded waterfall; and of the future – a militaristic authoritarian regime. Eventually, as Boonmee feels he is to pass away, he is taken to the cave where he believes his first life to have begun. The title, in this way, is wonderfully disingenuous. To recall past lives (*raleuk chat*) immediately orients the spectator towards a Buddhistic interpretation of the film. No doubt, if we were to seek out evidence to support such an interpretation, we could find it without too much trouble. Indeed, Weerasethakul claims that the initial impetus for the film (and project) came from a book he was given by a priest from the temple in his hometown. The book was by a man called Boonmee, the title *A Man Who Can Recall His Past Lives*. Yet the film does not explore reincarnation to any significant degree. If *Uncle Boonmee* has a Buddhistic world view, this is incidental. The recalling of past lives becomes something else entirely. For instance, there is one visual venture into the past. A princess, who, ashamed of her ugliness, visits a waterfall. While there, she has a tryst with a particularly licentious catfish. Clearly, this is not simply a direct memory of one of Boonmee's past lives, but an indirect memory that condenses tonalities, stories, reminisces: a mythical past in general. Then there is the dream of the future. The events are narrated in voice-over by Boonmee, but the images appear as photogrammes, and the images are contemporary: Thai soldiers with civilian-clothed prisoners. Crucially, these visual images return us to a moment earlier in the film when Boonmee told his sister about killing communist sympathisers for the Thai government during his youth.

In other words, the memories of the past and the dreams of the future are functions of Boonmee's present, are dimensions of the present. This is seen most clearly at the beginning of the film. His family returning home from the city. The appearance of the ghost of his wife. His monstrous son emerging from the forest where he disappeared years before. *Uncle Boonmee Who Can Recall His Past Lives* explores the variable present. It is the final scene, the doubled sequence, that gives us the skeleton key with which to explore the film in this way … and in so doing reorients a theological interpretation towards the political, the philosophical. The present becomes the staging ground for the past and the future. Everything happens in the present.

In his *Cinema* books, Deleuze names this kind of filmic organisation 'peaks of the present', a film composed of chronosigns through which certain (inexhaustible) temporal strategies undo causality. Thus the question 'can the present ... stand for the whole of time?' and the response 'Yes, perhaps, if we manage to separate it from its own actual quality ...' – the quality of the present as now (C2: 100). In this type of film 'there is no longer a future, present and past in succession, in accordance with the explicit passage of presents which we make out' (C2: 100). Rather, 'there is a present of the future, a present of the present and a present of the past, all implicated in the event, rolled up in the event, and thus simultaneous and inexplicable' (C2: 100). Here 'time is revealed inside the event, which is made from the simultaneity' of presents, 'from these de-actualised peaks of present' (C2: 100). 'It is', concludes Deleuze, 'the possibility of treating the world or life, or simply a life or an episode, as one single event which provides the basis of the implication of presents' (C2: 100). In this sense, uncle Boonmee can recall his past lives within the life he has lived, that singularity which opens up onto the universal, which captures his deeds and misdeeds, stories told to him when he was young, cool (and not so cool), TV shows shot in 16mm, dreams and hallucinations. His hopes for the future beyond him. His very real lives within his very real life, where what is actual and what is virtual are indiscernible. Life is not, the film seems to say, a simple case of identity. I is not simply I: one thing after another from birth to death. There is something more fundamental. We are in the present, but that present is a function of the universe ... of a temporal infinity.

The last moments of the film – the doubling of the present – are then curious in another respect. For Boonmee is dead. The central point around which the film accumulated has disappeared, the circumference has been breached. The memories, the ghosts, the returns, the dreams, the hallucinations, necessarily evaporate. And yet the film continues ... indeed, even when the film finishes, the undertaking continues. *Uncle Boonmee Who Can Recall His Past Lives* being just one element of Weerasethakul's *Primitive* project. In this way the individual is also left behind. Weerasethakul has said that instead of filming the book given to him by the priest, he made a more personal film. But perhaps this film, this project, is genuinely impersonal ... or depersonalised. The present itself is what is at stake. For the spectator. The way the past and future are implicated in the present we inhabit. The way we experience memory, explore the past ... the way we experience the future ... in the now ...

39

Russkiy kovcheg/Russian Ark

Sheets of the past

Frame III.39 *Russian Ark* (Alexander Sukurov, Russia | Germany | Japan | Canada | Finland | Denmark, 2002)

Alexander Sukurov's *Russian Ark* has everything to excite an aficionado of time travel movies: a spectacular temporal enfolding; a vast array of characters, fictional, fictionalised and real; strange situations and baroque settings, both historical and imaginary; ravishing beauty and permeating unease; mystery and revelation; self-reflexivity, intertextuality, and an inventive filmic process at once spontaneous and rigorous. An unnamed twenty-first-century Russian filmmaker – Sukurov himself? – arrives in the past from our present. He hooks up with a fellow traveller in time, the nineteenth-century French aristocrat Marquis de Custine, and together they wander the St Petersburg's Hermitage

– Winter Palace of the Czars, grand museum of Mother Russia. Leaping this-way and that-way in time, the Unnamed and the Marquis encounter a cascade of moments spanning some three hundred years of Russian history: the founding St Petersburg; the (renamed) city under threat of destruction during the Second World War; Nicholas II, Anastasia and family on the morning of revolution. *Russian Ark* abounds in many such cinematic pleasures. Yet the film not only celebrates the possibilities of time travel in the movies; it also disrupts the genre through an ungrounding.

The general principle of time travel concerns an immediate encounter with temporal paradox. No longer is time merely chronological: a past begetting the present begetting a future. No longer is time simply homogeneous: a chain of presents – the present a now preceded by a now that has passed, to be superseded by a now to come. Rather, the present interfolds with pasts and futures; pasts and futures interfold with the present. A traveller jumps from one time to another (from a present to the past or the future; from the past or the future to a present) disturbing homogeneous chronological time with non-chronological relations, generating temporal paradox. In this way, the as-it-was or yet-to-come are reconfigured or revealed, in turn transforming the as-it-is. Time travel, in other words, creates or averts a temporal crisis – sometimes even averting the very crisis it created. Thus the tendency of the narration: to mend time, put time back together as it was or reconstitute it as it should be. To re-impose order upon the chaos that has arisen. Yet *Russian Ark* neither creates nor averts a crisis. The travellers are witnesses, seers – sometimes of a relative past, sometimes of a relative future. They do not intervene and what they witness will not transform their relative presents. We encounter here a fascinating reversal. *Russian Ark* does not disturb chronological time with non-chronological relations. The film rather considers time as fundamentally non-chronological. Temporal paradox is not introduced into the narration through time travel, but is exposed as being the essence of time. An always there; and, being so, irresolvable. Chronological time is a ruse, mere appearance, a chimera. Time is – as Deleuze puts it in *Cinema 2* – a time-image and composed of sheets of the past.

Sheets of the past: '[b]etween the past as a pre-existence in general and the present as infinitively contracted past', writes Deleuze, there are 'all the circles of the past' (C2: 99). In this way, temporality is captured from the perspective of pure pastness (rather than the past being a function of the present, as in the movement-image). With the time-image the now is effaced and pasts appear as moments of coexistent singularity arranged non-chronologically. There is no cause and effect, just events that resonate with each other, backwards and forwards. These sheets of the past are seen in exemplary fashion in *Russian Ark*, the film creating an extraordinary encounter for the time travellers with historical events as mise-en-scène. It was André Bazin who first apprehended such a function of mise-en-scène in the cinema – and Deleuze will develop his argument with respect to the time-image, and sheets of the past. Yet approaching Bazin already requires us to acknowledge a theoretical position dependent upon an 'evolution' of filmmaking, one both technical and artistic, arising from two intertwined propositions and two reciprocal consequences (Bazin, 1997: 23). First proposition: resist montage. It is only after we have discovered the function of montage to concretise associations (after Kuleshov and Eisenstein) that we can turn away from it. We thus encounter a 'refusal to break up the action' and rediscover the long take (the sequence-shot, as Bazin names it), allowing us to 'analyse the dramatic field in time' (Bazin, 1997: 34). Second proposition: deep focus becomes depth-of-field. Deep focus can be used to create (after Renoir and Welles/Toland) a 'composition in depth' by way of introducing planes of coexistent action (Bazin, 1997: 34). 'One shot sequences in depth', writes Bazin, will thus give 'new meaning' to the image (Bazin, 1997: 36). First consequence: 'a sense of the ambiguity of reality' (Bazin, 1997: 36). Hollywood-esque realism is undermined by uncertainty – and is so aligned with the neo-realist project (after Visconti and Rossellini). Second consequence: the 'theatricalization of cinema' ('the exact opposite of a passive recording of theatre') (Bazin, 1997: 69). Cinema must (after Dreyer and Hitchcock) reveal the illusion of reality as the reality of illusions – thus allowing the audience the role of judgement with respect to filmic events. These consequences are 'bound up with the very essence of the mise-en-scène' captured through the long take and depth-of-field (Bazin, 1997: 102).

Such a conception of mise-en-scène is immediately apparent in *Russian Ark*. The long take and moving camera form a sequence-shot that provides the foundation upon which everything occurs in-depth through multiple planes, which generate theatricalisation and ambiguity. Early on in *Russian Ark*, Unnamed and Custine encounter a window into the chambers of Peter the Great and his entourage. Voices are heard, actions performed by those inside, but these occur at a distance, movements and sounds obscured by dark glass and old stone in the mid-ground while the camera snakes around attempting to achieve a better visual and sound apprehension (though it never succeeds). Why is the Czar angry? Is he always angry? We never really know: this realism propagates opacity, indeterminacy and ambiguity. Custine and Unnamed climb a dark and tortuous spiral staircase. They emerge into a vast space divided into discrete sections which the camera will pass one by one along a lateral track, right to left: men turning wooden wheels and working a massive concertina system; Roman soldiers in plate armour, a throne of gold with a woman in robes; dancers dancing; an orchestra playing in the pit; then out into a sumptuous theatre, an audience of nobles and Catherine the Great.

The camera now reorients through ninety degrees, revealing a stage, partitions now planes of an exposed composition-in-depth, lead characters, secondary players and mechanical scenery in motion. Such a movement through space in time is pedagogy, a signalling of the theatricalisation of the entire film. 'Has all this been staged for me?', asks Unnamed at the very beginning of the movie; 'What kind of play is this?'

Yet seeing these events as a reciprocity of realist ambiguity and theatrical illusion goes only so far. A film composed with long takes, for Bazin, should 'not exclude the use of montage' – this would result in 'primitive babbling' (Bazin, 1997: 35). Montage must bring a secret order to ambiguity and illusion. Depth-of-field remains in the service of 'continuity', in 'the specific effects that can be derived from unity of image in space and time' (Bazin, 1997: 34; 35). In *Russian Ark*, the long take babbles (this lasts the entirety of the film), and depth-of-field propagates a baroque cascade of elements that overwhelm the screen. People are everywhere and everything happens at once. Accordingly, Deleuze writes that 'neither a function of theatricality nor one of reality seems to exhaust this complicated problem' (C2: 109). Rather, 'sequence shot' and 'depth of field create ... a certain type of direct time-image that can be defined by [pure] memory' (C2: 107; 109); sheets of the past.

Appearing between the past in general and the immediate present as the edge of the past, these sheets are manifold: from the moment of the Unnamed and Custine as focal point to a receding limit – the Winter Palace and Hermitage from 1732 giving way to St Petersburg from 1700; the art collected from Europe created in preceding periods giving way to – as will be seen – mythical time. Between such limits and the focal point appear all the sheets of the past. Each sheet will have 'its own characteristics, its "tones", its "aspects", its "singularities", its "shining points" and its dominant themes' (C2: 99). These sheets will be arranged in 'non-chronological time', moments between which the narration will 'jump' (C2: 99). Finally, these sheets create coexistence, they are 'inextricable' happenings – there is no cause and effect; sheets of the past rather reveal the conditions for and disrupt cause and effect through selection, resonance and a multiplicity of connections (C2: 99). The time travellers traverse these sheets of the past, one after another, from arrival in the early 1800s to the encounter with Peter the Great in the early 1700s to Catherine the Great directing her theatrical production in the 1760s. They jump back and forth between sheets: on to the twenty-first century; then the German blockade of Stalingrad; the Persian Ambassador presented to the court of Nicholas I. Catherine again (this time as an old lady with her grandchildren); Nicholas II and family at breakfast with whispers of the coming revolution. There is no chronological continuum here, and thus no actions to be performed – the travellers are seers jumping between moments of the past – but never depicted as coming from or returning to their relative presents. They are adrift in pure memory. In the final moment of the film the Unnamed finds the Neva has flooded, the Hermitage is an Ark preserving concurrent pasts afloat on the waters of time – the myth of Noah experienced anew. Resonances, reverberations, echoes: *Russian Ark* produces a coexistence of sheets of the past.

40

Er shi si cheng ji/24 City

Powers of the false

Frame III: 40 *24 City* (Zhang Ke Jia, China | Hong Kong | Japan, 2008)

Chengdu, in China's Sichuan province, is a city caught up in the country's economic boom, the result of the ongoing transformation from a centrally planned to market economy. On what was once the outskirts of the city is Factory 420. It was founded in the late 1950s to produce components for the aerospace industry in the wake of the Korean War, its purpose a state secret. It was thus built to be a city-in-and-of-itself, apart from Chengdu, having its own schools, restaurants, cinemas, its workers brought in from all over the country. In the post-Cold War period Factory 420 was retooled for peacetime products, white goods. This, however, was the beginning of its end, a slow decline leading to the current events of the film. Factory 420 is to be demolished and its remaining workers laid off. In its place will rise 24 City, a premier development of state-of-the-art apartments, a complex for the middle classes in ascension. The film itself consists predominantly of face-to-cameras, static long takes of interviews with the workers and their families. The film begins with He Xing, an employee, reminiscing about his time as an apprentice to master tooler Wang. Then there is Guan Fenijo, head of security at the time of Mao's Cultural Revolution. Hou Linju, a woman who was made redundant several years previously. Hao Dali, an ageing secretary permanently connected to a saline drip. Vei Dong, assistant to the General Manager and intimately involved in the selling of the factory land to the new developers. There is Little Flower, darling of the factory floor. There is Zhao Gang, a factory trainee who, after a wee taste of the life of a worker, escaped – as he sees it – to become a TV presenter. There is Su Na, a 'shopper' for the Chengdu elite, who dreams of an apartment in the new 24 City complex, but who remembers the life her mother had as a worker there too.

Zhang Ke Jia thus structures the film as a journey, from the past to the present. The film seamlessly transitions from workers steeped in the ideology of communist China to the young generation and their modern (Chinese version of) consumer capitalism with dreams of affluence. We cannot but feel impressed by the selfless dedication of the older generation and their authentic wish for the betterment of the state … and horrified at the consequences of such an environment – the lost child abandoned at a port during the workers' journey to Factory 420. We cannot but be impressed by the way the people have moved away from such conscious slavery … and horrified by the unconscious slavery and disdain for the past of the new generation. It is this kind of ambiguity that permeates the film. There is no nostalgia for the past, nor is there a celebration of the present. Or rather, nostalgia and hope for the future are beautifully balanced. What, then, is the point of the film? What, then, is Zhang Ke Jia's political position? These things remain unclear. Indeed, it is this ambiguity that creates the power of *24 City*.

A far more curious aspect: some of the interviews are fake. Fake in the sense that they are 'acted' by 'actors' speaking 'lines' composed out of interviews with 'real' people. But only some; some interviews are with 'real life' people. In a particularly fascinating move, Little Flower's story tells of how she was named such after a movie starring Joan Chen. Little Flower herself is played by that actress. Zhang Ke Jia may be accused of undercutting realism, as if this were a crime … as if this were not his intention. However, we would like to claim this is exactly the point. This is why the two methods are present. We never quite know exactly when the 'true' transitions to the 'fake'. This gives the spectator a retroactive crisis. Towards the end of the film it is clear that some the interviews have been manipulated. But when did this begin? In other words, undermining the sense of 'truth' is exactly the point of the film. To understand this cinematic process more fully we can turn to Deleuze, to his cinematic concept of 'powers of the false' (C2: 131).

In the cinema of realism, specifically, and the classical cinema in general, narration works by getting characters' actions and situations to interrelate, events dovetail and there is resolution. As Deleuze puts it, '[t]his is truthful narration in the sense that it claims to be true, even in fiction' (C2: 127). In the modern, modernist cinema, however, 'narration ceases to be truthful' (C2: 131). This kind of film proceeds by the 'series', a serial form rather than a flowing form (C2: 133). Deleuze writes that the 'narration is constantly being completely modified, in each of its episodes ... as a consequence of disconnected places and de-chronologised moments' (C2: 133). In short, 'truth is not to be achieved, formed, or reproduced; it has to be created. There is no other truth than the creation of the New: creativity, emergence ...' (C2: 146–7). What does this amount to? What we could call the untruth. A cinema that 'will have destroyed every model of the true so as to become creator and producer of truth: this will not be a cinema of truth but the truth of cinema' (C2: 151). Powers of the false.

What does this mean? Rather than *24 City* presenting the truth, the film undermines and ungrounds such strategies. By deliberately presenting the 'untruth' (which is not the same as a lie, but simply the avoidance and complexification of 'the truth') virtual correlates overwhelm the actual images. In other words, the film does not think for the viewer. It stymies its own image of thought as truth to become an invitation for the viewer's thinking. But, as Deleuze warns us, 'the power of the false is delicate' (C1: 147). Just because it sets up the conditions for us to think the film, this does not mean we will. *24 City* is only an invitation.

41

I'm Not There

Bodies of attitude

Frame III.41 *I'm Not There* (Todd Haynes, USA | Germany | Canada, 2007)

Bob Dylan: the American singer/songwriter. In *I'm Not There*, Dylan is played by six different actors: Christian Bale, Cate Blanchett, Marcus Carl Franklin, Richard Gere, Heath Ledger, and Ben Whishaw. Five white actors, and one black; one woman, and five men; five adults and one child. Each character has a name designed by director Todd Haynes to express a different aspect of Dylan and echo antecedents, real and fictional both within and without the film: Woody Guthrie, Arthur Rimbaud, Jude Quinn, Billy McCarty, Jack Rollins/Father John, Robbie Clark. Fake, poet, martyr, outlaw, prophet and actor. Woody Guthrie is travelling through the USA, hopping trains and relying on the kindness of strangers to survive. Playing the blues, he carries his guitar in a case with the slogan 'This machine kills fascists'. Arthur Rimbaud is a tripped-out poet – undergoing an intense interrogation. Jude Quinn now plays electric guitar with a band – a scandal to the folk audience that made Quinn famous. Now hanging with The Beatles, and poet Allen Ginsberg, Jude is seen as a sell-out, and descends into a drug-induced oblivion. Billy McCarty is an old outlaw in the old West, a man who has taken advantage of being thought killed by Pat Garrett, now living a quiet life. Jack Rollins is a folk musician – whose story is told in a documentary. In hiding after identifying himself with a killer, he turns to God and emerges as a minister who performs gospel music with the new name of Father John. Robbie Clark is a young actor portraying Jack Rollins in a biopic called *Grain of Sand*.

Haynes creates what Deleuze would name a body of attitude. The actors do not perform an act of mimesis, but expose and accentuate Dylan. Guthrie, Rimbaud, Quinn, McCarty, Rollins/Father John and Clark do not attempt 'to reconstitute a presence of bodies, in perception and action, but to carry out a primordial genesis of bodies' (C2: 201). The bodies of Dylan, where 'disparate sets overlap and rival each other, without being able to organise themselves according to sensory-motor schemata. They fit over each other, in an overlapping of perspectives which means that there is no way to distinguish them even though they are distinct and incompatible' (C2: 203). Haynes cuts from one scene to another, exploring one facet of a character; jumps from one image to another, creating a fragmented body. In this way, the character becomes a multiplicity and the body is 'dispersed in "a plurality of ways of being present in the world", of belonging to sets, all incompatible and yet coexisting' (C2: 203). This body of attitude is a noosign. Here the body is that which 'forces us to think, and forces us to think what is concealed from thought, life' (C2: 189).

42

Politist, adjectiv/Police, Adjective

Bodies of gest

Frame III.42 *Police, Adjective* (Corneliu Porumboiu, Romania, 2009)

So 'police' as an adjective, a word that modifies a noun ... yet with no noun to modify. Something is missing ... but what? Which word does 'police' prefigure? It is tempting to specify immediately: 'officer'. Perhaps, however, we should resist this temptation. What has the title deliberately done? In not specifying the noun, it foregrounds an indeterminacy, in the sense of an in/finite delay. In this way, the title becomes significant through what it leaves unsignified. First, this can be seen as an indicator of the centrality that language will have. Words become politicised. Second – and, I maintain, far more importantly – the missing noun becomes a structural device in the film's form. And it is here, with the way the missing noun structures the images, that a far more radical political reading of *Police, Adjective* appears. The transition between, or clarification of, these two politics takes place in the (now famous) penultimate scene of the film. Cristi has been called into Captain Anghelache's office. The meeting is to review the case Cristi has (reluctantly) been working on.

A young plainclothes police officer, Cristi has been tasked with following Alex, a teenage student suspected of being a drug dealer. Cristi soon ascertains that Alex just smokes a little weed with his mates. It is nothing. Porumboiu films these sequences in long takes, endless followings and waitings (the film form beautifully, and bravely, capturing the longueurs of the investigation). But Cristi comes under increasing pressure to arrest the kid, to get a result (as a more mainstream police procedural might put it). However, he feels this would not be in anyone's interest, least of all for Alex, who would get a police record and ruin his chances in life. So Cristi tries to find out who is supplying the drugs. He gets nowhere. The trouble is, the more time he invests in the case, the more the demand for an arrest. So we find ourselves in Captain Anghelache's office. Cristi tries to get the case dropped, citing that it would be bad for his conscience if Alex were arrested. So begins one of the most exceptional scenes in recent cinema. Captain Anghelache asks his secretary for a copy of the Romanian dictionary and looks up the words 'conscience', then 'morality', 'law', 'state', 'police'. The crucial aspect of this line of flight through signifiers is in the resonance with an earlier scene. Cristi returns home, late from work, and while eating his tea his wife repeatedly listens to a track by a Romanian singer. For Cristi, the words in the song are just meaningless. His wife sees them as affective, intensive, words used as poetry. Their conversation then turns to the way in which words are ascribed official definitions by the Romanian Academy. Back to Captain Anghelache's office. The concepts in play become the tools of the state, an ideological weapon to bring Cristi back in line. And just to make sure, Anghelache raises the stakes from the ideological to the repressive ... if Cristi doesn't capitulate, he will be fired. Cut. The final scene is of a whiteboard with Cristi planning a stake-out to arrest Alex.

It would be tempting to see the film, ultimately, as a tragedy. A tragedy for justice and a tragedy for Cristi, his personal ethical code abandoned – or crushed – owing to the pressure of the state. In this way we would be following a broadly Hegelian approach. Hegel, in *Aesthetik*, frames the conflict between ethics and the law as the dialectics of justice (Hegel, 1988). His example is Sophocles' *Antigone*. The play revolves around Antigone wishing to bury and honour her dead brother. However, King Creon has pronounced him a traitor; his body should be left to decay on the battlefield. Here we have divine law verses a human law, or an ethical code coming up against the state. In *Antigone*, it ends in tragedy … Antigone – and almost everyone else – dead. It is at this point that Creon understands, finally, that this conflict has been nothing but trouble … and so ushers in a new era for justice. Here, for Hegel, is the dialectic in action: thesis, antithesis and synthesis. There is resolution, not between good and evil, but between two contradictory positions.

It would seem, then, that *Police, Adjective* follows Antigone and the Hegelian dialectic. Director Corneliu Porumboiu explores the way in which the individual is circumscribed in a battle between a personal ethics and the collective law. However, this reading of the film seems inadequate. For a start, the final sequence is not played for tragedy. From the ideological/repressive diktat of Captain Anghelache to Cristi's submission: a simple cut. There are no scenes of Cristi in torment, agonising over what to do. There is no staring out over the sea/city with emotive music. Just a cut. And yet this is not the most significant aspect of the denouement. Rather, in the final sequence, the planning of the stake-out, we do not see Cristi. The camera frames the whiteboard as plans are drawn up. It is as if Cristi has disappeared. It is as if Cristi has become the missing noun. It is in this way that the film reconfigures its coordinates with regard to the political situation. In other words, the Hegelian reading of the film can be bypassed. Let us turn, to explore this, to Deleuze's taxonomy of cinema, albeit via Deleuze's collaboration with Félix Guattari in *Kafka*. They write: '[i]f justice doesn't let itself be represented, this is because it is desire. Desire could never be on a stage where it would sometimes appear like a party opposed to another party (desire against the law), sometimes like the presence of the two sides under the effect of a superior law that would govern their distribution and their combination' (K: 50). Rather, for Deleuze and Guattari, the characters discover the 'functioning of a polyvalent assemblage of which the solitary individual is only a part' (K: 85). Rather than conflict, 'it is one and the same desire, one and the same assemblage, that presents itself as a machinic assemblage of content and as a collective assemblage of enunciation' (K: 85).

In short, Cristi should not be treated as a hero who undergoes trials and is ultimately sacrificed at the altar of the state. Cristi is not a Christ figure. Rather, the situation is the exact reverse. Cristi is already police. What we get is merely the appearance of an abandonment of a personal ethics for state law. Deleuze and Guattari: 'The statement may be one of submission, or of protestation, or of revolt and so on; but it is always part of the machine' (K: 82). Thus '[t]he question is thus much more complicated than simply a question about two abstract desires, a desire to repress and a desire to be repressed … Repression, for both the represser and the repressed, flows from this or that assemblage of power-desire, from this or that state of the machine … in a connection more than in a hierarchy' (K: 56). Cristi, in essence, aligns himself with Captain Anghelache and the collective desire of the state, and in so doing, disappears.

If we have begun with *Kafka*, it is only because Deleuze and Guattari are exploring what they call a 'minor literature', a plane of composition Deleuze will reconfigure as 'minor cinema' in the *Cinema* books. The minor appears within the major, or classical, culture, disrupting it from within. In this way it is inherently political. And Deleuze writes, with regard to 'modern political cinema', that it is as if it 'were no longer constituted on the basis of a possibility of evolution and revolution, like the classical cinema, but on impossibilities, in the style of Kafka: the intolerable' (C2: 219). Quoting Jean-Luc Comolli, Deleuze clarifies: it is about 'the impossibility of escaping from the group and the impossibility of being satisfied with it' (C2: 219). In this way, Cristi's disappearance is crucial in the context of minor cinema. Deleuze writes: 'if there were a modern political cinema, it would be on this basis: the people no longer exist, or not yet ... the people are missing' (C2: 216). What does this mean, the people are missing? 'This acknowledgement of a people who are missing is not a renunciation of political cinema, but on the contrary the new basis on which it is founded ... art, and especially cinematographic art, must take part in this task: not that of addressing a people, which is presupposed already there, but of contributing to the invention of the people' (C2: 217).

Does a film of minor cinema create a people where the people are missing? Deleuze is deliberately ambiguous because the results can never be seen in advance. No one can foresee the results of these cultural moments at the beginning. It is only in the midst of, or at the end of, their time that the revolutionary results can be felt ... and by then, the moment had passed, the problem had changed. In *Police, Adjective* the people are missing. The noun is missing. Cristi is missing. In making Cristi disappear, Porumboiu resists giving the film a resolution. A resolution creates a people, embodied in the main character. The spectator is thus forced to think beyond (and not with) the film. For Deleuze, this is the task of modern political cinema which has as its time-image the noosign. Noosigns constitute a new image of thought, tear thinking away from the domain of thought (the already thought, the movement-image, classical cinema) and explore the unthought. The unthought: that what cannot (yet) be thought. In *Police, Adjective* this unthought appears through the body as gest. 'It is no longer a matter of following and trailing an everyday body, but of making it pass through a ceremony, of introducing it into a glass cage or a crystal, of imposing a carnival or a masquerade on it which makes it into a grotesque body ... until at last the disappearance of the visible body is achieved' (C2: 190). Isn't this just the trial that Cristi's body undergoes? The everyday body that is seen in the first part of the film exists until the ceremony in Anghelache's office, and thereafter, it disappears. This is Cristi's body as gest – in its collective

Section III

enunciation. 'The gest is necessarily social and political, following Brecht's requirements, but it is necessarily something different as well … It is bio-vital, metaphysical and aesthetic' (C2: 194).

43

Dogville

Cinema of the brain

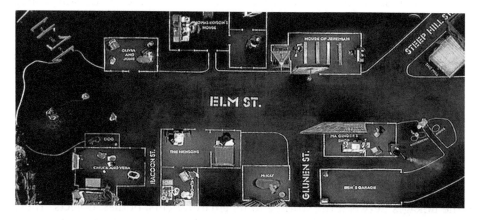

Frame III.43 *Dogville* (Lars von Trier, Denmark | Sweden | UK | France | Germany | the Netherlands | Norway | Finland | Italy, 2003)

'This is the sad tale of the township of Dogville' – so intones the gnarled mellifluous voice of the narrator, over the first shot of the film: a god's-eye view of Elm Street, and the shacks that border it. Prior to this we have been presented with two intertitles. The first: 'The film "DOGVILLE" as told in nine chapters and a prologue'. The second: 'PROLOGUE (which introduces us to the town and its residents)'. Looking down, we see the roads marked out by white chalk lines upon a black sound stage, with the street names written in. Similarly, the shacks are simple outlines drawn upon the ground, and labelled 'House of Jeremiah', 'Olivia and June', 'Thomas Edison's House'; although there is real furniture within each. A bush is drawn and marked, and so is a sleeping dog – yet among these elements walk real characters dressed in Depression-era clothes. The camera will enter into this environment, and track these people – who are unaware of the ellipses of set and scenery – as they interact. The surrounding world is the purest black or the purest white – for night and day, one becoming the other at the flick of a switch. Doors that do not exist creak open, polite knocks are heard as a character raps upon an invisible wall; raking and hoeing produces the sound of soil turning over. As the film progresses, it is accompanied by the narrator's voice, which interweaves with those of the characters, and always maintains a presence in the sound field to explicate events, tells us about the characters and their actions, explaining what has happened in the past and warning us about the future, although the narrator appears as lost and is as opinionated as the characters. And just as promised – we will encounter nine chapters proper, each with a subtitle – the final one reading: 'Chapter NINE In which Dogville receives the long awaited visit and the film ends'.

Director Lars von Trier ensures we are always aware of the storytelling function. This is a movie – this is a story. Intertitles, the black/white and chalk environment, the soundscape of the narrator's voice and invisible objects are the aspects of the mise-en-scène that forefront such a process. Intertitles are reintroduced but do not serve to stand in for speech or description, but introduce a novelistic function which foregrounds the film as a story. The black and white screen introduces extreme rarefaction into the frame, but also acts as a colour-image, destroying the coordinates of the environment as an organic situation. The lack of building structures and walls, doorways, vegetation, streets and objects rendered in chalk lines creates similar problems, which the film ignores. Finally, the sound images (narrator's voice, invisible objects) exposes the linkages between the world and its environments, bodies, objects. These are the noosigns of *Dogville*: a cinema of the brain, where the brain becomes the screen, and the storytelling function of cinema is made visible. And in being made visible, the image must be read. Deleuze writes: a movie can explore the 'identity of the brain and world' where 'landscapes are mental states, just as mental states are cartographies' (C2: 205). In *A Thousand Plateaus*, Deleuze (and co-author Félix Guattari) compare mapping with tracing, cartography with decalomania. Mapping prepares us for an exploration; while tracing is merely a copying out – 'organised, stabilized, neutralised ... multiplicities' (TP: 15). Mapping is a 'reverse, but non-symmetrical, operation'; mapping undoes tracing, not only sustaining but propagating multiplicity – and the method is to 'combine several maps' (TP: 15). This is *Dogville* – a mapping of cinema screen upon the brain of the audience. *Dogville* is a cinema of the brain.

44

Enter the Void

Lectosigns

Frame III.44 *Enter the Void* (Gaspar Noé, France | Germany | Italy, 2009)

Like a storm, raging through the synapses of the brain. Like a cloud, millions of star systems orbiting around a galactic central axis. A dispersive amorphous map of smoke pulsates: purples morph into orange morph into white morph into red. Like an eye – a big, bloodshot eye – staring down at you, looking into your skull, gazing into your mind. Like jellyfish swarming in the night sea, thousands of teeming tentacles in the invisible movement of the water. Like a toy kaleidoscope, turning the lenses under the sheets when everyone else is asleep, when you were a child. Like the centre of a flower, the stigma effervescent, open; the stamen vibrating, reaching out. Like being inside the still, quiet centre of a violent hurricane. Like red blood exploding in slow motion out of the dark hole of a wound. Like blood diffusing into water.

Enter the Void has some of the most potent cinematic images ever created – beginning with Oscar's trip-out with a toot on a wee pipe of DMT

(Dimethyltryptamine): a six-minute real-time odyssey of abstract shapes overwhelming a willing consciousness. This pattern image – which is at the centre of the film's opening sequence – is a beautiful expression of an intensive state: a formless, dispersive cinematic duration. Oscar has seen his sister, Linda, out of the Tokyo apartment where they both live and is awaiting the arrival of Alex, his friend. Director Gasper Noé utilises the point-of-view shot, aligning camera perception with the perception of the character – even inserting a black frame every few seconds mimicking the blinking of Oscar's eyes. Similarly, the speech and thoughts of Oscar are rendered in the same blank voice-over, sometimes making the status of speech and thought indeterminate. Noé will sustain this method of shooting Oscar both before and after the DMT trip, when Alex will arrive and they will walk the streets of Tokyo towards the club where Victor is waiting for a drug deal. The only exception to this rule will be the DMT trip sequence, which begins and ends by cutting in with blurred staccato images of Oscar lying on his unkempt bed, zoned out. An out-of-body experience, a body looking at itself from a disjunctive position, a hallucination, a fantasy. After the trip, after the stroll through Tokyo to the club and Victor, Oscar will be shot by the police in the toilet of The Void. As he dies, his consciousness appears to leave his body; the camera gazes down upon Oscar, curled up in shit, piss and pills, his blood seeping across the broken tiles. Accordingly, the DMT trip will become the impetus for the main section of the film. An out of body experience – Oscar traversing the past, present and future. A cavalcade of images from Oscar's past, the present where Linda, Alex and Victor live through the aftermath of Oscar's passing, and various possible futures. Past, present and future interweave to create a fluid mosaic, fragments from the past, present and future, mental landscapes and disparate bodies – from the point of view of the dead Oscar. Finally, in a short coda – Oscar is reborn.

Enter the Void is an exceptional cinematic event: a time-image – which through its extreme cinematic processes can be said to explore in particularly productive circumstances what Deleuze names hyalosigns, chronosigns, and noosigns. Time-image fragments, narrations and narratives. In so doing, the film is an exemplary lectosign: an image which must and can only be interpreted, an image which is in itself an interpretation. 'I don't believe in life after death', comments Noé, '[b]ut I still enjoyed the idea of doing a movie that would portray that collective dream, that collective need … You just say, well, it's in literature and books … That's what all religions rely on … But those are brainwashing tools' (Lambie, 2010). For Noé, the image of life after death is a fiction, a way to tell a story, and the way to create a very powerful time-image from noosigns, chronosigns and hyalosigns.

A hyalosign is the '*description*' of an image on-screen – a fragment – the 'most restricted circuit of the actual image and *its* virtual' (C2: 69). This actual and virtual of the hyalosign has three aspects: a description of the immediate image, a description of an image that is passing into the past, and a description of an image coming from the future. Each of these descriptions concerns the temporal dimensions of a fragment: actual with its virtual, an exchange of actual and virtual, and the virtual sustaining the disconnection between actuals. The in-itself, the passing and the becoming of description are the dimensions of the hyalosign: 'making presents pass, replacing one by the next while going towards the future, but also preserving all the past, dropping it into an obscure depth' (C2: 87). These hyalosigns can be described as 'mirrors face to face', 'the limpid and the opaque' and 'the seed and the environment' (C2: 71). Each performs an exchange between the actual on-screen image in the present and its virtual connections in relation to the immediate present, an immediate passing, and an immediate future. With mirror images bodies and backgrounds appear multitudinous – and in this way the actual propagates indiscernibility enacted by the virtual linkages between elements. In *Enter the Void*, Oscar – after his DMT trip – goes into the bathroom of his apartment. A switch is snapped on, and this is the first proper sight we have of the character, rendered in bright, unforgiving light. He looks at himself in the mirror, pours cold water into his cupped hands and splashes it into his face. This is a point-of-view shot, and the image stutters as Oscar blinks, and is obscured as he rubs the water into his face, off his face. Later in the film – this shot will be revisited. This time, however, the shot is back to front (the light switch has switched sides). In this way, it is as if – after Oscar's death – he has gone through the looking glass, into a fictional world, an indeterminate world of images of thought. The limpid and opaque concerns the passing of the present where one image becomes opaque as another becomes limpid, the limpid actualised in the present corresponding to an opaque retention of the past as virtual. Noé will create such exchanges using strange match cuts. These occur when the floating camera enters into an object and appears somewhere else: the circle of a lamp echoes the circle of a plug hole, and either side we have passed from one event to another. Or more immediate exchanges. Oscar is sucking on the breast of a lover, and the film cuts to baby Oscar sucking on the breast of his mother. Finally, the present is a seed, the future a virtual environment in relation to that seed, a virtual succession which subsists and insists within the seed image; correspondingly, an actual environment may refer to a virtual seed – one is 'pure virtuality' in respect of the other (C2: 79). Oscar has been lent a copy of the *Bardo Thödol*, the *Tibetan Book of the Dead*, by Alex. Oscar asks what the book is about. As they descend the exo-staircase of the apartment block, Alex tells him the book deals with what happens after death. First, you experience yourself leaving your body behind. Second, you explore moments from your past. Third, you search out and are drawn towards a new body to inhabit for reincarnation. It is clear that the book – or at least Alex's synopsis of the book – will provide the trace for Noé's film. That Oscar will die, explore the present, past and future. 'Dying would be the ultimate trip' – says Oscar, and it is thus that the DMT sequence similarly is a seed image for the environment of the film. Seed and environment, limpid and opaque, mirrors face to face: the hyalosign – the 'indiscernibility … of the real and the imaginary, or of the present and the past, of the actual and the virtual' (C2: 69).

Hyalosigns coalesce in narration. This coalescence is not a direct connection of actual image to actual image, but rather an indirect connection of actual to actual via the virtual. This is the chronosign, and it will have – once again – three signs. The first sign of actual–virtual narration is 'peaks of the present' – images which explore the way in which any present moment is fundamentally composed of many heterogeneous presents (C2: 100). Perhaps this is a narration that can make time 'inexplicable', one that is distributed between different presents which are all possible in themselves, but together are impossible. (C2: 101). In *Enter the Void*, Oscar's disembodied perception will follow the lives of Linda, Alex and Victor in the aftermath of his death. Noé shoots using a crane which will allow the camera to hover above the action and to pass at incredible speeds above the streets of Tokyo to explore simultaneous events. Linda fucking Mario while Alex is attempting to call her about her brother's death, Alex on the phone leaving the message. We will see different presents that are contradictory. 'I want 2 live' is written by Alex on concrete using charcoal; when we see this again after a uncut instance, the message reads 'I want to die'. In one sequence, Oscar lives. In the morgue, someone knocking. The hospital staff discover Oscar is alive. On the trip home Linda rants and raves: 'That thing is not my brother'; 'That thing is fucking disgusting'; 'There's no way I could put up with him'. If peaks of the present concern simultaneous presents, sheets of the past explore the way in which memories are 'no longer confused with the space which serves as its place' (C2: 100). Instead, memories explore time itself – no longer functioning as a repository of the present, but as the pure pastness of spaces as disparate non-causal events. *Enter the Void* will revel in sheets of the past, jumping from one moment to another through resonance, repeating the same images, sometimes in difference, sometimes the same but in another context. Oscar travels back in time and sees himself (shot from behind) and Linda as children. In the back seat of a car, their parents in the front seats. Suddenly, a car crash – mother and father instantly killed. Later, Linda joins Oscar in Tokyo and they ride a roller coaster – the ride ends with the car smash. These events are not connected in a linear fashion, but as echoes, sheets of the past. A taxi trip through the streets of Tokyo at night – ends with the car crash. A conversation lying on the grass in a park, now brother and sister are finally together, remembering a time they discussed never parting, cut to when they were children and they made the pact. Linda pretends not to remember. An image of Linda being taken away by social services. Her screaming and crying. The back of the car: Linda screaming her throat raw: 'No no mummy, no no daddy don't leave.' Deleuze refers to sheets of the past and peaks of the present as the 'order of time' in that they undermine the linear chronology, the continuity of past, present and future (C2: 155). The third avatar of the chronosign is the 'power of the false' and Deleuze delineates this function as the 'series of time' (C2: 126, 155). A serial organisation once again disrupts the continuity of time that constructs a film as a narration where the present is a product of the past and the future a consequence, yet here the narration does not unground the order of time, but creates images as events permeated by the future, events along a line of flight, each of which has a virtual presence with all the others. Deleuze puts it thus: 'the power of the false exists only from the perspective of a series of powers, always referring to each other and passing into one another' (C2: 133). All of time resonates through its futurity. Oscar will be reborn. In the coda at the end of the film – Oscar is reborn to his own mother. Noé: 'at the end, when you see the baby coming out from the mother's belly … you see the face of the mother, so you don't know if you're seeing his original birth. He's recreating a false memory of that traumatic moment that was his birth when he discovered light and oxygen. Or is he just getting into a loop, and your perception of time is only likened to how your brain is built' (Lambie, 2010).

The cinematic trajectory of the time-image is: image (hyalosigns) → narration (chronosigns) → narrative (noosigns), where the narrative is the story arising from the narration composed of images. And the story, writes Deleuze, will 'replace filmstock, in a virtual film which now only goes on in the head' (C2: 215). Noosigns are narratives emerging from cinematic matter-images; noosigns 'force … us to think' (C2: 189). Noosigns are the narrative as that which is eternally discordant: 'problematic and problematizing' (LS: 64). This storytelling function of the noosign is discordant thought engendered by the world and its bodies. Noosigns are the very emergence of the world and its bodies as discordant images. Thought is not engendered as a consequence of a given, actual sensory-motor linkage between the character and the mise-en-scène, but rather through the absence of such relations. In the absence of an actual link and in the constitution of virtual relinkage, thought becomes us. Deleuze names the poles 'world' and 'the body'; and the three signs corresponding to these poles are the body of attitude, the body of gest and the cinema of the brain. Thought appears through the body as attitude through being 'dispersed in "a plurality of ways of being present in the world", of belonging to sets, all incompatible and yet coexisting' (C2: 203). Oscar will enter the bodies of others. He will enter the head of Mario and see with his eyes as he fucks Linda, his sister. He will enter the head of his sister, and this entry will transform into a dream for Linda where Oscar is alive once more. He will enter the head of his father while he fucks his mum, see from his mother's perspective as young Oscar watches from a doorway while she and her husband make love. The body of gest 'is no longer a matter of following and trailing an everyday body, but of making it pass through a ceremony, of introducing it into a glass cage or a crystal, of imposing a carnival or a masquerade on it which makes it into a grotesque body ... until at last the disappearance of the visible body is achieved' (C2: 190). Such is the condition of Oscar's body from the very beginning of the film. The film effaces Oscar: the point-of-view shot becoming the point of view of a dead man. What is a body, asks Deleuze in *Nietzsche and Philosophy*. 'We do not define it by saying that it is a field of forces, a nutrient medium fought over by a plurality of forces ... there is no "medium", no field of forces or battle' (NP: 37). A body is a genesis of forces: 'Every force is related to others', and thus what 'defines a body is this relation ... Every relationship of forces constitutes a body – whether it is chemical, biological, social or political' (NP: 37). Accordingly, we pass into the cinematic environment of the mise-en-scène. As Deleuze writes, 'landscapes are mental states'; thus the mise-en-scène is 'the brain' (C2: 188, 205). The love hotel sequence that collapses Tokyo into the UV model, the gliding, out-of-body experience expressing Oscar's mind/spirit, the repetition and differences of the escapes into the past, the hallucinations of Oscar's DMT trip... all rendered in long takes, blurrings, false continuities ... the sonics a mishmash of whispers, blank voices, uterine soundscapes.

Time-images are 'the plane of composition that restores the infinite to us', created from 'a finite composite sensation' (WP: 197). Frame, shot, montage, colour and sound – all the coordinates of cinema – are attacked and, in being attacked, destroyed. Everything begins anew, a new conception and cineosis of the image, narration and narrative; hyalosigns, chronosigns and noosigns – each an exploration of actual–virtual correlates. Hyalosigns, chronosigns and noosigns are simultaneities appearing as a lectosign: a film that not only demands to be seen, but necessitates interpretation. Lectosigns are the pure virtual: ∞.

We can thus only interpret the final coda, and only encounter it as an interpretation. Shot from the point of view of the newborn baby, the images are blurred. Oscar buries his face into his mother's breast.

A blurred, flickering, indistinct image – then darkness once again.

A black screen: darkness. Silence. Breathing ...

[C]ertain philosophical problems pushed me to seek out solutions in cinema, even if this only serves to raise more problems.
  All research, scholarly or creative, participates in such a relay system.
(TRM: 285)

Select bibliography

Angelucci, Daniala (2012/2014) *Deleuze and the Concepts of Cinema* (*Deleuze Studies*, vol. 8, no. 3), trans. S. Marchetti, Edinburgh: Edinburgh University Press.

Aristotle (1984a) 'Categories', trans. J. L. Ackrill, in Jonathan Barnes (ed.), *The Complete Works of Aristotle*, rev. edn, Princeton: Princeton University Press, 3–24.

Aristotle (1984b) 'Metaphysics', trans. W. D. Ross, in Jonathan Barnes (ed.), *The Complete Works of Aristotle*, Princeton: Princeton University Press, 1,552–728.

Artaud, Antonin (1972) 'Witchcraft and the cinema', in *Antonin Artaud Collected Works: Vol. 3*, London: Calder & Boyars.

Atkin, Albert (2008) 'Peirce's final account of signs and the philosophy of language', in *Transactions of the Charles S. Peirce Society*, vol. 44. no. 1, pp. 63–85.

Badiou, Alain (2015) *The Communist Hypothesis*, trans. D. Macey and S. Corcoran, London and New York: Verso.

Badiou, Alain (2000) *The Clamor of Being*, trans. L. Burchill, Minneapolis and London: University of Minnesota Press.

Bazin, André (1997) *What Is Cinema? Vol. I*, trans. H. Gray, Berkeley, Los Angeles and London: University of California Press.

Bergson, Henri (1991) *Matter and Memory*, trans. N. M. Paul and W. S. Palmer, New York: Zone Books.

Bergson, Henri (1998) *Creative Evolution*, trans. A. Mitchell, New York: Dover.

Bickerton, Emilie (2009) *A Short History of Cahiers du cinema*, London and New York: Verso.

Bogue, Ronald (2003) *Deleuze on Cinema*, New York and London: Routledge.

Boucher, Geoff (2010) 'The directors: Rodrigo Cortés builds suspense in *Buried*', *Los Angeles Times*, 12 Sept., < http://articles.latimes.com/2010/sep/12/entertainment/la-ca-buried-20100912 > (last accessed 20 September 2010).

Carroll, Noël (1988) *Mystifying Movies: Fads and Fallacies in Contemporary Film Theory*, New York: Columbia University Press.

Carroll, Noël (2008) *The Philosophy of Motion Pictures*, Malden, MA, Oxford and Carlton: Blackwell.

Colman, Felicity (2011) *Deleuze and Cinema: The Film Concepts*, Oxford and New York: Berg.

Chion, Michel (1994) *Audio-Vision: Sound on Screen*, trans. C. Gorbman, New York: Columbia University Press.

Comolli, Jean-Louis and Jean Narboni (1996) 'Cinema/ideology/criticism', trans. S. Bennett, in Antony Easthope (ed.), *Contemporary Film Theory*, London and New York: Longman, pp. 43–52.

Deamer, David (2011) 'A Deleuzian cineosis: cinematic semiosis and syntheses of time', *Deleuze Studies*, vol. 5, no. 3, pp. 358–82.

Deamer, David (2009) 'Cinema, Chronos/Cronos: becoming an accomplice to the impasse of history', in J. A. Bell and C. Colebrook (eds), *Deleuze and History*, Edinburgh: Edinburgh University Press, pp. 161–87.

Deledalle, Gérard (2000) *Charles S. Peirce's Philosophy of Signs: Essays in Comparative Semiotics*, Bloomington and Indianapolis: Indiana University Press, 2000.

Deleuze, Gilles (1991) *Bergsonism*, trans. H. Tomlinson and B. Habberjam, New York: Zone Books.

Deleuze, Gilles (2002) *Cinema 1: The Movement-Image*, trans. H. Tomlinson and B. Habberjam, London: Athlone Press.

Deleuze, Gilles (2010) *Cinéma 1: L'image-mouvement*, Paris: Les Éditions de Minuit.

Deleuze, Gilles (2001) *Cinema 2: The Time Image*, trans. H. Tomlinson and R. Galeta, Minneapolis: University of Minnesota Press.

Deleuze, Gilles (2009) *Cinéma 2: L'image-temps*, Paris: Les Éditions de Minuit.

Deleuze, Gilles (2004) *Desert Islands and Other Texts: 1953–1974*, trans. M. Taormina, Los Angeles and New York: Semiotext(e).

Deleuze, Gilles (2004) *Difference and Repetition*, trans. P. Patton, London and New York: Continuum.

Deleuze, Gilles (2011) *Différence and Répétition*, Paris: Épiméthée.

Deleuze, Gilles (2004) *The Logic of Sense*, trans. M. Lester with C. Stivale, ed. C. V. Boundas, London: Athlone Press.

Deleuze, Gilles (2006) *Nietzsche and Philosophy*, trans. H. Tomlinson, London, New Delhi, New York and Sydney: Bloomsbury.

Deleuze, Gilles (2006) *Two Regimes of Madness: Texts and Interviews 1975–1993*, trans. A. Hodges and M. Taormina, ed. D. Lapoujade, New York: Semiotext(e).

Deleuze, Gilles and Claire Parnet (2002) *Dialogues II*, trans. H. Tomlinson and B. Habberjam, New York: Columbia University Press.

Deleuze, Gilles and Félix Guattari (2003) *Anti-Oedipus: Capitalism and Schizophrenia*, trans. R. Hurley, M. Seem and H. R. Lane, London and New York: Continuum.

Deleuze, Gilles and Félix Guattari (2004) *A Thousand Plateaus: Capitalism and Schizophrenia*, trans. Brian Massumi, London and New York: Continuum.

Deleuze, Gilles and Félix Guattari (2008) *Kafka: Toward a Minor Literature*, trans. D. Polan, Minneapolis: University of Minnesota Press.

Deleuze, Gilles and Félix Guattari (2009) *What Is Philosophy?*, trans. G. Burchell and H. Tomlinson, London and New York: Verso.

Easthope, Antony (ed.) (1996) *Contemporary Film Theory*, London and New York: Longman.

Edelstein, David (2006) 'Now playing at your local multiplex: torture porn', *New York Magazine*, 6 Feb., < http://nymag.com/movies/features/15622 > (last accessed 5 December 2015).

Eisenstein, Sergei (1977a) 'A dialectical approach to film form', in Jay Leyda (ed.), *Film Form: Essays in Film Theory*, San Diego, New York and London: Harvest, pp. 45–63.

Eisenstein, Sergei (1977b) 'Achievement', in Jay Leyda (ed.) *Film Form: Essays in Film Theory*, San Diego, New York and London: Harvest, pp. 179–95.

Eisenstein, Sergei (1977c) 'The cinematographic principle and the ideogram', in Jay Leyda (ed.), *Film Form: Essays in Film Theory*, San Diego, New York and London: Harvest, pp. 28–44.

Eisenstein, Sergei (1977d) 'Through theatre to cinema', in Jay Leyda (ed.), *Film Form: Essays in Film Theory*, San Diego, New York and London: Harvest, pp. 3–17.

Farias, Priscila and João Queiroz (2003) 'On diagrams for Peirce's 10, 28, and 66 classes of signs', *Semiotica* 147 (1/4), pp.165–84.

Farias, Priscila and João Queiroz (2004a) '10cubes and 3N3: using interactive diagrams to model Charles Peirce's classifications of signs', *Semiotica* 151 (1/4), pp. 41–63.

Farias, Priscila and João Queiroz (2004b) 'Images, diagrams and metaphors: hypoicons in the context of Peirce's 66-fold classification of signs', < www.dca.fee.unicamp.br/projects/artcog/files/Farias&QueirozSemiotica.pdf > (last accessed 21 November 2011).

Farias, Priscila and João Queiroz (2006) 'A diagrammatic approach to Peirce's classifications of signs', < www.library.utoronto.ca/see/SEED/Vol6-1/Farias_Queiroz.doc > (last accessed 21 November 2011).

Fontanier, Pierre (2009) *Les figures du discourse*, Malesherbes: Champs classiques.

Gottlieb, Sidney and Christopher Brookhouse (eds) (2002) *Framing Hitchcock: Selected Essays from the 'Hitchcock Annual'*, Detroit: Wayne State University Press.

Hegel, G. W. F. (1988) *Aesthetics: Lectures on Fine Art*, trans. T. M. Knox, Oxford: Clarendon Press.

Heidegger, Martin (1972) *What Is Called Thinking?*, trans. J. Gray, New York: Harper & Row.

Hughes, Joe (2008) 'Schizoanalysis and the phenomenology of cinema', in I. Buchanan and P. MacCormack (eds), *Deleuze and the Schizoanalysis of Cinema*, London and New York: Continuum.

Kennedy, Barbara M. (2002) *Deleuze and Cinema: The Aesthetics of Sensation*, Edinburgh: Edinburgh University Press.

Kierkegaard, Søren (2009) *Concluding Unscientific Postscript*, trans. A. Hannay, Cambridge: Cambridge University Press.

Kimberley, Matthew and Jason N. Dittmer (2015) 'To boldly go where no man has gone before: complexity science and the *Star Trek* reboot', in Matthew Jones and Joan Ormrod (eds), *Time Travel in Popular Media: Essays on Film, Television, Literature and Video Games*, Jefferson, NC: McFarland.

Klossowski, Pierre (2009) *Nietzsche and the Vicious Circle*, trans. D. W. Smith, London: Continuum.

Lambie, Ryan (2010) 'Gaspar Noé interview: *Enter the Void*, illegal substances and life after death', 21 September, at *Den of Geek*, < http://www.denofgeek.com/movies/16358/gaspar-no%C3%A9-interview-enter-the-void-illegal-substances-and-life-after-death > (last accessed 5 December 2015).

Lampert, Jay (2006) *Deleuze and Guattari's Philosophy of History*, London and New York: Continuum.

Lapsley, Robert and Michael Westlake (2006) *Film Theory: An Introduction* (2nd edn), Manchester: Manchester University Press.

Lay, Samantha (2002) *British Social Realism: From Documentary to Brit-Grit*, London and New York: Wallflower.

MacCormack, Patricia (2014) 'Introduction', in Patricia MacCormack (ed.), *The Animal Catalyst: Towards Ahuman Theory*, London and New York: Bloomsbury, pp. 1–12.

Marrati, Paola (2008) *Gilles Deleuze: Cinema and Philosophy*, trans. A. Hartz, Baltimore: Johns Hopkins University Press.

Martin-Jones, David (2006) *Deleuze, Cinema and National Identity: Narrative Time in National Contexts*, Edinburgh: Edinburgh University Press.

Merrell, Floyd (1995) *Semiosis in the Postmodern Age*, West Lafayette, IN: Purdue University Press.

Meyer, Bonnie (2008) 'The implications of Peirce's marriage of semiotics and pragmatism', *Cognito-Estudoa*, Sao Paulo, vol. 5, no. 2, julho–dezembro, pp. 152–71.

McNamara, Patrick (1996) 'Bergson's matter and memory and modern selectionist theories of memory', *Brain and Cognition* 30, pp. 215–31.

Miller, Tony (2004) 'Introduction', in Tony Miller and Robert Stam (eds), *A Companion to Film Theory*, Oxford: Blackwell, pp. 1–8.

Miller, Tony and Robert Stam (eds) (2004) *A Companion to Film Theory*, Oxford: Blackwell.

Monks Kaufman, Sophie (2013a) 'Metro Manila', in *Little White Lies*, 19 September, < http://www.littlewhitelies.co.uk/theatrical-reviews/metro-manila-24874 > (last accessed 21 September 2013).

Monks Kaufman, Sophie (2013b) 'Sean Ellis', in *Little White Lies*, 18 September, < http://www.littlewhitelies.co.uk/features/interviews/sean-ellis-24851 > (last accessed 21 September 2013).

Myer, Clive (2004) 'Playing with toys by the wayside: an interview with Noel Burch', *Journal of Media Practice*, vol. 5, no. 2, pp. 71–80.

Müller, Ralf (1993) 'On the principles of construction and the order of Peirce's trichotomies of signs', *Transactions of Charles S. Peirce Society*, vol. 30, no. 1, 135–53.

Nietzsche, Friedrich (2006) 'On the uses and disadvantages of history for life', in *Untimely Meditations*, ed. D. Breazeale, trans. R. J. Hollingdale, Cambridge: Cambridge University Press, pp. 57–124.

Nietzsche, Friedrich (2003) *The Gay Science*, ed. B. Williams, trans. J. Nauckhoff, Cambridge: Cambridge University Press.

Nietzsche, Friedrich (2008) *Thus Spoke Zarathustra*, trans. G. Parkes, Oxford: Oxford University Press.

O'Toole, Robert (2005) 'Deleuze's abuse of the history of philosophy', *Transversality*, < http:// blogs.warwick.ac.uk/rbotoole/entry/deleuzes_abuse_of/> (last accessed 29 November 2011).

Olsen, Len (2000) 'On Peirce's systematic division of signs', *Transactions of the Charles S. Peirce Society*, vol. 36. no. 4 (Fall), pp. 563–78.

Peirce, Charles Sanders (1965) *Collected Papers of Charles Sanders Peirce: Volume I and II*, ed. C. Hartshorne and P. Weiss, Cambridge, MA: Belknap Press of Harvard University Press.

Peirce, Charles Sanders (1974) *Collected Papers of Charles Sanders Peirce: Volume V and VI*, ed. C. Hartshorne and P. Weiss, Cambridge, MA: Belknap Press of Harvard University Press.

Peirce, Charles Sanders (1966) *Collected Papers of Charles Sanders Peirce: Volume VII and VIII*, ed. A. W. Burks, Cambridge, MA: Belknap Press of Harvard University Press.

Peirce, Charles Sanders (1966) *Charles S. Peirce: Selected Writings (Values in a Universe of Chance)*, ed. P. P. Wiener, New York: Dover.

Peirce, Charles Sanders and Victoria Lady Welby (1977) *Semiotic and Significs: The Correspondence between Charles S. Peirce and Victoria Lady Welby*, ed. Charles S. Hardwick and James Cook, Bloomington and London: Indiana University Press.

Pisters, Patricia (2011) 'Synaptic signals: time travelling through the brain in the neuro-image', *Deleuze Studies*, vol. 5, no. 2, Edinburgh: Edinburgh University Press, pp. 261–74.

Pisters, Patricia (2012) *The Neuro-Image: A Deleuzian Film-Philosophy of Digital Screen Culture*, Stanford: Stanford University Press.

Rodowick, D. N. (1997) *Gilles Deleuze's Time Machine*, Durham and London: Duke University Press.

Rose, Steve (2013) 'Metro Manila – review', *The Guardian*, 19 September < http://www. theguardian.com/film/2013/sep/19/metro-manila-review > (last accessed 21 September 2013).

Rushton, Richard (2008) 'Passions and actions: Deleuze's cinematographic cogito', *Deleuze Studies* vol. 2, no. 2, Edinburgh: Edinburgh University Press.

Sanders, Gary (1970) 'Peirce's sixty-six signs?', *Transactions of the Charles S. Peirce Society*, vol. 6. no. 1, pp. 3–16.

Short, T. L. (2004) 'The development of Peirce's theory of signs', in Cheryl Misak (ed.), *The Cambridge Companion to Peirce*, Cambridge: Cambridge University Press, pp. 214–40.

Sinnerbrink, Robert (2011) *New Philosophies of Film: Thinking Images*, London and New York: Bloomsbury.

Somers-Hall, Henry (2013) *Deleuze's Difference and Repetition: A Philosophical Guide*, Edinburgh: Edinburgh University Press.

Truffaut, François (1954) 'A certain tendency in French cinema', < http://www.newwavefilm. com/about/a-certain-tendency-of-french-cinema-truffaut.shtml > (last accessed 9 February 2016).

Tsang, Hing (2013) *Semiotics and Documentary Film: The Living Sign in the Cinema*, Boston and Berlin: de Gruyter.

Weiss, Paul and Arthur Burks (1945) 'Peirce's sixty-six signs', *The Journal of Philosophy*, vol. 42, no. 14 (5 July), pp. 383–8.

Žižek, Slavoj (2001) *The Fright of Real Tears: Krzysztof Kieślowski between Theory and Post-Theory*, London: BFI Publishing.

Zola, Émile (1964) *The Experimental Novel and Other Essays*, trans. B. M. Sherman, New York: Haskell House.

Filmography

24 City (Zhang Ke Jia, China | Hong Kong | Japan, 2008)
Ajami (Scandar Copti and Yaron Shani, Germany | Israel, 2009)
Apocalypse Now (Francis Ford Coppola, USA, 1979)
Black Swan (Darren Aronofsky, USA, 2010)
Breathless (Jean-Luc Godard, France, 1960)
Brooklyn's Finest (Antoine Fuqua, USA, 2009)
Buried (Rodrigo Cortés, Spain, 2010)
Despicable Me (Pierre Coffin and Chris Renaud, USA, 2010)
Despicable Me 2 (Pierre Coffin and Chris Renaud, USA, 2013)
Director's Video Diary of Timecode (Jeff Brown and Glen Janssens, USA, 2000) on *Timecode* DVD
Diving Bell and the Butterfly, The (Julian Schnabel, France | USA, 2007)
Doctor Who – Bad Wolf (Joe Ahearne, UK, 2005)
Doctor Who – Born Again (Euros Lyn, UK, 2005)
Doctor Who – Castrovalva (Fiona Cumming, UK, 1982)
Doctor Who – Deep Breath (Ben Wheatley, UK, 2014)
Doctor Who – Journey's End (Graeme Harper, UK, 2008)
Doctor Who – Logopolis (Peter Grimwade, UK, 1981)
Doctor Who   Planet of the Spiders (Barry Letts, UK, 1974)
Doctor Who – Robot (Christopher Barry, UK, 1974–5)
Doctor Who – Spearhead from Space (Derek Martinus, UK, 1970)
Doctor Who – The Caves of Androzani (Graeme Harper, UK 1984)
Doctor Who – The Christmas Invasion (James Hawes, UK, 2005)
Doctor Who – The Day of the Doctor (Nick Hurran, UK, 2013)
Doctor Who – The Deadly Assassin (David Maloney, UK, 1976)
Doctor Who – The Eleventh Hour (Adam Smith, UK, 2010)
Doctor Who – The End of Time: Part 1 (Euros Lyn, UK, 2009)
Doctor Who – The End of Time: Part 2 (Euros Lyn, UK, 2010)
Doctor Who – The Enemy Within (Geoffrey Sax, USA | UK, 1996) aka *Doctor Who: The Movie*
Doctor Who – The Night of the Doctor (John Hayes, UK, 2013)
Doctor Who – The Parting of the Ways (Joe Ahearne, UK, 2005)
Doctor Who – The Power of the Daleks (Christopher Barry, UK, 1966)
Doctor Who – The Stolen Earth (Graeme Harper, UK, 2008)
Doctor Who – The Tenth Planet (Derek Martinus, UK, 1966)
Doctor Who – The Time of the Doctor (Jamie Payne, UK, 2013)

Doctor Who – The Twin Dilemma (Peter Moffatt, UK, 1984)
Doctor Who – Time and the Rani (Andrew Morgan, UK, 1987)
Dogville (Lars von Trier, Denmark | Sweden | UK | France | Germany | the Netherlands | Norway | Finland | Italy, 2003)
Don Quixote (Orson Welles [unfinished])
Enter the Void (Gaspar Noé, France | Germany | Italy, 2009)
Fish Tank (Andrea Arnold, UK | the Netherlands, 2009)
Five (Abbas Kiarostami, Iran | Japan | France, 2003)
Four Lions (Christopher Morris, UK, 2010)
Four Times (Michelangelo Frammartino, Italy | Germany | Switzerland, 2010)
Harry Potter and the Deathly Hallows: Part 1 (David Yates, UK | USA, 2010)
Harry Potter and the Deathly Hallows: Part 2 (David Yates, USA | UK, 2011)
Human Centipede (First Sequence), The (Tom Six, the Netherlands, 2009)
I'm Not There (Todd Haynes, USA | Germany | Canada, 2007)
Inception (Christopher Nolan, USA | UK, 2010)
Innocence (Lucile Hadzihalilovic, Belgium | France | UK | Japan, 2004)
Jurassic Park (Steven Spielberg, USA, 1993)
Killer Inside Me, The (Michael Winterbottom, USA, 2010)
Lambeth Walk – Nazi Style (Charles Ridley, UK, 1942)
Lifeboat (Alfred Hitchcock, USA, 1944)
Life is War – Making of Naqoyqatsi (Unattributed, USA, 2002) on *Naqoyqatsi* DVD
Lion King (Roger Allers and Rob Minkoff, USA, 1994)
Machinist, The (Brad Anderson, Spain | USA, 2004)
Made in Dagenham (Nigel Cole, UK, 2010)
Making of Five (Abbas Kiarostami, Iran, 2005)
Making of Triangle, The (Danielle Lomas, UK, 2009) on *Triangle* DVD
marxism today (prologue) (Phil Collins, UK | Germany, 2010)
Metro Manila (Sean Ellis, UK | Philippines, 2013)
Minions (Kyle Balda and Pierre Coffin, USA, 2015)
Monsters (Gareth Edwards, UK, 2010)
Mother (Joon-ho Bong, South Korea, 2009)
Naqoyqatsi (Godfrey Reggio, USA, 2002)
Police, Adjective (Corneliu Porumboiu, Romania, 2009)
Pulp Fiction (Quentin Tarantino, USA, 1994)
Rear Window (Alfred Hitchcock, USA, 1944)
Rope (Alfred Hitchcock, USA, 1948)
Russian Ark (Alexander Sukurov, Russia | Germany | Japan | Canada | Finland | Denmark, 2002)
Scott Pilgrim vs. the World (Edgar Wright, USA, 2010)
Screaming Man, A (Mahamat-Saleh Haroun, France | Belgium | Chad, 2010)
Se7en (David Fincher, USA, 1995)
Secret in Their Eyes, The (Juan José Campanella, Argentina | Spain, 2009)
Self Made (Gillian Wearing, UK, 2010)
Slackistan (Hammad Khan, Pakistan, 2009)
Source Code (Duncan Jones, Canada | France | USA, 2011)
Star Trek – First Contact (Jonathan Frakes, USA, 1996)
Synecdoche, New York (Charlie Kaufman, USA, 2008)
Terrorist, The (Santosh Sivan, India, 1998)
Timecode (Mike Figgis, USA, 2000)
Triangle (Christopher Smith, UK | Australia, 2009)
Triumph of the Will (Leni Riefenstahl, Germany, 1935)
Uncle Boonmee Who Can Recall His Past Lives (Apichatpong Weerasethakul, Thailand | UK | France | Germany | Spain | the Netherlands, 2010)

untitled (Phil Collins, UK | Germany, 2010)
Wandering Cloud, The (Tsai Ming-liang, France | Taiwan, 2005)
War of the Worlds (Steven Spielberg, USA, 2005)
White Material (Claire Denis, France | Cameroon, 2009)
Z (Costas-Gravas, France | Algeria, 1969)

Index

Note: where there are multiple page references against an index entry, page numbers in **bold** indicate the more significant discussions.